THE ~~PELICAN~~

THE POOR LAW REPORT OF 1834

S. G. CHECKLAND, Professor of Economic History in the University of Glasgow since 1957, was born in Ottawa in 1916. While at Birmingham University he was President of the National Union of Students. He has been Senior Lecturer in Economic Science in the University of Liverpool and lecturer in history at Cambridge. In 1960 and 1964 he was a member of the Institute for Advanced Study at Princeton. His interests in urban history are reflected in his membership of the East Kilbride (New Town) Development Corporation 1964–8, and in his chairmanship of the board of management of *Urban Studies*. He is a Senate Assessor on the Court of the University of Glasgow. In addition to many articles and reviews in learned journals he is author of *The Rise of Industrial Society in England, 1815–1885* (1964), *The Mines of Tharsis: Roman, French and British enterprise in Spain* (1967), and *The Gladstones, A Family Biography, 1764–1851* (1971) (Scottish Arts Council Book Award). An historiographical study of economic history is in progress, provisionally entitled *The Economic Content of History*.

His wife, E. O. A. CHECKLAND, has been a schoolteacher and a tutor in economic history at the Universities of Liverpool, Cambridge and Edinburgh. She researched a good deal of *The Gladstones* and is doing much of the primary work on *Scottish Banking: A History, 1695–1973* on which she and her husband are currently engaged. Philanthropy in Glasgow in the nineteenth century is her special interest. The Checklands have five children and two grandchildren.

THE POOR
LAW REPORT
OF
1834

═

Edited with an Introduction by
S. G. AND E. O. A. CHECKLAND

PENGUIN BOOKS

Penguin Books Ltd, Harmondsworth, Middlesex, England
Penguin Books Inc., 7110 Ambassador Road, Baltimore, Maryland 21207, U.S.A.
Penguin Books Australia Ltd, Ringwood, Victoria, Australia

—

First published in 1834
Published in Pelican Books 1974

—

Introduction and Notes Copyright © S. G. and E. O. A. Checkland, 1973

—

Made and printed in Great Britain by
Hazell Watson and Viney, Ltd,
Aylesbury, Bucks
Set in Monotype Fournier

To E. D. C.

whose business is poverty

CONTENTS

INTRODUCTION

I. THE CHALLENGE OF THE POOR LAW

THE English Poor Law Report of 1834 is one of the classic documents of western social history. Together with the thirteen folio volumes of Appendices with their nearly 8,000 pages, it is the record of the attempt by Parliament, within the first industrializing society, to comprehend the condition of the labouring poor and to formulate a policy. It was inspired by the fears of the day, guided by contemporary social philosophy, and inhibited by the primitive state of social inquiry.

In conjunction with the debate and the studies it has provoked, the Report has not only provided a basis for understanding the condition of the English poor in the 1830s; it is also a paradigm of social attitudes in a much wider sense. The other great welfare discussions of the time – those concerned with the Factory Acts and the sanitation movement – are of course of great importance in the study of the condition of the people and the actions of the Government. But the debate over the Poor Law is more fundamental because it involved taking up positions on social discipline. This challenge scarcely arose with the other great social reforms; in the case of the Poor Law it was paramount. For behind the immediate attitudes and statements in the Report and the evidence there lay a complex of concepts about the nature of man and society. Indeed in any inquiry into the condition of the poor this must be so. If we seek a time perspective on the relations in an industrializing society between social casualties, social discipline and social science, a study of the English poor in the 1830s provides a unique opportunity.

In the broadest sense the verdict of the Poor Law Inquiry of 1834 was clear. It was that there should be a new rigour in the treatment of the poor, and consequently in the lives of most of the labouring population who could expect to be dependent, at some time in their lives, on public assistance.

As we look back upon it some 140 years later we are aware of an immense shift in outlook. The prevailing view in the England of the 1830s, though it could take some account of environmentalism, was basically individualistic and moralistic. It rested upon the notion of personal autonomy through self-help. It was the world view that derived from the age of emergent industrialization, of relatively small-scale enterprise in which the owner-manager was common, of markets which, though not perfect, were much more difficult to rig than they are now. Today the dominant thought-idiom is environmentalist; its theoretical bases lie in sociology and psychology. With the development of industrial-urban society to its present complexity the realization has been forced upon us that men cannot reasonably be thought of as standing each as a discreet entity, each responding of his own volition to the changing situation in which he lives.

Yet any 'common-sense' scrutiny of any society reveals the dangers of such a situation. Because of the weakening of the idea of the autonomy and integrity of the individual (those great bulwarks of liberal philosophy), it is much easier today to subject him to manipulations that may be used as a substitute for social discipline of the kind that lay behind the Poor Law Report of 1834. Where there holds no concept of social responsibility relating effort to reward, it is doubtful whether society can remain coherent, at least in its present unregenerate state. Moreover, at the level of the individual it may well be that personality formation and stability make essential some sense of personal autonomy and self-respect. Political belief in the efficacity of individualism is far from dead. In Britain in the 1970s, under its Conservative government, there is a revival of concepts, embodied in a range of policy measures, that stress individual responsibility. But at the same time payment in augmentation of incomes for the least well paid has been introduced in the form of Family Income Supplements.

The assumptions of the Poor Law Report and its evidence may now seem naïvely culture-bound. But as one reads through it and ponders on the elements that went into its making, it throws out a dual challenge: to understand the situation out of which it arose and, by contrast, to try to make explicit the assumptions that lie behind our own views on the poor today.

2. THE PRE-INDUSTRIAL POOR

The Commissioners who prepared the Poor Law Report had to try to understand a set of arrangements that had been in evolution, on a local basis, for at least two and a half centuries.[1] It rested on an interplay between the intentions of legislators at the centre and the actions of implementors in the parishes, taking place as society moved from a feudal basis to an industrial one. Over this long period ideas and practices had accumulated by accretion: in English society, well embarked upon urbanization and industrialization, the poor were treated under a set of arrangements that were an extraordinary mixture of archaism and adaptation. Anxious though the Commissioners were to plunge into the discussion of the problem as it pressed in the 1830s, they felt it necessary to give an outline of the historical background.[2] Even Benthamite thinkers, eager to construe the immediate situation and to legislate for it, were aware that the practices they were scrutinizing were deeply rooted in the English past.

The schoolmen of the Middle Ages, living in an hierarchic society based upon the ownership of agricultural land and a peasantry tied to it, had asserted the responsibility of the better-off to assist the less fortunate through charitable giving. Indeed, the poor performed a social and religious role by challenging the wealthier to remember that fraternal duty. The rich were expected to worship God by giving, and to ensure their own felicity in an after-life by so doing. Nor was the feudal-Christian view so curious as it might seem to later ages, for the theory of society then held assumed that most men, by and large, had a place in the life of the village and manor. Those who did not had a claim on their more fortunate fellows. Those who held property did so on condition that they recognized the duties that went with it.

In those countries where the commercial and the incipient industrial revolutions were more rapidly gestating there was much debate on the poor, and some provision for them, especially in the larger towns. It was in England that the most developed system appeared, embodied in the acts of 1597 and 1601, especially the latter, the famous 'Act of Elizabeth'.[3]

The Tudor treatment, in lengthy evolution over the course of the sixteenth century,[4] rested first upon a distinction between the able-bodied poor and the 'impotent' (infants, aged persons, invalids, lunatics, and others unable to support themselves). The impotent were endowed with both a moral and a legal claim upon their parish of birth for a minimal maintenance. With respect to the able-bodied the law was much more complex. It had two facets. First, it was designed to keep them *in situ* so that they might not wander abroad and congregate in dangerous 'routs'.

Second, it provided, in the parish of birth, a claim upon local landholders. A rate was to be levied upon all occupiers of land within the bounds of the parish. These two provisions were the response of a government confronted with a frightening increase in the number of men no longer capable of maintaining themselves as the older system of village and manorial life decayed. Elizabeth and her advisers were anxious to dampen the rate of economic and social change: they appear to have hoped that a combination of geographical immobility of labour and parish provision would stabilize a potentially dangerous situation.

This duality was paralleled by another: that between, on the one hand, a realization, however dim, that unemployment might arise from defects in the economy and not from the fecklessness of the individual, and, on the other hand, a reassertion of the need for strong measures of discipline over the able-bodied. The Tudor debate on unemployment was sophisticated enough to take some account of the effects of bad harvests and slack trade upon job opportunities and incomes. The principle that had appeared in an earlier Tudor Poor Law statute, that of 1572, that the parish should 'set the poor on work' (e.g. provide employment under supervision within a workhouse) was reasserted.[5] But there is some obscurity on the entitlement to relief of men who could not be provided for in this way. On the principle of social discipline there was no equivocation: the justices were told to 'correct' those who were wilfully idle.

The principle of official control had already been adopted in the code affecting the working conditions of labour, embodied in the Statute of Artificers of 1563.[6] The power of regulating maximum rates of pay, first introduced after the Black Death (the Statute of Labourers, 1351)[7] was continued, though in a more flexible form, with the justices of the peace instructed to regulate such maxima in terms of changes in the cost of living.

The Elizabethan policy towards labour was conceived in strongly paternalistic terms: to cast such a framework of control over labour behaviour was entirely consistent with the view taken of the responsibility of the state. It was the duty of princes both to cherish their people and to impose order upon them. Yet in a country that was under great tension, with no standing army, there was also the element of fear; it was prudential to immobilize the poor and to provide them with a minimal standard of living. Indeed the nature of the social bond in Tudor times and later was a highly complex affair. For paternalism and fear in governing circles were both present in a society in which a new commercialized agriculture, based upon enclosure and the dispersal of monastic lands, operated alongside the older and more easy-going arrangements.

The early Stuarts, who inherited the two codifying Elizabethan statutes shortly after they were passed, attempted a central supervision. This was never easy or wholly effective; it collapsed during the Civil Wars of the 1640s. Thereafter overseers and magistrates dealt with the poor on a purely local basis. The way was now open for the growth of an extraordinary diversity in the 15,535 parishes of England.[8] In the course of time, and especially under an act of 1796, the poor acquired the right of appeal against the overseers to the justices of the peace. The latter, very largely the landed gentry, discharged their duty to the poor along with their other responsibilities. This arrangement, consisting of a statutory prescription operating locally without central supervision, was unique in Europe. Even Scotland continued to rely upon voluntary assessment of the parish landowner.[9]

In the seventeenth century there were efforts in some towns to make work for the poor by providing stocks of materials such as iron for nailmaking or flax for spinning, to be worked on in workhouses that served also as 'houses of correction'. But such provision had an inherent tendency to perversion. The difficulties of using men in such a position as a labour force are obvious enough. Such institutions could not attract and retain the kind of governor who could resist the tendency, always present, for the element of correction to become dominant. There was also much corruption over the purchase of paupers' food and other expenditures. Such 'workhouses' became little more than prisons presided over by inadequate or venial men. Most overseers put out the pauper children as 'apprentices' to anyone who would take them off their hands; indeed they had powers to force householders to take such children.[10]

The paternalistic tradition deriving from feudal society was exemplified in the attempts in Elizabeth's later years to regulate the distribution of the corn supply when the harvest was deficient. The magistrates had powers to search farmers' granaries for supplies hoarded against a further price rise and to proceed against corn dealers for the medieval offences of forestalling, engrossing and regrating. This duty of the magistrates has recently been described as an essential element in a 'moral economy of provision'.[11] It was codified in the Book of Orders of 1630. The Civil Wars damaged this provision as it did the central control of the Poor Law and the regulation of wages. But a popular memory of both persisted long afterwards; indeed labourers are to be found in the 1820s and 1830s appealing to this paternalistic tradition, though, to be sure, they believed the justices to have a duty to fix minimum rather than maximum wages.

In 1662, two years after the restoration of the Stuart monarchy, Parliament passed the Poor Law Amendment Act which, taken together with the Statute of 1601, served as the framework of the English Poor Law system until 1834. The 1662 Statute, commonly known as the Act of Settlement, codified existing practice, and reasserted the power of parish overseers, when complaint had been made to the justice of the peace, to remove to their parish of birth any incomers who had no settlement.[12] In this way the parish basis of Poor Law relief was reaffirmed. Arguments about the settlement and removal of paupers became a continuous element in parochial affairs. But the enforcement of settlement, like the collection of the poor rate and its dispersal, became a matter of great diversity in which both callousness and kindness could play their parts in different measure, depending on local conditions and the personalities of overseers, the larger ratepayers and the county justices. Handbooks published for the guidance of such men were lengthy and complex.[13]

It would seem that by 1660 the balance was changing between dependence upon private charity and recourse to the overseers. Professor Jordan held that from Tudor times to the later seventeenth century the belief in the necessity and efficacy of private charity, which had stood so long in the way of a compulsory provision for the poor, was such that benevolent free giving was more important than Poor Law relief.[14] Indeed it may be that the Tudor Poor Law was conceived not as a continuous thing, but as a 'reserve' provision, to be activated only when private giving proved inadequate. But then came a relative drying up of private charity leaving only recourse to the parish.

By the early eighteenth century the feeling was once more growing that the able-bodied poor, no longer disciplined by the workhouse, should be brought under control.[15] In spite of the early failure of workhouse provision, Knatchbull's permissive Act of 1722 provided for a new programme of workhouse building. Less than 200 such houses were set up in a minute proportion of the number of parishes.[16] But the old difficulties reappeared; once more the workhouse was discredited. Moreover, opinion seems to have veered again away from employment in the workhouse to attempts to find employment for paupers outside it. This resulted in Gilbert's Act of 1782.[17] In those parishes which adopted the powers it provided the workhouse became a poorhouse containing only the aged and infirm. For the able-bodied, work was to be found outside the poorhouse and, if necessary, subsidized from the poor rates. Thus relief could be given to the able-bodied out-of-doors. The act further provided that parishes might join in 'unions' in order to create more viable units. Though at no time did more than 1,000 of the 15,535 parishes apply the act, it represented a basic reversal of official attitude since 1722. At the same time as this official approval and implementation of outdoor relief, opinion was moving away from the restraint on labour mobility involved in the Settlement Act: Adam Smith was one of its most incisive and weighty critics in his *Wealth of Nations* of 1776.[18]

But in spite of the debate over Gilbert's Act and the Law of Settlement the condition of the poor does not seem to have been a matter of major concern until the last decades of the eighteenth century. The apparent lack of emphasis on the problem of the poor is consistent with other evidence about the state of the people. Broadly the life of the labourer continued to be local or regional, not all that different from what Chaucer might have recognized in the fourteenth century. According to Peter Laslett, England was 'a one-class society where overall, nation-wide class conflict could scarcely arise';[19] this view is also taken by Harold Perkin.[20] There were no great price fluctuations of the kind so disturbing in the later fourteenth and in the sixteenth centuries, at least down until the 1770s. Severe mortality crises had ceased: famine and plague no longer had their old terrors, though people could still of course die of malnutrition or even starvation. Population was certainly on the increase, responding to factors as yet imperfectly understood, among which was the ability of the economy to generate jobs and incomes. But in spite of growth, population was not pressing all that seriously on the means of subsistence.

Yet we cannot assume, from the apparent lack of concern, that the lot of the workers was an easy one. There was much in the life of the countryside that was harsh, not only delimiting the lives of the peasants but, as Marx believed, brutalizing them. The truth is that our techniques of assessment of the quality of human life, involving of course the question of criteria, are still so underdeveloped and unscientific that we must always exercise great caution in speaking of improvement or deterioration.

These difficulties are reflected in the problem of assessing the amount and form of class tension before serious industrialization. Hobsbawm and Rudé assert that even before 1750 'the basic tripartite division of the English land – a small number of very large landowners, a medium number of tenant farms employing hired labour, and a large number of wage-workers' was already in existence.[21] Hobsbawm further states that 'By the 1790s the . . . decay of the village poor had reached catastrophic proportions in parts of southern and eastern England.'[22] Thompson stresses food shortages, insisting that 'dearth was real dearth'. It would seem, from him, that the 'moral economy' had begun its long death by the 1750s. But, he argues, it remained a reality for the labourers, who derived a 'sense of legitimation' from 'the paternalistic model' (that is to say the outlook of the ruling class in earlier generations as reflected in the Book of Orders of 1630).[23] This consensus and consciousness among the labourers, according to Thompson, was so strong as, on occasion, to override fear or deference towards those of the landed class who were departing from the moral economy.

3. THE IMPACT OF THE INDUSTRIAL REVOLUTION

Whatever the trend in the condition of the labourer through most of the eighteenth century, there can be no doubt that in the forty years down to the Poor Law Inquiry in the early 1830s there were great structural changes in the economy and in society. Though there was no English census until 1801 it is clear that the population had been growing significantly, from some 5·5 million in 1700 to 8·9 million in 1801; in the next thirty years it grew to 13·9 million.[1] An accelerating increase in thirty years of some 5 million, or 57 per cent, could only mean great adjustments and great stress. In 1798 the Reverend T. R. Malthus sounded the alarm with his *Essay on the principle of population as it affects the future improvement of society*. Malthus argued that there was always a tendency for population to press on the food supply, with the labourer being employed under ever-deteriorating conditions of diminishing returns to effort on the land.

In response to the need for food much of English cereal agriculture was rationalized through the enclosure movement, authorized by some 4,000 private acts of Parliament.[2] Over large parts of the country, especially in the midlands and the south, the traditional co-operative agriculture of the open fields had survived to the late eighteenth and early nineteenth centuries. Through enclosure the landlords were able to create larger and more efficient units, more appropriate to the new farming technology. In this way agricultural output kept up with the growth of population, keeping Britain more or less self-supplying.

The peasant, though compensated to some degree for the rights to which he could establish title, was on the whole adversely affected. Whereas he could often scrape along with the older village system, using its diverse facilities – open fields, meadows, common rights and the like – in the new situation his scope was much narrower. There was a decline also in the old system of having labourers lodging in the farm-house, using a servants' hall, and so preserving something of the old familial relationship as well as securing maintenance especially in bad times. The old annual hirings gave place to monthly or even weekly ones. The peasant with no real title was, of course, the most vulnerable to the new situation. With the continuing relentless increase in labourers' numbers and the rationalization of farming there was created a surplus of labour which could neither find wage-employment nor adapt to the new situation through improvisation. For the old diverse village life was going, while the Settlement Laws, tying a man to his parish, remained. Moreover agriculture had always been erratic in terms of yield, and consequently in terms of incomes, prices and employment; it did not cease to be so.

With the outbreak of the French wars in 1793 were added the difficulties of war at sea and blockade. Price inflation damaged the labourers' position further, for they had no means, through trade union activity, or any other, of exerting pressure to push their money wages up. Presumably recruitment to the forces eased this labour surplus for a time, but with the coming of peace in 1815 the survivors, perhaps some 300,000 of them, returned home having fought for English liberties, to be forced into an even more constricted situation than the one they had left. Deflation and economic contraction came with the post-war difficulties. Change went relentlessly on, destroying cottage industries, an essential rural support: local smiths, glove-makers, spinners and weavers, saddlers and leather workers all found their employment shrinking. Through all this the parish and the village, still largely isolated and inward-looking, continued to be the background of the farm labourers' life and the only unit of government with which they had any effective contact.

So was consolidated the characteristic English system, so important for all subsequent agricultural history and so distinctive in comparison with other countries, of landowners, tenant farmers and labourers for the most part landless.

To these immense challenges the overseers in the agricultural parishes had to find a response. They did not do so corporately, or with any guidance from the centre. They extemporized. This they did, by and large, in a single direction, that of easing the conditions of relief. The sums spent on the poor grew from an average in the year 1783–5 of just under £2 million to £5·7 million in 1815–16 and in 1820–21 some £7 million.[3] This increase took place under what became known as the Speenhamland system. It derived its name from the policy adopted by the magistrates of Berkshire meeting at the Pelican Inn in the village of Speenhamland. Faced with two bad harvests, in 1794 and 1795, they were frightened that the proposal before them of regulating wages by setting minima would simply have the effect, in the face of general grain shortage, of increasing prices further. Instead they adopted the only available alternative, drawing up a scale of relief.[4] It was based upon the minimum necessary to maintain a labourer and his family; this the justices made adjustable to changes in the price of bread. By the general adoption of this system in the agricultural shires the allowance system in augmentation of wages was greatly extended. Indeed, it might be argued that Speenhamland removed the control on poor relief in a way analogous to the effects of the suspension of cash payments in 1797 in opening the banking and credit system to infinite extension. Speenhamland was an attempt to alleviate poverty without prescribing an increase in wages, for, in addition to the inflationary objection, the latter would be difficult to reverse when the labourers' condition eased. But it was a formula that could only accentuate the natural tendency to slackness in the award of relief. The distinctions between labourer and pauper and between wages and relief were placed in jeopardy. A classic account of the problem was given in 1797 by Sir Frederick Morton Eden.[5]

For many industrial workers, as for the farm labourer, there was a deterioration of life. Whereas much of earlier textile manufacture could take place in the countryside using rural water power, with the adoption of the steam engine the trend to the towns was accelerated. City slums and factory life awaited the farm labourer who could overcome the restraints on movement and offer his unskilled labour to industry.[6] Moreover employment could be highly erratic as the economy developed the characteristic instability that comes with fixed capital and reliance on foreign markets. Many older skills were made obsolescent. To all this workers could find little collective response, for trade union organization was effectively illegal until the law was partly relaxed in 1824.

Yet not all workers found themselves so badly placed. By and

large the more skilled a man was, the more able he was to improve
his income and his way of life. The gap between the rough and
the respectable, of which sociologists write today, was present in
industrial revolution times as now.

But though there was some scope for self-improvement there is
great difficulty in assessing changes in the condition of life. On the
land, it has been argued, the adversities of the labourers down to
the 1830s may have been exaggerated.[7] Quantitative assessment of
enclosure and close regional scholarship have, at the very least,
qualified the more dramatic view of the proletarianization of the
labourer. The post-war decline of the yeoman (the owner working
his land himself or with the aid of his family) was not catastrophic.
It would appear that the major decline of small owners and small
farmers did not take place between 1760 and 1830, but before 1760,
with a possible slight recovery in the first three decades of the
nineteenth century.[8] Even the landless and semi-landless cottagers
were not so ruthlessly treated as has been believed. Where the
improved agriculture was adopted new jobs were often created.

4. THE NEW ETHOS

Simultaneous with these changes affecting the workers a new
ethos was asserting itself in that part of society mainly responsible
for introducing the new industrial way of life – the middle-class
innovators, inventors and investors. In place of the hierarchical-
paternalistic view that had dominated the thinking of the schoolmen of the Middle Ages and had been continued under the Tudors
and early Stuarts, and which still had a place in the attitudes of some
at least of the landed class, a new view of man and society was
gaining ground. This asserted the autonomy of the individual, his
responsibility for his actions, and his honourable title to the
economic gains to which they might give rise, provided he traded
within the law. This justification had its reciprocal; it was that
those who did not make economic gains, or were unable to maintain themselves in the face of changes, had failed in their responses.
One further step remained to complete the individualist ethos;
it was to cast a general air of moral approval over economic success.

Combined with the new attitude towards the individual there had
developed by the 1830s a sense of precariousness about society.

This was expressed in the form that there was a delicate balance between institutions and their operation, and the behaviour of the labouring classes. There was a feeling that any concession to idleness might bring about a rapid and cumulative deterioration in the labourers' attitude towards work. This produced a growing sensitivity towards the Poor Law.

With the rise of the new individualism many of the insights into human need upon which the fathers of the church and the schoolmen had insisted were weakened and even abandoned. At the very time when society was imposing unprecedented strains on the mass of its members, the concept of the need of the individual for group support was being lost, at least by a large part of society, especially the most active and innovatory. For the notion of a society based upon the operation of enlightened self-interest led to a loss of appreciation of the need of the individual to locate himself within a group and to assimilate himself to it; psychological support was being withdrawn when it was most needed.

The development of philosophy and social science was of course affected by the notion of individualism. The consequent atmosphere was such that sociology, with its concern with group behaviour, could hardly emerge. On the other hand the idiom of individualism, combined with the concept of the market, meant that political economy could make great progress among the intelligentsia. The classical political economy of Adam Smith, Malthus,[1] and David Ricardo[2] provided a quasi-scientific basis for a theory of individual behaviour.

All this, of course, had implications for the attitude taken towards the poor. It reaffirmed the 'rightness' of the existing structure of incomes and employment, insofar as it had arisen from the operation of market forces, or was altered by them. But the thought-idiom of the new political economy brought a further implication. Though the market provided the mechanism of allocation both of goods and resources, the new political economy argued also in terms of the 'allocative shares', viz. the rewards received for land, labour and capital (in the form of rent, wages and profits) for their respective contributions to the product. To treat labour thus as a factor of production made possible a great advance in theoretical comprehension; at the same time, in conjunction with the notion

that all factors should be mobile so as to be able to move from one
use to another in response to market demand, it led to a dehumaniz-
ing of the notion of labour. Moreover, in individualist thinking
the provision of poor relief for the able-bodied would have the
further effect of placing a premium upon idleness and thus promote
a deterioration of standards and of personality which would spread
until a large part of the labour force was debauched. Malthus and
Ricardo shared this view and propagated it.

The classical political economy by and large stood for minimal
economic and social control, placing its faith in the market mechanism. But there was another school of thinkers whose emphasis was
somewhat different; that of Jeremy Bentham and his followers.[3]
For them the test of institutions and policies was that of efficiency
and effectiveness, judged in terms of the greatest happiness of the
greatest number, the guiding canon of utilitarianism. This led to an
emphasis on the need for uniformity of concepts and procedures
and a strong direction from the centre, instead of relying on the
traditional units of county and parish. The Benthamites were not
frightened by the need for state action, though, by and large, they
accepted the economists' advocacy of free enterprise (there was
indeed some degree of common membership between the two
groups). The Benthamite and the economists' views of the Poor
Law largely converged; both saw it as in need of reform both in
terms of efficiency and the reduction of outdoor relief. For the
Benthamite the great need was to reassert control over a chaotic
system.

But though there were such ideas at work favouring a more hard-
headed and perhaps callous attitude towards the poor, there was
also present a contrary influence. It has become known as the
humanitarian movement. The ending of the slave-trade in 1807 and
of slave-owning in 1833, the reduction of penalties for criminal
offences especially those of a capital nature, the abolition of the
pillory, the movement for prison reform, a dawning compassion
for the insane, the first acts to regulate conditions in mines and
factories were all in gestation or operation in the first half of the
nineteenth century. For this ambivalence between the belief in the
need for greater rigour in the Poor Law and greater concern for
human values there were several reasons. The problem of poor

relief was greater in scale than any of the others and it related directly to work incentives among the labour force.

Many of the landowners, both nobility and gentry, continued in the paternalistic vein of earlier days, approving of the Speenhamland Poor Law provision in the parishes and accepting the pauper, as in the past, as an integral part of the rural scene. For the most part the landed men were hostile to political economy. These traditional supporters of the old 'moral economy' were also thinking in practical terms: they were conscious of the need for social peace in the shires. They particularly resented the rise of the economists with their demand for free trade involving the abolition of agricultural protection in the form of the corn laws. For this was seen as an intrusion into the affairs of the countryside, a threat to farming incomes and, more remotely, an opening of the gates to uninhibited industrialization. Nevertheless a good many landed men by the 1830s were wondering whether the administration of the Poor Law in the parishes had become too slack.

There were others, even among the professional and business classes, who were repelled by a too-mechanistic view of society that looked upon the economy and the poor in such remote terms. Moreover, like some of the landed nobility and gentry, such men could hardly fail to be aware of the tensions now present in English society.

By 1830 the attitudes of the landed men and the rising commercial and industrial classes had created a situation in which two concepts of society conflicted. Significant elements of both groups were loath to see the old paternalism vanish, partly on the ground of justice and partly because of fear of protest and disturbance. But the ascendant view among the businessmen and their associates, together with the intellectuals who followed the new political economy, though they were aware of the social disruption and economic instability that must result, was in favour of economic growth through the market mechanism, keeping governmental intervention of all kinds, at national or parish level, to a minimum. This of course meant mounting an attack on the old Poor Law.

5. PROTEST AND VIOLENCE

The links between poverty and protest in the industrial revolution are only beginning to be explored. Since before the end of the wars against Napoleon there had been disturbances of one kind or another. In 1811 the 'Luddites', followers of 'Captain Ludd', had broken machinery and disturbed the peace in industrial areas; their object was to demonstrate their solidarity against their employers and to resist wage reductions. There were bad harvests in 1816–17 and 1819, bringing high food prices and violent strikes. The hosiery frame-workers of Nottingham and Leicester smashed the machines they regarded as their enemies. There was demagoguery among the workers and signs of panic in the owning class. The Lancashire 'blanketeers' marched on London; the red flag was carried. Habeas corpus was suspended in 1817–18, and the Government had recourse to spies and to the amateur Yeomanry to re-inforce the army. The most famous episode of English urban disturbance, that of Peterloo, took place in 1819. A crowd assembled to hear Orator Hunt; nineteen of them were killed when the Yeomanry charged. The Six Acts of 1819 made mass meetings in the open air subject to the licence of the magistrates, and increased the taxation of the cheap press, giving power to the courts to confiscate newspapers judged to be seditious or blasphemous. Agricultural labourers in East Anglia and the southern shires rioted in 1816 and 1822; in 1830–31, some 20 of the 60 or so counties of England were disturbed to greater or lesser degrees by rick burnings, menaces for money, and threats of violence to Pooɪ Law overseers and others. The initial rejection of the Reform Bil. in 1831 brought acts of violence against the bishops and mob action at Nottingham and Bristol; the centre of the latter city was sacked.[1]

The significance of all this for the study of the Poor Law inquiry lies in the challenges it poses as to the nature of such protests, their relationship to class consciousness, and the extent to which they derived from the state of Poor Law practice.

At the extremes two views are possible. It is argued that the situation of the farm labourer was such as 'to make some sort of rebellion inevitable'.[2] Such a statement emphasizes the extent and intensity of disturbance, with the possibility of it becoming general. 'Perhaps', wrote Hobsbawm and Rudé, 'its great tragedy was that it never succeeded in linking up with the rebellion of mine, mill and city.' At the same time the consciousness of the labourers of their condition is stressed, together with their sense of responsibility: 'The rising', we are told, 'was a massive, collective and peaceful assertion of the labourers' rights as men and citizens.'[3] This approach maximizes the oppressive nature of the regime in dealing with protest, arguing that politicians, officialdom and the military were more prone to violence than were the workers. This kind of thinking rests upon the attitude that protest, because it occurs, is a symptom of tension meaningful for society as a whole, that the 'crowd' which carries it out is rational and controlled, free of any tendency to pass into a 'mob', and that the authorities in dealing with the situation should have taken this into account.

The opposing view is that the protests, though frightening to contemporaries, were not all that formidable or concerted, but were a discrete set of incidents, spasmodically related to the worst times and the most adversely affected groups, and encapsulated within particular regions. The question might well be asked by those who take this view: if the labourers had developed a serious consciousness of oppression, and of their role and their solidarity, why then did not the envisaged link-up take place? (Rudé says that of the many disturbances in 1830–31 it was only the Reform movement that had any sort of revolutionary potential.)[4] By extension this approach argues that regrettable though the need for public discipline may have been, protest was on a modest scale, not comparable to what has occurred in other societies. It is possible also to point to the relatively brief period of the trouble.

To date it is the maximizers of protest who have done most of the work and have set the tone of the discussion. In the debate over the standard of living the liberal-positivists have had protagonists capable of balancing the debate; perhaps the same is necessary in this equally difficult but important aspect of social history.

The Poor Law Report and its Appendices contain a good many references to the disturbances of 1830–31, the kind of action taken by the protesters, and the effect on the outlook of those who felt themselves vulnerable. There is little doubt that in many parishes landowners, farmers, overseers and magistrates were shaken by the outburst. The evidence suggests that the effect of disturbance

and the threat of it was to further weaken the willingness of overseers and magistrates to deny the claims made upon them by the
poor. Indeed the authors of the Poor Law Report believed that the
'paroxysm subsided' 'partly under the application of force, but
much more under that of bribes', that is to say, higher payments to
the poor.[5] The authors further believed that even in the face of a
general surplus of capital, agriculture was starved of it because
of the destruction of confidence .

6. THE AVAILABLE ALTERNATIVES

What courses were open to those concerned with the question of
the English poor in the early 1830s? There were two general
possibilities: some radical departure from the existing system
of relationships (that is to say revolutionary change), or a programme of ameliorative self-help within the existing structure of
society, with or without a reassertion of social discipline by a
return to rigour in the administration of the Poor Law.

No generalized solution was forthcoming from the farm labourers
nor could it be expected. The disturbances were not revolutionary in
intent. There was no demand that proprietors give up the land;[1]
land reform was a notion held by urban idealists. It did not enter
the heads of the labourers that they could run agriculture, through
collectives or any other means. Rather, the labourers demanded
better wages, more secure employment and greater sympathy and
support from the Poor Law overseers; at a deeper level it may be
that they sought the nostalgic and perhaps romanticized ideal of
a stable moral order in the countryside. To this aspiration there
was much in the make-up of their masters – nobility, gentry and
farmers – that responded; this was the programme of Cobbett, that
arch radical-conservative.[2] But for its realization it was necessary
that English agriculture, within the larger context of the economy,
should thrive to such a degree as to make necessary its already
large and still growing labour force. In an industrializing society
with a rationalizing and improving agriculture this could not
be.

As a possible alternative the state might try to provide employment in the shires. But the long sad tale of decay and corruption
that had accompanied past attempts to set the poor to work under

the parish aegis meant that some other form of sponsorship was necessary for such a programme; none was available.

Nor could the radical thinkers of the day offer a convincing programme.[3] Robert Owen's fundamental notion was that of a 'scientific arrangement of the people, united in properly constructed villages of unity and co-operation'.[4] Sturges Bourne's Committee of 1817, according to Owen, debated for two whole days whether he should be examined, and then refused him a hearing. The majority of the Committee were clearly embarrassed in dealing with 'a new system in principle, spirit and practice, for the government of the human race'.[5] The other socialists writing in the 1820s, Thompson, Gray, Bray and Hodgskin, were unable to provide the baffled workers, or indeed the intellectuals, with a programme.[6] To do so would have involved a challenge to the pattern of ownership and authority, and so to the general social and political structure.

Much middle-class thought went into suggestions for amelioration through self-help. There were advocates of the provision of small plots for the peasantry so that they might practise spade husbandry, thus augmenting their diet and their self-respect. The savings-bank movement achieved some success in its efforts to induce habits of thrift and foresight. Support was given to schemes of emigration. There was a good deal of effort in the direction of education, some of it taking the form of preparation for Bible-reading so that the worker might become aware of a beneficent God who rewarded virtue in this world or the next. Some 'education' emphasized the Malthusian precepts of continence among bachelors and the delay of marriage until the groom could support its legitimate fruits.

Thomas Chalmers, the Scottish divine, who had served in 'the most plebeian parish in Glasgow', attracted sympathetic attention with his apparent success with the poor. In reviewing the Poor Law Committee Report of 1817 he condemned the English Poor Law system, arguing that anyone in need should be supported by their families or friends, so that neither the able-bodied nor the aged should come to expect a public provision. For, in Chalmers's view, the effect of English Poor Law practice had been to kill independence of spirit as shown in the willingness to work and to save.[7] He believed that the best approach to the problem was to encourage families to give aid to their members, for neighbours to sustain one another, and for this pattern not to be intruded upon and destroyed by payments made from the parish, which too easily came to be regarded as a natural right.[8] Labourers should be encouraged to give for the support of their own parish poor. The middle class of Glasgow might also make a modest monetary contribution, but instead of being called upon merely for money, they should voluntarily serve as deacons, administering parish funds to assist cases in which mutual aid was not enough, and proceeding by strict investigation. In this way Chalmers placed his faith in the twin principles of independence among the labourers and a spirit of mutualism in aiding their own poor, together with an active committed participation by the middle class.[9] His ideas seem to have approximated to those of Cobbett in that both sought a reunion of social classes. But they differed in that Chalmers believed that the workers might, largely by their own efforts, sustain themselves, and under supervision, take care of their own, an attitude that must have seemed to Cobbett totally unrealistic.

But these were all *ad hoc* and limited treatments of the problem of the poor. By the early 1830s the commitment of Britain to industrialization had gone so far that there could be no question of turning back; equally there could be no serious possibility of introducing a socialist or other collectivized society, nor even of trying to modernize the traditional pattern of state regulation of commerce and industry (mercantilism) to control economic growth, incomes and employment. The only long-term hope for the poor lay in the extension of the market economy.

It is hard to see how the passing of England (or indeed any other country) from an agrarian to an urban-industrialized basis could have been other than painful, with a good many casualties. Thus was the dilemma that stretched back to Tudor times sharpened: how were the poor to be helped in their immediate needs without making the problem even more difficult in the longer term?

In the upshot the Government reacted to the protests of 1830–31 as it had to others earlier, treating them as a law-and-order situation. Some two years later it set up a major inquiry into the working of the Poor Law.

7. THE POOR LAW INQUIRY

In February 1832, three months before the great storm over the Reform Bill ended in its passing, the Whig Government appointed a Royal Commission directed to 'make a diligent and full inquiry into the practical operation of the laws for the relief of the poor in England and Wales ... To report whether any, and what, alterations, amendments, or improvements may be beneficially made in the said laws, ... and how the same may be best carried into effect'.[1]

The Commission of nine was presided over by Charles Blomfield, the Tory Bishop of London; he had the support of J. B. Sumner, the moderate Bishop of Chester who had pondered the problems of poverty as related to the grand design of the Deity.[2] A further priest of the Church of England brought the clerical representation to three. A veteran of the subject, Sturges Bourne, was a member; he had been chairman of the 1817 Poor Law Committee and had devoted most of his political career to the problem. The intellectual luminary was Nassau Senior,[3] who as holder of the short-tenure Drummond Professorship of Political Economy at Oxford had delivered in 1830 'Three Lectures on the Rates of Wages ...' In them he had shown himself to be a Malthusian, a believer in the inefficacity of trade unions in raising wages, and an opponent of the Poor Laws, especially relief to the able-bodied. Perhaps more notable than Senior in the long run, was Edwin Chadwick, then thirty-two; he was to become one of the best known and most controversial men of his generation in the field of social improvement. The remaining two members were men of no apparent distinction.

It was Senior as the most technically competent in matters of political economy and the Poor Law who supervised the investigation and kept contact with the Cabinet. Chadwick certainly made an original contribution to the Report and to the act to which it gave rise.[4] He has been seen as the quintessential Benthamite, eager to put his country's institutions to the utilitarian test of promoting the greatest happiness of the greatest number, and vigorously to amend them if they failed it. There can be little doubt that the Commissioners shared the new ethos of self-help, strongly biasing them against a liberal provision for the poor. They expected to find certain evils rampant; they were fearful of an indigent and debauched working class. It was all the more important that their investigations be carried out as objectively as possible.

The procedure for the gathering of data was a two-part one.[5] The Commissioners drew up three questionnaires, two of which were circulated in rural districts and the third in the towns. But the Commissioners soon became aware of the inadequacies of the replies, both in quantity and quality. A little over ten per cent of the parishes replied (there was no compulsion), corresponding to about one fifth of the population. There were important elements of ambiguity in the questions, which added to the difficulty of interpretation. The result was an enormous collection of data that was extremely difficult to construe. It was decided, therefore, to send out Assistant Commissioners who should 'ascertain the state of the poor by personal inquiry among them, and the administration of the Poor Laws by being present, at the vestries and at the sessions of the magistrates'.[6] They were to take the replies to the questionnaire with them. They were told that because it was impossible to visit all the parishes in England and Wales they should use their own discretion in the choice of parishes. They were to dwell 'principally on those facts from which some general inference may be drawn and which form the rule rather than the exception'[7] – a curiously naïve invitation to preconception. The Assistant Commissioners were further briefed with a set of topics to be inquired into; these, like the original questionnaires, were too diffuse and imprecise to give rise to aggregative knowledge, but rested on the Commissioners' views of what was important.

There were twenty-six Assistant Commissioners. They undertook an arduous unpaid task. Indeed the Commissioners could not find as many Assistants as they needed, and had to do a good deal of doubling-up of districts. The Assistants visited some 3,000 places, about one fifth of the Poor Law authorities. They were philanthropically minded amateurs, warned by the Commissioners to keep their expenses down. It may well be that they themselves were the result of a biased self-selection, for it is likely that they would be men motivated by a sense of the need to do something about the Poor Law. The Rev. Henry Bishop and Edwin Chadwick appeared both as Commissioners and Assistant Commissioners. In the latter character Chadwick was by far the most assiduous: his evidence is equal to that of any other two Assistant Commissioners.[8]

The complete range of information is contained in the thirteen volumes of Appendices to the Report. For the Commissioners decided that everything should be published, confident that such a procedure would support, in the public mind, their conclusions and recommendations. This immense storehouse of raw data has only lately been used by scholars. The materials are arranged under five headings: the parish reports of the Assistant Commissioners, the returns to the parish questionnaires (five volumes from rural areas and two from the towns), miscellaneous communications from various individuals on sundry topics including emigration, medical dispensaries and the administration of the Poor Law in the North of England, communications from the counties on labour rates and vagrancy, and, finally, communications describing Poor Law practice in various foreign countries.

There has been a good deal of criticism of the Report as an exercise in social inquiry. It is well, however, to remember the conditions under which the Commission worked. There was an almost total lack of experience and precedent in survey technique.[9] It was impossible to apply scientific principles to the collection of evidence, for none existed. Indeed the question – 'how does a society take an objective view of itself in social terms?' had hardly yet been posed. (The Select Committee on the Factory Acts was gathering its evidence about the same time and encountered many of the same difficulties.) In addition there was the pressure from the Government for speed, for it wanted a quick result. The Assistant Commissioners were urged to move briskly through the parishes. Indeed the Report was written before all the evidence had arrived, let alone been studied.[10] There was an interval of a mere six months between the circulation of the questionnaire to the sending of the evidence to the printers.[11]

In addition to the need for speed there was also that of practicality. The Commissioners were aware that the Government expected them to produce the basis for a reform. A kind of teleology would thus operate: the very need for a programme could hardly have failed to affect the writing of the Report, giving it greater simplification and directness. Into the spirit of this necessity men like Senior and Chadwick readily entered. Finally, among the difficulties in the way of a scientific procedure was the complexity of the problem, the number of parish units into which it fell, and the state of mind of those of whom inquiry was to be made. The Commissioners, daunted by the mountain of material their questionnaires and Assistants had produced, were 'unwilling to incur the responsibility of selection'.[12]

Vast though the task was, the Commissioners would have had to go a good deal further if they were to gain a full grasp of the problem. There was no systematic information either about unemployment or wage levels – both inseparable from the problems of Poor Law policy. It is true that the Report contains many references to these matters, but they are local and *ad hoc*. Hardly surprisingly, the Commissioners did not conceive of themselves as inquiring into the economy as a whole. The result was that it was impossible to judge the pressures bearing upon the poor. This meant that moralism and the attempt to distinguish between the deserving and the undeserving poor were not controlled by a proper view of the forces to which they were subject.

How would sociologists and economists of our own day, could they be transported back to the early 1830s, design an inquiry to discover the condition of the poor and the impact of the relief system upon them? To ask such a question is perhaps to make us somewhat less critical of the Commissioners and their Assistants. They did not lack scientific canons: they altered and amplified their questionnaire in the light of experience. They had some of the Assistant Commissioners make pilot investigations. They presented in their printed volumes of Appendices all that had been brought before them. The Commissioners were proud of their work: they believed themselves to be tendering to His Majesty 'the most extensive, and at the same time the most consistent, body of evidence that was ever brought to bear on a single subject'.[13]

But they did not make any serious calculations; they relied rather on impressionistic interpretation. Because they did not sufficiently standardize their questions at the outset, but rather allowed their respondents great scope for variation in reply, they could not easily summate the flood of answers. Indeed it is hard to imagine what Nassau Senior and the other Commissioners thought they were going to do with such a deluge of data in the age of the quill pen. Modern scholars, especially Mark Blaug,[14] have reworked some of the evidence in quantitative terms, and have concluded that within it are clues that, had they been detected, might have controlled the operation of preconception.

8. THE PARISH AS PROJECTED BY THE COMMISSIONERS: THEIR REMEDIES

There can be no doubt that the Commissioners began, as we all must do, with generalized assumptions. Both moralism and environmentalism were present. As to the former, the Commissioners believed it to be a natural law of civil society that 'the effects of each man's improvidence (or indeed misbehaviour of any kind) are borne by himself and his family'.[1] Even though the parish might give some temporary relief, this only compounded the situation, making it worse than before. Their emphasis, therefore, was to try to seek out and assess failure in social responsibility.

Environmentalism was present in the fact that the Commissioners did not regard the pauper as inherently an inferior person, but rather as corrupted by the system of relief under which he lived; he was not by nature brutish, requiring strong discipline (for after all he was English), but rather was rendered incapable of self-respect and self-control by the Poor Law system. Where it was well operated (that is to say with firmness and concern) the labourer responded by raising his conduct to a new level. The Commission reported with approval cases of well-run parishes in country and town. They implied that cases had been found in which parishes in a similar situation in the same region produced very different responses from the labourers, depending on parish policy. The solution to the condition of the poor lay in improving the context within which they lived, the parish.

The Commissioners argued that the descent into indigence and social decay was cumulative. Pauperism could all too easily become accepted; pauper hostility to the independent labourer could develop, breaking down the resistance of the stronger-minded, until in the end the parish population was reduced to idleness.

On the general result of their inquiries the Commissioners were clear. Immediately after their historical preliminaries they condemned parish practice. 'It is now our painful duty to report', they wrote, 'that in the greater part of the districts we have been able to examine, the fund, which the 43 Elizabeth directed to be employed in setting to work children and persons capable of labour, but using no daily trade, and in the necessary relief of the impotent, is applied to purposes opposed to the letter, and still more to the spirit of that law, and destructive to the morals of the most numerous class, and to the welfare of all.'[2]

The first half of the Report is devoted to demonstrating this, and to its corollary – a condemnation of the idea of the able-bodied having, as of right, a claim upon society for maintenance. The second half (after disposing of certain false cures) goes on to recommend remedies. The Report concludes with a statement that economic solutions to the nation's ills are but secondary. The influence among the Commissioners of their clergymen colleagues is apparent in the insistence that improvement in the Poor Law was a mere preliminary to the promotion of religious and moral education among the labouring classes. As soon as the cancer of the Poor Law has been brought under control, urged the Commissioners, the nation should turn to a programme of religious and moral instruction addressed to the labourer now redeemed from the incubus of outdoor relief.[3]

The Commissioners found and presented much evidence of social decay – idleness, dishonesty, evasion, drunkenness, dirty homes and dirty people, ragged children, poaching, smuggling, etc., all compounded in a continuous battle of wits and tempers with the overseers and reflected in damage to veracity, industry, frugality, and the domestic virtues. In this, Marxist historians have followed the Commissioners. Engels, having observed the bad effects of practice as set out in the Report, wrote that the 'description of the working of the old Poor Law is by and large, true enough since the relief encouraged idleness and promoted the increase of "superfluous population"'.[4] As Hobsbawm puts it, the Speenhamland system was 'disastrous' for 'it pauperised, demoralised, and immobilised the labourer'.[5] He considers it to have been a last attempt 'to maintain a traditional rural order in the face of the market economy'. By this he appears to mean that the overseers and justices were trying, by mistakenly generous payments, to preserve the interest of their class by insulating the labourer from the impact of social change.

It is worthwhile constructing the model of a badly administered parish to which the Commissioners, by their preconceptions and their inquiries, were led. It began with the over-prolific labourer, fathering perhaps eight or ten children.[6] The overseers felt obliged to accept man, wife and children as a charge on the parish rate. Under the allowance system the local farmer would get the man's labour for much less than the going wage, thus keeping wages lower than they would otherwise have been. The labourer might in addition get assistance with his rent. All in all, though an inferior worker, the man would thus do well. Indeed he might be better off than another who had followed the advice of Malthus and remained single or kept his family small. If he were not otherwise employed he might be required to work for the parish breaking stones for road-making or digging gravel or other tasks; this, however, all too readily became a form of idleness. Often the single man was discriminated against by the farmers in hiring men, for it was in the interest of all to give the available jobs to married men in order to reduce the pressure on the parish. As a result, the single man was tempted to marry and so bring more children to the parish charge. Thus parish, farmer and married labourer all had an interest in a perverted system; insidiously deceived by their own circumstances, all were content with arrangements that permitted a cumulative excess of population, a lowering of wages, a continuous disincentive to work and a constant discouragement to personal budgeting and saving.

The parish could thus be subject to a spiral of rising poor-rates and declining labour productivity. The point could be reached at which farmers, at last caught between the two, would find that their net profit after payment of the poor-rate had been destroyed. They would cease to make any improvements or even to do proper maintenance and would finally abandon their tenancies, leaving their farms uncultivated and exhausted. In this phase a rapid acceleration of decay could occur, for each abandoned farm meant both more unemployed and less property capable of being rated for the poor. As in the case of the parish of Cholesbury in Buckinghamshire there could be an almost total abandonment of farming. There 'the parish officers threw up their books', and the poor assembled in a body around the door of the clergyman while he was in bed, asking for advice and food.[7] Only one such case of near total breakdown was discovered by the Commissioners, but they hinted at many parishes that were well begun on such a decline. They insisted that it could rapidly be cumulative. Even where there was not such a galloping deterioration farming was in general being starved of capital in a situation of capital glut because of the lack of confidence in farm investment.[8]

The Commissioners believed that, for the most part, the families of the impotent, though enjoined by the 43 Elizabeth to care for their natural dependants, were not being made by the overseers to do so; rather such persons, contrary to the 'natural affections', were put upon the parish.[9] The Commissioners favoured a policy of encouraging or even forcing labouring families to take care of their own.

A further evil lay in bastardy.[10] The law permitted any pregnant spinster to 'swear her child' to any adult male she might choose. The result was often grievously unfair to men so accused, but they had no recourse. They would then be charged with the maintenance of the child. But in most cases the parish had little or no success in collecting the sums thus awarded by the justices, for the men concerned would evade payment, often by leaving the parish.

In the lax state of the law the Commissioners believed that the poorhouses (or as they ought properly to be called, the workhouses) were grossly mismanaged, especially, judging from the examples given, in the larger towns.[11]

Finally, among the abuses was the state of the Settlement Laws.[12] Their object had always been to control geographical mobility by restricting the conditions under which a labourer could acquire a Settlement in any parish but that of his birth. Fraud, deception and all manner of deviousness were promoted by the terms on which a labourer who wanted to move could obtain a Settlement. The labourer who did not wish to seek work elsewhere found confirmation in a set of laws that rested on the assumption that he should not. The result was to discourage men from moving from areas of unemployment to those where there were jobs. The Commissioners thought it likely that had the labourers in the Home Counties been willing and able to move, the influx of Irish into London would have been on a much smaller scale.[13]

In addition to all this, the pauper could bring about conflict between the overseers (elected by the vestry) and the justices, consisting largely of the landed gentry. For the Poor Law allowed appeal from the overseers to the justices, thus providing the labourer with a marvellous opportunity for divisive action. For the overseers (usually men of lesser substance, though occasionally a larger farmer would take on the task with a view to reducing the poor rates)[14] were closer to the parish, aware of the limitations of its finance and experienced in the effects of a weakening of control over payments. The magistrates were more removed from the problem, with no real knowledge of the life of the labourer. With an inappropriate sense of money values and their nerves shaken by the risings of 1830–31, they were often more amenable to the pleas of the poor. Moreover the parish rates were levied not on owners (among which the justices were often the largest group) but on occupiers – the farmers. After humiliating rebuffs by the justices the overseers would tend to act not on the basis of their own judgement, but would anticipate what they thought the magistrates would enforce upon them. In a good many cases, indeed, the paupers hastened such capitulation by threatening the overseers with the displeasure of the magistrates. Frustrated overseers not unnaturally became surly and sometimes even cruel in their treatment of the poor. They became, moreover, the centre and focus of village raillery and of threatened violence.

The Commissioners concluded that in the rural districts the greater the sums dispensed in poor rates or in private charities, the greater the discontent. They supported this with the concept of rising expectations: each concession to the pauper led to his accepting and assimilating it and then asking for more.[15]

This, then, was the way in which the Commissioners saw the Old Poor Law as capable of acting. They did not see all the abuses as appearing in every parish, nor even in any. But this was their picture of the elements of the old Poor Law, their inter-relationships, and their tendency.

*

The remedies proposed by the Commissioners derived directly from their analysis of the problem. Because the 'master evil' of the Old Poor Law was outdoor relief, and the great object was to 'dis-pauperize', such relief had to be cut away. Accordingly, except for medical attention, all able-bodied persons or their families should cease to receive 'all relief whatever ... otherwise than in well-regulated workhouses'.[16] Such workhouses should be paid for and operated, as before, by parishes or unions of parishes. But there was need for the expression of a single will, bringing uniformity and explicitness of practice. A central Board should be set up 'to control the administration of the Poor Laws' (e.g. the workhouses). It should be provided with assistant commissioners. The Board would 'frame and enforce regulations for the government of the workhouses',[17] including the standard of provision for the paupers, applying, so far as was practicable, uniformity throughout the country.

The Board and the parishes were to be guided by the principle that paupers receiving relief within the workhouse should be in a 'situation' which 'on the whole shall not be made really or apparently so eligible as the situation of the independent labourer of the lowest class'.[18] This was the famous principle of 'less eligibility' whereby the standard of living in the workhouse must be inferior to that of the lowest-paid worker. The Board would have authority to combine parishes for the purpose of managing or building workhouses (of the 15,535 parishes 12,034 had less than 800 inhabitants and 6,681 less than 300). It would also 'incorporate parishes', e.g. authorize them to appoint and pay permanent officers and to carry out building operations. Such officers should be suited to their task (e.g. should be 'professionals'); for in the Commissioners' view dependence upon intuition in Poor Law management was as unsound as such reliance in navigating a ship or operating a steam engine.[19] To this end the Board should set up the qualifications required, and have the power both to recommend persons and to remove those they thought unfit.[20] The Board and the parishes were to treat the cost of relief given within the workhouse as a loan, and seek to recover it from the labourer where possible.

In addition the treatment of parish apprentice children was to be considered by the Board and suggestions for their treatment made.[21] The Commissioners recommended that Settlement be abolished.[22] The Bastardy Acts were to be changed, requiring the mother of an illegitimate child to support it, and abolishing any claim on the putative father.[23] The Board would encourage parishes to make payments from the poor rates to subsidize emigration.[24]

Finally, the Board would submit an annual report to the Government on all its activities, and on the state of the poor.

This programme had a classic simplicity, combining an attack on the central evil of the allowance system with administrative reform, involving the setting up of a national supervising body, yet retaining local participation.

9. THE CRITICS OF THE REPORT

The Poor Law Report of 1834 and the act based upon it have inspired heated and sustained criticisms. These have been of two kinds: charges of heartless coercion and of unscientific procedures. Marxist authors have viewed the new policy in terms of the abuse of a proletariat. Engels in 1844 described the authors of the Report as wishing 'to force the poor into the Procrustean bed of their preconceived doctrines. To do this they treated the poor with incredible savagery.'[1] For Maurice Dobb the new Poor Law 'set the seal on unfettered free trade in the labour market'.[2] Hobsbawm refers to the Act as 'that ruthless piece of legal-economic coercion'.[3] Others have stressed the failure of the authors of the Report to follow proper procedures. R. H. Tawney impaled the Report on the phrase, 'brilliant, influential and wildly unhistorical'.[4] The Webbs criticized the lack of quantification, and themselves defaulted in this respect; in addition they regarded most of the Assistant Commissioners as vitiated observers.[5] Mark Blaug has written: 'The Poor Law Commissioners of 1834 ... deliberately selected the facts so as to impeach the existing administration [of the Poor Laws] on predetermined lines ... what little evidence they did present consisted of little more than picturesque anecdotes of maladministration.'[6]

It can hardly be denied that the abuses described in the Report existed: no-one has accused the Commissioners or their Assistants of making up the cases they presented. The real problem is threefold: how do we ascertain how serious and how general they were, their trend over time, and their future potential for economic and social deterioration? The Commissioners believed that the abuses built into the system were widespread, that they had been continuously growing for three decades, and that they 'appear to contain ... elements of an almost indefinite extension'. These three levels of objection provide us with tests by means of which to attempt a judgement between the Commissioners and their critics on the matter of diagnosis.

There can be no doubt that the Commissioners in their fact-gathering were looking for bad practice rather than good. Yet the good is also there. There are well-conducted parishes and there are independent-minded labourers, though both are usually presented in order to point up the contrast with the bad. Had the Assistant Commissioners chosen different parishes, those less 'interesting' in terms of what they were looking for, would the flavour of the Report have been different? What of the other four fifths of the parishes that did not bother to reply? Did they abstain because they were not so greatly exercised over the problem as were those that did? We can only learn the answer to such questions as studies of particular parishes and regions become available.

Blaug, unlike Engels and other Marxist commentators, insists that 'hardly any of the dire effects ascribed to the old Poor Law stand in the light of the available empirical knowledge'.[7] Moreover, he says, 'the Speenhamland system has not always been as imprudently administered as has been thought'.[8] Somewhat puzzlingly, however, he adds in his second article, 'But I accepted the general picture which they (the Commissioners) presented of the old Poor Law, in particular the practice of giving outdoor relief to employed workers in the form of supplements to earned wages, the amount of the supplement being proportionate to the ruling price of bread.'[9]

A careful reading of the Report shows that the Commissioners, in some parts of it at least, were a good deal less flatly spoken than their critics have implied. Some of the general statements made refer to the 'pauperized districts', and not to the country as a whole, though, on the other hand, the Commissioners made no effort to define, much less list, such districts. There is a good deal of use of qualifying phrases like 'in many places', 'in some of the districts', 'sometimes', 'appears to', or 'seems'. The Commissioners have suffered a great deal from commentators like Engels, who prepared their own paraphrases of the Report (in Engels's case based upon the table of contents) and presented these as literal abstracts of its conclusions.[10]

It could be argued that in order to make the case for a legislative programme the Commissioners did not have to demonstrate general breakdown in the English parishes, but only that the evils described were sufficiently general and dangerous to require action. For such a demonstration the technique of presenting massed evidence, with selections embodied in the Report, is perhaps not unacceptable.

On the trend in outdoor relief, Blaug's conclusion is that here the Commissioners went badly wrong: had they done the necessary calculations they would have discovered that Speenhamland allowances had not in fact been on the increase since the Select Committee on Labourers' Wages of 1824, but that there had been a considerable reduction in such payments in the course of the intervening years.[11] He concludes that the practice of wage subsidy was largely confined to areas where the growth of industry was too weak to lever wages upwards. He identifies eighteen counties as the 'hard core' of the problem.[12]

The Commissioners recognized that the absolute sum spent on poor relief as recorded in the Parliamentary Return for 1832, being some £7 million, was less than that for 1817 at £7·9 million. But they argued that 1817 was a year of extraordinary distress and high prices making the figures for that year uncharacteristically high.[13] They made no attempt to calculate relief per head of population, as adjusted to price changes.[14] Moreover they believed that the hidden subsidy to wages was very much greater in 1832 than it had been in 1817. There is no way of testing this assertion on the evidence provided; perhaps parish inquiries will produce new light. The result, the Report argued, was increasing deterioration in the pauperized districts.

This was not the only kind of *a priori* thinking practised by the Commissioners. They held the ideal of an 'independent' peasantry, free of parish subsidy, and maintaining itself by its earnings, a prosperous proletariat. They looked back to a time, presumably

before 1795, in which landlords and farmers concerned themselves
much more intimately with their labourers and did not seek to
buy quiescence from the poor-rates. The Commissioners, in
condemning the Old Poor Law, did not have as their objective
the demolition of the last defences of the poor against the market
economy, but rather the removal of a debilitating influence that
made it impossible for them to respond to its opportunities. The
Commissioners sought the restoration of a spirit of independence
among the labourers, through the sale of their services by bargains
made with their employers.

This attitude was reinforced by a general set of notions about the
economy. The Commissioners persuaded themselves that, by and
large, those who sought employment could find it. They did so
not by considering the economy as a whole, but by studying those
parishes where rigour of administration had been practised or had
been newly introduced: they concluded from these examples that
men whose relief was withdrawn could find other means of employment. 'One of the most encouraging of the results of our inquiry',
says the Report rather paradoxically, 'is the degree to which the
existing pauperism arises from fraud, indolence or improvidence.'[15]
It seems that there was indeed some scope for men to find jobs in
some areas. But it was a dangerous and unwarranted step to conclude, as did the Commissioners, that this was true generally.

10. THE POOR LAW AMENDMENT ACT AND ITS IMPLEMENTATION

The Government, with the understandable intention of making
things easier for itself and harder for its opponents, produced a Bill
that was much less explicit than the Report. It provided, as proposed, a Poor Law Board, in the form of a new set of Poor Law
Commissioners, and passed most of the tasks to it. The Bill contained no reference to a workhouse test in the form of less eligibility,
but left this implicit and discretionary with the Commissioners.
Though the Bill originally contained the stipulation that allowances
in aid of wages were to cease on 1 June 1835, this clause was dropped. In its place the Commissioners were given discretion to
regulate outdoor relief as they saw fit, through directives. Indeed,
very little of the principles of implementation were set out, but

were left to the new Commissioners. On the other hand the Bill implied that the Commissioners were to take the Report as their guiding light. The Bill became the Poor Law Amendment Act in August 1834, some two months after the presentation of the Report.[1]

Only on administration was the Act explicit. The Commissioners were to supersede the old system of overseers with a new one of elected guardians; parishes, where appropriate, were to be grouped into unions and be provided with workhouses. The Commissioners were to conduct a general surveillance, evolving policy directives as they went along, but aiming at limiting parish discretion and promoting standardization of treatment. Illegitimate children became the responsibility of the mother unless the father's identity could be proven. The Settlement Laws, though altered in detail, remained in principle.[2]

Thus it was that the Government, though it accepted the prescriptions of the Report, left the principal policy questions at the discretion of the Commissioners. This meant, of course, that the struggle over implementation had to be fought not by the Government in Parliament, but by the Commissioners in the parishes.

Installed in their headquarters in Somerset House the three Commissioners, with twelve Assistant Commissioners, began their immense task of reorganization. They started with the most heavily pauperized districts of southern England. Chadwick, who had very much hoped to become a Commissioner, was instead made Secretary, a post he occupied for fourteen years. In spite of a few scattered disturbances, things went smoothly for some two years, helped by good harvests and by the welcome of farmers and landowners. Indeed, effective organization among rural workers ended with the Tolpuddle martyrs in 1834; it was not to revive until the 1870s. Boards of Guardians were set up, parishes were combined in unions and the conditions of relief were tightened. The Commission appointed two agents to act as a kind of labour exchange, linking northern industrialists looking for workers to the rural parish authorities in the south. There were bitter charges that this was an attempt to hold down wages and weaken labour organization in the factories. But the work went steadily on: by July 1837 only 1,300 of the parishes of England (less than 10 per cent) had not been provided with Boards of Guardians.[3]

It was when the Commissioners sent their Assistants to the industrial North, to reorganize parish relief there, that the real storm broke.[4] For in 1837 the relatively good times of the mid 1830s collapsed in a major depression. An anti-Poor Law movement sprang up, drawing support from the factory reform movement. The enemies of the New Poor Law condemned the offer of the workhouse, the 'Bastille', to the unemployed men. There was resistance too among local officials, magistrates and ratepayers, who believed that the workhouse formula was irrelevant in the face of large-scale urban-industrial unemployment. Highly emotional things were said at public meetings and in some places there were riots. Resistance to the spirit of the Report as it was feared it would be expressed in the letter of instructions from the Commissioners gave the Poor Law an important place in the history of mass agitation in the England of the 1830s and 1840s.

The policy of the Report, if it was to meet the needs of the nation, required the fulfilment of four major assumptions. The first was that the concept of the 'well regulated' workhouse was capable of implementation. The second was the view that the wages of those in employment would be high enough to make possible the enforcement of the margin of 'less eligibility' so that treatment in the workhouses would not be inhuman. The third required that the unemployed, under the goad of rigour, would be able to find employment. Fourthly, there was the idea that the workhouse could be so used as to induce a decisive psychological effect on the pauper.

Each of these assumptions was, to greater or lesser degree, falsified. All too soon cases came to the public notice of abuse and deterioration in workhouses. The authors of the Report had, undoubtedly, forgotten the lessons of Tudor times and of the act of 1722, underestimating the insidiousness of workhouse decay and overestimating the supervisory capacity of the Boards of Guardians and the Assistant Commissioners. Less eligibility, so clear as a principle, became blurred in practice, for there were too many low-paid workers for a differential to be maintained in their favour over the workhouse inmates. The ease with which employment could be found, especially in some parts of the country, had been greatly overestimated. Finally the concept of psychological renewal under the discipline of the workhouse was based upon too simple a view of the paupers' motivation.

These limitations became ever more apparent as the anti-Poor Law agitation gained momentum. Its great strength lay in the industrial cities of the North, though for a time there appeared to be effective support in Wales, Cornwall and London.

In their attempts to implement the act the Poor Law Commission, and especially Chadwick, have been charged with dogmatism and inhumanity.[5] But, under pressure from the Home Secretary, they desisted, especially in the North. Indeed the Commission failed to draft effective orders upon which enforcement might have been based. By 1844, in spite of a renewed effort by the Commissioners in 1842 to bring the North into greater uniformity with the South, a kind of stalemate had been reached. The Anti-Poor Law Movement was thus deprived of its great complaint, for the anticipated inhumanity failed to appear, at least on the scale expected. From the later months of 1838 the energies of the members of the Anti-Poor Law Movement were largely turned towards Chartism, depriving the opposition to the Commission of its political dynamic.

Yet the 'Three Bashaws of Somerset House' continued to be a standing target. They and the New Poor Law were much satirized. Under the burdens of overwork, unpopularity and internal divisions, the morale of the Commission deteriorated. In particular there was the continuous problem of supervising the workhouse masters. In 1845 the scandal of the Andover workhouse broke; its inmates were found to have been reduced to gnawing rotten bones.[6] In 1847 the Poor Law Commission was replaced by a Poor Law Board, whose president was to be a minister of the Crown, sitting in Parliament.

Speenhamland, in the old sense of making up wages according to a scale related to the cost of living, did end. But the allowance system took a new form. It was used largely to augment small, irregular earnings.[7] In effect many Boards of Guardians granted relief more or less as under the Act of Elizabeth of 1601, especially in the textile areas of Lancashire and the West Riding of Yorkshire.

The Guardians, for the most part, acted under motives of prudence, humanity and economy. They had no wish to encourage disturbance. They knew better than the authors of the Poor Law Report that it was impossible to refuse outdoor relief in the industrial towns in times of trade depression. They learned too, as had earlier parish custodians, that keeping paupers and their families in a workhouse was almost invariably more expensive than giving relief to tide them over. The Guardians must also have known that, even with assistance, the life of the labourer who was on the poverty line was precarious and debilitating.

*

So it was that the assertions of the Report proved inadequate to the complexities of the real situation. To the failure of the remedies it proposed at least four elements contributed: firstly, those who felt themselves or their fellows entitled to relief made an effective protest; secondly, the new Poor Law Commissioners (weakened in their will by the Government itself) did not draft and impose the necessary orders; thirdly, the Boards of Guardians in the parishes, acting pragmatically, tempered rigour with mercy and caution; and finally, the middle class, as represented for example by Lord Overstone, the banker, did not take so simple a view of the problem as had the authors of the Report.[8] The Poor Law revolution by legislation sought by the latter largely failed, especially in its principal object of ending outdoor relief. The theories of the political economists and the Benthamite administrators were frustrated in the sense that local improvisation and diversity continued to be part of the English response to the unemployed.

Perhaps it is not too much to say that the Government, having sensed from the public reaction to the New Poor Law some of the realities and complexities of which the Report had lost sight, responded in a sensible way, allowing the conceptual clarity of the Report to be clouded by the need for practicality, mercy and a recognition of the dangers of dogma in the face of protest. Nevertheless, something of an administrative revolution had been consolidated, for the Government was never to give up the centralized jurisdiction of the Poor Law imposed by the Act of 1834.

Yet in spite of so modified a practical application of the Report of 1834, the 'myth' it contained of the need for rigour continued in men's minds. More than sixty years later, in 1895, the leading economist of the day, Alfred Marshall, giving evidence to the Royal Commission on the Aged Poor, said: 'It seems to me that whenever I read Poor Law literature of today I am taken back to the beginning of the century ... You can trace the economic dogmas of present Poor Law literature direct from those times.'[9] As late as the next great Poor Law Commission, that of 1905–9, J. S. Davy, Assistant Secretary of the Local Government Board, could insist that though a man in need through no fault of his own was entitled to sympathy, '... he must stand by his accidents; he must suffer for the general good of the body politic ... what you have to consider is, not this or that pauper, but the general good of the whole community'.[10]

October 1971

S.G.C.
E.O.A.C.

A NOTE ON SOCIAL HISTORY
AND THE POOR LAW

THE historian concerned with the Poor Law finds in it an epitome of the fundamental problem of his craft. He must try to establish the facts, and at the same time apply to them a frame of reference that is true, manageable and meaningful.

So far as the facts are concerned, even a rudimentary knowledge of the struggles of sociologists to extract truth from contemporary observation of phenomena still in train brings an oppressive sense of the difficulties involved; how desperate the prospects seem for an understanding of the departed past! Not least of the difficulties is the strong emotive air that can so easily surround social inquiry. For those who concern themselves with such matters, whether in modern or historical terms, often come to the subject in a committed search for answers to problems of human amelioration, and quite properly so.

At the same time, in order to assess what might appear to be a single phenomenon, the treatment of the poor, it is essential to attempt an understanding of the wider picture of which it is a part. All serious students of the economics of development have had impressed upon them the fact that there exist intimate and involved relationships between land tenure, the volume and price of the food supply, population, employment, real wages, and the condition of the labourer and the pauper.

But there are even deeper problems. There have been two main sets of protagonists in social history as in other aspects of history. Those historians who stand in the liberal intellectual tradition derived from the market economy seek to practise a positive history, free of value-judgements about the nature of society and its long-run course. They reject over-arching historical theses, regarding them as vitiating any objective approach to the facts. The result is often somewhat monographic and non-committal. The great questions of long-term movements are left open; there is therefore always scope for the contingent and the unforeseen and there is never a warrant for the wholesale manipulation of the facts about society towards a goal derived from a theory. By contrast, those historians who start from a Marxist or other historicist viewpoint take from it a generalized clue to the mechanisms and course of history. Whereas the liberal-positivist historian thinks in terms of the interaction of interests through the market mechanism, with a strong equilibristic tendency, and gives perhaps too little attention to sociology, the historicist thinks in on-going terms with relationships continuously evolving through identifiable stages. The Marxist is also much concerned with sociological aspects, basing his approach upon environmental conditioning.

It is true that one historian, W. W. Rostow, has tried to formulate a 'liberal' form of historicism, based upon the notion of societies moving towards the critical conjuncture of 'take-off', without necessary class struggle.[1] But, though, as with Marx, Rostow's insights and vocabulary are borrowed by many historians and economists, the general reaction has been to find his schema inadequate. For the Marxist, the poor are an index of the point that has been reached in the development of the internal contradictions of capitalism; for the liberal historian the poor are simply part of the continuous adjustment of society in response to changing conditions.

The Marxist has a leaning towards the idea of the inherent equality of natural men and indeed their capacity for perfection. The man who becomes a pauper is thus seen as a victim of a defective society, deprived by it of the realization of his potential. Liberal historians, on the other hand, would like to believe that they, by contrast, start without pre-conceptions about the nature of man. But some, especially those of the older tradition, seem to have shared the view, at least in part, that humble men have an intrinsic nobility. Beveridge, contemplating the villein as he saw him in the manorial court records, wrote, 'There remains . . . an impression of the independence of spirit in our ancestors battling their way to freedom in daily work from the trammels of serfdom.'[2] But it is perhaps a fair indictment of most liberal historians that, for the most part, they have been satisfied with superficial mechanisms for integrating the labourer and the pauper into their thinking. Towards the poor they have taken a somewhat unsympathetic and uninquiring attitude, often treating them as mere social residuals who have failed in the process of economic and social selection.

The French historian, Georges Lefebvre used the expression, 'history from below' in order to draw an antithesis to 'history from above'.[3] The latter is the kind of history that derives from the writings of men of the intelligentsia or in positions of responsibility and authority. Such historical material includes statutes and their preambles of intention, discussions and analyses of ideas by individuals, and public inquiries into economic and social problems (the official reports on the factories, the mines, sanitation, etc., and including that on the Poor Law). The starting point for the writing of all such documents is, because of the social position and assumptions of their authors, far removed from the poor; *per contra* they are impregnated with the preconceptions of other classes. 'History from above', moreover, is usually associated with a generalized institutional approach rather than with a concern with the evolution of the community that is being studied, and the groups, including the poor, of which it is composed.

'History from below', on the other hand, tries to remedy this bias by going directly to evidence deriving from the commonality. In it, the contrast between liberal-empiricist and Marxist-historicist is apparent. On the whole, Marxist historians have been more concerned than have liberal historians to try to understand the workers and the poor directly. This applies not only to the observation and measurement of the cost of living, wages, housing and the like, but also, especially in more recent years, to the role of class-consciousness. Indeed it is one of the criteria of the Marxist concept of class that men should be aware of their place in society and react to it. This dual concern with the workers, encompassing both their objective conditions of life and their state of consciousness, has provided two of the great driving forces behind modern social history. It is to be found in the work of E. J. Hobsbawm,[4] George Rudé,[5] E. P. Thompson,[6] and others. It has, of course, an important bearing on the study of the poor. But such work, especially on consciousness, is made difficult by the lack of direct evidence deriving from the labourers and the poor themselves. Even the student of workers' consciousness must rely to a great degree upon sources that derive 'from above', including the Poor Law Report.

The practitioners of 'history from below', if they are to make manageable the task they have set for themselves, must have recourse to the computer. For, because such scholars are seeking to understand situations composed of a great number of individuals and incidents, correlating the characteristics of these and relating them to regional and national experience in terms of employment, earnings, prices, etc., mechanization by means of the computer is necessary. One of the recent meeting-grounds between the liberal-positivist and the Marxist or radical approaches has been the study of social dissatisfaction, aspirations for social change, and the conditions of revolution.[7] It is perhaps here that collective history, the study of the experience of large numbers of persons or social units, has gone furthest. There is, however, among some radical historians in the United States the view that quantitative history 'embodies a particularly subtle and pernicious form of conservative bias'.[8] This, it is thought, is because aggregates dehumanize, and because they lead to an evasion of moral and political responsibility, in short to what such radicals would regard as the failings of liberal-positivism. On this argument, to computerize the poor would be to lose real contact with them.

These problems will almost certainly become more serious when the study of Poor Law history is brought under the new discipline of mechanized quantification. So far, however, the challenge has hardly arisen; a recent survey of work in Britain on economic and social history scarcely mentions the Poor Law;[9] the same is true of the American discussion.

Both liberal-positivist and Marxist scholars, in spite of their difference in approach, must take account of the views of the other. This is enforced by the active debate between them. Indeed the tension between the two points of view provides one of the main driving forces to further understanding. Yet a good many historians, indeed perhaps most, prefer not to be exclusive but to borrow eclectically from both, especially in considering so long and complex a story as that of the English poor.

NOTES TO THE INTRODUCTION

SECTION 2

1. See Sidney and Beatrice Webb, *English Local Government*, vols. VII–IX, *English Poor Law History*, London, 1929. Re-issued 1963. For a convenient treatment see J. D. Marshall, *The Old Poor Law, 1795–1834*, Economic History Society pamphlet, London, 1968.

2. *Report*, pp. 73–81.

3. For text see A. E. Bland, P. A. Brown and Richard H. Tawney, eds., *English Economic History, Select Documents*, London, 1914, pp. 380–81.

4. See John Pound, *Poverty and Vagrancy in Tudor England*, London, 1971; A. G. R. Smith, *The Government of Elizabethan England*, London, 1967, pp. 73–81; P. Ramsay, *Tudor Economic Problems*, London, 1963.

5. F. Aydelotte, *Elizabethan Rogues and Vagabonds*, Oxford, 1963, pp. 68, 69.

6. M. R. G. Davies, *The Enforcement of English Apprenticeship, 1563–1642*, Cambridge, Mass., 1956.

7. R. H. Hilton, 'Peasant Movements in England before 1381', *Economic History Review*, 1949, pp. 117–36.

8. For the administration of the parish see W. E. Tate, *The Parish Chest*, 3rd ed., Cambridge, 1960.

9. See R. H. Campbell and J. B. A. Dow, *Source Book of Scottish Economic and Social History*, Oxford, 1968, chapter VI; A. A. Cormack, *Poor Relief in Scotland*, Aberdeen, 1923; Sir George Nicholls, *A History of the Scotch Poor Law in connection with the condition of the People*, London, 1856, p. 33.

10. J. J. and A. J. Bagley, *The English Poor Law*, London, 1968, p. 17.

11. E. P. Thompson, 1971, pp. 132–6. 'The Moral Economy of the English Crowd in the Eighteenth Century', *Past and Present*, February, 1971, pp. 76–136.

12. For the text see Sir Charles Grant Robertson, *Select Statutes, Cases and Documents*, London, 1949, pp. 53–60.

13. J. R. Poynter, *Society and Pauperism, English Ideas on Poor Relief, 1795–1834*, London, 1969, p. 1.

14. W. K. Jordan, *Philanthropy in England, 1480–1660*, London, 1959, chapters IV–V; *The Charities of London*, London, 1960; *The Charities of Rural England*, London, 1960. See also David Owen, *English Philanthropy, 1660–1960*, Oxford, 1965.

15. For the eighteenth century and its preliminaries see Dorothy Marshall, *The English Poor in the Eighteenth Century*, London, 1965.

16. Charles Wilson, *England's Apprenticeship, 1603–1763*, London, 1965, p. 350.

17. See Michael E. Rose, *The English Poor Law, 1780–1930*, Newton Abbot, 1971, pp. 26–8. This is an excellent documentary introduction. On the

general course of opinion see A. W. Coats, 'Economic Thought and Poor Law Policy in the Eighteenth Century', *Economic History Review*, 1960, pp. 39–51; 'Changing Attitudes to Labour in the Mid-Eighteenth Century', *Economic History Review*, 1958.

18. Andrew Skinner, ed., Adam Smith, *The Wealth of Nations*, 1776, Pelican Classic, 1970, pp. 238–45.
19. Peter Laslett, *The World We Have Lost*, London, 1965, p. x.
20. Harold Perkin, *The Origins of Modern English Society, 1780–1880*, London, 1969, p. 37.
21. E. J. Hobsbawm and George Rudé, *Captain Swing*, London, 1969, p. 15.
22. E. J. Hobsbawm, *Industry and Empire*, Penguin Books, 1969, p. 104.
23. Thompson, 1971, p. 109.

SECTION 3

1. For a useful and cautionary account of the mechanisms see M. W. Flinn, *British Population Growth, 1700–1850*, Economic History Society pamphlet, 1970.
2. For the general background see J. D. Chambers and G. E. Mingay, *The Agricultural Revolution, 1750–1880*, London, 1966.
3. Rose, 1971, pp. 40–41.
4. ibid., pp. 33–5; *Report*, pp. 68–73.
5. Sir Frederick Morton Eden, *The State of the Poor*, London, 1797, New ed., London, 1966.
6. For the movement of labour see A. Redford, *Labour Migration in England*, 2nd ed., Manchester, 1964.
7. J. D. Chambers, 'Enclosure and labour supply in the Industrial Revolution', *Economic History Review*, 1953. Reprinted in E. J. Jones, ed., *Agriculture and Economic Growth in England 1650–1815*, London, 1967, pp. 94–127.
8. See G. E. Mingay, *Enclosure and the Small Farmer in the Age of the Industrial Revolution*, Economic History Society pamphlet, London, 1968, especially pp. 31–2.

SECTION 4

1. cf. Anthony Flew, ed., Thomas Robert Malthus, *An Essay on the Principle of Population*, 1798, Pelican Classic, London 1970. For the Poor Law see chapter V.
2. cf. R. M. Hartwell, ed., David Ricardo, *On the Principle of Political Economy and Taxation*, 1821, Pelican Classic, London, 1971. For the Poor Law see pp. 126–8.
3. cf. J. B. Brebner, 'Laissez-faire and State Intervention in Nineteenth Century Britain', *Journal of Economic History*, Supplement, 1948; David Roberts, 'Jeremy Bentham and the Victorian Administrative State', *Victorian Studies*, 1958–9.

SECTION 5

1. George Rudé, 'English Rural and Urban Disturbances on the Eve of the First Reform Bill, 1830–1831', *Past and Present*, July, 1967, pp. 87–102.
2. Hobsbawm and Rudé, 1969, p. 16.
3. ibid., p. 19.
4. Rudé, 1967, p. 102.
5. *Report*, p. 149.

SECTION 6

1. Hobsbawm and Rudé, 1969, p. 16.
2. See William Cobbett, *Legacy to Labourers*, London, 1835; G. D. H. Cole and M. Cole, eds., *The Opinions of William Cobbett*, London, 1945. For Cobbett's attack on the Poor Law Bill see Rose, 1971, pp. 93–4.
3. For the radical underground press see Patricia Hollis, *The Pauper Press, A Study in Working-Class Radicalism of the 1830s*, Oxford, 1970.
4. John Butt, ed., *Life of Robert Owen, written by himself*, London, 1971. pp. 131, 155.
5. ibid., p. 156.
6. S. G. Checkland, *The Rise of Industrial Society in England, 1815–1885*, London, 1964, p. 407.
7. *Edinburgh Review*, February 1818. Reprinted in G. C. Wood, ed., *Dr. Chalmers and the Poor Laws*, Edinburgh, 1911.
8. Evidence before the Committee of the House of Commons on the Irish Poor Law, 1830, reprinted in Wood, 1911.
9. See Stewart Mechie, *The Church and Scottish Social Development 1780–1870*, London, 1960, chapter 4.

SECTION 7

1. *Report*, p. 67.
2. Poynter, 1969, pp. 229–30.
3. See Marion Bowley, *Nassau Senior and the Classical Economists*, London, 1937.
4. S. E. Finer, *The Life and Times of Sir Edwin Chadwick*, London, 1952, Book Two, chapters III, IV, Book Three, chapters I, II, III.
5. *Report*, p. 67.
6. See *Extracts from the Information Received by His Majesty's Commissioners as to the Administration and Operation of the Poor Laws*, London, 1833, p. 411. This volume gives an extensive selection of the evidence in convenient form.
7. ibid., p. 412.
8. *Report*, Appendices, vols. A.2, A.3.
9. M. J. Cullen, *Social Statistics in Britain, 1830–1852*, Edinburgh University Ph.D. thesis, 1971, discusses the state of social inquiry in terms of the 'statistical movement'; not surprisingly the Poor Law has little place in the 'movement'.

10. Poynter, 1969, p. 318.
11. *Report*, p. 70.
12. ibid., p. 69.
13. ibid., p. 72.
14. Mark Blaug, 'The Myth of the Old Poor Law and the Making of the New', *Journal of Economic History*, 1963, pp. 151–84; 'The Poor Law Re-examined', ibid., 1964, pp. 229–45. For a critique of Blaug's approach see James Stephen Taylor 'The Mythology of the Old Poor Law', *Journal of Economic History*, 1969, pp. 292–7.

SECTION 8

1. *Report*, p. 156.
2. ibid., p. 82.
3. ibid., p. 496.
4. W. O. Henderson and W. H. Chaloner, eds., Frederick Engels, *The Condition of the Working Class in England in 1844*, London, 1958, p. 323.
5. Hobsbawm, 1969, p. 104.
6. For a provisional refutation of the Malthusian view that the allowance system had the effect of increasing marriage and birth rates see James P. Huzel, 'Malthus, the Poor Law and Population in Early Nineteenth-Century England', *Economic History Review*, December 1969, p. 451.
7. *Report*, Appendix C, Communications, pp. 181–6.
8. ibid., p. 149.
9. ibid., p. 115.
10. ibid., pp. 258–74. See U. R. Henriques, 'Bastardy and the New Poor Law', *Past and Present*, 1967, pp. 103–29.
11. *Report*, p. 124.
12. ibid., pp. 242–251.
13. ibid., p. 247.
14. ibid., p. 183.
15. ibid., p. 123.
16. ibid., p. 375.
17. ibid., p. 418.
18. ibid., p. 335.
19. ibid., p. 401.
20. ibid., p. 466.
21. ibid., p. 466.
22. ibid., p. 473.
23. ibid., p. 479.
24. ibid., p. 490.

SECTION 9

1. Henderson and Chaloner, eds., Engels, 1958, p. 323.
2. Maurice Dobb, *Studies in the Development of Capitalism*, London, 1946, p. 275.

3. In Asa Briggs and John Saville, eds., *Essays in Labour History in Memory of G. D. H. Cole*, London, 1960, p. 124.
4. R. H. Tawney, *Religion and the Rise of Capitalism*, London, 1926; Pelican Books, 1938, p. 211.
5. J. D. Marshall, 1968, pp. 17–18.
6. Blaug, 1963, p. 177.
7. Blaug, 1963, p. 176.
8. ibid., p. 176.
9. Blaug, 1964, p. 229.
10. Henderson and Chaloner, eds., Engels, 1958, p. 375.
11. Blaug, 1963, p. 161.
12. ibid., p. 160.
13. *Report*, p. 128.
14. See J. D. Marshall, 1968, p. 26 for a table adjusting the figures in terms of population and prices.
15. *Report*, p. 393.

SECTION 10

1. For the important clauses see Rose, 1971, pp. 95–100.
2. ibid., pp. 191–3.
3. Élie Halévy, *The Triumph of Reform*, London, 1927, p. 285.
4. For the regional implementation of the new Poor Law in the North see R. Boyson, 'The New Poor Law in North-East Lancashire, 1834–71', *Transactions of the Lancashire and Cheshire Antiquarian Society*, 1960; Wilfred Proctor, 'Poor Law Administration in the Preston Union, 1838–1848', *Transactions of the Historical Society of Lancashire and Cheshire*, 1966; E. C. Midwinter, *Social Administration in Lancashire, 1830–1860*; *Poor Law, Public Health and Police*, Manchester, 1969. For a highly readable account of the politics of the attempt to apply the Act in the North, see N. C. Edsall, *The Anti-Poor Law Movement, 1834–44*, Manchester, 1971. More generally, see M. E. Rose, 'The Anti-Poor Law Movement in the North of England', *Northern History*, I, 1966.
5. For a general discussion of hardship see D. Roberts, 'How cruel was the Victorian Poor Law?', *Historical Journal*, 1963, pp. 97–107.
6. See Finer, 1952, Book Six, chapter II.
7. Rose, 1966, p. 609.
8. See D. P. O'Brien, ed., *The Correspondence of Lord Overstone*, Cambridge, 1971, vol. I, pp. 48–51.
9. Rose, 1971, pp. 247–8.
10. From Maurice Bruce, *The Coming of the Welfare State*, London, 1961, p. 85.

NOTE ON SOCIAL HISTORY AND THE POOR LAW

1. W. W. Rostow, *The Stages of Economic Growth. A non-communist manifesto*, Cambridge, 1960.

2. Lord Beveridge, 'Westminster Wages in the Manorial Era', *Economic History Review*, 1955, pp. 18–35.

3. For an early attempt to combine the two, see J. L. and Barbara Hammond, *The Town Labourer, 1760–1832*, London, 1917; *The Village Labourer, 1760–1832*, 1927; *The Skilled Labourer, 1760–1832*, 1919.

4. See E. J. Hobsbawm, *Primitive Rebels*, Manchester, 1959; *Labouring Men*, London, 1964; with George Rudé, *Captain Swing*, London, 1969.

5. George Rudé, *The Crowd in History*, London, 1964; *Paris and London in the Eighteenth Century: Studies in Popular Protest*, London, 1970. Part One, The 'Pre-Industrial Crowd'.

6. E. P. Thompson, *The Making of the English Working Class*, London, 1963; 'The Moral Economy of the English Crowd in the Eighteenth Century', *Past and Present*, February 1971, pp. 76–136.

7. David S. Landes and Charles Tilly, *History as a Social Science*, Englewood Cliffs, N. J., 1971, pp. 39–47.

8. ibid., pp. 14, 15.

9. *Research in Economic and Social History*, published for the Social Science Research Council, London, 1971. There are a few exceptions to this statement, for example James P. Huzel, 'Malthus, the Poor Law, and Population in Early Nineteenth-Century England', *Economic History Review*, December 1969, pp. 430–51, where the author tries to isolate the Poor Law factor as a variable, and closely studies two parishes in Kent.

FURTHER READING

THE POOR LAW

J. J. and A. Bagley, *The English Poor Law*, London, 1968.

M. Blaug, 'The Myth of the Old Poor Law and the Making of the New', *Journal of Economic History*, 1963.

M. Blaug, 'The Poor Law Re-examined', ibid., 1964.

Sir Frederick Morton Eden, *The State of the Poor*, London, 1797; New ed., London, 1966.

N. C. Edsall, *The Anti-Poor Law Movement 1834–44*, Manchester, 1971.

James P. Huzel, 'Malthus, the Poor Law and Population in early nineteenth-century England', *Economic History Review*, 1969.

Dorothy Marshall, *The English Poor in the eighteenth century*, London, 1965.

J. D. Marshall, *The Old Poor Law 1795–1834*, London, 1968.

J. R. Poynter, *Society and Pauperism, English Ideas on Poor Relief, 1795–1834*, London, 1969.

Michael Rose, *The English Poor Law, 1780–1930*, 1971.

Sidney and Beatrice Webb, *English Local Government*, vols. VII–IX, London, 1927; re-issued 1963.

BACKGROUND READING

Marion Bowley, *Nassau Senior and the Classical Economists*, London, 1937.

Maurice Bruce, *The Coming of the Welfare State*, chapter IV, London, 1961.

J. D. Chambers and G. E. Mingay, *The Agricultural Revolution 1750–1880*, London, 1966.

Frederick Engels, *The Condition of the Working Class in England in 1844*, W. O. Henderson and W. H. Chaloner, eds., London, 1958.

S. E. Finer, *The Life and Times of Sir Edwin Chadwick*, London, 1952.

M. W. Flinn, *British Population Growth, 1700–1850*, London, 1970.

R. M. Hartwell *et al.*, *The Long Debate on Poverty*, London, 1972.

E. J. Hobsbawm, *Labouring Men*, London, 1964.

E. J. Hobsbawm and George Rudé, *Captain Swing*, London, 1969.

Patricia Hollis, *The Pauper Press: a study in working class radicalism of the 1830s*, Oxford, 1970.

S. Leon Levy, *Nassau W. Senior, critical essayist, classical economist and adviser to governments, 1790–1864*, London, revised ed., 1970.

Thomas Robert Malthus, *An Essay on the Principle of Population*, 1798; Anthony Flew, ed., Pelican Classics, London, 1970.

David Owen, *English Philanthropy 1660–1960*, London, 1965.

E. P. Thompson, *The Making of the English Working Class*, London, 1963.

A NOTE ON THE TEXT

As the Commissioners themselves pointed out in the 'Statement of Proceedings', the publication of the Poor Law Report in 1834 was a very hurried affair and consequently the first edition suffered in several important respects. A considerable portion of the Appendices was still in the press when the Report was published, and many of the references to the Appendices were left blank. Also, the editing and proof-reading of the Report were so hurried that many inconsistencies in the text were overlooked.

In 1905, on the occasion of the setting up of the Royal Commission on the Poor Law and the Relief of Distress, H.M. Stationery Office published a new edition of the 1834 Report with a revised index (which has been included in the Pelican Classics edition). Though the general layout is rather clearer, the opportunity was not taken to improve the footnotes, nor to remove the inconsistencies of editorial style – indeed, the 1905 edition introduced new irregularities.

With the Pelican Classics edition, therefore, an attempt has been made to correct these shortcomings. All footnotes referring to the Appendices have been removed, and a more consistent and more modern attitude has been taken to the presentation and punctuation of the text, which in the two previous editions present serious problems of readability. However, the precise wording and spelling of the Report remain unchanged, and it is hoped that by these means the text has been presented in a way clearer and more intelligible to the reader, but with no loss of the Report's character or period 'flavour'.

As there is probably insufficient indication within the text of where the reader is, headings for sections, taken from the contents pages, and enclosed in square brackets, have been inserted where appropriate.

Facsimile of the title page of the first edition of
Report of the Royal Commission on the Poor Laws, 1834

REPORTS

FROM

COMMISSIONERS:

TWENTY-TWO VOLUMES.

—*(9.)*—

POOR LAWS.

Session
4 February——15 August 1834.

VOL. XXVII.

CONTENTS

CHARACTER OF PERSONS WHO DISTRIBUTE AND AWARD RELIEF:

LEGISLATIVE MEASURES CONSIDERED BUT NOT RECOMMENDED:

REMEDIAL MEASURES

PRINCIPLE OF ADMINISTERING RELIEF TO THE INDIGENT:

PRINCIPLE OF LEGISLATION:

AGENCY FOR CARRYING INTO EFFECT THE INTENTIONS OF THE LEGISLATURE – A CENTRAL BOARD OF CONTROL:

ADMINISTRATION AND OPERATION

OF

THE LAWS

FOR

THE RELIEF OF THE POOR

REPORT OF COMMISSIONERS

TO THE KING'S MOST EXCELLENT MAJESTY

We, the Commissioners appointed by Your Majesty to make a diligent and full inquiry into the practical operation of the Laws for the Relief of the Poor in England and Wales, and into the manner in which those laws are administered, and to report our opinion whether any and what alterations, amendments, or improvements may be beneficially made in the said laws, or in the manner of administering them, and how the same may be best carried into effect, humbly certify to Your Majesty, in manner following, our proceedings in the execution of Your Majesty's Commission, and the opinions which they have led us to form.

Our first proceeding was to prepare questions for circulation in the rural districts, and afterwards in the towns. Considerable alterations were made in the rural questions, after the earlier answers received by us showed that some of the questions were imperfectly understood, or that additional inquiries might be usefully made. Appendix B contains copies of our questions with their different variations. The town questions, having been prepared after those for rural districts had received their last amendments, were never altered.

As we were directed to employ Assistant Commissioners in the prosecution of our inquiry, our next business was to frame instructions for them. For the purpose of facilitating their preparation, two of the Commissioners made excursions into the country, in order to ascertain by actual experience the sort of duties which the Assistant Commissioners would have to perform. Assisted by that experience and by the information contained in the answers to our circulated questions, we prepared the instructions for Assistant Commissioners, which are contained in the Supplement to this Report. We then proceeded to the appointment of Assistant Commissioners; a task by no means easy, as the office was one requiring no ordinary qualifications, necessarily involving a great sacrifice of time and labour, likely to be followed by much hostility, and accompanied by no remuneration. The difficulty of discovering a greater number of fit persons whom we could induce to act, by confining the number of Assistant Commissioners, forced us to assign to them much larger districts than would have been in other respects advisable. And different accidents, which prevented several persons who had undertaken the business from proceeding in it, in some cases forced us to confide to one person districts which had been intended for two, and to leave some altogether unvisited. One of these was South Wales, to which two persons were successively appointed, each of whom was subsequently prevented from acting.

Our Commission did not extend beyond England and Wales. Mr Tufnell and Mr Johnston, however, made inquiries for us in Scotland; Mr Le Marchant in Guernsey; Captain Brandreth in Flanders; and Mr Majendie in France. We have inserted their reports in the Appendix, together with some valuable information respecting the public provision made for the poor, and the state of the labouring classes, in the continent of Europe and in America, which have been communicated by the Foreign Office, and by Count Arrivabene, M. Thibaudeau, M. de Chateauvieux, and from other sources.

So much time was taken up in the preparation of questions and instructions, and in the appointment of Assistant Commissioners, that few of them proceeded on their mission before the middle of August 1832.

They were directed to make their reports by the end of the following November. Very few reports, however, were received until the beginning of January 1833. In the mean time we had received returns to our circulated queries so numerous, that it became a question how they should be disposed of.

The number and the variety of the persons by whom they were

furnished, made us consider them the most valuable part of our evidence. But the same causes made their bulk so great as to be a serious objection to their publication in full. It appeared that this objection might be diminished, if an abstract could be made containing their substance in fewer words, and we directed such an abstract to be prepared. On making the attempt, however, it appeared that not much could be saved in length without incurring the risk of occasional suppression or misrepresentation. Another plan would have been to make a selection, and leave out altogether those returns which appeared to us of no value. A very considerable portion, perhaps not less than one half, are of this description; their omission would have materially diminished the expense of copying and printing, and the remainder would have been more easily consulted and referred to when unincumbered by useless matter.

But on a question of such importance as Poor Law amendment, we were unwilling to incur the responsibility of selection. We annex, therefore, in Appendix B, all the returns which we have received. In order to diminish, as far as possible, the inconvenience arising from their number, they are so arranged that the answer to any one of the fifty-three questions may be read as a separate subject without the attention being distracted by the intervention of other matter, the answer from each parish occurring in the same portion of each page. The only alterations which we have permitted have been the omission of disquisitions on matters perfectly irrelevant, and the insertion, in a different part of the Appendix, of some passages which were too long to appear in a tabular form.

The Report of the Assistant Commissioners, though less voluminous than the returns, forms altogether a large mass; and a large body of testimony consists of the communications made to us from every part of England, and from some parts of America, and of the continent of Europe.

We felt it to be of the utmost importance that we should ourselves be masters of the contents of all this evidence, and that those whose conduct may be influenced by our suggestions should be enabled to examine all grounds on which they are founded. For these purposes, it was necessary that it should be in print; any use of it in manuscript being exceedingly fatiguing, and the complete use impossible. We obtained, therefore, the permission of the Lord Chancellor, and of the Speaker of the House of Commons, that it should be printed by the Parliamentary printers, in anticipation of the orders of the two Houses; and it was accordingly placed in the printer's hands in the beginning of February, 1833.

In the mean time we received a communication from Your Majesty's Principal Secretary of State for the Home Department, directing us to 'transmit, in detail, the information which we had received as to the administration and operations of the Poor Laws, in some of the parishes in which those laws have been administered in various modes, and particularly any returns to our inquiries, showing the results of the various modes adopted in those parishes'. On the receipt of this letter we requested the Assistant Commissioners to furnish us with such extracts from the evidence collected by them as they thought most instructive.

The papers received in consequence of these applications were subsequently published, and obtained an extensive circulation. It has, we believe, been supposed that these extracts were selected by us, and contained the most striking parts of our evidence. Both these suppositions are erroneous. Neither on this occasion, nor on any other, have we exercised any discretion with respect to our evidence. We left the task of selection to the Assistant Commissioners, very few of whose reports we had then seen, and we transmitted to the Home Office what they chose to furnish. And on comparing the portions which they thought fit to extract with the whole of their reports, it will not be found that the extracts, strange as they must have appeared to any one unacquainted with the system which they describe, differ from the general tenor of the Appendix. For one part of the volume, however, we are responsible, since it was prepared in the offices of the Commission, and that is the index. As it was considered important that the extracts should appear as soon as they could be got ready, the index, to save time, was prepared from the proof sheets; and, as the paging of these sheets was subsequently altered to meet the corrections made by the Assistant Commissioners, all the references become inapplicable, and a few were ultimately passed over without correction. A graver complaint has been made of the index as containing expressions of opinion. We admit that the complaint is to a certain degree well founded: our apology is that, as is usually the case, we left the index to be prepared by others, and did not see it until the work had been for some time in circulation.

We have already stated that our Appendix was placed in the printer's hands in the beginning of February 1833. If it could have been printed, as we hoped, in three months, we should have been able to report before the end of the last session. The outline of this Report had been prepared in the beginning of that session, and all that was necessary was to add references to the evidence and to make those additions, qualifications, and exceptions which the reconsideration of that evidence might show to be necessary; but the vast bulk of the manuscripts, and the degree in which the Parliamentary printers were engaged by other matters, so prolonged the printing that not one fifth of it had been executed before the end of the session. It proceeded more rapidly after the prorogation, but even then so slowly, notwithstanding the exertions of the printers, that even now it is not completed. We have been forced, therefore, to take it as it was furnished to us week by week, using the proof sheets, unpaged and unindexed. And this is one of our apologies for the defects of this Report, and for the omissions and occasional false references which, with all our care, must, we fear, be found in it. If it had been possible to wait till the whole Appendix was in a perfect state, we could have completed our Report with far less labour and in a far more satisfactory manner. But that would have involved a delay of three months longer, a delay which might, in fact, have occasioned the postponement of remedial measures, so far as they are to be promoted by this Report, until the following year. Such a delay appeared to us a greater evil than the imperfections and inaccuracies to which the course which we have adopted must expose us.

It appears from this narrative that the magnitude of the evidence has been the great difficulty with which we have had to struggle. But we believe, on the other hand, that that very magnitude gives the principal value to our inquiry. All evidence is necessarily subject to error, from the ignorance, forgetfulness, or misrepresentation of the witnesses, and necessarily tinged by their opinions and prejudices. But in proportion as the number of witnesses is increased, those sources of error have a tendency to compensate one another and general results are afforded, more to be depended upon than the testimony of a few witnesses, however unexceptionable. The evidence contained in our Appendix comes from every county and almost every town, and from a very large proportion of even the villages in England. It is derived from many thousand witnesses of every rank and of every profession and employment, members of the two Houses of Parliament, clergymen, country gentlemen, magistrates, farmers, manufacturers, shopkeepers, artisans, and peasants, differing in every conceivable degree in education, habits, and interests, and agreeing only in their practical experience as to the matters in question, in their general description both of the mode in which the laws for the relief of the poor are administered, and of the consequences which have already resulted from that administration, and in their anticipation of certain further consequences from its continuance. The amendment of those laws is, perhaps, the most urgent and the most important measure now remaining for the consideration of Parliament; and we trust that we shall facilitate that amendment by tendering to Your Majesty the most extensive, and at the same time the most consistent, body of evidence that was ever brought to bear on a single subject.

In the hope of diminishing the difficulty of making use of this voluminous evidence, we have embodied a considerable portion of it in the following Report; and wherever it has been practicable, we have subjoined to our quotations references to the pages in the Appendix from which they were extracted. But as the Appendix, owing to the obstacles which we have already stated, is still incomplete, and much of it unpaged, many of our references are unavoidably left blank.

[PROGRESS OF THE LAW]

We do not think it necessary to prefix to the statement of the result of our inquiries any account of the provisions of the 43 Elizabeth, c. 2 [1601], or of the subsequent acts for the relief of the poor. Those acts are well known, and are to be found in almost every treatise on the Poor Laws, and we have inserted the 43 Elizabeth in the Supplement. But as the preceding acts are almost forgotten, and not easily accessible, and as they throw great light on the intentions of the framers of the 43 Elizabeth, we will shortly state the substance of some of the principal enactments of those which appear to us most to deserve attention.

The great object of our early pauper legislation seems to have been the restraint of vagrancy.

The 12 Richard II, c. 7 (1388), prohibits any labourer from departing from the hundred, rape, wapentake, city, or borough where he is dwelling without a testimonial, showing reasonable cause for his going, to be issued under the authority of the justices of the peace. Any labourer found wandering without such letter is to be put in the stocks till he find surety to return to the town from which he came. Impotent persons are to remain in the towns in which they be dwelling at the time of the act; or, if the inhabitants are unable or unwilling to support them, they are to withdraw to other towns within the hundred, rape, or wapentake, or to the towns where they were born, and there abide during their lives.

The 11 Henry VII, c. 2 (1495), requires beggars not able to work to go to the hundred where last they dwelled or were best known, or born, without begging out of the hundred.

The 19 Henry VII, c. 12 (1504), requires them to go to the city, town, or hundred where they were born, or to the place where they last abode for the space of three years, without begging out of the said city, town, hundred, or place.

The 22 Henry VIII, c. 12 (1531), directs the justices to assign to the impotent poor a limit within which they are to beg. An impotent person begging out of his limit is to be imprisoned for two days and nights in the stocks, on bread and water, and then sworn to return to the place in which he was authorized to beg. An able-bodied beggar is to be whipped, and sworn to return to the place where he was born, or last dwelt for the space of three years, and there put himself to labour.

Five years after was passed the 27 Henry VIII, c. 25 (1536). This statute is remarkable, both as having first introduced the system of compulsory charity, and as showing that the motive for its establishment was the desire and the difficulty of repressing vagrancy. It recites the preceding act and adds that no provision is made for the support of the impotent, nor for setting and keeping in work the said valiant beggars; and then enacts that the head officers of every city, shire, town, and parish, to which such poor creatures or sturdy vagabonds shall repair in obedience to that act, shall most charitably receive the same and shall keep the same poor people, by way of voluntary and charitable alms, within the respective cities, shires, towns, hundreds, hamlets, and parishes, by their discretion, so that none of them of very necessity shall be compelled to beg openly, and shall compel the said sturdy vagabonds and valiant beggars to be kept to continual labour in such wise as they may get their own living by the continual labour of their own hands, on pain that every parish making default shall forfeit 20s. a month. It then directs the head officers of corporate towns, and the churchwardens and two others of every parish, who are to remain in office only one year, to collect voluntary alms for the purpose of relieving the impotent poor, and that such as be lusty be kept to continual labour. Every preacher, parson, vicar, and curate, as well in their sermons, collections, bidding of the beads, as in the time of confession and making of wills, is to exhort, move, stir, and provoke people to be liberal for the relief of the impotent, and setting and keeping to work the said sturdy vagabonds.

The money collected is to be kept in a common box in the church, or committed to the custody of a substantial trusty man as they can agree on, to be delivered as necessity shall require. Almsgiving, otherwise than to these common boxes or common gatherings, or to fellow parishioners or prisoners, is prohibited on forfeiture of ten times the amount given. And all persons bound to distribute ready money, victuals, or other sustentation to poor people, are to dispose of the same, or the value thereof, to such common boxes. The overplus of the collection of wealthy parishes is to be applied in aid of other parishes within the same city, borough, town, or hundred.

A sturdy beggar is to be whipped the first time, his right ear cropped the second time, and if he again offends, to be sent to the next gaol till the quarter sessions and there to be indicted for wandering, loitering, and idleness, and if convicted, shall suffer execution of death as a felon and an enemy of the commonwealth.

It appears that the severity of this act prevented its execution. Such at least is the reason assigned for its repeal by the 1 Edward VI, c. 3 (1547), which recites that partly by foolish pity and mercy of them which should have seen the said goodly laws executed, and partly from the perverse nature and long-accustomed idleness of the persons given to loitering, the said goodly statutes have had small effect, and idle and vagabond persons, being unprofitable members or rather enemies of the commonwealth, have been suffered to remain and increase, and yet so do; and as a milder punishment enacts that an able-bodied poor person who does not apply himself to some honest labour or offer to serve even for meat and drink, if nothing more is to be obtained, shall be taken for a vagabond, branded on the shoulder with the letter V and adjudged a slave for two years to any person who shall demand him, to be fed on bread and water and refuse meat, and caused to work by beating, chaining, or otherwise. If he run away within that period, he is to be branded on the cheek with the letter S and adjudged a slave for life; if he run away again, he is to suffer death as a felon. If no man demand such loiterer, he is to be sent to the place where he says he was born, there to be kept in chains or otherwise at the highways or common work, or from man to man, as the slave of the corporation or inhabitants of the city, town, or village in which he was born; and the said city, town, or village shall see the said slave set to work, and not live idly, upon pain, for every three working days that the slave live idly by their default, that a city forfeit £5, a borough 40s., and a town or village 20s., half to the King and half to the informer. If it appears that he was not born in the place of which he described himself as a native, he is to be branded on the face, and be a slave for life.

It appears also that taking surety of the impotent poor that they would repair to the places where they were born, or had dwelt for the three previous years, was not effectual. The officers, therefore, are directed to convey the impotent poor on horseback, cart, chariot, or otherwise, to the next constable, and so from constable to constable till they be brought to the place where they were born or most conversant for the space of three years, there to be kept and nourished of alms. 'Provided always, that if any of the said impotent persons be not so lame or impotent but that they may work in some manner, and refuse to work, or run away and beg in other places, then their city, town, or village, is to punish them according to their discretion, with chaining, beating, or otherwise.' The statute also orders the curate of each parish, every Sunday after reading the gospel, to exhort his parishioners to remember the duty of Christian charity in relieving them which be their brethren in Christ, born in the same parish, and needing their help.

This statute had a very short existence, for it was repealed by the 3 & 4 Edward VI, c. 16 (1550), and the 22 Henry VIII, c. 12, revived. The directions, however, that the impotent poor should be removed to the place where they were born or had been most conversant for three years, and that they should be kept to work, if capable of some manner of work and punished by chaining, beating, or otherwise if they refused were re-enacted.

The 5 & 6 Edward VI, c. 2 (1551), 'to the intent that valiant beggars, idle and loitering persons, may be avoided, and the impotent, feeble, and lame provided for, which are poor in very deed', confirms the 22 Henry VIII, c. 12 and 3 & 4 Edward VI, c. 16, and commands that they shall be put in execution; and then directs a book to be kept in every city, corporate town, and parish containing the names of the householders and of the impotent poor, and that yearly in Whitsun week the head officers of towns and the minister and churchwardens in every parish in the country shall appoint two persons to be collectors of alms for the relief of the poor, which collectors shall, the next or following Sunday at church, gently ask every man and woman what they of their charity will give weekly towards the relief of the poor, and write the same in the book and distribute what they collect weekly to the same poor and impotent persons, after such sort that the more impotent may have the more help, and such as can get part of their living the less, and by the direction of the collectors be put on such labour as they be able to do; but none to go or sit openly begging upon pain limited in the above statutes. If any one able to further this charitable work do obstinately and frowardly refuse to give, or do discourage others, the minister and churchwardens are to gently exhort him. If he will not be so persuaded, the bishop is to send for him, to induce and persuade him by charitable ways and means and so according to his discretion take order for the reformation thereof.

It is a curious example of the fear of our ancestors that statutes should grow into desuetude, and perhaps a proof that such a fate had actually befallen the 5 & 6 Edward VI that precisely the same enactments, with precisely the same preamble, are repeated by the 2 & 3 Philip and Mary, c. 5 (1555). But the act, however reiterated, seems to have been ineffectual. Neither the gentle askings of the collectors, the exhortations of the minister, nor the charitable ways and means of the bishop, appear to have persuaded the parishioners to entrust to the collectors the distribution of their alms.

The 5 Elizabeth, c. 3 (1563), therefore, after repeating the same preamble and the same enactments, goes on to enact that if any person of his froward, wilful mind shall obstinately refuse to give weekly to the relief of the poor according to his ability, the bishop shall bind him to appear at the next sessions; and at the said sessions the justices there shall charitably and gently persuade and move the said obstinate person to extend his charity towards the relief of the poor of the parish where he dwelleth; and if he will not be persuaded, it shall be lawful for the justices, with the churchwardens, or one of them, to tax such obstinate person, according to their good discretion, what sum the said obstinate person shall pay weekly towards the relief of the poor within the parish wherein he shall dwell; and if he refuse, the justices shall, on complaint of the churchwardens, commit the said obstinate person to gaol, until he shall pay the sum so taxed, with the arrears.

The next statute, the 14 Elizabeth, c. 5 (1572), is remarkable as a proof of the inefficacy of the previous statutes, and as showing how short an interval elapsed between giving to the justices power to tax at their sessions an obstinate person at the complaint of the minister, the churchwardens, and the bishop, and the giving to them discretionary power to tax every inhabitant in their divisions, and to direct the application of the sums so taxed.

It begins by a recital that all the parts of this realm of England and Wales be presently with rogues, vagabonds, and sturdy beggars exceedingly pestered, by means whereof daily happeneth in the same realm horrible murders, thefts, and other great outrage, to the high displeasure of Almighty God and to the great annoyance of the common weal.

And then, 'as well for the utter suppressing of the said outrageous enemies to the common weal, as for the charitable relieving of the aged and impotent poor people in manner and form following,' it enacts that all persons thereafter set forth to be rogues and vagabonds or sturdy beggars shall for the first offence be grievously whipped, and burnt through the gristle of the right ear with a hot iron of the compass of an inch about; for the second, be deemed felons; and for the third, suffer death as felons without benefit of clergy.

Among rogues, vagabonds and sturdy beggars are included all persons whole and mighty in body, able to labour, not having land or master, nor using any lawful merchandise, craft, or mystery; and all common labourers, able in body, loitering and refusing to work for such reasonable wages as is commonly given.

And forasmuch as charity would that poor, aged, and impotent persons should as necessarily be provided for as the said rogues, vagabonds, and sturdy beggars repressed, and that the said aged, impotent, and poor people should have convenient habitations and abiding places throughout this realm to settle themselves upon, to the end that they nor any of them should hereafter beg or wander about, [it enacts] that the justices of the peace shall within their several divisions and authorities make inquiry of all aged, poor, impotent, and decayed persons born within their said divisions and limits, or which were there dwelling within three years next after this present Parliament, living by alms, and register their names; and when the number of poor people forced to live upon alms be by that means known, the said justices shall appoint within their said divisions meet places, by their discretion, to settle the same poor people for their abidings, if the parish within which they shall be found shall not or will not provide for them, and set down what portion the weekly charge towards the relief and sustentation of the said poor people will amount unto, and that done, shall by their good discretions tax and assess all the inhabitants dwelling within the said divisions to such weekly charge as they and every of them shall weekly contribute towards the relief of the said poor people, and shall appoint collectors, who shall gather the same proportion, and make delivery of so much thereof, according to the discretion of the said justices, to the said poor people, as the said justices shall appoint them. If any person able to further this charitable work shall obstinately refuse to give, or discourage others, he shall be brought before two justices, to show the cause of such refusal or discouragement, and to abide such order therein as the said justices shall appoint, and if he shall refuse to do so, they shall commit him to gaol until he shall be contented with their said order and do perform the same.

It then provides that the justices, out of the surplus of such collections (the impotent being first provided for), shall settle to work the rogues and vagabonds that shall be disposed to work (i.e. capable of working) born within the said counties or there abiding for the most part within the said three years, there to be holden to work to get their livings, and to live and be sustained only upon their labour and travail. And:

that the justices in sessions within any of the counties, cities, or towns where collection of money cannot presently be had, may license some of the poor, or any other for them, to gather, within such other town, parish, or parishes of the county as the said justices shall name within the division of the licensing justices, charitable donations and alms at the houses of the inhabitants. And the inhabitants of every such parish to which such poor shall be so appointed, shall be coacted and bound, under such pain as to the said justices shall seem convenient, to relieve the said poor in such sorts as the said justices shall appoint.

Even its kindness is mixed with much severity, for:

if any of the said poor people refuse to be bestowed in any of the said abiding places, but covet still to hold on their trade of begging, or after they be once bestowed in the said abiding places, depart and beg, then the said person so offending, for that first offence shall be accounted a rogue or vagabond, and suffer as a rogue or vagabond in the first degree of punishment; and if he do the second time offend, then be esteemed a rogue or vagabond, and suffer as a rogue or vagabond in the last degree of punishment (that is, suffer death as a felon); and if any of the said aged and impotent persons, not being so diseased, lame, or impotent but that they may work in some manner of work, shall be by the overseers of their said abiding place appointed to work, and refuse, they are to be whipped and stocked for their first refusal, and for the second refusal to be punished as in the case of vagabonds in the said first degree of punishment.

The 14 Elizabeth, c. 5, does not appear to have been expressly repealed, as far as the relief of the impotent is concerned. It was replaced in that respect by the 39 Elizabeth, c. 3 (1597), and with respect to able-bodied vagrants, by the 39 Elizabeth, c. 4. That statute, which is in fact merely a continuation of the 39 Elizabeth, c. 3, directs that every rogue and vagabond (among whom are included 'all wandering persons and common labourers, being persons able in body, using loitering, and refusing to work for such reasonable wages as is taxed or commonly given in such parts where such persons do or shall happen to dwell or abide, not having living otherwise to maintain themselves'):

shall, on his apprehension, be openly whipped until his body be bloody, and shall be forthwith sent from parish to parish the next strait way to the parish where he was born, if the same may be known by the party's confession or otherwise; and if the same be not known, then to the parish where he last dwelt before the punishment by the space of one whole year, there to put him or herself to labour as a true subject ought to do; or, not being known where he or she was born or last dwelt, then to the parish through which he or she last passed without punishment, to be by the officers of the said village where he or she so last passed through without punishment, conveyed to the house of correction of the district wherein the said village standeth, or to the common gaol of that county or place, there to remain or be employed in work until he or she shall be placed in some service, and so to continue by the space of one whole year; or, not being able of body, until he or she shall be placed to remain in some almshouse in the same county or place. [And] if any of the said rogues shall appear to be dangerous to the inferior sort of people where they shall be taken, or otherwise be such as will not be reformed of their roguish kind of life, it shall be lawful to the justice of the limits where any such rogue shall be taken, to commit that rogue to the house of correction, or otherwise to the gaol of that county, there to remain until the next quarter-sessions; and then such of the same rogues so committed as by the justices of the peace there present, or the most part of them, shall be thought fit not to be delivered, shall be banished out of this realm and all other the dominions thereof, and, at the charge of that county, shall be conveyed into such parts beyond the seas as shall be at any time hereafter for that purpose assigned by the Privy Council, or otherwise be judged perpetually to the galleys of this realm, as by the same justices or the most part of them shall be thought fit and expedient.

The 27 Henry VII, c. 25 [1536], which imposed a fine on the parish in which the impotent poor should not be relieved, and directed the surplus collection of rich parishes to be applied for the relief of poor parishes within the same hundred, the 1 Edward VI, c. 3 [1547], which directed the curate of any parish to exhort his parishioners to relieve those born in the same parish, and needing their help, and the 5 & 6 Edward VI, c. 2 [1551], which directed the parson, vicar, or churchwardens of each parish to appoint collectors and to gently ask for contributions in the church, were all so many steps towards making the relief of the poor a parochial charge. And it appears that the ecclesiastical division of parishes was preferred to any civil division, on account of the part which the clergy were required to take in the business.

The 14 Elizabeth, c. 5 [1572], appears to have deviated from this plan; and as it vested the power of assessment in the justices, it threw the burden, not on each parish, but upon all the inhabitants of the divisions within the jurisdiction of the assessing justices. The 39 Elizabeth, c. 3 (1597), returned to the parochial system; and it differs so little in its provisions from the well-known 43 Elizabeth, c. 2, the basis, but certainly not the origin, of our present system, that we do not think it necessary to state its substance. The following clause, however, deserves to be cited, both on account of its importance, and from its not having been re-enacted:

No person or persons whatsoever shall go wandering abroad and beg in any place whatsoever, by license or without upon pain to be esteamed, taken, and punished as a rogue: Provided always, and this present act shall not extend to any poor people which shall ask relief of victualling only in the same parish where such poor people do dwell, so the same be in such time only and according to such order and direction as shall be made and appointed by the churchwardens and overseers of the poor of the same parish, according to the true intent and meaning of this act.

[ADMINISTRATION OF THE LAW]

It is now our painful duty to report that in the greater part of the districts which we have been able to examine, the fund which the 43 Elizabeth directed to be employed in setting to work children and persons capable of labour but using no daily trade, and in the necessary relief of the impotent, is applied to purposes opposed to the letter, and still more to the spirit of that law, and destructive to the morals of the most numerous class, and to the welfare of all.

The subject may be divided, with respect to the mode of relief, into in-door relief, or that which is given in the workhouse, and out-door relief, or that which is not given in the workhouse; and with respect to the objects of relief, into those who are, and those who are not able-bodied.

I

OUT-DOOR RELIEF OF THE ABLE-BODIED

The great source of abuse is the out-door relief afforded to the able-bodied on their own account, or on that of their families. This is given either in kind or in money.

i

Out-door relief of the able-bodied in kind

The out-door relief of the able-bodied, when given in kind, consists rarely of food, rather less unfrequently of fuel, and still less unfrequently of clothes, particularly shoes; but its most usual form is that of relieving the applicants, either wholly or partially, from the expense of obtaining house-room. As this last mode of relief is extensively prevalent, and productive of important consequences, both direct and indirect, we shall dwell on it at some length.

Partial relief from the expense of obtaining house-room is given, or professed to be given, whenever the occupant of a cottage or an apartment is exempted on the ground of poverty from the payment of rates. In a few places, among which are Cookham (Berks.), and Southwell and Bingham (Notts.), every tenement is rated, and the whole rate is collected; but as a general statement it may be said that the habitations of the labourers are almost always exempted from rates when the occupant is a parishioner, and are frequently exempted when he is not a parishioner. The distinction thus made between parishioners and non-parishioners is one among the many modes in which the Law of Settlement and the practice of relief narrow the market and interfere with the proper distribution of labour. It perhaps is better that all the labourers should be exempted than that those who have sought work at some distance from their homes should be thus punished for their enterprise and diligence. But the evil effects of a general exemption of all who plead poverty are shown by Mr Bishop, in his report from St Clement's, Oxford.

The only peculiarity (in that parish, as distinguished from the neighbouring parishes) is to be found in the extent of the speculation for building small tenements, and in some of the circumstances which have attended that speculation.

It is impossible to estimate, with anything like accuracy, the number of new houses, but there are whole streets and rows built in the cheapest manner.

The rents are, in fact, levied to a considerable degree upon those who pay rates. In the first place, by the abstraction of so much property from rateable wealth, the remainder has to bear a heavier burden; secondly, the rents are carried to as great a height as possible, upon the supposition that tenements so circumstanced will not be rated; the owner, therefore, is pocketing both rate and rent; and thirdly, the value of his property is increased precisely in the proportion that his neighbour's is deteriorated, by the weight of rates from which his own is discharged. Neither is this all; as it is always regarded by the tenant as a desirable thing to escape the payment of rates, the field for competition is narrowed, and a very inferior description of house is built for the poor man. In order to make out a case for the non-payment of rates, it is necessary to have inconveniences and defects; and thus it happens that a building speculation, depending upon freedom from rates for its recommendation, always produces a description of houses of the worst and most unhealthy kind. Those who would build for the poor with more liberal views, and greater attention to their health and their comfort, are discouraged, and a monopoly is given to those whose sole end is gain by whatever means it may be compassed.

In a great number of cases, the labourer, if a parishioner, is not only exempted from rates but his rent is paid out of the parish fund. North Wales is a district of comparatively good administration; but the following extracts from Mr Walcott's report show both the extent of these practices in that country, and some of their effects:

The payment of rent out of the rates is nearly universal; in many parishes it is extended to nearly all the married labourers. In Llanidloes out of £2,000 spent on the poor, nearly £800, and in Bodedern out of £360, £113, are thus exhausted. In Anglesea and part of Carnarvonshire, overseers frequently give written guarantees, making the parish responsible for the rent of cottages let to the Poor. I annex a copy of one from a parish officer, on behalf of the parish, from himself as overseer, to himself as landlord:

Copy of Guarantee for Rent of Pauper's Apartment

WE, the Overseers of the Poor of the parish of Llanfacbraeth, will pay the rent of A. Jones, pauper of our parish, to W. Hughes, of Bodedern, the sum of £1 5s. yearly, commencing tomorrow the 13th November, 1827, for an apartment of a house in Bodedern.

(Signed)   *William Hughes*

I examined William Hughes, who stated that he signed the above on behalf of the parish, and was the person mentioned in the body of it.

Paupers have thus become a very desirable class of tenants, much preferable, as was admitted by several cottage proprietors, to the independent labourers, whose rent, at the same time, this mode of relief enhances. Of this I received much testimony; amongst others, an overseer of Dolgelly stated that there were many apartments and small houses in the town not worth to let £1 a year, for which, in consequence of parochial interference with rents, from £1 14s. to £2, was paid; and the clerk to the Directors of Montgomery House of Industry mentioned an instance of a person in his neighbourhood who obtained ten cottages from the landowner at a yearly rent of £18, and re-let them separately for £50; eight of his tenants were parish paupers.

This species of property being thus a source of profitable investment, speculation, to a considerable extent, has taken that direction; and it is further encouraged by exempting pauper cottages from rates, or paying them out of the parochial funds, a mode of relief as universal as the last.

In general, all the tenements in a parish are rated, but the rates are very rarely collected from the smaller class, except in the case of non-parishioners. One or two instances will suffice to show the extent to which the exemption is carried.

The middle division of Welch Pool contains 535 tenements, which are all rated; but of this number 207 are at a rent not exceeding £6 a year, from which no rate is obtained; and the Rev. Mr Trevor states, as to the town of Carnarvon, that whole streets have been built on speculation by three or four persons, the houses in which are let under £4 a year, and pay no rates. Except the landlords, few doubted but that the rent in these cases is augmented by the amount of rate remitted; and there was much complaint that this class of proprietors not only escaped contributing to the burdens of a parish, but actually increased them, by creating a cottier pauper population. In and near towns the proprietors are of all classes, chiefly however builders and tradesmen. The following is the evidence on these points of the vicar of Bangor in Carnarvonshire: he states that the proprietors of cottages are persons who, having saved small sums, build cottages as a means of procuring the highest interest for their money; that at least the half of the town of Bangor consists of cottages, many of which are exempted from rates on account of the poverty of the occupier, there being no law to compel the owner to pay the rates; that a law to that effect seems very much wanted, and that the poor tenant is given to understand by his landlord that his cottage will be free from rates, and thus is induced to give a higher rent for it.

The proposition of rating the owner of small tenements is one of great popularity, and was received with delight by parish officers. I met with only one dissentient, an assistant overseer, who on further examination proved to be a proprietor of several exempted cottages. On the other hand, the assistant overseer of the township of Bangor, in Flintshire, also a proprietor, said that he was so convinced of the expediency and advantage of rating the landlord, that he would cheerfully assent to an enactment for the purpose, although it would lessen the value of his property.

The practice in Suffolk is thus stated by Mr Stuart:

The payment of rent is a mode of furnishing relief which few parishes recognize, yet it is unquestionably a very frequent way of giving relief, not always to the extent of paying the whole rent, but of giving some assistance towards it. It is in general difficult to ascertain the length to which this practice is carried, as in the entry of the charge in the parish books it is usually described as relief 'in distress', without specifying the purpose for which it is granted. It is most prevalent in towns and large villages, in which tradesmen, who are commonly the owners of cottages, have a greater influence in the distribution of the poor fund. There is no kind of property which yields a higher rent, or of which the rent is better paid, than that of houses occupied by the lower orders. When the landlord once adopts rigorous measures to enforce his demands, the parish takes good care that the payment shall afterwards be regularly made, under the plea of avoiding the expense which would be incurred if a whole family were thrown on it for support by being deprived of their goods. An overseer mentioned the following case, for the purpose of convincing me of the policy and necessity of paying rent. A baker with a family of eight children had his rent of £13 a year, paid for him by the parish, besides an allowance of 2s. 6d. a week for his children. It was determined to discontinue the payment of rent; his goods were immediately distrained, he lost his business, and he and his family were obliged to be taken into the workhouse. It was soon found that it cost the parish about 5s. per head per week, or about £130 a year, to maintain them in this way, and it was judged most prudent to hire a house for him and buy furniture for the purpose of setting him up in his trade again. The parish, after having incurred all this expense and outlay, have again been obliged to return to the payment of his rent, which is now £12 4s. a year, and to his former out-allowance. It is evident that when the landlord has such an easy remedy for securing his claims, he can command any rent he chooses to ask, which the poor man does not scruple to agree to pay, provided the outward appearance of the house is suitable to a person in his condition, for the parish is particular in this point.

The following is an extract from Mr Maclean's report from Surrey and Sussex:

The practice of paying rent is, I may say, universal; for although in but few parishes it is acknowledged, and in many the parish officers seemed suprised at my questions, and referred to the books, where nothing is entered as rent, still I found that it is frequently paid indirectly, i.e., though the pauper does not feel that he can ask the vestry or the parish officer to pay his rent, yet he knows that an application for a pound or two to enable him to pay it or to stay a threatening execution will not be made in vain. The other indirect modes in which rent is paid, are either by an allowance of 1s. a week for the third child, which is retained by the parish officer for that purpose, by an exemption from the rate, or by an application to the vestry from time to time, which is so invariably successful, that those with families do not think it necessary, by foresight or industry, to lay by any thing to meet the demand. To enumerate all the parishes in which one or other of these practices exists would be to name nearly every parish which I have visited.

In Pulborough parish 1s. a week is allowed for the third child, but this is retained by the parish officer to pay rent.

In the purely agricultural parish of West Grinstead, containing a population of 1,292, the amount of rent entered in the parish books last year amounted to £267 11s. 6d.

In the similar parish of Shipley, with a population of 1,180 the amount entered last year was £254 14s. 2d.

At Horsham the same custom prevailed, and has done so for years. I attended the select vestry there, and found Mr Simpson, the clergyman (who always attends), in the chair. The applications were numerous, and were, with few exceptions, for the payment of a half or a whole year's rent, and were in every case granted without apparently any regard to the size of the applicant's family or his earnings; indeed, relief is given in addition for the third child. No entry is made in the parish books as 'rent'; but it is charged under the head of 'weekly relief', and amounted to upwards of £200 last year.

In the parish of Steyning, with a population of 1,436, near £120 was paid last year for rent. If a man has two children, it has been the custom for the last twenty years and upwards to pay his rent, to the amount of 1s. a week; and this is not considered to furnish a sufficient ground upon which to discontinue his allowance of 1s. 6d. a week for the third child.

The parish of Epsom pays rent to the amount of £50 a year, the rule being to pay none. The chief applicants are those who have large families, or persons of idle and dissolute character.

Mr Tweedy states that –

The practice of giving relief by payment of rent is found to prevail in a greater or less degree throughout the West Riding, though the opinion is gaining ground that it is a mode of relief mischievous in its effects, and liable to great abuse.

There can be no question that the renting of cottage property by overseers, and the consequent exemption of it from the poor-rate, has more or less, according to the circumstances of each case, a tendency to increase the rate at which other cottage property is let. And when one pauper has been accustomed to receive it, another thinks himself ill used if it be not allowed to him also. The example becomes contagious, insomuch that I find in some places, where the greatest abuse has existed, young people destitute of all means of livelihood have married, and come immediately to the overseers to demand work, and with it, what in their slang language is called 'harbour', that is a house.

'In Millbrook, Southampton,' says Colonel Hewitt, 'it was imagined that houses letting under £10 a year are not rateable, which was found to act as an encouragement to the building of small tenements, and introduced into the parish a very objectionable description of residents.'

2
Out-door relief of the able-bodied in money

The out-door relief afforded in money to the able-bodied on their own account, or on that of their families, is still more prevalent. This is generally effected by one of the five following expedients, which may be concisely designated as: 1. Relief without Labour. 2. The Allowance System. 3. The Roundsmen System. 4. Parish Employment. 5. The Labour-Rate System.

I. RELIEF WITHOUT LABOUR

By the parish giving to those who are or profess to be without employment a daily or a weekly sum, without requiring from the applicant any labour. Sometimes relief (to an amount insufficient for a complete subsistence) is afforded, without imposing any further condition than that the applicant shall shift, as it is called, for himself, and give the parish no further trouble. In many districts the plan has become so common as to have acquired the technical name of 'relief in lieu of labour'.

Mr Villiers, in his report from the counties of Warwick, Worcester, Gloucester, and the North part of Devon, states that –

The practice of granting small sums of money to able-bodied men without requiring labour in return, is adopted in some parishes in each county: in the Atherstone and Stratford division in Warwickshire, in the Halfshire hundred in Worcestershire, and in the Slaughter hundred of Gloucestershire; and is known to be in use in other parts of these counties. This practice is favoured by parish officers, from a notion that the parish must gain the difference between the cost of the pauper's maintenance, or the minimum allowed by the scale, and what the pauper consents to take; it is also supposed that it may give the pauper an opportunity to seek work for himself, which he could not if he was employed by the parish.

In the Stratford division, the overseer of Alverston stated that there were young men receiving 2s. 6d. and 3s. a week, and that though it was barely sufficient for their support, and that they lived in lodgings at 6d. a week, yet they greatly preferred it to more pay with labour, as it afforded them time for depredations of various sorts, from which the farmers each year became great sufferers. At Kidderminster, in Worcestershire, young able men were observed to receive small sums of money, such as 1s. 6d. and 2s., and it was said that the convenient form in which relief was thus afforded them was their chief inducement in seeking it, and that they would not accept it in any other shape. At Stow-on-the-Wold, in Gloucestershire, the overseer and church-warden stated that this practice had been adopted after the failure of many others, and with great expectation of its advantage, since by it relief was granted without the trouble of finding employment for the pauper, and upon the condition that the application would not be immediately repeated. They stated, however, that it had completely failed, as the same men soon returned, and they were again compelled to relieve them. The object in view is to save trouble and present expense; the result proves a bounty upon idleness and crime, and is, in the end, not less expensive.

But it is more usual to give a rather larger weekly sum and to force the applicants to give up a certain portion of their time by confining them in a gravel-pit or in some other enclosure, or directing them to sit at a certain spot and do nothing, or obliging them to attend a roll-call several times in the day, or by any contrivance which shall prevent their leisure from becoming a means either of profit or of amusement.

In a still greater number of instances the relief is given on the plea that the applicant has not been able to obtain work; that he has lost a day or a longer period, and is entitled, therefore, to receive from the unlimited resources of the parish what he has not been able to obtain from a private employer.

2. ALLOWANCE

By the parish allowing to labourers, who are employed by individuals, relief in aid of their wages.

The word *allowance* is sometimes used as comprehending all parochial relief afforded to those who are employed by individuals at the average wages of the district. But sometimes this term is confined to the relief which a person so employed obtains on account of his children, any relief which he may obtain on his own account being termed 'payment of wages out of rates'. In the following report we shall use the word *allowance* in its former or more comprehensive sense.

In some places allowance is given only occasionally, or to meet occasional wants; to buy, for instance, a coat or a pair of shoes, or to pay the rent of a cottage or an apartment. In others it is considered that a certain weekly sum, or more frequently the value of a certain quantity of flour or bread, is to be received by each member of a family.

The latter practice has sometimes been matured into a system, forming the law of a whole district, sanctioned and enforced by the magistrates, and promulgated in the form of local statutes, under the name of *scales*.

The following are copies of some of the scales:

County of Cambridge

The Churchwardens and Overseers of the Poor are requested to regulate the incomes of such persons as may apply to them for relief or employment, according to the price of bread; namely,

A single woman, the price of	3	quartern loaves per week.
A single man	4	,,
A man and his wife	7	,,
,, ,, and one child	8	,,
,, ,, and two children	9	,,
,, ,, and three ,,	11	,,

Man, wife, four children and upwards, at the price of two quartern loaves per head per week.

It will be necessary to add to the above income in all cases of sickness or other kind of distress, and particularly of such persons or families who deserve encouragement by their good behaviour, whom parish officers should mark both by commendation and reward.

By order of the Magistrates assembled at the
Shire Hall, Cambridge, December 15th, 1821,
Robert Gee,
Clerk to the Magistrates.

TOWN OF CAMBRIDGE

The Churchwardens and Overseers of the Poor are requested to regulate the incomes of such persons as may apply to them for relief or employment, according to the price of fine bread; namely,

A single woman, the price of · ·	$3\frac{1}{2}$ quartern loaves per week
A single man · · · ·	$4\frac{1}{2}$ · ,,
A man and his wife . . .	8 · ,,
,, · ,, and one child · ·	$9\frac{1}{2}$ · ,,
,, · ,, and two children ·	11 · ,,
,, · ,, and three ,, ·	13 · ,,

Man, wife, four children and upwards, at the price of $2\frac{1}{2}$ quartern loaves per head per week.

It will be necessary to add to the above income in all cases of sickness or other kind of distress; and particularly of such persons or families who deserve encouragement by their good behaviour, whom parish officers should mark both by commendation and reward.

By order of the Magistrates assembled at the Town Hall, Cambridge,

A. Chevell,
November 27, 1829.   Clerk to the Magistrates.

ESSEX. DIVISION OF CHELMSFORD, 1821

At a special meeting of the magistrates acting in and for the said Division, held at the Justice Room, in the Shire Hall, on Friday the 15th day of June, 1821.

It was resolved,

That the undermentioned scale of relief, for the assistance of the overseers of the poor within the said division in relieving the necessitous poor, be recommended: That they do provide each person in every family with the means of procuring half a peck of bread flour per week, together with 10d. per head for other necessaries, if the family consist of two only; 8d. per head, if three; 6d. per head, if four; and 5d. per head, if more than four.

N.B. The above-mentioned sums are exclusive of fuel.

By order of the Magistrates,
T. Archer, Clerk

Price of Flour per Peck.	NUMBER IN FAMILY								
	2.	3.	4.	5.	6.	7.	8.	9.	10.
s. d.	s. d.	s. d.	s. d.	s. d.	£ s. d.	£ s. d.	£ s. d.	£ s. d.	£ s. d.
1 6	3 2	4 3	5 0	5 10	7 0	8 2	9 4	10 6	11 8
1 9	3 5	4 7½	5 6	6 5½	7 9	9 0½	10 4	11 7½	12 11
2 0	3 8	5 0	6 0	7 1	8 6	9 11	11 4	12 9	14 2
2 3	3 11	5 4½	6 6	7 8½	9 3	10 9½	12 4	13 10½	15 5
2 6	4 2	5 9	7 0	8 4	10 0	11 8	13 4	15 0	16 8
2 9	4 5	6 1½	7 6	8 11½	10 9	12 6½	14 4	16 1½	17 11
3 0	4 8	6 6	8 0	9 7	11 6	13 5	15 4	17 3	19 2
3 3	4 11	6 10½	8 6	10 2½	12 3	14 3½	16 4	18 4½	1 0 5
3 6	5 2	7 3	9 0	10 10	13 0	15 2	17 4	19 6	1 1 8
3 9	5 5	7 7½	9 6	11 5½	13 9	16 0½	18 4	1 0 7½	1 2 11
4 0	5 8	8 0	10 0	12 1	14 6	16 11	19 4	1 1 9	1 4 2
4 3	5 11	8 4½	10 6	12 8½	15 3	17 9½	1 0 4	1 2 10½	1 5 5
4 6	6 2	8 9	11 0	13 4	16 0	18 8	1 1 4	1 4 0	1 6 8
4 9	6 5	9 1½	11 6	13 11½	16 9	19 6½	1 2 4	1 5 1½	1 7 11
5 0	6 8	9 6	12 0	14 '7	17 6	1 0 5	1 3 4	1 6 3	1 9 2
5 3	6 11	9 10½	12 6	15 2½	18 3	1 1 3½	1 4 4	1 7 4½	1 10 5
5 6	7 2	10 3	13 0	15 10	19 0	1 2 2	1 5 4	1 8 6	1 11 8
5 9	7 5	10 7½	13 6	16 5½	19 9	1 3 0½	1 6 4	1 9 7½	1 12 11
6 0	7 8	11 0	14 0	17 1	1 0 6	1 3 11	1 7 4	1 10 9	1 13 4
6 3	7 11	11 4½	14 6	17 8½	1 1 3	1 4 9½	1 8 4	1 11 10½	1 15 5
6 6	8 2	11 9	15 0	18 4	1 2 0	1 5 8	1 9 4	1 13 0	1 16 8
6 9	8 5	12 1½	15 6	18 11½	1 2 9	1 6 6½	1 10 4	1 14 1½	1 17 11
7 0	8 8	12 6	16 0	19 7	1 3 6	1 7 5	1 11 4	1 15 3	1 19 2

HUNDREDS of UTTLESFORD, CLAVERING, and FRESHWELL, in the County of ESSEX*

*A man and his wife, with four children and upwards, to be allowed the price of two quartern loaves each, weekly.

Parish officers are desired to regulate allowances according to the price of fine bread, viz.

Quartern Loaves		9d.	9¼d.	9½d.	9¾d.	10d.	10¼d.
		s. d.	s. d.	s. d.	s. d.	s. d.	s. d.
Single Woman –	3	2 3	2 3¾	2 4½	2 5¼	2	2 6¾
„ Man – –	4	3 0	3 1	3 2	3 3	3 4	3 5
Man and Wife –	7	5 3	5 4¾	5 6½	5 8¼	5 10	5 11¾
„ and 1 Child –	8	6 0	6 2	6 4	6 6	6 8	6 10
„ and 2 Children	9	6 9	6 11¼	7 1½	7 3¾	7 6	7 8¼
„ and 3 „ –	11	8 3	8 5¾	8 8½	8 11¼	9 2	9 4¾
„ and 4 „ –	12	9 0	9 3	9 6	9 9	10 0	10 3
„ and 5 „ –	14	10 6	10 9½	11 1	11 4½	11 8	11 11½
„ and 6 „ –	16	12 0	12 4	12 8	13 0	13 4	13 8

It will be necessary to increase the above allowances in some cases, and the deserving should be particularly encouraged.

By order of the Magistrates of the Walden Division, 1826.

Thos. Hall, clerk

ARUNDEL BOROUGH, NOV. 19, 1830

At a meeting of the inhabitants, held this day, the masters agreed to give able-bodied men 2s. per day, wet and dry, and an allowance of 1s. 6d. per week for every child (above two) under 14 years of age.

Lads from 14 to 16, 8d. per day; lads from 16 to 18, 1s. per day; young men from 18 to 21, 1s. 6d. per day, from this time to Lady-day.

It was also agreed that from Lady-day to Michaelmas the able-bodied men should have 14s. per week, wet and dry, with a like allowance of 1s. 6d. per week for every child (above two) under 14 years of age; the boys, from 14 to 16, 9d. per day; from 16 to 18, 1s. 2d. per day; and young men from 18 to 21, 1s. 8d. per day.

Agreed to by the Magistrates assembled at their meeting this day.

In perhaps a majority of the parishes in which the allowance system prevails, the earnings of the applicant, and, in a few, the earnings of his wife and children, are ascertained, or at least professed or attempted to be ascertained, and only the difference between them and the sum allotted to him by the scale is paid to him by the parish. The following extracts from Mr Tweedy's report from Yorkshire, and Mr Wilson's from Durham, show the mode in which this branch of the allowance system is extending itself over the North of England:

In Gisburn the rule and practice of the town is to inquire into the circumstances of each case, and to make up the wages of a man and his family to 1s. 6d. per head. This rule is adopted, because it is the rule by which the magistrates govern themselves on application to them. The course of the magistrates is to inquire of a weaver (for instance) how many pieces he can weave per week, and how much he gets for it. A man will say, perhaps, he can weave three pieces in a week, and would get 1s. 3d. a piece for weaving them; then if he had a family of a wife and four children, they would allow him 5s. 3d. a week... A man had a sickly wife, and was allowed 5s. a week for her and for a woman to attend her. She died, and in about a year he married again; and on the very day of his marriage, said, 'Now I have married again, I'll work Gisburn another round'; and he has been as good as his word, having had three children by the second wife, on account of which he received £2 11s. from January to September in last year.

At Dent, in the same neighbourhood, 'relief to the able-bodied is afforded by payments of a weekly or monthly sum in the name of a pension, the amount of which is regulated according to the number of a man's family, after the rate of two shillings a head per week; poor people, especially those who have become pensioners, marry early, more frequently under twenty years of age than above; they are induced to this, no doubt, from a reliance upon relief from the poor rate. Instances have been numerous in which this had been known to be the case, and in a majority of cases relief is applied for on the birth of the first child; the most profligate and dissolute are amongst this class, and if they get a little extra pay at any time, they spend it in drinking, leaving their families to be maintained by the township.'

At Kettlewell (in Craven) and the neighbourhood, the same system prevails. 'The rule of the magistrates is to allow so much as will yield one shilling and sixpence a head per week, and the overseers take this rule therefore as their guide. The overseer has sometimes called upon little farmers for their rates, and found that they had no provisions of any kind in the house, nor money to buy any; while on the other hand, he has not unfrequently been obliged to give relief to men who, there is no doubt, could have procured work if they had exerted themselves; they speak of it as a matter of right, and, if what they ask be not granted, they threaten to appeal to the magistrate; and, as he lives *fifteen* miles off, the overseers are often induced to yield to their demands, on account of the expense of meeting the claim before him.'

The places above-named are within the jurisdiction of one bench of magistrates.

At Pateley Bridge many are relieved in degree when the wages they earn are not sufficient. It is reckoned that 1s. 9d. per head for each member of the family is necessary, except for infants, and that rule the overseers act upon. One magistrate, however, allows 2s. 6d. each for husband and wife, and 1s. 6d. for each child. Relief is demanded as a matter of right, and sometimes with insolence. An instance is mentioned as occurring some years ago, in which a man came and said, 'We have been getting married; can you find us a house?' and another instance occurred two years ago, in which a man came out of Craven, and claimed relief a few weeks after marriage, and was insolent in his demand.

At Knaresborough the paupers are chiefly weavers of linen and flax dressers; if they are wholly out of work, the rule is to allow a man and his wife 6s. a week, and 9d. for each child; a single man 3s. a week. This rate is allowed, because the magistrates allow it; but in fact, in many cases, it amounts to *more* than a man, when trade is flourishing, could earn. If a man has partial work, they give him 1s. 6d. or 2s. a week, or as little as they can satisfy him with, knowing that, if he goes before the magistrate, he will allow him such a sum as, with his earnings, will make up the rate above mentioned. Immediately that a man is out of work now, he comes for relief; and if he be not relieved at once he goes to a magistrate who grants a summons and makes a memorandum upon it directing the overseer to relieve him in the meantime.

'In Darlington, in the county of Durham', says Mr Wilson,

allowances to able-bodied labourers are graduated according to the numbers of their families; and whenever the wages of any class of labourers (for example, of the linen weavers, who have latterly been the most distressed) fall below the amount appointed by the scale, the difference is made up as a matter of course by the parish. The scale awards 2s. a head a week to heads of families, and 1s. 6d. for each of the children under 12 years of age. This is the minimum of allowance paid by the parish in all cases. Suppose a single man to earn 2s. a week, he could put forward no claim to relief.* Suppose another, earning the same wages,

* 'I merely mean to state that 2s. is the utmost weekly pension or allowance *gratuitously* given to a single able-bodied labourer. An applicant of this description, if he said that he could not live on his wages, would probably be taken

but possessing besides a wife and six children, then 2s. a head for himself and his wife, and 1s. 6d. a head for each of his children, give a total amount of 13s. weekly. In this second case the family man has a recognized claim on the parish for an allowance for 11s. weekly, making up his earnings of 2s. by the above-mentioned graduated scale.

Some remarkable instances of this occurred on Wednesday, January 9th, at the meeting of the parish committee. One applicant owned he had earned 21s. during the last fortnight; but because he had not applied within the last month to the parish, and his average during that period had not been made up (he had four children) he now applied to have the deficit made up, which was done accordingly.

Another man was earning 9s. a week; he had six children; 4s. were handed over the table to him immediately.

A third had seven children, with himself and his wife, making nine in family. He stated that his average earnings were 9s. a week. Last week he had been out of work for a day or two, and consequently had earned only 5s. The parish had found two days' work for him, which made up his earnings to 7s.; 7s. 6d. additional were handed to him over the table.

I need not report a dozen similar cases, which were dispatched like the foregoing, in my presence. Yet do people in this district talk as glibly as any of the abuses of the Poor Laws in the south.

The abuses of the South are, however, still more striking.

'I was able', says Mr Villiers, 'to examine some parishes in nearly every magisterial division in the county of Warwick, in the three principal hundreds of the county of Worcester, and in the adjoining parts of Gloucestershire; and I communicated personally with the overseers and other officers from the hundreds and principal towns in North Devon.'

In each of these counties the relief is regulated upon the same general principle, namely, to relieve all claimants according to their alleged actual necessities; and in each a separate table of relief, varying with the condition of the pauper and the price of bread, has been drawn up and published by the magistrates for the guidance of overseers.

Allowance of money to men, regulated by the number of their

into the poor-house, or set to work by the parish at perhaps 5s. a week; but he would not receive *for doing nothing* more than 2s. a week, while the sums which a married labourer receives for doing nothing increase with the birth of every additional child.'

families, was seldom, if ever, denied. The exceptions are in some few parishes where by a better system of management the labourers have been encouraged to maintain their own children. The system is defended by some persons, and by others it is not considered as a mode of supplying the deficiency in wages from the rates. A magistrate lamented to me that a practice of paying the wages out of the rates did exist in the southern and eastern counties, and was happy to think that it had never been adopted in his division; but he admitted and defended the custom of allowing a sum for the third or fourth child of every labourer. In one parish I asked the overseer if it would be possible for a man and his family to be earning a guinea a week, and receiving allowance for his children; he said, 'Certainly, as we never suppose that a man earns more than the farmers usually give.' Upon asking several other overseers why such inquiry was not made, the reply generally was, that they either had not time, or that it was not usual, and that should they refuse the allowance applied for they would be summoned before a magistrate, who would order it.

The statement of the vestry clerk of Old Swinford was that men with families were in the habit of being relieved who were known to earn 16s. or 18s. a week, and that unless it were shown that the earnings of the family amounted to 25s. a week allowance was not refused. This I was hardly able to credit at first, but he stated that when the trade was good, people were able to earn these wages, and that it had been considered since that time as a standard for allowance. The character of a large portion of these people was described as being reckless and dissolute beyond any others. They were said to be living almost promiscuously, and that large families, legitimate or not, were considered by them as an advantage. Nails are manufactured in their houses, and children, who can be employed early in this trade, become a source of profit to the parents if the trade is good, and if it should fail they are maintained by the parish.

In these districts the truck system has been practised, and doubtless continues to be so; and consequently the owners of the tommy shops, being the manufacturers, are frequently the persons who are expected to regulate the distribution of relief to their own men.

The following are extracts from the valuable answers of Mr Russell, a magistrate residing in Swallowfield, in the counties of Berks. and Wilts., to our printed queries:

The parish gives the labourers, out of the poor-rates, what they call sometimes their 'make up', and sometimes their 'bread money'.

The bread money is calculated weekly, at the price of two gallon loaves for the husband, one for the wife, and one for each of the children, be the number what it may; and to whatever extent the earnings of the family may fall short of that sum, the difference is made up in money. This allowance is given in compliance with an order made many years ago by the magistrates of this county (Berks.), and, practically, is in all cases enforced by them. I have known a magistrate on an application made by a pauper for his bread money exclaim that no such thing as bread money was recognized by the bench, and then make an order, with the mere omission of the term, for the precise amount demanded.

No attention is paid to either the character of the applicant or the causes of his distress. In fact he is considered entitled to it without pleading any distress.

The bread money is hardly looked upon by the labourers in the light of parish relief. They consider it as much their right as the wages they receive from their employers, and in their own minds make a wide distinction between 'taking their bread money' and 'going on the parish'.

In other parishes the labourer is not supposed to earn more than a given sum. If that sum be less than the sum to which the size of his family entitles him, he receives the difference from the parish.

At Thaxted, Essex, the overseer states:

. . . that allowance is regulated by the price of flour; that the magistrates direct half a peck of flour for each individual of the family, besides 6d. each for the father and mother and 4d. for each child. If wages do not amount to this, they are to be made up out of the poor-rate. A man's weekly earnings are reckoned at 8s. If he makes more, still he receives his allowance, in order that industry may not be discouraged.

In the answers to which we have referred, Mr Russell states that:

In the Berks. portion of Swallowfield the invariable usage, both in winter and in summer, was to make up the bread money from the actual earnings of the whole family. In the Wiltshire portion they take the man's earnings, let them have been as high as they may, at the fixed rate of day work only, allowing him the benefit of the difference; and under the influence of the panic struck by the fires, our portion has so far yielded to the importunity of the farmers as to adopt this practice during the winter months. For instance, if a family consist of a man,

his wife and six children, their bread money for nine loaves at 1s. 6d. a
loaf is 13s. 6d. a week. Suppose, as often happens in the winter, that
the man has earned 12s. in the week, and the wife and children nothing,
then, according to the rate which used to prevail with us all the year
round, and which still prevails in summer, the family will receive a
'make up' of 1s. 6d.; but according to the practice which we now follow
in the winter, the man's earnings, though really 12s., will be taken at
the ordinary rate of only 9s., and he will receive 4s. 6d. in money.
Whatever the wife and any of the children may earn, whether in summer or in winter, their real earnings are taken as a set-off against
their loaf.

It is to be observed that even in those parishes in which the
amount of allowance is supposed to depend on that of the applicant's earnings, the inquiry as to the amount of those earnings is
never carried back further than the current or the previous week
or fortnight. The consequence is, that many of those who at particular periods of the year receive wages far exceeding the average
amount of the earnings of the most industrious labourer, receive
also large allowances from the parish. Mr Cowell and Mr Bishop
found a parish in the Bedford Level, in which a recently drained
tract of fertile land requires more labour than the settled inhabitants can provide; and the average yearly earnings of a labourer's
family are from £60 to £70; but during a frost, and generally
from November to March, almost every labourer comes on the
parish. When they commented on these facts in their conversation with a resident magistrate, his answer was, 'Why, what are we
to do? They spend it all, and then come and say they are starving;
and you must relieve them.' 'In our vestry', says Mr Russell,
'which meets every Monday, the calculation is confined to the
earnings of the past fortnight. No further retrospect is ever taken
either for or against the claimant. In some parishes I believe the
account is settled once a week instead of once a fortnight.'

Sometimes the inquiry does not go back even to the beginning
of the week at the end of which the claim is made.

'A case was mentioned to me', says Mr Stuart,

of nine men who had been able to earn 15s. each by taskwork, in three
days, and who came to the parish for the other three days of the week,
during which they had no employment. The overseer, aware of the

profitable work in which they had been engaged, offered 1s. a day for the lost days instead of 1s. 6d. a day, which would have been their allowance according to the scale. This the men rejected, left the work which they then had, and went to a magistrate to complain. The magistrate sent an open note by the complainants, appealing to the humanity of the overseer. The men, aware of the contents of the note, backed the recommendation of the magistrate by threats, which induced the overseer to comply.

Again, there are other parishes in which no inquiry whatever is made respecting earnings, but the birth of a child endows the parent with an allowance, whatever be his income.

'At Laughton, Sussex', says Mr Majendie,

I attended the vestry with one of the principal farmers. One of his labourers, who was in constant employ at 17s. per week, came for his 'pay', for a third child just born, at 1s. a week for six months; it will then be raised to 1s. 6d. a week. The plan of allowance, without inquiry into earnings, is justified on the ground that if the same allowance were not made to all it would cramp industry.

In Westoning, Bedfordshire,

There is scarcely one able-bodied labourer in the employment of individuals but what receives regular relief on account of his family. A married man and his wife, without any child, receive 5s. per week if he be out of employment; for one child, he is allowed 1s. whether in or out of employment; for two children, 2s. and so on in proportion to the number of children under 10 years; above 10 years, each boy out of employment is allowed from 1s. 6d. to 3s. 6d.

Mr Walcott states that in North Wales,

No single able-bodied man in the employment of individuals ever obtains parochial relief.

Married agricultural labourers in work and with only three children, although in many cases their rents are paid and the rates remitted, yet are very rarely considered entitled to regular weekly relief; but if out of work, or with more than three children, in nearly every parish they obtain it on those grounds.

The allowance is usually 1s. a week for each child above the third. Overton is the only parish I heard of entirely free from the abuse of relieving the able-bodied in the employ of individuals. It is there considered contrary to law, justice, and humanity.

The rule of commencing relief with the fourth child is, however, by no means inflexible; for example in Kerry a very well-managed parish, a great portion of the labourers support four, five and six, children, without any parochial assistance, and wages are not higher there than in many other places where it is given.

The effect of thus placing the married and unmarried man on a different footing as to relief, is clearly to encourage early and improvident marriages, with their consequent evils. Of this there was no lack of evidence; the answers to inquiries on this subject being, that such marriages are now much more common amongst the labouring and lower classes than formerly; that the great majority of young men marry under twenty-four years of age, and frequently under twenty-one. That such is one of the effects of the practice, is evident from the circumstance that in the parish of Kerry, where a married man is not certain of obtaining relief, even with five or six children, the labourers (according to the testimony of a very intelligent and long-resident magistrate, Mr Pugh) do not marry earlier than they did twenty or twenty-five years ago.

In the northern division of Devonshire, says Mr Villiers,

The practice of granting allowance for children is so general and confirmed that the pauper is in the habit of giving formal notice to the overseer of the pregnancy of his wife. Should the overseer refuse the application for the fixed sum allowed for the second, third, or fourth child, the magistrates' single inquiry on his appearance before them under a summons would be as to the custom of the parish or the hundred. 'At what number does allowance begin with you?' is the common mode of putting the question, as I was repeatedly assured by overseers. The previous or present earnings of the pauper, or of any of his family, are never mentioned.

It is to be observed also that under the scale system a child is very soon considered as an independent claimant for relief, and entitled to it though residing with his parents, and though they may be in full work and high wages. At Friston, Suffolk, Mr Stuart states that 'a child is entitled to relief, at the rate of 3s. a week, on his own account from the age of fourteen'.

At Bottisham, Cambridge, says Mr Power,

A boy of sixteen receives 2s. 6d. for the week; lives at home with his father; the family consists of his father, mother, brother, and himself. His father and brother are both now doing work at full wages for Mr Jenyns the magistrate. From the overseer: 'Seventeen is the age at which we consider a young man entitled to separate relief, as an unemployed labourer; his pay then is 3s. 6d.; this boy is relieved, not as a labourer out of employ, but at the instance of Mr Jenyns, who has been for some time past endeavouring to obtain him a service.' From Mr King afterwards: 'The allowance to our young single men out of employment used to be 2s. 10d., according to scale, four quartern loaves, present price 8½d. Last November they came to the sessions in a body to complain of the insufficiency, and it was then raised to 3s. 6d. This sum they receive when above a certain age, although residing with their families. One family consisting of man, wife, and seven children, are entitled to, and at this time receiving, 19s. 6d. from the parish, several of the sons being grown up. At Little Shelford a worse case than this was given me by the acting overseer, of one family, a man, wife, and four sons, living together, receiving 24s. weekly from the parish. The woman was receiving 3s. a week at that time in the family of Mr Finch, the clergyman, as Mrs Finch informed me.

3. THE ROUNDSMAN SYSTEM

By the parish paying the occupiers of property to employ the applicants for relief at a rate of wages fixed by the parish, and depending not on the services, but on the wants of the applicants, the employer being repaid out of the poor-rate all that he advances in wages beyond a certain sum. This is the house row, or roundsmen, or billet, or ticket, or stem, system.

According to this plan, the parish in general makes some agreement with a farmer to sell to him the labour of one or more paupers at a certain price, and pays to the pauper, out of the parish funds, the difference between that price and the allowance which the scale, according to the price of bread and the number of his family, awards to him. It has received the name of the billet or ticket system, from the ticket signed by the overseer, which the pauper, in general, carries to the farmer as a warrant for his being employed and takes back to the overseer signed by the farmer as a proof that he has fulfilled the conditions of relief. In other cases the parish contracts with some individual to have some work performed for him by the paupers at a given price, the parish paying the paupers.

In many places the roundsman system is effected by means of an auction. Mr Richardson states that in Sulgrave, Northamptonshire, the old and infirm are sold at the monthly meeting to the best bidder, at prices varying, according to the time of the year from 1s. 6d. a week to 3s.; that at Yardley, Hastings, all the unemployed men are put up to sale weekly, and that the clergyman of the parish told him that he had seen ten men the last week knocked down to one of the farmers for 5s. and that there were at that time about seventy men let out in this manner out of a body of 170.

The following extracts, from the answers to our printed queries for the rural districts, are further examples of all these forms of relief:

GREAT HENNY, ESSEX: *William Newport*, Churchwarden; *Edward Cook*, overseer.

Having so many labouring men, the income from the land will not allow us to give more than is sufficient for the best characters to subsist upon, and we are obliged to give the same to the worst. A man of bad character, on account of which he is not employed, having two children or more, applies to the parish at the end of the week for relief, through loss of time, and has the same money given him as the honest labourer receives of his master for his labour for the same week.

HARLOW, ESSEX: *Isaac Rogers*, overseer.

We are obliged to maintain the family if the man is idle.

CASTLE HEDINGHAM: *Ashurst Majendie*, Deputy Lieutenant, member of vestry.

Rent was at one period paid by the parish, by which an artificial price was kept up; since the practice has been discontinued, the rent of cottages has fallen.

GOUDHURST, KENT: *Giles Miller*.

Every man having more than three children upon his hands comes to the parish for support for all above the third; it is granted as a matter of course.

The word 'scale' is unknown, but the thing exists as effectually as if it were published by authority at every petty sessions. Every parish officer and pauper knows that a man with his wife and three children is entitled to have his wages 'made up' (such is the phrase) to 12s. a week and is entitled to 1s. 6d. per week for every child beyond three, and without entering into any very rigid account as to the average of his earnings. Extra receipts are supposed to go for clothes and extra payments: in reality, they too often go to the beer shop.

NONINGTON, KENT: *W. O. Hammond*, J.P.

There are at this time (May) twelve or fifteen able men disengaged in this parish. The thrashing is over sooner than usual, owing to a deficient crop. The woods are cleared, and pea-hoeing is also finished. The men out of work are allowed at the rate of 6s. for man and wife, with 1s. a head for children. Under the circumstances, the following plan has been adopted: A married man, having two children, receives 8s. from the poor-rate. He takes at the vestry a ticket inscribed with the name of an occupier in the parish. For this person he is required to work four days, *and the employer is pledged to set him at no necessary or essential occupation.* This reservation must be obviously ineffectual. The remaining two days the man is at liberty to earn anything elsewhere if he can. The tickets are allotted by rotation. The system cannot be justified on principle or practice. So long as it lasts, necessary work will wait for the turn of a ticket man. The land will become foul, the labourer half employed and half paid, and the parish imposed upon.

PRESTON, near FAVERSHAM, KENT: *Giles Hilton*, Preston House.

No regular system for the attached; when unattached, a man, wife and four children, usually obtain the full weekly wages of the attached; with six children, I have known most undeserving parents get 18s. a week all the winter and the greater part of the summer. The practice of partly paying for work done for individuals did prevail, but the pauper, learning the practice, could seldom be made to do a fair day's work.

STOGUMBER, SOMERSET: *Charles Rowcliffe.*

An allowance is made, *unhappily*, beginning at three children. I consider that nearly all the work is partly paid for by the parish, and that this fact is a crying evil, working great mischief and distress, and carelessness and indifference about his family, in the mind of the labourer.

HOGSTHORPE, LINCOLN: *John Kirkham*, late contractor; *Joseph Eldin*, churchwarden.

The practice of work being done for individuals and partly paid for by the parish has proved more injurious than any measure ever adopted, having brought numbers of the most hale labourers on the list of paupers, who previous to that would have shuddered at the thought of coming to a parish, but are now as contented to receive relief as they were before in a state of labouring independence; the most wages the best labourers could then obtain were no more than from 3s. to 4s. per week, the remainder was made up out of the rates, according to their families. This system is now abolished, and the labourer gets fair wages.

BYFIELD, NORTHAMPTON: *Charles Wetherell*, Rector; *T. Carter*, J.P.

'Head money' is given indiscriminately to all families of labouring men with more than two children under ten years of age, without inquiring into their earnings, at the rate of 1s. each for those exceeding two; latterly many petty tradesmen have laid claim to it and their claims have in too many instances been acceded to.   *T. C.*

Relief is given generally, according to a scale which the deputy overseer obtains at the magistrates' petty sessions.   *C. W.*

ENSTONE, OXFORD: *William Gardener, F. Elton*

All that apply to the vestry for employment have half their money, or more, out of the poor-rates. They allow, with all the earnings, 5s. per week to the man and his wife and 1s. 6d. per head for the children, many or few; half from the master and the rest from the rates.

A married man and his wife, with no child, will receive 5s. per week; a single man, perhaps 3s. 6d. and 4s.; half from the master and the rest from the poor's rates.

ODDINGTON Parish, and PLOUGHLEY Hundred, Oxford: *Philip Serle*, clerk and J.P.

I am sorry to say that all our able-bodied labourers who have more than two children receive regular allowance from the parish, and this is the case generally in the neighbourhood. In some of the adjoining parishes it is carried to such a length that I have known a labourer receive 2d. per diem where he worked, and the rest of his wages made up from the poor's book. The children are usually sent round, and paid wholly by the overseer.

(Vale of TAUNTON), BAGBOROUGH, BISHOP'S LYDEARD, COMBE-FLOREY, COTHELSTONE, KINGSTON, SOMERSET: *E. J. Esdaile*.

All farm labourers, during the whole or a part of the year, receive a portion of their wages out of the poor's rates.

HASILBURY BRYAN, DORSET: *Henry Walter,* Rector.

In 1821–22 the overseers had been in the habit of sharing out the pauper labourers amongst the farmers (including themselves), and of paying for the work done by them *wholly* out of the poor's rates; and as certain magistrates in the Blandford division (to which this parish then belonged) declined interfering to check this abuse, the answerer felt it his duty to appeal to the two sessions in 1823, and at the July sessions at Shaftesbury he obtained a verdict which put an end to the practice. The custom, however, of 'making up the pay' of able-bodied labourers from the poor-rates still continues. So lately as the 25th July last, the answerer being told by the overseers that a complaint was lodged against the parish for not affording relief to an able-bodied labourer in addition to his wages, whose family consisted of a wife and four little children, but who paid nothing for living in a house belonging to the parish; he accompanied them to the petty sessions, and respectfully informed the magistrates that he should feel it his duty to advise his neighbours to resist any order requiring the parish to pay such allowance; to which it was replied, that they felt it was *their* duty, and should sign the order. Eventually, however, they did not sign it, but their signature was withheld on grounds unconnected with the principle opposed, and that principle was still avowed and maintained.

WELFORD, GLOUCESTER: *William Welch,* assistant overseer.

The labourers changed their service much more frequently when they were paid a part of their money by the overseers (called head-money), which was an order from the magistrates, and persisted in by them till we established a poorhouse, which has nearly done it away, and the labourers are becoming more respectable.

Magistrates, when applied to, always make their orders according to the head-money system, taking the labourer's earnings at the usual day-work price without regard to the conduct or ability of the labourer.

4. PARISH EMPLOYMENT

By the parish employing and paying the applicants for relief.

The 43 Elizabeth [1601] does not authorize relief to be afforded to any but the impotent, except in return for work. And much as this part of the statute has been neglected, its validity is recognized by the Judges. In the King *v.* Collett; 2 Barnewell and Cresswell, 324, Lord Tenterden decided it to be the duty of overseers to provide work, if possible, before they afforded relief. And whatever may be the difficulty of finding *profitable* work, it is difficult to suppose the existence of a parish in which it would not be *possible* to provide some work, were it merely to dig holes and fill them again. But though such is the law, it appears from the Parliamentary Returns, that payment for work is the most unusual form in which relief is administered. The Poor Rate Returns for the year ending 25 March 1832 state that out of £7,036,968 expended in that year for the relief of the poor, less than £354,000, or scarcely more than one twentieth part, was paid for work, including work on the roads and in the workhouses. This may easily be accounted for.

In the first place, to afford relief gratuitously is less troublesome to the parochial authorities than to require work in return for it. Wherever work is to be paid for there must be superintendence; but where paupers are the work-people much more than the average degree of superintendence is necessary. In ordinary cases all that the superintendent inquires is whether the workman has performed an average day's work; and where the work is piece-work, he need not make even that inquiry. The practice of his trade fixes the market price of the work, and he pays it without asking whether the workman has been one hour or one day in performing it, or whether it exceeds or falls below his wants. But the superintendent of pauper labourers has to ascertain not what is an average day's work, or what is the market price of a given service, but what is a fair day's work for a given individual, his strength and habits considered; at what rate of pay for that work, the number of his family considered, he would be able to earn the sum necessary for his and their subsistence; and lastly, whether he has in fact performed the amount which, after taking all these elements into calculation, it appears that he ought to have performed. It will easily be anticipated that this superintendence is very rarely given; and that in far the greater number of the cases in which work is professedly required from paupers, in fact no work is done. In the second place, collecting the paupers in gangs for the performance of parish work is found to be more immediately injurious to their conduct than even allowance or relief without requiring work. Whatever be the general character of the parish labourers, all the worst of the inhabitants are sure to be among the number; and it is well known that the effect of such an association is always to degrade the good, not to elevate the bad. It was among these gangs, who had scarcely any other employment or amusement than to collect in groups and talk over their grievances, that the riots of 1830 appear to have originated. And thirdly, parish employment does not afford direct profit to any individual. Under most of the other systems of relief, the immediate employers of labour can throw on the parish a part of the wages of their labourers. They prefer, therefore, those modes of relief which they can turn to their own account, out of which they can extract profit under the mask of charity.

In those parishes in which labour is the condition on which relief is granted we have found great differences with respect to the kind and the duration of the labour required, and the amount of its remuneration. In Cookham, in Putney, and in many of the metropolitan parishes, the work is irksome, the hours of labour are equal to those which a private employer would exact, and the pay less than he would give. In others the amount of labour required is far less than that which an independent labourer must afford; but the pay is diminished so far as is consistent with the supposed wants of the applicant. Thus, at Kimpton, Hants, 'the single young men are employed by piece-work, but are restricted to earn only 2s. 6d. a week, and are then at liberty to go where they like. In the same place children are employed in picking stones by task, and are allowed to earn the price of a gallon of bread and 6d. over per week, which they can do in about four days.' At Gamlingay, Cambridge, 'the paupers are employed in collecting stones, at the price of 2d. a bushel, until they have earned the sum allotted to them by the bread scale; they then do as they please for that week'. At Uckfield, Sussex, instead of a part of each week, 'they are required to work a part of each day, so as to earn the sum which is considered necessary for their subsistence'; a sum which, according to the magisterial scale of the Uckfield bench, appears to be for a single man, 4s.; man and wife, 7s.; man, wife, and one child, 8s. 6d.; with two children, 10s.; and for each child above two, the value of a gallon of flour. In a parish in Suffolk, 'twenty acres were hired by the parish and dug by the paupers at piece-work, the price being proportioned to their families. Either the work was completed by two or three o'clock, and the rest of the day spent in idleness, or the men consumed the whole day in the lazy performance of the work of a portion of the day.' In Pollington, Yorkshire, 'they send many of them upon the highways, but they only work four hours per day; this is because there is not employment sufficient in that way; they sleep more than they work, and if any but the surveyor found them sleeping, they would laugh at them. In Rancliffe they employed a man in the winter of 1830–31 to look over them; but they threatened *to drown* him, and he was obliged to withdraw. If a man did not like his work, he would say, "I can have 12s. a week by going on the roads, and doing as little as I like." In Carlton, from £30 to £40 was paid to men last year (1831) for doing nothing.' In the parish of Mancetter, in the county of Warwick, the overseer stated that young able men received 2s. 6d. a week, and the magistrates would not allow the parish to employ them more than three days in the week, in order that they might get work for themselves. Upon inquiry, it appeared that their characters soon became so infamous that no person would employ them, having devoted their spare time to thieving and poaching. In the township of Atherstone, Mr Wellday, a manufacturer, impatient of contributing his property to the encouragement of vice and idleness by paying men without exacting labour, purchased some water-carts himself for the purpose of giving employment to paupers. The magistrates refused to allow them to be used after twelve o'clock in the day, in order that these men might procure work for themselves; they were also described as becoming the most worthless characters in the town.

In some of the agricultural districts, the prevalent mismanagement in this respect has created in the minds of the paupers a notion that it is their right to be exempted from the same degree of labour as independent labourers. In the parish of Swallowfield (Berks.), the paupers summoned the overseers before the magistrates. They had been

offered task-work at the gravel-pit at 8d. a yard, or 1s. a load for digging and sifting without loading. This had been considered a fair price with loading. The complainants contended before the magistrates that by what they considered 'a right', they ought not to be employed on the part of the parish more than from eight in the morning until four in the afternoon, although when working for farmers they were usually kept at work from six in the morning until six at night in summer, or from daylight until dark in the winter. This, which they claimed as 'their right', had, in fact, been the previous practice in the parish, and was and is in a greater or less degree the existing practice in adjacent parishes.

In the course of the examination of Mr Price from Great Farringdon (Berks.), he was asked:

How did you enforce work on the in-door paupers? – Chiefly by admonition. Their labour was, as might be expected, very slack comparatively. I, however, insisted that they should work during the same time as the independent labourers. This they resisted, and appealed to the magistrates against this usage. The ground of their appeal was that it was a thing unknown before in this parish, or any other, that parish labourers should work as long or as hard as the other classes of labourers.

But in many places, while the labour required by the parish is trifling, the pay equals or exceeds that of the independent labourer. Eastbourne, in Sussex, is a striking example. In this place, in which the average wages earned from individuals by hard work are 12s. a week, the parish pays for nominal labour as much as 16s. a week. Two families alone received from it, in the year ending Lady Day 1832, £92 4s.; and the wives of the few independent labourers regret that their husbands are not paupers. At the parish farm, occupied by the incorporated parishes of the Isle of Wight, 240 men were employed at one time in the year 1830 at the same wages as those usually given by the farmers; they scarcely did any work, and twice left the farm in a body to threaten the directors. Their wages were consequently raised.

In the parish of Hartland, says Mr Villiers,

Mr ——, who had occupied land there for seventeen years informed me that the magistrates were in the habit of ordering the same wages for the men working on the roads not superintended as were paid to the labourers in the employ of the farmers; and that on this account, as well as that the poor liked to watch for the wrecks in the winter, they did not seek for work out of the parish.

Mr Richardson states that in Northamptonshire,

The plan generally in use in the agricultural villages is, upon the man's applying to the overseer for work, to send him upon some part of the parish roads, where he is expected to work – not the farmer's hours, or anything like them, but to begin at eight, to leave at twelve for dinner, an hour, and to leave the roads finally at four. It is the business of the overseer or the surveyor of the roads, a farmer or a tradesmen, who, paid or not, has his own business to attend to, to see that the men are actually working. While he is present, and the farmers take credit to themselves for riding up once or twice a day to the roads, the men bestir themselves a little; but the moment his back is turned, a man who gives himself any trouble is laughed at by his companions. As the overseer at Kettering told me, their remark is, 'You must have your 12s. a week, or your 10s. a week, whether you work or not; I would not be such a fool as to work – blast work – damn me if I work,' &c.; and, of course, under these circumstances, they do anything but work; if there is a wood near, as at Glapthorne and some other places round Oundle, they run into the wood to steal firing, which they hide and carry off at a convenient time; and universally they are in the habit of stealing turnips, or posts, or any little thing of that sort that comes to hand.

In short, where there were many able-bodied men employed on the roads, there everybody complained of petty thefts, pilfering, poaching, &c., as the natural consequences.

Whatever the previous character of a man may have been, he is seldom able to withstand the corruption of the roads; two years occasional employment there ruins the best labourer. Moreover, in very many instances, the difference between parish pay for pretending to break stones on the road, and the real wages given by the farmer, does not amount to more than 1s. a week; and, if the man has a family entitling him to receive a given sum by the scale as head-money, he receives as much from the parish as he would from any other employer. Accordingly, the labourers who are only occasionally employed are nearly indifferent to pleasing or displeasing their employer; they quit with the remark which I heard at least a dozen times from different overseers 'I can get as much on the roads as if I worked for you.'

The following extracts from Mr Okeden's and Mr Majendie's reports afford examples of all these systems, sometimes separate and sometimes in combination.

At Urchfont, a parish in the district of Devizes, the population of which is 1,340, and the annual poor-rates about £1,450, there are above

50 men out of employ for 45 weeks every year. To these the parish pays 3s. a week each during that time, and inquires no further about their time or labour; thus creating an annual item of expense of nearly £400.

At the parish of Bodicott, in the district of Bloxham, a printed form is delivered to those who apply for work. The labourer takes this to the farmers in succession, who, if they do not want his labour, sign their names. The man, on his return, receives from the overseer the day's pay of an industrious labourer, with the deduction of 2d. The same system takes place in other parishes.

In the parish of Sidford Gore, in the same district, where the poor-rates are under £650 per annum, £114 was paid last year in six months to men who did not strike one stroke of work for it.

At Deddington, during the severe winter months, about sixty men apply every morning to the overseer for work or pay. He ranges them under a shed in a yard. If a farmer or any one else wants a man, he sends to the yard for one, and pays half the day's wages; the rest is paid by the parish. At the close of the day the unemployed are paid the wages of a day, minus 2d. I could multiply instances of this application of the scale to the superfluous labourers; but to do so would only waste your time.

At Rotherfield, in East Sussex, 120 men were out of employ in the winter 1831–32, and various modes were attempted to dispose of them. First they were set to work on the parish account; single men at 5s.; men with families at 10s. per week; the pay being the same as farmers' pay, the men left the farmers in order to get the same pay with less work. Then they were billeted among the farmers at 1s. per day from the farmers, and 8d. from the parish. This was changed to 1s. from the parish, and 8d. from the farmer. The men so billeted did not keep the proper hours of work; then the farmers' men, finding that they who worked the regular hours were paid no more than those who were irregular, gave up their employment to become billeted men, and the farmers were induced to throw their men out of employ to get their labour done by the parish purse. The billeting system having failed, a 6d. labour-rate was made: it soon failed. Magistrates now recommend 6d. in the pound to be deducted from the full rate, and that the occupier should be allowed to pay that proportion of his rate by employment of the surplus hands.

The labourers are much deteriorated. They do not care whether they have regular work or not; they prefer idle work on the roads. The magistrates at the Uckfield bench told the overseer, the year before last, that if the men made complaint they should be allowed at the rate of 2s. 4d. per head for each member of the family.

At Burnash, in East Sussex, in the year 1822, the surplus labourers were put up to auction, and hired as low as 2d. and 3d. per day; the rest of their maintenance being made up by the parish. The consequence was, that the farmers turned off their regular hands, in order to hire them by auction when they wanted them. The evil of this system was so apparent, that some occupiers applied to the magistrates, who recommended it should be given up. During the last year, the following plan has been adopted: the names of the occupiers are written on pieces of paper, which are put into a bag; the labourer draws out a ticket, which represents 10s. worth of labour, at fair wages; next week the labourer draws another master, and this is repeated till the occupier has exhausted the shilling rate. This has continued two winters; much fraud is mixed up with the practice. Some farmers turn off their labourers in order to have ticketed men; other occupiers refuse to pay the rate, and against them it is not enforced.

5. THE LABOUR-RATE SYSTEM

By an agreement among the rate-payers that each of them shall employ and pay out of his own money a certain number of the labourers who have settlements in the parish, in proportion, not to his real demand for labour, but according to his rental or to his contribution to the rates, or to the number of horses that he keeps for tillage, or to the number of acres that he occupies, or according to some other scale. Where such an agreement exists, it is generally enforced by an additional rate, imposed either under the authority of the 2 & 3 William IV, c. 96 [1832], or by general consent on those who do not employ their full proportion. This may be called the labour-rate system. We shall consider it more at length in a subsequent portion of this Report.

Widows

In all the cases which have been mentioned, relief is professed to be afforded on the ground of want of employment, or of insufficient wages; but a class of persons have, in many places, established a right to public support, independently of either of these claims. These are widows, who, in many places, receive what are called pensions, of from 1s. to 3s. a week on their own account, without any reference to their age or strength, or powers of obtaining an independent subsistence, but simply as widows. In such places, they receive an additional allowance if they have children. The allowance for each child is generally about 1s. 6d. a week in rural districts unless the child be illegitimate, in which case it is more frequently 2s. or more.

II

OUT-DOOR RELIEF OF THE IMPOTENT

THE out-door relief to the impotent (using that word as comprehending all except the able-bodied and their families) is subject to less abuse. The great source of Poor Law maladministration is, the desire of many of those who regulate the distribution of the parochial fund to extract from it a profit to themselves. The out-door relief to the able-bodied, and all relief that is administered in the workhouse, afford ample opportunities for effecting this purpose; but no use can be made of the labour of the aged and sick, and there is little room for jobbing if their pensions are paid in money. Accordingly, we find that even in places distinguished in general by the most wanton parochial profusion the allowances to the aged and infirm are moderate.

The out-door relief of the sick is usually effected by a contract with a surgeon which, however, in general includes only those who are parishioners. When non-parishioners become chargeable from illness, an order for their removal is obtained, which is suspended until they can perform the journey; in the mean time they are attended by the local surgeon, but at the expense of the parish to which they belong. This has been complained of as a source of great peculation, the surgeon charging a far larger sum than he would have received for attending an independent labourer or a pauper in the place of his settlement. On the whole, however, medical attendance seems in general to be adequately supplied, and economically, if we consider only the price and the amount of attendance.

The country is much indebted to Mr Smith, of Southam for his exertions to promote the establishment of dispensaries for the purpose of enabling the labouring classes to defray, from their own resources, the expense of medical treatment. Some valuable remarks on this subject, by the Rev. P. Blakiston and Dr Calvert, will be found in Appendix C. It appears to us, that great good has already been effected by these dispensaries, and that much more may be effected by them; but we are not prepared to suggest any legislative measures for their encouragement.

It appears from the whole evidence, that the clause of the 43 Elizabeth [1601] which directs the parents and children of the impotent to be assessed for their support is very seldom enforced. In any ordinary state of society we much doubt the wisdom of such an enactment. The duty of supporting parents and children, in old age or infirmity, is so strongly enforced by our natural feelings that it is often well performed, even among savages, and almost always so in a nation deserving the name of civilized. We believe that England is the only European country in which it is neglected. To add the sanction of the law in countries where that of nature is found sufficient, to make that compulsory which would otherwise be voluntary, cannot be necessary; and if unnecessary, must be mischievous. But if the deficiencies of parental and filial affection are to be supplied by the parish, and the natural motives to the exercise of those virtues are thus to be withdrawn, it may be proper to endeavour to replace them, however imperfectly, by artificial stimulants, and to make fines, distress warrants, or imprisonment act as substitutes for gratitude and love. The attempt, however, is scarcely ever made.

GENERAL REMARKS ON OUT-DOOR RELIEF

We have dwelt at some length on out-door relief because it appears to be the relief which is now most extensively given, and because it appears to contain in itself the elements of an almost indefinite extension; of an extension, in short, which may ultimately absorb the whole fund out of which it arises. Among the elements of extension are the constantly diminishing reluctance to claim an apparent benefit, the receipt of which imposes no sacrifice, except a sensation of shame quickly obliterated by habit, even if not prevented by example; the difficulty often amounting to impossibility on the part of those who administer and award relief of ascertaining whether any and what necessity for it exists; and the existence in many cases of positive motives on their parts to grant it when unnecessary, or themselves to create the necessity. The first and third of these sources of maladministration are common to the towns and to the country; the second, the difficulty of ascertaining the wants of the applicant, operates most strongly in the large towns, and is well displayed in the following extract from the report of Mr Chadwick, on the eastern division of the Metropolis:

George Huish, Assistant Overseer of the Parish of Saint George's, Southwark.

I have lived in the parish upwards of forty years, and have served office upwards of twelve years, and before that time I had cognizance of much parochial business with a relation.

The most injurious portion of the Poor Law system is the out-door relief. I do not serve a day without seeing some new mischiefs arise from it. In the smaller parishes, persons are liable to all sorts of influences. In such a parish as ours, where we administer relief to upwards of 2000 out-door poor, it is utterly impossible to prevent considerable fraud, whatever vigilance is exercised.

Has the utmost vigilance been tried? – One man to every twenty would be required to watch the paupers living out of the parish, and one man to watch every hundred living within the parish; which is an expense of inspection which could not be borne. Suppose you go to a man's house as a visitor: you ask, where is Smith (the pauper)? You see his wife or his children, who say they do not know where he is, but that they believe he is gone in search of work. How are you to tell, in such a case, whether he is at work or not? It could only be by following him in the morning; and you must do that every day, because he may be in work one day, and not another. Suppose you have a shoemaker who demands relief of you, and you give it him on his declaring that he is out of work. You visit his place, and you find him in work; you say to him, as I have said to one of our own paupers, 'Why, Edwards, I thought you said you had no work?' and he will answer, 'Neither had I any; and I have only got a little job *for the day.*' He will also say directly, 'I owe for my rent; I have not paid my chandler's shop score; I have been summoned, and I expect an execution out against me, and if you stop my relief, I must come home.' (That is, he must go into the workhouse.) The overseer is immediately frightened by this, and says, 'What a family that man has got! it will not do to stop his relief.' So that, unless you have a considerable number of men to watch every pauper every day, you are sure to be cheated. Some of the out-door paupers are children, others are women; but, taking one with another, I think it would require one man's whole time to watch every twenty paupers.

Does the practice of obtaining out-door relief extend amongst respectable classes of mechanics, whose work and means of living are tolerably good? – I am every week astonished by seeing persons come whom I never thought would have come. The greater number of our out-door paupers are worthless people; but still the number of decent people who ought to have made provision for themselves, and who come is very great, and increasing. One brings another; one member of a family brings the rest of a family. Thus I find, in two days' relief, the following names: 'John Arundell, a sawyer, aged 55; his son, William, aged 22, a wire-drawer; Ann Harris, 58, her husband is in Greenwich Hospital; her son John, and his wife, also came separately; so does their son, a lad aged 18, a smith.' Thus we have pauper father, pauper wife, pauper son, and pauper grandchildren, frequently applying on the same relief-day. One neighbour brings another. Not long since a very young woman, a widow named Cope, who is not more than 20 years of age, applied for relief; she had only one child. After she had obtained relief, I had some suspicion that there was something about this young woman not like many others. I spoke to her, and pressed her to tell me the real truth as to how so decent a young woman as herself came to us for relief; she replied that she was 'gored' into it. That was her expression. I asked her what she meant by being gored into it. She stated that where she was living there were only five cottages, and that the inhabitants of four out of five of these cottages were receiving relief, two from St Saviour's, and two from Newington parish. They had told her that she was not worthy of living in the same place unless she obtained relief too.

Indeed, the malady of pauperism has not only got amongst respectable mechanics, but we find even persons who may be considered of the middle classes, such as petty masters, small master bricklayers, and other such persons, who have never before been seen making application to parish officers, now applying. My opinion is that they apply in consequence of having witnessed the ease with which others who might have provided for themselves obtain relief. They naturally say, 'Why should we be content with half a loaf when we might have a whole one ?' A few days ago a man applied for relief, stating that he was in great distress. On inquiry, it was found that he held a situation as packer, and actually received wages of the amount of 20s. per week at the time he made the application and had been in the receipt of them for some time previous. We found that one woman had received relief from us for two years, whilst she was receiving from the East India Company a pension of £70 per annum. In one instance, we discovered that a man named James Peaton was receiving relief of six different parishes; he belonged to our parish, and he had picked out five other parishes which gave relief on the five other days. He made it his entire business to live on parish pensions, and he received one week's pension every day.

Since the inquiry has been made, I have stationed persons at well-known gin shops to observe the number of paupers who came and the money they spend; and from all their statements I have drawn the conclusion that £30 out of every £100 of the money given as out-door relief is spent in the gin-shops during the same day.

From the preceding evidence it will be seen how zealous must be the agency, and how intense the vigilance, to prevent fraudulent claims crowding in under such a system of relief. But it would require still greater vigilance to prevent the bona fide claimants degenerating into impostors; and it is an aphorism amongst the active parish officers that 'cases which are good today are bad tomorrow, unless they are incessantly watched'. A person obtains relief on the ground of sickness; when he has become capable of returning to moderate work, he is tempted, by the enjoyment of subsistence without labour, to conceal his convalescence, and fraudulently extend the period of relief. When it really depends upon the receivers whether the relief shall cease with its occasion, it is too much to expect of their virtue that they shall, in any considerable number of instances, voluntarily forego the pension.

The permanent officers appointed to make inquiries at the residence of the out-door paupers frankly acknowledge, that it is beyond the powers of any individuals to prevent an immense amount of fraud. We add the following instances from Mr Chadwick's report:

Mr Thorn, Assistant Overseer of the parish of Saint Giles, Cripplegate, London, states:

'The out-door relief in the city of London would require almost one man to look after every half dozen of able-bodied men, and then he would only succeed imperfectly in preventing fraud. They cheat us on all hands. I have had instances where the masters who have employed out-door paupers have given such answers to my inquiries as to leave no doubt in my mind that the master concealed the real amount of wages, for fear that if he caused the parish to reduce the man's allowance he should have to pay him higher wages. There is no protection whatever from the growing evil of the increase of the able-bodied out-door poor, which is one of the greatest evils of the system, but in finding them labour out of town.'

Mr Samuel Miller, Assistant Overseer in the parish of Saint Sepulchre, London, declares that:

'With respect to the out-door relief, there must, from the very nature of it, be an immense deal of fraud. There is no industry, no inspection, no human skill, which will prevent gross impositions belonging to this mode of relief.

'By far the greater proportion of our new paupers are persons brought upon the parish by habits of intemperance, and the others are chiefly pauper children or hereditary paupers.

'After relief has been received at our board, a great portion of them proceed with the money to the palaces of gin-shops, which abound in the neighbourhood.'

Mr William Weale, Assistant Overseer of the parish of Lambeth, whose chief business is the investigation of the cases of out-door paupers, after specifying the modes of examination, concludes by stating that after all

'However diligent an assistant overseer or an officer for inquiry may be, there are numerous cases which will baffle his utmost diligence and sagacity; the only test of these cases is making their condition more severe than that of the lowest class of labourers who obtain their livelihood by honest industry.'

Mr Luke Teather, another officer of great experience in the same business, adds that as

'It is the study of bad paupers to deceive you all they can, and as they study more their own cases than any inquirer can study each of the whole mass of different cases which he has to inquire into, they are sure to be successful in a great many instances. The only protection for the parish is to make the parish the hardest taskmaster and the worst paymaster that can be applied to.'

Another evil connected with out-door relief, and rising from its undefined character, is the natural tendency to award to the deserving more than is necessary, or where more than necessary relief is afforded to all, to distinguish the deserving by extra allowances. The scales which we have already quoted, promulgated by the magistrates for the county of Cambridge, by those for the town of Cambridge, and by the magistrates of the Walden division, Essex, all direct the parish officer to reward or encourage the deserving. The whole evidence shows the danger of such an attempt. It appears that such endeavours to constitute the distributors of relief into a tribunal for the reward of merit, out of the property of others, have not only failed in effecting the benevolent intentions of their promoters, but have become sources of fraud on the part of the distributors, and of discontent and violence on the part of the claimants.

Mr Masterman, who had served the office of headborough, and also the offices of churchwarden and overseer, in the parish of St Matthew, Bethnal Green, states:

The system of expenditure was bad in the favouritism exercised as to the parties to whom relief was given. Many of the landlords of the smaller tenements have always mustered their friends on the days of election, to get them appointed governors or guardians of the poor. When parties came to be relieved, who were tenants of the governors who sat at the Board, the governors have given testimony to their meritorious characters, and urged that they might have relief. I have been present when it has been proposed that 1s. 6d. should be given, when the landlord would say 'Oh, he a very good man, give him 3s.', and the 3s. has been awarded. The working of this system would naturally be that when one man's tenants were thus favoured, he would favour the tenants of the others in turn when they came to demand relief. Another consequence is that the landlord or his collector, when they collect the rent, are well aware that the tenant has had money which will pay it.

'I found', says Mr Chadwick,

that most attempts to administer public relief according to character, even when those attempts have been made under circumstances apparently the most favourable, have created great dissatisfaction. Character being made up of habits, and habits being made up of series of simple acts (which we sometimes find it difficult to determine on in our courts of law, even with all skilled appliances), it is not surprising that persons in wealthy or superior stations who have rarely the means of observing or knowing the daily arts of the labouring classes usually fail of estimating them so as to adjudicate justly according to the estimation of the claimants. The Rev. W. Bishop, the rector of Ufton, Berks., stated to me: 'When first I came to this parish, I instituted rewards for virtuous conduct amongst my parishioners, but I soon found that I did more mischief than good by the proceeding, and I was compelled to abandon it. I found that my parishioners, from their situation, knew more of the objects whom I selected for reward than I possibly could. They saw actions of which I could obtain no knowledge. With all my desire to do justice, there were actions which I forgot to take into account; and of those which I did take into account, they probably often made a more correct estimate than I could; under these circumstances, I probably was led to decide unjustly, and excited more ill feeling by my decisions than emulation by my rewards.' He gave up entirely the idea of rewarding according to character, and adopted other courses of proceeding.

In more rude hands, such attempts often excite fierce discontent by the inequalities of the distribution amongst claimants who conceive themselves at least equal in merit. Private charity, being usually dispensed to separate individuals, is unattended with the discontents arising from a comparison of the objects of bounty; but I did not find one magistrate of extensive experience who had found it practicable to take character into account, except on rare occasions. 'A man', it has been said, 'may be a very worthy, good sort of man, but so ought we all to be: and if every man who is so were to bring in his bill for being so, who would there be to pay it?'

A common consequence is that to satisfy the clamours of the undeserving, the general scale of relief is raised; but the ultimate result of such a proceeding appears always to be to augment the distress which it was intended to mitigate and to render more fierce the discontent which it was intended to appease. Profuse allowances excite the most extravagant expectations on the parts of the claimants, who conceive that an inexhaustible fund is devoted to their use, and that they are wronged to the extent of whatever falls short of their claims. Such relief partakes of the nature of indiscriminate alms-giving in its effects, as a bounty on indolence and vice; but the apparently legal sanction to this parochial alms-giving renders the discontent on denial the most intense; wherever, indeed, public charities are profusely administered we hear, from those who are engaged in their administration, complaints of the discontent and disorders introduced. Bedford is a town in which money is profusely dispensed in charity for the partial relief of the labouring classes, without any return of labour. The following is an extract from a communication on the subject by the Rev. James Donne, the vicar of St Paul's, Bedford:

The great Bedford Charity has a bad effect on the minds of all the working classes. They are discontented because they think that there is an ample provision for the poor whenever they are thrown out of work.

I have heard an engineer (Mr Bailey), resident in the town, say that he dare not employ a Bedford hand, they are so idle.

A stranger has lately contracted to light the town with gas. He declared that of all the places where he had undertaken such works, he never met with such idle workmen as the Bedford men. Thus they show by their actions that the charity is no real blessing to them, whatever it may prove to the next generation, who will have the benefit of all the improvements in our schools. But the class above the working people are also affected by this charity, to their injury. They conceive they shall be provided for in the almshouses if ever they come to poverty; and they are not careful and provident, but rather extravagant in their way of living.

In times of popular excitement the poorer sort will speak out and say the pauper's charity should be theirs, and if they had justice done them they need not work at all. And having such opportunities of education in our schools, they entirely neglect the religious education of their children at home. No doubt there are exceptions, but I believe the rule to be as I state it.

There are very few labouring men in my parish who save anything, and yet many contrive, who are beholden to the parish for their subsistence, to spend a good deal at the beer shop. Drunkenness has greatly increased the last two years. The beer houses are much frequented on Sundays.

It appears from all our returns, especially from the replies to question 53 of the rural queries, that in every district, the discontent of the labouring classes is proportioned to the money dispensed in poor's rates, or in voluntary charities. The able-bodied unmarried labourers are discontented, from being put to a disadvantage as compared with the married. The paupers are discontented from their expectations being raised by the ordinary administration of the system, beyond any means of satisfying them. 'They, as well as the independent labourers to whom the term poor is equally applied, are instructed', says Mr Chadwick, 'that they have a right to a "*reasonable* subsistence", or "a *fair* subsistence", or "an *adequate* subsistence". When I have asked of the rate distributors what "*fair*", or "*reasonable*", or "*adequate*" meant, I have in every instance been answered differently; some stating they thought it meant such as would give a good allowance of "meat every day", which no poor man (meaning a pauper) should be without; although a large proportion of the rate-payers do go without it.' It is abundantly shown in the course of this inquiry, that where the terms used by the public authorities are vague, they are always filled up by the desires of the claimants, and the desires always wait on the imagination, which is the worst regulated and the most vivid in the most ignorant of the people. In Newbury and Reading the money dispensed in poor's rates and charity is as great as could be desired by the warmest advocate either of compulsory or of voluntary relief; and yet, during the agricultural riots, many of the inhabitants in both towns were under strong apprehensions of the rising of the very people amongst whom the poor-rates and charities are so profusely distributed. The violence of most of the mobs seems to have arisen from an idea that all their privations arose from the cupidity or fraud of those entrusted with the management of the fund provided for the poor. Those who work though receiving good wages, being called *poor*, and classed with the really indigent, think themselves entitled to a share of the 'poor funds'. Whatever addition is made to allowances under these circumstances excites the expectation of still further allowances, increases the conception of the extent of the right, and ensures proportionate disappointment and hatred if that expectation is not satisfied. On the other hand, wherever the objects of expectation have been made definite, where wages, upon the performance of work, have been substituted for eleemosynary aid, and those wages have been allowed to remain matter of contract, employment has again produced content, and kindness become again a source of gratitude.

IN-DOOR RELIEF

IN-DOOR relief, that which is given within the walls of the poor-house, or as it is usually but very seldom properly denominated, the workhouse, is also subject to great maladministration. When Mr Chadwick's account of Reading was published many readers thought that the management of the workhouses, described by him, must be an exception to the general rule. It is probable that the smallness of those workhouses prevents their inmates from suffering so much from the misconduct of one another, as is the case in the larger workhouses. But in all other respects, in the absence of classification, discipline, and employment, and the extravagance of allowances, the Reading workhouses seem to be merely fair specimens of the ordinary workhouses in thriving towns. The description of many of the London workhouses, in the evidence collected by Mr Codd, is still less favourable than the report from Reading.

Mr W. Lee, who has for seventeen years held the office of master of the workhouse of St Pancras, containing more than a thousand inmates, says,

It is a common remark among our paupers that they live better in the house than they ever lived before; and looking to the cleanliness, the airiness and roominess of the apartments, the goodness of the beds and bedding, and the wholesomeness and quantity of the food, this is probably the case. There are 300 children; if we get them places they throw them up, or misconduct themselves so as to lose them, and return to the workhouse as a matter of course because they prefer the security and certainty of that mode of life to the slightest exercise of forbearance or diligence. As little or no classification can take place, the younger soon acquire all the bad habits of the older, and become for the most part as vitiated. This is peculiarly the case with respect to young girls. We are obliged to have many prostitutes among our inmates; they decoy the young girls with whom they have met in the house to leave it, and addict themselves to the same abandoned course.

Mr Bryand, clerk to the overseers of St James's, Westminster, states that the workhouse contains 811 persons, and that the parish has besides about forty refractory poor in places called farm-houses, who, in consequence of their bad character, are excluded from the regular establishment. The workhouse inmates, therefore, are people of comparatively good character; and Mr Bryand considers the workhouse to be better managed than most work-houses, or certainly as well.

He goes on to say,

Our paupers are allowed to leave the workhouse for one day in each week. It is a very common occurrence for both men and women, on the days that they are let out, to return in a state of intoxication. They are let out on the weekly days, about one o'clock, after dinner, and on festival days early in the morning; on these latter days, it not unfrequently happens that paupers, especially women, are brought into the house by constables or policemen before twelve o'clock in a beastly state of intoxication; they are received as a matter of course, and the care of the governor and matron is applied, not to their punishment, but to keeping them quiet and peaceable; if they can be rendered so, they are put to bed, and no further notice is taken of the case; if they cannot, and they are very violent and riotous, the heads of the house are obliged to have recourse to assistance to hold them or tie them down in their beds.

We have in the house many women who are known to be prostitutes; we have also notorious thieves. I recollect, in particular, W. Thomas and J. Selburn, now young men; both of them were brought up from infancy in the workhouse; these men are always supported either by the county or in the parish, except what they get by thieving. I am persuaded that parish poorhouses, as at present administered, have the effect of attracting paupers.

Mr Stephenson, vestry-clerk of St Margaret's and St John's, Westminster, says,

For cleanliness, diet, lodgings, and medical attendance, no house can be more remarkable than that of St Margaret's, and these advantages are extended to the bad as well as the good. The diet and accommodation of all are very superior to that which can be obtained by the most industrious of our independent labourers and mechanics.

He is asked how it happens that there are in that workhouse a hundred females between the ages of twenty-one and fifty, and answers that 'it arises from the bad character of the low population of

Westminster'. 'Then I conclude that many of these women are prostitutes?'

Yes, a large majority. They walk the streets until they are reduced to great distress, and then apply to be taken into the house; they remain with us until their strength is recruited, and they return to their former practices. Indeed, it very often happens that they go out worse than they came in, owing to their intercourse, within the walls, with older and more vicious characters.

The farm-houses to which Mr Bryand referred, as places of confinement for the persons whose character is so bad that they are excluded from the society of the thieves and prostitutes of the regular workhouse, are large establishments, containing sometimes as many as 500 persons, apparently with scarcely any attempt at discipline, and with scarcely any means of enforcing it if attempted.

Mr Fry, whose parochial establishment contains 270 persons, and among them many discharged convicts, uses 'mild remonstrance', unless they are much complained of by their fellow paupers, or act violently, in which case they are put into the black hole for *two or three hours*.

Mr Perry, whose premises contain from 280 to 500, says, 'The only way in which we can punish them for misconduct is by remonstrance or discharge, but we do not use any system of coercion.'

Mr Hall, the overseer of St Botolph, Aldgate, says,

We send our poor to farm-houses, paying 4s. 6d. per head per week for them; but it is the interest of the farm-house-keepers to give them so much liberty, on account of the consequent saving of provision, that their residence is not one of restraint nor their life one of hardship. It has been repeatedly said to me by paupers nominally confined in farm-houses that they got 2d. a day from the keepers of those houses to leave them for the day, by which means the keepers saved their food for the day; and I have constantly seen persons for whom I knew that we were paying to farm-houses wandering about the streets, sometimes in a state of intoxication, and often I have had them come to my house in such a state and insist, with much violence, upon getting further relief.

And yet the London workhouses are not likely to be comparatively ill-managed. The number of persons of leisure and intelligence, who have the power to expose their faults, and are interested in doing so, makes it probable that they are, in fact, comparatively well administered. And we find their general management favourably contrasted with that of the Oxford workhouses.

Mr Bishop's picture of the Oxford House of Industry is, indeed, alarming; but many of its worst features reappear in the descriptions of similar establishments scattered through our evidence. In some very few instances, among which Southwell, in Nottinghamshire, is pre-eminent, the workhouse appears to be a place in which the aged and impotent are maintained in comfort, and the able-bodied supported, but under such restrictions as to induce them to prefer to it a life of independent labour. But in by far the greater number of cases, it is a large almshouse, in which the young are trained in idleness, ignorance, and vice; the able-bodied maintained in sluggish sensual indolence; the aged and more respectable exposed to all the misery that is incident to dwelling in such a society, without government or classification; and the whole body of inmates subsisted on food far exceeding both in kind and in amount, not merely the diet of the independent labourer, but that of the majority of the persons who contribute to their support.

[PROGRESSIVENESS OF BURDEN]

IT is with still further regret that we state our conviction, that the abuses of which we have given a short outline, though checked in some instances by the extraordinary energy and wisdom of individuals, are, on the whole, steadily and rapidly progressive.

It is true, that by the last Parliamentary Return (that for the year ending 25 March 1832), the total amount of the money expended for the relief of the poor, though higher than that for any year since the year 1820, appears to fall short of the expenditure of the year ending 25 March 1818; the expenditure of that year having been £7,890,014, and that for the year ending 25 March 1832, £7,036,968. But it is to be remembered, first, that the year ending 25 March 1818 was a period of extraordinary distress among the labouring classes, especially in the manufacturing districts, in consequence of the high price of provisions, unaccompanied by a corresponding advance in wages; secondly, that in the year ending 25 March 1832 the price of corn was lower by about one third than in 1818, and that of clothes and of the other necessaries of life lower in a still greater proportion; so that, after allowing for an increase of population of one fifth, the actual amount of relief given in 1832 was much larger in proportion to the population than even that given in 1818, which has generally been considered as the year in which it attained its highest amount; and thirdly, that the statement of the mere amount directly expended, whether estimated in money or in kind, affords a very inadequate measure of the loss sustained by those who supply it. A great part of the expense is incurred, not by direct payment out of the rates, but by the purchase of unprofitable labour. Where rate-payers are the immediate employers of work-people, they often keep down the rates, either by employing more labourers than they actually want, or by employing parishioners, when better labourers could be obtained. The progressive deterioration of the labourers in the pauperized districts, and the increasing anxiety of the principal rate-payers, as their burthen becomes more oppressive, to shift it in some way, either on the inhabitants of neighbouring parishes, or on the portion of their fellow-parishioners who can make the least resistance; and the apparent sanction given to this conduct by the 2 & 3 William IV, c. 96 [1832], appear to have greatly increased this source of indirect and unrecorded loss. Our evidence, particularly Appendix D, is full of instances of which we will cite only those which have been drawn from the county of Cambridge, and are to be found in Mr Cowell's and Mr Power's reports. Mr Cowell's report contains the examination of a large farmer and proprietor at Great Shelford, who, on 500 acres situated in that parish pays 10s. per acre poor-rate, or £250 a year. In addition, though he requires for his farm only sixteen regular labourers, he constantly employs twenty or twenty-one. The wages of these supernumerary labourers amount to £150 a year, and he calculates the value of what they produce at £50 a year; so that his real contribution to the relief of the poor is not £250, the sum which would appear in the Parliamentary Returns, but £350. In the same report is to be found a letter from Mr Wedd, of Royston, containing the following passages:

An occupier of land near this place told me today that he pays £100 for poor-rates, and is compelled to employ fourteen men and six boys, and requires the labour of only ten men and three boys. His extra labour at 10s. a week (which is the current rate for men), and half as much for boys, is £130.

Another occupier stated yesterday that he held 165 acres of land, of which half was pasture. He was compelled to employ twelve men and boys, and his farm required the labour of only five. He is about to give notice that he will quit. Every useless labourer is calculated to add 5s. an acre to the rent of a farm of 100 acres.

It contains also a letter from Mr Nash, of Royston, the occupier of a farm in a neighbouring parish, stating that

The overseer, on the plea that he could no longer collect the money for the poor-rates without resorting to coercive measures, and that the unemployed poor must be apportioned among the occupiers of land in proportion to their respective quantities, had required him to take two more men. Mr Nash was consequently obliged to displace two excellent labourers, and of the two men sent in their stead one was a married man with a family sickly, and not much inclined to work; the other a single man addicted to drinking.

The subsequent history of these two men appears in Mr Power's report. One killed a favourite blood mare of Mr Nash's, and the other he was obliged to prosecute for stealing his corn.

Mr Power reports the evidence of Mr Charles Mash, of Hinxton:

He occupies a farm of 1,000 acres, one of the most highly cultivated in the country. They have the practice there of sharing among themselves all the labourers of the parish, according to an assessment of value. He finds this burthen a very oppressive one and injurious to him in many ways. He is paying about £1,200 a year for labour, and his farm being already in an excellent state, he cannot find work for a great portion of his men. He believes that by discarding those whom he does not want, he should save £200 of the sum above stated.

Injury often occurs to his property from the negligent conduct of such men as he is sometimes obliged to employ. He would rather pay some for their absence than their presence on his farm. By the necessity of employing so much labour, he has found himself much constrained, and to great disadvantage, in choosing his mode of cultivation. He has nevertheless, at this time, six more labourers than he can possibly employ to advantage. They are frequently obliged to remain idle on the farm because there is no dependence to be placed on their industry or attention to their work; and much of this arises from a consciousness in the men themselves that they are not wanted.

We believe, that if it were possible to ascertain the loss from all these sources during the year ending 25 March 1832, it will be found at least to approach the £7,036,968, which the Parliamentary Return states to have been directly expended.

From this pecuniary loss, indeed, must be deducted the pecuniary gain, such as it may be, obtained by those employers who have purchased the services of their labourers, for wages which an independent labourer would not have accepted; a gain which may at first sight be supposed to be considerable, since the endeavour to procure it has been one of the principal causes of the allowance system. Our inquiries have convinced us that the deduction which may fairly be made on this account, from the apparent charge of the poor-rates, is much less than it is commonly thought to be; that its amount is decreasing every day; and that, though in many instances much less is paid to the pauperized labourer by his employer, for his day or his week, than he could have received if he had been independent; yet that, even in these cases, the work actually performed is dearly paid for. We shall recur to this subject in a subsequent part of the Report.

[OBJECTIONS TO AMENDMENT]

It might have been hoped that under such circumstances a general feeling would have arisen that these abuses are intolerable, and must be put an end to at any risk or at any sacrifice. But many who acknowledge the evil seem to expect the cure of an inveterate disease, without exposing the patient to any suffering or even discomfort. They exclaim against the burthen as intolerable, but object to any amendment if it appears that it must be or may be attended by any immediate inconvenience.

And among all parties, labourers, employers of labourers, and owners of property, many are to be found who think that they *shall* suffer some immediate injury from any change which shall tend to throw the labouring classes on their own resources.

I

[ON THE PART OF LABOURERS]

The labourer feels that the existing system, though it generally gives him low wages, always gives him easy work. It gives him also, strange as it may appear, what he values more, a sort of independence. He need not bestir himself to seek work; he need not study to please his master; he need not put any restraint upon his temper; he need not ask relief as a favour. He has all a slave's security for subsistence without his liability to punishment. As a single man, indeed, his income does not exceed a bare subsistence; but he has only to marry and it increases. Even then it is unequal to the support of a family; but it rises on the birth of every child. If his family is numerous, the parish becomes his principal paymaster; for, small as the usual allowance of 2s. a head may be, yet when there are more than three children it generally exceeds the average wages given in a pauperized district. A man with a wife and six children, entitled, according to the scale, to have his wages made up to 16s. a week in a parish where the wages paid by individuals do not exceed 10s. or 12s., is almost an irresponsible being. All the other classes of society are exposed to the vicissitudes of hope and fear; he alone has nothing to lose or to gain.

'In Coggeshall, Essex', says Mr Majendie,

weekly wages are 8s.; but by piecework a good labourer may earn 10s. Now, consider the case of labourers with four children, for the subsistence of which family (according to the Chelmsford scale, which is the law of that district), 11s. 6d. is required. Of this sum the good labourer earns 10s., and receives from the parish 1s. 6d. The inferior labourer earns 8s., and receives from the parish 3s. 6d. The man who does not work, and whom no one will employ, receives the whole from the parish.

Other classes of society are restrained from misconduct by fear of the evils, which may result to their families. Parochial legislation rejects this sanction. Even in Barnard Castle, in Northumberland, Mr Wilson states that if any remonstrance is made on account of the applicant's bad character, the reply of the magistrate commonly is, 'the children must not suffer for it'.

The following answers are specimens of the feeling and conduct in the southern districts:

The answer given by the magistrates, when a man's bad conduct is urged by the overseer against his relief, is, 'We cannot help that: his wife and family are not to suffer because the man has done wrong.'

Too frequently petty thieving, drunkenness or impertinence to a master throw able-bodied labourers, perhaps with large families, on the parish funds, when relief is demanded as a right and, if refused, enforced by a magistrate's order without reference to the cause which has produced his distress, viz., his own misconduct, which remains as a barrier to his obtaining any fresh situation, and leaves him a dead weight upon the honesty and industry of his parish.

Mr Stuart states that in Suffolk children deserted by their parents are in general well taken care of, and that the crime of deserting them is largely encouraged by the certainty that the parish must support the family.

When I was present [he adds] at the committee of the Bulchamp House of Industry, early in October, a man came with four children and applied to have them admitted into the house during his absence at the herring fishing. He was a widower. He had earned the high wages of the harvest month, and besides had work afterwards; yet he had made no provision for the support of his family while he went to the fishing, neither would he undertake to reimburse the parish out of his wages for the expense to be incurred during his absence. The committee offered to take charge of two, and that he should provide for the others. This he refused, *and next day he left all his children to the parish.*

The whole charge on the parish of Tressingfield, within the year preceding the 26th September, was £77 3s. 6d. for deserted families.

At the sessions of Framlingham a man was brought up who had left his wife and family chargeable, to avoid an order for a bastard child. On the intercession of the parish officers, his confinement was limited to a fortnight; but it was impossible not to observe that the lenity of the parish was called forth entirely with a view to save it from additional expense, by keeping him the shortest possible time away from his family.

The overseer of the parish of Westhall, which lies near the coast, informed me that the farmers are frequently unable to find a sufficient number of labourers for their spring and October work, although they are burdened with the unemployed during the winter months. This arises from the temptation to go to herring and mackerel fishing at which a man in a moderately successful season may earn £7 to £8 in as many weeks. The families of these men are generally a burden on the parish during their absence, and it is very rarely indeed that any part of the expense can be recovered. When they are punished by being sent to gaol, it merely fills up the time till the high wages of harvest work can be obtained, or till the season for fishing returns.

Even the inconvenience which might fall on the husband by the punishment of his wife for theft is made the subject of pecuniary compensation at the expense of the injured parish. Under what other system could there be a judicial instrument concluding thus:

And whereas it appears to us that the wife of the said Robert Reed is now confined in the house of correction at Cambridge, and that he is put to considerable expense in providing a person to look after his said five children; we do therefore *order* the churchwardens and overseers of the poor of the said parish, or such of them to whom these presents shall come, to pay unto the said Robert Reed the sum of 11s. weekly and every week, for and towards the support and maintenance of himself and family, for one month from the day of the date hereof.

Given under our hands and seals this twentieth day of February, in the year of our Lord one thousand eight hundred and thirty-three.

It appears to the pauper that the Government has undertaken to repeal, in his favour, the ordinary laws of nature; to enact that the children shall not suffer for the misconduct of their parents, the wife for that of the husband, or the husband for that of the wife: that no one shall lose the means of comfortable subsistence, whatever be his indolence, prodigality, or vice: in short, that the penalty which, after all, must be paid by some one for idleness and improvidence, is to fall, not on the guilty person or on his family, but on the proprietors of the lands and houses encumbered by his settlement. Can we wonder if the uneducated are seduced into approving a system which aims its allurements at all the weakest parts of our nature – which offers marriage to the young, security to the anxious, ease to the lazy, and impunity to the profligate?

II

[ON THE PART OF EMPLOYERS]

THE employers of paupers are attached to a system which enables them to dismiss and resume their labourers according to their daily or even hourly want of them, to reduce wages to the minimum, or even below the minimum of what will support an unmarried man, and to throw upon others the payment of a part, frequently of the greater part, and sometimes almost the whole of the wages actually received by their labourers. Many of our correspondents from rural districts have replied to our question as to the effects of prohibiting allowance to those employed by individuals that 'they do not see the justice of forcing the farmer to pay to the unmarried wages equal to those of the married', that 'such an enactment would produce a rate of wages which would be ruinous to the farmers'; that 'the effect would be to prevent the tithe-owners and those who employ few labourers from paying their fair proportion of the wages of the parish'.

Similar feelings show themselves in the following answers:

Wymondham, Norfolk.

I fear the employers would discharge such men as could not maintain their families without high wages, and employ only single men, and such as have small families, who can do the work cheaper. Thus the former would become a heavy expense to the parish and *the latter would receive more than is necessary for a maintenance.*

Hawkhurst, Kent.

In this parish one of the effects of such a measure would be to shift from the tithe-holder (the lessee of the Dean and Chapter of C. C. Oxon.), who exacts a high tithe from the occupiers, a portion of that which he now pays as poor-rate upon the farmer in the shape of increased wages.

Boreham, Essex.

There has been much said upon this subject which, in my opinion, is very wrong, as it is quite contrary to reason that any person should pay a man for his work sufficient to support a whole family, which in some cases would be 20s. a week.

And even if they pay in rates what they would otherwise pay in wages, they prefer the payment of rates which recur at intervals, and the payment of which may, from time to time, be put off, to the weekly ready-money expenditure of wages. High rates too are a ground for demanding an abatement from rent; high wages are not. In Mr Richardson's instructive statement of the reforms effected by Mr Litchfield, in Farthingoe, Northamptonshire, we find that Mr Litchfield has been opposed not only by the labourers but by the farmers; first, because they grudged giving the labourer with no children 8s. a week; secondly, because they were afraid to displease the labourer who had two children and preferred head-money; and thirdly, because they were fearful lest, if the rates were lowered, their rents would be raised; and that they encouraged the labourers, at first openly, and afterwards covertly, in their attempts to deter Mr Litchfield by menaces and insult.

'When a valuer', says Mr Cowell, 'values a farm to an in-coming tenant, or fixes the rent from time to time (in these parts they have no lease), he says, "What are your poor-rates?"'

If the tenant answers, 'Rates are low, but wages are high', the valuer says, 'I have nothing to do with *wages*, that is your affair, but *rates* are a *positive thing*, and I allow for *them*.' This Mr Ellman considers a bad custom, as it holds out an inducement to the farmer to prefer low wages and high rates.

Mr Ellman stated this circumstance as accounting for the predilection of the farmers for the allowance system, which is so strong in this neighbourhood that I was told by a member of a family which has lately come into possession of considerable property in the county, the head of which has been anxious to eradicate the allowance system over his estates, that 'We can do little or nothing to prevent pauperism; the farmers will have it; they prefer that the labourers should be slaves; they object to their having gardens, saying, "The more they work for themselves, the less they will for us." They wish that every man should receive an allowance from the parish according to his family, and declare that high wages and free labour would overwhelm them!'

'One of the first inquiries', says Mr Meadows White, a solicitor of great experience in the purchase and sale of land in Suffolk,

in seeking to purchase an estate is, what is the amount of poor-rate? and again, are the poor well managed or not? and the answers in a great degree regulate the price. So in the present system if a tenant seek a renewal of his lease, a high rate is a bonus to him, for it is a sure plea for a reduced rent. And although when he has obtained a renewal he is interested in proportion to the length of his term in keeping down the rate, yet as the greater number of agricultural occupations are held on tenancies from year to year, the preponderance of interest is thought by the tenant to lie in a high rate, partly because he is short-sighted enough to fancy that as his fellow-parishioners share in it, it falls lighter on himself, and partly because he is long-sighted enough to see that though he pays the rate at first hand, yet it falls at last on his landlord in the shape of abatement of rent in the current year, and a reduced rent for the next.

'Tenants at will', says Mr Cogshill, 'too often think the more poor-rates, the less rent. Confidence between landlord and tenant seems quite lost. I have witnessed a great deal of this.'

The following replies to question 36 of our rural queries are further testimonies to the same effect:

I think the Poor Laws have not diminished the capital, but rather the rent of the landlord, as the tenant considers rents and rates as payment for the farm, and one can only be increased at the expense of the other.

The farmers are aware that (excepting in cases of long tenures and very sudden augmentation of rates) the burden does not at all affect them. It is a rent paid to the parish instead of the landowner.

It should be understood that poor's rates are deducted in all calculations for rent, and that landlords pay them, and not the farmers.

Capital is decreasing from the loose manner the laws are administered, and the tenants feeling that they do not in effect pay the rate, but the landlord. I cannot otherwise account for the apathy with which they view, and the tenacity with which in many instances they defend abuses.

III

ON THE PART OF PROPRIETORS

IN towns the allowance system prevails less, probably because the manufacturing capitalists form a small proportion of the ratepayers, and consequently have less influence in the vestries than the farmers in country places. But even in the towns it exists to a very formidable degree. The northern counties are least infested by it; but if we turn to Mr Wilson's report from Darlington and Barnard Castle, and Mr Henderson's from Preston, we shall see it creeping in, and enlisting the same private interests in its defence. To which it must be added that the persons who supply the workhouses, or whose shops are frequented by the poor, are more immediately benefited as tradesmen by parochial extravagance than as rate-payers by parochial economy.

The owners of rateable property might, at least, be expected to be favourable to any change which should avert their impending ruin. But we have seen that of the property liable to poor-rates, there is a portion, and a portion of considerable importance, less from its value than from the number of rate-payers among whom it is divided and their influence in vestries, which not only is in practice exempted from contributing to the parochial fund, but derives its principal value from the maladministration of that fund. This property consists of cottages or apartments inhabited by the poor. We have seen that in almost all places the dwellings of the poor, or at least of the settled poor, are exempted from rates, and that in a very large proportion the rent is paid by the parish. The former practice enables the proprietor often to increase the rent by the amount of rate remitted and always to be an owner of real property, and yet escape the principle burdens to which such property is subjected. The latter practice gives him a solvent tenant, and if he has influence with the vestry or with the overseer, a liberal one.

Of the higher classes of landlords, those who reside in towns seldom take much part in parochial government or have any distinct ideas as to the extent or the effects of its mismanagement, and the majority of those who have become familiarized with the abuses of the villages, seem to have acquired habits of thinking, and feeling and acting which unfit them to originate any real and extensive amendment, or even to understand the principles on which it ought to be based. To suppose that the poor are the proper managers of their own concerns, that a man's wages ought to depend on his services, not on his wants, that the earnings of an ordinary labourer are naturally equal to the support of an ordinary family, that the welfare of that family naturally depends on his conduct, that he is bound to exercise any sort of prudence or economy, that anything is to be hoped from voluntary charity, are views which many of those who have long resided in pauperized rural districts seem to reject as too absurd for formal refutation.

It appears, therefore, necessary to state at some length the effects of the existing system both to show how short-sighted are the views of those who think that they continue to profit by it, and to show, before we suggest any remedy, the absolute necessity that some remedy should be applied.

These effects may be considered, first, with respect to the owners of property; secondly, with respect to the employers of labour; and thirdly, with respect to the labourers and their families.

[OPERATION OF THE LAW AS ADMINISTERED]

===

I

EFFECTS ON PROPRIETORS

THE Committee appointed by the House of Commons in 1817 to consider the Poor Laws stated their opinion 'that unless some efficacious check were interposed, there was then every reason to think that the amount of the assessment would continue to increase, until at a period more or less remote, according to the progress the evil had already made in different places, it should have absorbed the profits of the property on which the rate might have been assessed, producing thereby the neglect and ruin of the land and the waste or removal of other property, to the utter subversion of the happy order of society so long upheld in these kingdoms'. In consequence of the recommendations of that Committee, a check was interposed by the 59 Geo. III, c. 12 [1818]. But though that act, by restricting the power of the magistrates to order relief, and by authorizing the removal of the Irish and Scotch paupers, the appointment of representative vestries and of assistant overseers, the rating the owners of small tenements, and the giving relief by way of loan, occasioned during the six years that immediately followed it a progressive diminution of the amount of the Poor Law assessment, its beneficial enactments appear to be no longer capable of struggling with the evil tendencies of the existing system. The year ending 25 March 1824 was the last year of regular improvement. And we have seen that the amount of relief now given, when estimated in commodities, is actually greater, and greater in proportion to our population, than it was when that report was made. It has increased still more when considered with reference to the value of the property on which it is assessed.

We are happy to say that not many cases of the actual dereliction of estates have been stated to us. Some, however, have occurred; and we have given in the extracts from our evidence the details of one, the parish of Cholesbury, in the county of Bucks. It appears that in this parish, the population of which has been almost stationary since 1801, in which, within the memory of persons now living, the rates were only £10 11s. a year, and only one person received relief, the sum raised for the relief of the poor rose from £99 4s. a year in 1816 to £150 5s. in 1831; and in 1832, when it was proceeding at the rate of £367 a year, suddenly ceased in consequence of the impossibility to continue its collection; the landlords having given up their rents, the farmers their tenancies, and the clergyman his glebe and his tithes. The clergyman, Mr Jeston, states that in October 1832 the parish officers threw up their books, and the poor assembled in a body before his door while he was in bed, asking for advice and food. Partly from his own small means, partly from the charity of neighbours, and partly by rates in aid, imposed on the neighbouring parishes, they were for some time supported; and the benevolent Rector recommends that the whole of the land should be divided among the able-bodied paupers, and adds 'that he has reason to think that at the expiration of two years, the parish in the interval receiving the assistance of rates in aid, the whole of the poor would be able and willing to support themselves, the aged and impotent of course excepted'. In Cholesbury, therefore, the expense of maintaining the poor has not merely swallowed up the whole value of the land; it requires even the assistance for two years of rates in aid from other parishes to enable the able-bodied, after the land has been given up to them, to support themselves; and the aged and impotent must even then remain a burthen on the neighbouring parishes.

Our evidence exhibits no other instance of the abandonment of a parish, but it contains many in which the pressure of the poor-rate has reduced the rent to half, or to less than half, of what it would have been if the land had been situated in an unpauperized district, and some in which it has been impossible for the owner to find a tenant.

Mr Majendie states that in Lenham, Kent, at the time of his visit, some of the land was out of cultivation. A large estate has

been several years in the hands of the proprietor, and a farm of
420 acres of good land, tithe-free and well situated, had just been
thrown up by the tenant, the poor-rate on it amounting to £300
a year. He mentions another place in which a farm well situated,
of average quality, was in vain offered at 5s. an acre, not from
objection to the quality of the land, but because men of capital
will not connect themselves with a parish in which the poor-rates
would keep them in a constant state of vexation and anxiety.
He states that in Ardingly those farmers who have any capital
left withdraw from the parish as soon as their leases expire. One
of them admitted to him that it was out of the power of the landlords to relieve them.

Mr Power, after mentioning the universal complaint in Cambridgeshire that substantial tenants cannot be found at the lowest
assignable rents, goes on to say that Mr Quintin, a gentlemen of
considerable landed property in the county, told him that he had
a farm at Gransden for which he could not get a tenant even at
5s. an acre, though land from which thirty bushels of wheat an
acre had been obtained. 'Downing College', he adds, 'has a
property of 5,000 acres in this county, lying principally in the
parishes of Tadlow, East Hatley, Croydon, and Gamlingay; it is
found impossible, notwithstanding the lowering the rents to an
extreme point, to obtain men of substance for tenants. Several
farms of considerable extent have changed hands twice within the
last five years, from insolvency of the tenants in some cases, in
others from the terror of that prospect. The amount of arrears at
this time is such as only a collegiate body could support. I draw
from authentic sources, being myself a fellow of the college.' In
the same county Mr Power found that at Soham, a total absorption of the value of the land in twelve or fourteen years was anticipated; and Mr Cowell, that at Great Shelford the same result
was expected to take place in ten.

Mr Pilkington's description of several places in Leicestershire
is equally alarming. In Hinkley he found the poor-rate exceeding £1 an acre and rapidly increasing, and a general opinion
that the day is not distant when rent must cease altogether. On
visiting Wigston Magna in November 1832 he was informed
that the value of property had fallen one half since 1820 and was

not saleable even at that reduction. It does not appear, indeed, that it ought to have sold for more than two or three years' purchase, the net rental not amounting to £4,000 a year, and the poor-rate expenditure growing at the rate of £1,000 increase in a single year. And on his return to that neighbourhood three months after, the statement made to him was that property in land was gone; that even the rates could not be collected without regular summons and judicial sales, and that the present system must ensure, and very shortly, the total ruin of every individual of any property in the parish. We cannot wonder, after this, at the statement of an eminent solicitor at Loughborough that it is now scarcely possible to effect a sale of property in that neighbourhood at any price.

The following answers, taken from a multitude of others of a similar nature, contained in Appendix B, are to the same effect:

Annual value of the real property, as assessed April 1815, £3,390. Annual value of the real property, as assessed November 1829, £1,959 5s. It has undoubtedly fallen in value since the last valuation, i.e. in the last two years, and the population has been more than trebled in 30 years: 1801, 306; 1811, 707; 1821, 897; 1831, 938: and that in spite of an emigration of considerable amount, at the parish expense, in 1829. The eighteen-penny children will eat up this parish in ten years more unless some relief be afforded us.

If some material change does not very soon take place, the time is not far distant when the whole rent will be absorbed in the poors'-rates.

Much land in the hands of proprietors wanting tenants. Our poors'-rate being high, makes *farms in other parishes more desirable than in this*.

In the adjoining parish, the owners of untenanted farms who are not farmers fear to occupy, and prefer the loss of rent to the unlimited expense in poor rate which would overwhelm the profits of one not perfectly experienced in farming, and the parochial concerns it involves.

In the neighbourhood of Aylesbury, there were 42 farms untenanted at Michaelmas last; most of these are still on the proprietors' hands; and on some no acts of husbandry have been done since, in order to avoid the payment of poor-rate. I attribute these circumstances principally to the operation of the Poor Laws.

In the parish of Thornborough, Bucks., there are at this time 600 acres of land unoccupied, and the greater part of the other tenants have given notice of their intention to quit their farms, owing entirely to the increasing burthen of the poors'-rate.

We have made these quotations for the purpose of drawing attention not so much to the immediate evils which the landowners of the pauperized districts are undergoing as to the more extensive and irremediable mischiefs of which these are the forerunners. It appears to us that any parish in which the pressure of the poor-rates has compelled the abandonment of a single farm is in imminent danger of undergoing the ruin which has already befallen Cholesbury. The instant the poor-rate on a given farm exceeds that surplus which, if there were no poor-rate, would be paid in rent, the existing cultivation becomes not only unprofitable but a source of absolute loss. And as every diminution of cultivation has a double effect in increasing the rate on the remaining cultivation, the number of unemployed labourers being increased at the same instant that the fund for payment of rates is diminished, the abandonment of property, when it has once begun, is likely to proceed in a constantly accelerated ratio. Accordingly, it appears from Mr Jeston's statement that scarcely a year elapsed between the first land in Cholesbury going out of cultivation and the abandonment of all except sixteen acres.

II

EFFECTS ON EMPLOYERS OF LABOURERS

[*Agricultural*]

THE effects of this system on the immediate employers of labour in the country and in the towns are very different. To avoid circumlocution, we will use the word 'farmers' as comprehending all the former class of persons, and the word 'manufacturers' as comprehending all the latter; and as they are the least complicated, and most material, we will begin by considering the effects produced on the farmers. The services of the labourer are by far the most important of all the instruments used in agriculture.

In the management of live and dead stock much must always be left to his judgement. Only a portion, and that not a very large portion, of the results of ordinary farm labour is susceptible of being immediately valued so as to be paid by the piece. The whole farm is the farmer's workshop and storehouse; he is frequently obliged to leave it, and has no partner on whom he can devolve its care during his absence, and its extent generally makes it impossible for him to stand over and personally inspect all the labourers employed on it. His property is scattered over every part, with scarcely any protection against depredation or injury. If his labourers, therefore, want the skill and intelligence necessary to enable them to execute those details for which no general and unvarying rules can be laid down; if they have not the diligence necessary to keep them steadily at work when their master's eye is off; if they have not sufficient honesty to resist the temptation to plunder when the act is easy and the detection difficult, it follows that neither the excellence or abundance of the farmer's agricultural capital, nor his own skill or diligence, or economy, can save him from loss or perhaps from ruin.

Now it is obvious that the tendency of the allowance system is to diminish, we might almost say to destroy, all these qualities in the labourer. What motive has the man who is to receive 10s. every Saturday, not because 10s. is the value of his week's labour, but because his family consists of five persons, who knows that his income will be increased by nothing but by an increase of his family, and diminished by nothing but by a diminution of his family, that it has no reference to his skill, his honesty, or his diligence — what motive has he to acquire or to preserve any of these merits? Unhappily, the evidence shows not only that these virtues are rapidly wearing out, but that their place is assumed by the opposite vices; and that the very labourers among whom the farmer has to live, on whose merits as workmen and on whose affection as friends he ought to depend, are becoming not merely idle and ignorant and dishonest, but positively hostile; not merely unfit for his service and indifferent to his welfare, but actually desirous to injure him.

One of the questions circulated by us in the rural districts was whether the labourers in the respondent's neighbourhood were supposed to be better or worse workmen than formerly? If the answers to this question had been uniformly unfavourable, they might have been ascribed to the general tendency to depreciate what is present; but it will be found, on referring to our Appendix, that the replies vary according to the poor-law administration of the district. Where it is good the replies are, 'much the same', 'never were better', 'diligence the same, skill increased'. But when we come within the influence of the allowance and the scale, the replies are, 'they are much degenerated, being generally disaffected to their employers: they work unwillingly and wastefully': 'three of them would not do near the work in a day performed by two in more northern counties': 'one third of our labourers do not work at all, the greater part of the remainder are much contaminated; the rising population learn nothing, the others are forgetting what they knew'. 'They are constantly changing their services. Relying upon parish support, they are indifferent whether they oblige or disobey their masters, are less honest and industrious, and the mutual regard between employer and servant is gone.' 'The system of allowance is most mischievous and ruinous, and till it is abandoned the spirit of industry can never be revived. Allowance-men will not work. It makes them idle, lazy, fraudulent, and worthless, and depresses the wages of free labour.' 'With very few exceptions, the labourers are not as industrious as formerly; and notwithstanding the low rate of wages now too generally paid, it costs as much money in the end to have work performed as it did sixteen years ago.' 'The Poor Laws are perhaps better administered in this parish than in many others; but such a resource in view as parish relief prevents the labourer's exertions, and the young men from laying by anything in their youth. The latter marry early, because they can get no relief unless they have children; this, of course, raises the rates. An instance occurred a short time since, of a labourer marrying, and going from the church to the poorhouse, not having money to pay the fees! By old experienced individuals it is supposed one labourer, forty years ago, would do more than two of the present day.'

The reports of the Assistant Commissioners are full of the same evidence. In the pauperized districts we find sometimes the labourers, or rather those who ought to be the labourers, absolutely refusing work; sometimes we find them bribed by additional pay from the parish to take profitable work; but always they are represented as so inferior to the non-parishioners as to render their services, though nominally cheap, really dear, and generally dear in proportion to their apparent cheapness.

Mr Okeden states that in Wiltshire the farmer finds his labourers idle and insolent, and regardless of him, and his orders, and his work. They openly say, 'We care not, the scale and pay-table are ours.' Mr Majendie states that in Ardingly, Sussex:

Labourers refuse work, unless of a description agreeable to them; they say, 'Why should we be singled out for hard labour, instead of working for the parish?' A winter ago the clergyman offered 2s. a day to three labourers; they refused to work unless they had extra pay for remaining after half-past four, saying, that the parish did not require more than that of them. In the last hay harvest a man, inferior to the average labourers, refused 10s. a week from a farmer, saying, that he could do better with the parish.

At Eastbourne, in December 1832, four healthy young men, receiving from 12s. to 14s. per week from the parish, refused to work at threshing for a farmer at 2s. 6d. and a quart of ale per day. The fishermen, secure of pay without labour, refuse to go out to sea in the winter: one has said, 'Why should I expose myself to fatigue and danger, when the parish supports my family and pays my rent?' The masters are obliged to send to Hastings to get men for their boats. In May 1832 a respectable fisherman said, 'I fear that, like many of my neighbours, I shall be obliged to sell my boat and come upon the parish for want of hands to man her; I cannot get men here, as they like better their allowance from the parish. I therefore board a Hastings man, and give him as much profit as I get myself, but this ruins me.'

At Rochford, Essex, the overseers make up wages to 1s. 9d. per head to families, by the magistrate's order, and this the labourers demand as their right. Good ploughmen are not to be found. The labourers say, they do not care to plough, because that is a kind of work which, if neglected, will subject them to punishment, and, if properly done, requires constant attention, and the lads do not even wish to learn. Nine able-bodied young men were in the workhouse last winter; such was their character that they were not to be trusted with threshing.

Mr Power states the evidence of Mr King, the overseer, and a large occupier of land at Bottisham (Cambridgeshire), who refers the increase of rates in that neighbourhood, not to any increase of population, or diminution of demand, but to the effects of the existing system on the habits of the labourers:

He complained of their deficiency in industry, arising from their growing indifference, or rather partiality, to being thrown on the parish: when the bad season is coming on, they frequently dispose of any little property, such as a cow or a pig, in order to entitle themselves to parish wages. That very evening (says Mr Power) on which I saw him, one of his men swore at him, and said he did not want his work or his wages; he could do better on the parish.

It is unnecessary to multiply quotations, all of which would be to the same effect.

So much for the effects of the present system on the industry and skill of the agricultural labourers. Its effects on their honesty are well described by Mr Collett in his evidence before the House of Commons Committee of 1824, on Labourers' Wages:

Were I to detail the melancholy, degrading, and ruinous system which has been pursued, with few exceptions, throughout the country, in regard to the unemployed poor, and in the payment of the wages of idleness, I should scarcely be credited beyond its confines. In the generality of parishes, from five to forty labourers have been without employment, loitering about during the day, engaged in idle games, insulting passengers on their road, or else consuming their time in sleep, that they might be more ready and active in the hours of darkness. The weekly allowances cannot supply more than food; how, then, are clothing, firing, and rent to be provided? By robbery and plunder; and those so artfully contrived and effected, that discovery has been almost impossible. Picklock keys have readily opened our barns and granaries; the lower orders of artificers, and even in one or two instances small farmers, have joined the gang, consisting of from ten to twenty men; and corn has been sold by sample in the market of such mixed qualities by these small farmers, that competent judges have assured me, it must have been stolen from different barns, and could not have been produced from their occupations. Disgraceful as these facts are to a civilized country, I could enumerate many more, but recital would create disgust.

And yet this was said in the year 1824 – a time to which those who witnessed the events of 1830, in the disturbed districts, or those who examined their effects, must look back as a period of comparative comfort. Partly under the application of force, but much more under that of bribes, that paroxysm subsided; but what must be the state of mind of those who have to calculate every winter whether they may expect to be the victims of its return? Waste of capital and waste of time may be estimated, but at what rate are we to value the loss of confidence? What would each resident in a disturbed district then have given to have saved to himself and his family, not merely the actual expense, but the anxiety of that unhappy period? No complaint is more general than that of the difficulty of finding the means of profitable investment. The constantly increasing capital of the country, after having reduced interest and profits to lower rates than any persons now living can recollect, after having choked all the professions, and overflowed in all the channels of manufactures and commerce, is still seeking employment, however hazardous and however distant. One business alone is described as ill-supplied with capital, and that is the business which is of all others the most healthy, the most independent, and the most interesting. It appears that men are anxious to withdraw themselves and their capital from an employment in which so indefinite an outgoing as an ill-managed poor-rate is to be supplied, in which such instruments as pauper labourers are to be employed, and such events as those of 1830 are to be provided against.

It must be carefully remembered, however, that these evils are gradually evolved. Ultimately, without doubt, the farmer finds that pauper labour is dear, whatever be its price; but that is not until allowance has destroyed the industry and morals of the labourers who were bred under a happier system, and has educated a new generation in idleness, ignorance, and dishonesty. In the meantime wages are diminished and even of those wages a part is paid by others; the principal outgoing of the farm is reduced, and as long as the produce remains the same, the occupier, if himself the owner, or a leaseholder, gains the benefit of the difference between what he formerly paid in wages and what he now pays, subject only to the deduction of his additional expenditure in rates; a deduction which, if he were the only rate-payer, would of course be at least equal to his new gains, but which may be trifling if he is only one of many rate-payers, some of whom, such as the tithe-owner and the tradesman, are to a very small extent immediate employers of labour. This accounts for the many instances in our evidence, some of which we have already cited, and others of which we shall cite hereafter, of the indifference of the farmers in some places to Poor Law expenditure, and in other places of their positive wish to increase it. If, indeed, the occupier is a tenant from year to year, or at will, the general tendency towards the equalization of profits will prevent his long retaining this advantage. Offers will be made for his farm, and he will be forced to leave it or to pay an increased rent, which will leave his profits no greater than they were before the payment of wages out of rates began. But it is to be observed that if the tenant without a lease is the person who gains least by the introduction of these abuses, he is also the person who has the least motive and the least power to resist them: he has little motive, because the varying amount of his rent forms a sort of shifting ballast, tending always to keep his profits steady; he has little power, because there are always bidders for his farm, ready to pay the utmost rent that can be afforded, without reference to the means employed. Whether these means are the adoption or the continuance of abuses, he will be forced by competition, unless his landlord, or his landlord's agent, has knowledge and forbearance far beyond the usual average, either to pursue them, or, what is practically the same, to leave his tenancy to some one who will pursue them. This is explained in the following answers from Mr Hillyard, President of the Farming and Grazing Society of Northampton, and from Mr Robert Bevan, J.P.

If a system of allowances is adopted in a parish, the consequences are, the whole of the labourers are made paupers; for if one occupier employs labourers that have an allowance, other occupiers will send the labourers to the parish officers, otherwise he pays part of the other occupiers' labour.

One impoverished farmer turns off all his labourers; the rest do the same, because they cannot employ their own shares and pay the rest too in poor-rates. Weeds increase in the fields, and vices in the population. All grow poor together. 'Spite against the parson' is now ruining a neighbouring parish in this way.

Even the leaseholder, unless his term is so long as to put him in the situation of a landlord, has strong motives to introduce abuses; he can reap the immediate benefit of the fall of wages, and when that fall has ceased to be beneficial, when the apparently cheap labour has become really dear, he can either quit at the expiration of his lease, or demand on its renewal a diminution of rent; he has a still stronger motive to continue them when once introduced, as every amendment involves immediate expenditure, of which his successor, or rather his landlord, will obtain the principal advantage. The most favourable state of things is when the farmer is himself the proprietor. The owner of land, unless it be covered with cottages occupied by the poor, never has any permanent interest in introducing Poor Law abuses into the parish in which that land is situated. He may, indeed, be interested in introducing them into the neighbouring parishes, if he can manage, by pulling down cottages, or other expedients, to keep down the number of persons having settlements in his own parish. Several instances have been mentioned to us, of parishes nearly depopulated, in which almost all the labour is performed by persons settled in the neighbouring villages or towns; drawing from them, as allowance, the greater part of their subsistence; receiving from their employer not more than half wages, even in summer, and much less than half in winter; and discharged whenever their services are not wanted. But with the exception of similar cases, a good administration of the Poor Laws is the landlord's interest; and where he is a man of sense, is acquainted with what is going on, and being an occupier is allowed a vote, he may be expected to oppose the introduction of allowance, knowing that for giving up an immediate accession to his income he will be repaid by preserving the industry and morality of his fellow-parishioners and by saving his estate from being gradually absorbed by pauperism. Even when that system has been introduced, he may, in some stages of the disease, refuse to allow his labourers to be infected by it; pay them full wages, and insist on their taking nothing from the parish. Such conduct, however, can seldom be hoped for; both because it must be exceedingly difficult to preserve a set of labourers uncontaminated by the example of all around them; and because the person who pursues it must submit to pay his proportion of the rates, without being, like the other farmers, indemnified.

[*Manufacturing*]

The effects of the system on the manufacturing capitalist are very different. The object of machinery is to diminish the want not only of physical, but of moral and intellectual qualities on the part of the workman. In many cases it enables the master to confine him to a narrow routine of similar operations in which the least error or delay is capable of immediate detection. Judgement or intelligence are not required for processes which can be performed only in one mode, and which constant repetition has made mechanical. Honesty is not necessary where all the property is under one roof, or in one inclosure, so that its abstraction would be very hazardous; and where it is, by its incomplete state, difficult of sale. Diligence is insured by the presence of a comparatively small number of over-lookers, and by the almost universal adoption of piece-work.

Under such circumstances, it is not found that parish assistance necessarily destroys the efficacy of the manufacturing labourer. Where that assistance makes only a part of his income, and the remainder is derived from piece-work, his employer insists, and sometimes successfully, that he shall not earn that remainder but by the greatest exertion. We have seen that in agriculture this is impossible, and that, consequently, the allowance system becomes ultimately mischievous to the farmer who adopts or submits to it; but the manufacturer, who can induce or force others to pay part of the wages of his labourers, not only appears to be, but actually may be, a pure gainer by it; he really can obtain cheap labour. On whom, then, does the loss fall? Partly, of course, on the owners of rateable property, partly on the labourers who are unmarried, or with families of less than the average number, and who are, in fact, robbed of a portion of the natural price of their labour, but principally on those manufacturers who do not enjoy the same advantages. A manufactory worked by paupers is a rival with which one paying ordinary wages, of course, cannot compete, and in this way a Macclesfield manufacturer may find

himself undersold and ruined in consequence of the maladministration of the Poor Laws in Essex.

This is well stated in the following answer from Castle Donington, Leicestershire; though the answerer himself, probably an
agriculturist, perceives more clearly the evil to the landowner than
to other manufacturers.

The system of eking out the wages of manufacturing operatives
from the parish funds is pregnant with great evils, and is not adopted in
this parish. In several places in this county those evils are severely
felt; and where once a parish has embarked upon this system, the
greatest difficulty is experienced in returning to a better. From the
practice of parish officers, when trade is perhaps suffering under temporary depression, soliciting work for the number of men on their hands
from the various manufacturers (at any price), and making up the remainder necessary for the support of their families out of the poor's-rate
good trade becomes in a great measure annihilated. Stocks become too
abundant; and when a demand revives, the markets are not cleared before a check is again experienced; the same practice is renewed by the
parish officers, and thus the wily manufacturer produces his goods, to
the great emolument of himself, half at the cost of the agricultural
interest. This is particularly the case in the manufacture of hosiery.
Thus land in several places in this county will not let for more than the
poor's-rate, and its value as property is altogether destroyed.

The following extracts from Mr Villiers's and Mr Cowell's
valuable reports may be used in confirmation of these remarks,
if any confirmation is thought necessary:

Ribbon-weaving is carried on to a great extent in all the villages
around Coventry. Work is given out by the manufacturers to persons
who are termed undertakers, who contract for it at a certain price, and
the amount of their profit depends upon the rate at which they can procure labour; they consequently seek it at the lowest possible price, and
for this purpose it is said they often employ persons who are dependent
on the country parishes, which of necessity, if done to any extent, must
affect the rate of wages in the trade as much as if the competition arose
in a foreign country.

In the replies of the vestry clerk of Birmingham, he states that
relief is given occasionally according to the number of children, but not
given to eke out the wages of able-bodied persons *wholly* employed.

Upon inquiring the meaning of the words *not wholly employed*, it was explained to refer to those persons whose masters had certified that they only enabled them to earn a half of the average rate of wages in any branch of manufacture. On this subject Mr Lewis, the governor of the workhouse at Erdington, who has the management of the poor at Aston, the immediately adjoining parish to Birmingham, and now included within the borough, stated that he was in a manufacturing house for 15 years at Birmingham and that he is well acquainted with the practices of different masters, and that from his own knowledge he could state that what are termed 'small masters' in this town, i.e., those employing one or two journeymen, and who also work for some of the other masters, were in the constant habit of employing men who were receiving allowances from the parish, and that many in consequence were able to undersell other masters who were paying the full wages themselves.

The practice of paying the wages of manufacturers out of the rates is strongly illustrated in the case of Collumpton, at a short distance from Tiverton, where the weaving of serge and cloth is carried on by two manufacturers, on whose employment many of the poor in that town have chiefly depended for support: one of these manufacturers, however, receives at present regular annual payments from the parishes in the neighbourhood to employ their paupers, the sums paid being less than the cost of their support by the parishes. The same system is not adopted by the parish of Collumpton: the result, therefore, with regard to the poor at large is not to diminish the amount of pauperism, but to change its locality; for the first effect of such a measure was to increase the number of persons unemployed at Collumpton, and consequently to reduce wages; it was operating also with injustice to the other manufacturer.

On conversing with a manufacturer at Tewkesbury, I found that he regretted the great fall in wages, but said that, as a capitalist, he had no choice between reducing the wages of his men and giving up his business, and that if a certain proportion of the operatives were obliged to take lower wages, the wages of the rest must also fall, since otherwise the master who employed those at reduced wages would get possession of the market. He said that he could always calculate, out of a given number of workmen, what proportion working at low wages would bring down the rest; and that if any circumstance caused a fall in one district, wages must fall in all other districts producing the same article. He admitted that this would equally be the case, if the operatives, in any number, were relieved by the parish.

The stocking manufacturers in Nottinghamshire have been enabled to saddle others with paying a portion of the wages of their handicraftsmen, in the same manner as the farmers have done.

Stockings are made in all the neighbouring parishes in a circle round Nottingham of twenty or more miles in diameter, in the cottages of the journeymen, who rent frames at 1s. per week each, which they hire from a capitalist, who possesses, perhaps, several hundred, and the capitalist gives the operative work to do, and pays him wages. The operative, in whatever parish he may be, is informed that his wages must be lowered, and in consequence applies to the parish; his master at Nottingham furnishes him with a certificate that he is only receiving (suppose) 6s. a week; and thus the parishes were induced to allow him 4s. or 5s.

Mr Caddick, the former assistant overseer of Basford, which is a few miles from Nottingham, told me that this system was universal, and went into a calculation, proving that by means of it master manufacturers were enabled to sell stockings at a profit, though the selling price did not cover the prime cost, if the parochial addition to the wages paid by the master was to be taken as an element of the prime cost, as it undoubtedly ought to be.

At Southwell I heard of instances in which the master manufacturer had combined with his men to give them false certificates of the amount of their wages, so that they might claim a larger sum from the parish.

Whole branches of manufacture may thus follow the course not of coal-mines or of streams, but of pauperism; may flourish like the funguses that spring from corruption, in consequence of the abuses which are ruining all the other interests of the places in which they are established, and cease to exist in the better administered districts, in consequence of that better administration.

III

EFFECTS ON LABOURERS

BUT the severest sufferers are those for whose benefit the system is supposed to have been introduced, and to be perpetuated; the labourers and their families. In treating this branch of the subject, we will consider separately the case of those who are, and of those who are not, actually recipients of relief.

2
Effects on those not actually relieved

First, with respect to those who are not actually relieved. We have seen that one of the objects attempted by the present administration of the Poor Laws is to repeal *pro tanto* that law of nature by which the effects of each man's improvidence or misconduct are borne by himself and his family. The effect of that attempt has been to repeal *pro tanto* the law by which each man and his family enjoy the benefit of his own prudence and virtue. In abolishing punishment, we equally abolish reward. Under the operation of the scale system – the system which directs the overseers to *regulate* the incomes of the labourers according to their families – idleness, improvidence, or extravagance occasion no loss, and consequently diligence and economy can afford no gain. But to say merely that these virtues afford no gain, is an inadequate expression: they are often the causes of absolute loss. We have seen that in many places the income derived from the parish for easy or nominal work, or, as it is most significantly termed, 'in lieu of labour', actually exceeds that of the independent labourer; and even in those cases in which the relief-money only equals, or nearly approaches, the average rate of wages, it is often better worth having, as the pauper requires less expensive diet and clothing than the hard-working man. In such places a man who does not possess either some property or an amount of skill which will ensure to him more than the average rate of wages is of course a loser by preserving his independence. Even if he have some property he is a loser, unless the aggregate of the income which it affords and of his wages equals what he would receive as a pauper. It appears accordingly, that when a parish has become pauperized, the labourers are not only prodigal of their earnings, not only avoid accumulation, but even dispose of, and waste in debauchery, as soon as their families entitle them to allowance, any small properties which may have developed on them, or which they may have saved in happier times. Self-respect, however, is not yet so utterly destroyed among the English peasantry as to make this universal. Men are still to be found who would rather derive a smaller income from their own funds and their own exertions, than beg a larger one from the parish. And in those cases in which the labourer's property is so considerable as to produce, when joined to his wages, an income exceeding parish pay, or the aggregate of wages and allowance, it is obviously his interest to remain independent.

Will it be believed that such is not merely the cruelty, but the folly of the rate-payers in many places, that they prohibit this conduct – that they conspire to deny the man who, in defiance of the examples of all around him, has dared to save, and attempts to keep his savings, the permission to work for his bread? Such a statement appears so monstrous, that we will substantiate it by some extracts from our evidence.

Sir Harry Verney, in a communication which will be found in App. C says,

In the hundred of Buckingham, in which I act as a magistrate, many instances occur in which labourers are unable to obtain employment, because they have property of their own. For instance, in the parish of Steeple Claydon, John Lines, formerly a soldier, a very good workman, is refused employment, because he receives a pension. The farmers say that they cannot afford to employ those for whom they are not bound by law to provide. In order to prevent John Lines from being out of work, I am frequently obliged myself to give him employment.

Mr Courthope, of Ticehurst, Sussex, in his excellent answers to our queries, replies to the question, 'Could a poor family lay by anything?'

If the single man could procure regular work, and could be induced to lay by as he ought to do, I think an industrious man might in a few years secure an independence, at the present wages of the country; but if an industrious man was known to have laid by any part of his wages, and thus to have accumulated any considerable sum, there are some parishes in which he would be refused work till his savings were gone; and the knowledge that this would be the case acts as a preventive against saving.

Mr Wetherell, the rector of Byfield, Northamptonshire, replies to the same question:

With a family, it is scarcely possible he should lay by anything out of his earnings, and if he could, he dare not let it be known, lest he should be refused employment under the present system of the poor laws, though he is industrious and honest.

Mr Chadwick thus reports the evidence of Mr Hickson, a manufacturer at Northampton and landholder in Kent:

The case of a man who has worked for me will show the effect of the parish system in preventing frugal habits. This is a hard-working, industrious man, named William Williams. He is married, and had saved some money to the amount of about £70 and had two cows; he had also a sow and ten pigs. He had got a cottage well furnished; he was a member of a benefit club at Meopham, from which he received 8s. a week when he was ill. He was beginning to learn to read and write, and sent his children to the Sunday-school. He had a legacy of about £46, but he got his other money together by saving from his fair wages as a waggoner. Some circumstances occurred which obliged me to part with him. The consequence of this labouring man having been frugal and saved money, and got the cows was that no one would employ him, although his superior character as a workman was well known in the parish. He told me at the time I was obliged to part with him, 'Whilst I have these things I shall get no work; I must part with them all; I must be reduced to a state of beggary before any one will employ me.' I was compelled to part with him at Michaelmas; he has not yet got work, and he has no chance of getting any until he has become a pauper; for until then, the paupers will be preferred to him. He cannot get work in his own parish, and he will not be allowed to get any in other parishes. Another instance of the same kind occurred amongst my workmen. Thomas Hardy, the brother-in-law of the same man, was an excellent workman, discharged under similar circumstances; he has a very industrious wife. They have got two cows, a well-furnished cottage, and a pig and fowls. Now he cannot get work, because he has property. The pauper will be preferred to him, and he can qualify himself for it only by becoming a pauper. If he attempts to get work elsewhere, he is told that they do not want to fix him on the parish. Both these are fine young men, and as excellent labourers as I could wish to have. The latter labouring man mentioned another instance of a labouring man in another parish (Henstead), who had once had more property than he, but was obliged to consume it all, and is now working on the roads.

We have already quoted from Mr Cowell's report a letter from

Mr Nash, of Royston, in which he states that he had been forced by the overseer of Reed to dismiss two excellent labourers, for the purpose of introducing two paupers into their place. Mr Nash adds that of the men dismissed, one

was John Walford, a parishioner of Barley, a steady, industrious, trustworthy, single man, who, by long and rigid economy, had saved about £100. On being dismissed, Walford applied in vain to the farmers of Barley for employment. '*It was well known that he had saved money, and could not come on the parish, although any of them would willingly have taken him had it been otherwise.*' After living a few months without [having] been able to get any work, he bought a cart and two horses, and has ever since obtained a precarious subsistence, by carrying corn to London for one of the Cambridge merchants; but just now the current of corn is northward, and he has nothing to do; and at any time he would gladly have exchanged his employment for that of day labour, if he could have obtained work. No reflection is intended on the overseers of Barley; they only do what all others are expected to do; though the young men point at Walford, and call him a fool, for not spending his money at the public-house, as they do; adding that then he would get work.

The same report contains the following statement from Mr Wedd, an eminent solicitor of Royston, who was himself personally acquainted with the details of the case:

An individual who had risen from poverty and accumulated considerable personal property, bequeathed legacies to a number of labourers, his relations. Circumstances delayed for several months the collecting in the testator's estate. The overseer's deputy of one parish, in which some of the legatees were labourers, urged to the agent of the executors the payment, on the ground that it would benefit the parishioners, as, when the legacies were paid, they would not find employment for the legatees, because they would have property of their own. The legatees afterwards applied for money on account of their legacies. It was then stated that some of them, who lived in a different parish, had been refused employment because they were entitled to property.

Mr Richardson states that in Northamptonshire, in those parishes in which labour-rates, or agreements in the nature of labour-rates, exist:

Objections are constantly made to the allowing persons possessing any property to be counted on the rate. [That is, to be admitted on the number of those, the employment of whom exempts *pro tanto* a rate-payer from the burden of the labour-rate.] At Culworth, a man of the name of James Nuld, who had never applied for parish relief, was objected to partly *on that ground*, and partly because he kept a pig. At Eydon the same thing had taken place. One of the delinquents had qualified himself immediately as a pauper, by selling his house. At Middleton Cheney, a man with any property was neither employed on the rate nor relieved.

Those who are guilty of a still more important act of prudence and self-denial – that of deferring the period of marriage – are punished sometimes by being refused permission to work, sometimes by being allowed to work only a given number of days in each week, and sometimes by being paid for a full week's labour only a portion, often not half or a third, of what they see their married fellow-workmen receive. The principal evidence to this effect is to be found in the returns to our printed queries, and there is much in the reports of the Assistant Commissioners.

Mr Power states that in Gamlingay (Cambridgeshire) the wages paid to men employed by individuals are about 6s. a week to single men; to married men with children, from 9s. to 10s., with further allowance from the rates, according to the number of the family; and mentions, as a general remark, that when the farmer employs the young single man, it is seldom or never by the grate, but at daily wages, little above those of parish employ-ment.

'At Nuneaton', says Mr Villiers,

the overseer mentioned a case which had only occurred a few days before to himself, in an application made to him by a lad to procure him relief from the parish. His answer to him was, 'Go away and work, you foolish boy'; the boy's answer was, 'Ah, but, Sir, I married yesterday, and I expect the parish to find me a place to live in.' On examining a labourer at Holsworthy, he said that he was only receiving 4s. a week from the parish for his work upon the roads; but that he did not complain of the smallness of the allowance, since he knew what numbers there were then depending on the parish. Upon asking him to what he attributed this increase of number, he replied, that the reason was evident, 'since', to use his expression, 'the young folks married up so terrible early in these days.' On asking him if he could account for this, he said, 'that many of them thought they should be better off if they were married than if they were single, and get more regular employment from the farmers'. He said that he was sixty-eight years of age, and that he remembered a very different state of things; that 'when he was a young man, the farmers preferred a man who was single to a married man, and that he was used to live in the house with them; that men didn't use to marry till they had got a character as good workmen, and had put by some of their earnings'; and that if any man applied to the parish, he was pointed at by all who knew him, as a *parish bird*; but that it was very different now.

Mr Stuart states that in Suffolk:

The policy of most parishes is to employ the married men in preference to the single, and that when the single are employed, their wages are generally less. The farmers frequently said that they considered it bad management not to make this distinction, yet none complained more of early marriages.

Messrs Wrottesley and Cameron state that in West Wycombe (Bucks.):

The notion of wages as a contract beneficial to both parties seems to be nearly obliterated. The rate of weekly wages paid by the parish is, to a single man under twenty, 3s.; above twenty, 4s.; married men without children, 5s.; and so on. We asked what wages the farmers gave; the answer was, the same as the parish. We asked if piece-work was common: 'There is very little of it; it does not answer.' 'Why not?' 'We have got too many people, and want to employ them.' 'You mean that men would do too much work if employed by the piece?' 'That is just what I mean.'

Mr Richardson states that in Northamptonshire:

As the farmers have, under the scale system, a direct inducement to employ married men rather than single, in many villages, particularly in the southern district, they will not employ the single men at all; in others they pay them a much lower rate of wages for the same work, in the hope of driving them to seek work out of the parish. Instead of this, they marry directly, knowing that if they cannot maintain themselves, the parish must do it for them, and that the farmers will be more ready to give work to men likely to become burthensome, than to those who are not. The usual remark they make is, 'Well, I'll go and get a wife, and then you must do something for me.'

He adds that:

Sometimes single men are not counted on the labour-rate. A clergy-man of Culworth gave me an instance of a labourer who told him that he had married only because, under the labour-rate, he could not get work without. If they are admitted, it is at a lower rate than married men? 'Of course, Sir,' as I have often heard from the overseers, who seemed a little surprised at my putting the question.

We will close our instances of this conduct by the following law enacted by a vestry:

At a Vestry Meeting, holden in the Parish Church of Edgefield, on Monday, April 8, 1833,

Resolved, – That the rate of wages for able-bodied men be reduced to 4s. per week; that 1s. per week be given to each wife, and 1s. for each child per week. If there is not any children, allow the wife 1s. 6d. per week.

Agreed for three months from this date, to commence Monday 15th. [Here follow 15 signatures.]

All the previous testimony has been given by persons belonging to the higher orders of society. Some, however, has been furnished by the labourers themselves; and we quote the following passages from the reports of Mr Villiers and Mr Chadwick, to show what effects are attributed to the existing system by the very class to whom it professes to extend its bounty and protection.

'After observing', says Mr Villiers,

so many instances of an almost necessary connection between the con-dition of the people and the mode of administering relief by the parish, I examined persons of different classes with regard to the interests which might be supposed to be involved in the continuance of the present system in the agricultural districts; and on this point the follow-ing evidence of some labourers themselves, who were wholly un-prepared, and unacquainted with the object of my inquiry, is not unimportant. They were examined in the presence of two gentlemen, one a proprietor, and the other an occupier of land in Worcestershire and Gloucestershire.

Thomas Bayce, labourer, stated that he was not settled in the parish in which he worked; that he was upwards of fifty years of age, and that neither he nor his father had ever received relief from any parish;

that he knew many labourers were getting pay from the parish, and that many were relieved who were not so badly off as others who would not demand it; but that people did not care to go to the parish now as they used when he was a young man. Upon being asked his opinion of the roundsmen system, he answered in the following manner: 'That is the very worst thing that has ever happened for the labourers of this country; that is the way our wages are kept down. A farmer wants to get some work done; he proposes starving wages to the labourer. If the labourer refuses to take them, the farmer says, "Very well, I do not want you", and sends to the overseer and gets a man, whom he pays what he likes, and then the parson and the shopkeeper are made to pay the rest. And if a man is not in his own parish, he will often take less than he can live upon sooner than be sent back to his own parish where he is not wanted.' Upon being asked how he came to have been always employed, and (as he had previously said) earning sometimes 14s. a week, he said that all farmers were not alike, and that some farmers knew the value of a labourer who was honest and hard-working, and that his character might be learnt of any farmer with whom he had ever worked; but he added, 'This is not always the case, for I have seen many a man employed, not because he has a good character, but because he has a large family; and there are many who know that to be the case.'

J. Stanton, aged fifty, was a married man; had no children at present; he was a tenant of half an acre of land; he stated that it never took him from his other work, (as if he had much to do); he got some single man to work for him, as there were always some unemployed; the farmers always preferring to employ the men with large families, to keep them off the parish. One of the gentlemen present asked this man whether he would not prefer to see a man get employment who had children to support, than a single man who had only himself to provide for. His answer was in these words: 'To speak openly, Sir, I consider that a man ought to be paid for his work, and not for his family; and that if I had done a good day's work, I should sooner have the value of it myself than see another man paid because he has got children.' He was then asked if he had heard of men marrying with the view to obtain regular employment from the farmers, or more relief from the parish: he said, 'There are many, Sir, who do think that they shall be better off if they have a family, and I have heard them often say so.' He was asked if the labourers thought that the more industrious they were, the more encouragement they would receive: 'No, they do not do that, because we see many a man get parish pay whether he is industrious or not.' He continued, 'But, Sir, what is the use of a man working hard if he has got no master to oblige, paid half by the parish and half by the farmer? How would a man be better off if he were to work ever so hard? It would be better for us to be slaves at once than to work under such a system.' I asked him if some of the labourers did not prefer the system as a means of being idle, or of only doing half a day's work; he said he believed that might be the case sometimes, and added, 'Where is the wonder; when a man has his spirit broken, what is he good for?'

Gibson, labourer, stated that he was seventy years of age; he had brought up a family of six children, and had never applied to the parish, but on one occasion, to assist him to pay his rent in time; he knew many a man who was receiving parish relief, not so badly off as he had been himself, but that there were so many now with large families, that he hardly thought they could keep off the parish; 'but', he added, 'what is man to do, Sir; for if he has not a family, he has a bad chance of getting steady work in his own parish.'

Charles James, labourer. He had four children; he had never received parish relief; on being asked what he thought of the rounds-men system, he said, 'it completely ruined the labourer,' and added, 'and people may say, Sir, what they like, but there are one set of farmers who always will keep it up as long as they are allowed to do so; and it is no use their saying they do not approve of it, when last week farmer —— turned off all his men, and in the same week took the same men all back from the parish, and now he pays them half the wages that he did.'

Cockerell, labourer, said that he lived with his father-in-law, who was a very old man, that he often heard him remark 'what a sad change there was now in men going on the parish, and that he remembered the time when a man would rather starve than apply; but that nowadays, a man was more employed because he went on the parish than because he was industrious and strived to keep off.'

On another occasion, the gentleman at whose house I was stopping, being doubtful of the encouragement offered to early marriage from the mode of administering the Poor Laws, proposed to obtain, if possible, the opinion of the first labourers to be met with in the fields; an opportunity soon occurred; four men were working together near a farm-house; upon questioning them as to the wages they were earning, one among them, who informed us that he was thirty years of age and unmarried complained much of the lowness of his wages, and added, without a question on the subject being put to him, that if he was a married man, and had a parcel of children, he should be better off, as he should either have work given him by the piece, or receive allowances for his children. He was immediately joined by two of the other men, who said 'Yes, Sir, that is how it is; a man has no chance now unless he is a family man.' The other, an old man, who was nearly eighty years of age, said, 'that he was yet able and willing to work, but that he was obliged to go upon the parish because the farmers gave all the work they could to men who had families. When he was young, there was no such thing as that. The men proceeded to reckon what was allowed to families according to their numbers; and they spoke of the system with great irritation. That it tends in no degree to make the class happy and contented may be inferred from this part of the country having been the scene of considerable riot and outrage in 1831.

Thomas Pearce, labourer in husbandry, of the parish of Govington, Sussex; Examined.

WITNESS has worked all his life for Mr Noakes, of Wannoch.

At first the witness, who appeared to be a stout, hard-working young man, was examined as to the diet and usual mode of living of the labourers of that district. His evidence was confirmatory of that which is elsewhere stated, as to the modes of living of the labouring classes, and as to the superiority of the condition of paupers.

In your parish are there many able-bodied men upon the parish? – There are a great many men in our parish who like it better than being at work.

Why do they like it better? – They get the same money, and don't do half so much work. They don't work like me; they be'ant at it so many hours, and they don't do so much work when they be at it; they're doing no good, and are only waiting for dinner-time and night; they be'ant working, it's only waiting.

How have you managed to live without parish relief? – By working hard.

What do the paupers say to you? – They blame me for what I do. They say to me, 'What are you working for?' I say, 'For myself.' They say, 'You are only doing it to save the parish, and if you didn't do it, you would get the same as another man has, and would get the money for smoking your pipe and doing nothing.' 'Tis a hard thing for a man like me.

If you want anything from the parish, should you get it sooner than a man who has not worked so hard? – No, not a bit; nor so likely as one of those men.

What would they say to you? – They would say that I didn't want it, and that I had a piece of ground, and was well off. They're always giving to men who don't deserve it, whilst they are refusing to those who do.

Is it worse in your parish than in others? — No, it is the same in them all. There is partiality everywhere. If I was to offend my master, and he was to turn me away, none of the others would give me work; and if I go to the parish, they would put me on the roads. There's not one in our place that looks on me the better for my work, but all the worse for it.

What would be thought of a plan, of making all go either wholly on or wholly off the parish, so that the men should not be paid half in wages and half as a pauper? — I do not know; but my master (Mr Noakes) says that he would take his full part of men; and if all the others did the same, there would be no men on the road, except an old man or two just to let the water off. But some of the farmers like to poke the men on the roads, so as to make the blacksmith and the wheeler and the shopkeepers come in, which helps the rates.

But do not the workmen see that the farmers do this to serve their own turn, and pay less in wages? — Yes, that is how it is. A farmer, when he wants his stock in, will say, 'I want to keep my cattle going; I won't take away my cattle men, but I'll get some extra men from the roads.' And so he does; and when he has got his stock in, he says, 'Now you may go, and the parish may keep you.' He will get these men to do an extra day or two's work, but he won't give them more than the parish gives; for which reason they do not like to go, as they do not work half so hard for the parish.

Would it, do you think, be a good thing to prevent the farmers using the parish to keep a stock of hands ready for these extra jobs? — I do not know how that would be, as I never seed it tried; but I think he would make the farmers keep more men for constant, which would be a good thing, as they would find more work for them. The land is not near done here as it should be, for want of hands.

Piece-work is thus refused to the single man, or to the married man if he have any property, because they can exist on day wages; it is refused to the active and intelligent labourer, because he would earn too much. The enterprising man, who has fled from the tyranny and pauperism of his parish to some place where there is a demand and a reward for his services, is driven from a situation which suits him, and an employer to whom he is attached, by a labour-rate or some other device against non-parishioners, and forced back to his settlement to receive as alms a portion only of what he was obtaining by his own exertions. He is driven from a place where he was earning, as a free labourer, 12s. or 14s. a week, and is offered road-work, as a pauper, at sixpence a day, or perhaps to be put up by the parish authorities to auction, and sold to the farmer who will take him at the lowest allowance.

Can we wonder if the labourer abandons virtues of which this is the reward? If he gives up the economy in return for which he has been proscribed, the diligence for which he has been condemned to involuntary idleness, and the prudence, if it can be called such, which diminishes his means just as much as it diminishes his wants? Can we wonder if, smarting under these oppressions, he considers the law and all who administer the law as his enemies, the fair objects of his fraud or his violence? Can we wonder if, to increase his income, and to revenge himself on the parish, he marries, and thus helps to increase that local over-population which is gradually eating away the fund out of which he and all the other labourers of the parish are to be maintained?

2
Effects on labourers actually relieved

But, though the injustice perpetrated on the man who struggles, as far as he can struggle, against the oppression of the system, who refuses, as far as he can refuse, to be its accomplice, is at first sight the most revolting, the severest sufferers are those that have become callous to their own degradation, who value parish support as their privilege, and demand it as their right, and complain only that it is limited in amount, or that some sort of labour or confinement is exacted in return. No man's principles can be corrupted without injury to society in general; but the person most injured is the person whose principles have been corrupted. The constant war which the pauper has to wage with all who employ or pay him, is destructive to his honesty and his temper; as his subsistence does not depend on his exertions, he loses all that sweetens labour, its association with reward, and gets through his work, such as it is, with the reluctance of a slave. His pay, earned by importunity or fraud, or even violence, is not husbanded with the carefulness which would be given to the results of industry, but wasted in the intemperance to which his ample leisure invites him. The ground on which relief is ordered to the idle and dissolute is that the wife and family must not suffer for the vices of the head of the family; but as that relief is almost always given into the hands of the vicious husband or parent, this excuse is obviously absurd. It appears from the evidence that the great supporters of the beer-shops are the paupers. 'Wherever', says Mr Lawrence of Henfield, 'the labourers are unemployed, the beer-shops of the parish are frequented by them.' And it is a striking fact, that in Cholesbury, where out of 139 individuals only thirty-five persons, of all ages, including the clergyman and his family are supported by their own exertions, there are two public-houses. 'Hundreds of instances', says Mr Okeden,

came under my observation, in which the overseers knew that the wages and parish allowance were spent in two nights at the beer-houses, which ought to have been the week's subsistence of the whole family. Still no steps are taken; the scale is referred to, and acted on, and the parish actually supports and pays for the drunken excesses of the labourers. The character and habits of the labourer have by this scale system been completely changed. Industry fails, moral character is annihilated and the poor man of twenty years ago, who tried to earn his money and was thankful for it, is now converted into an insolent, discontented, surly, thoughtless pauper, who talks of 'right and income', and who will soon fight for these supposed rights and income, unless some step is taken to arrest his progress to open violence. Some rude efforts he may, at first, make to shake off his state of servitude: but he finally yields to the temptations of the pay-table and the scale, feels his bondage, puts off his generous feelings of industry, and gratitude, and independence, and

. . . to suit
His manner with his fate, puts on the brute.

'With the exception', says Mr Millman of Reading,

of decent persons reduced by inevitable misfortune, as is the case with some of our manufacturers, whose masters have totally failed, and who are too old, or otherwise incapable of seeking elsewhere their accustomed employment, I should state in the most unqualified manner that the cottage of a parish pauper and his family may be at once distinguished from that of a man who maintains himself. The former is dirty, neglected, noisome: the children, though in general they may be sent to school at the desire of the clergyman or parish officers, are the least clean and the most ragged at the school; in short, the degree of wretchedness and degradation may, in most instances, be measured by the degree in which they may burthen the parish. Unless some few tenements, inhabited by the lowest and usually the most profligate poor, the refuse of society, the cottages in my parish which it is least agreeable to enter are those of which the rent is paid by the parish, in which the effect of our exertions, and of the liberality of the landlords to cleanse on the alarm of cholera, was obliterated in a very few weeks.

Mr Chadwick states in his report that in every district he found the condition of the independent labourer strikingly distinguishable from that of the pauper, and superior to it, though the independent labourers were commonly maintained upon less money.

The assistant overseer of Windsor examined:

What is the characteristic of the wives of paupers and their families? – The wives of paupers are dirty and nasty and indolent; and the children generally neglected and dirty and vagrants, and immoral.

How are the cottages of the independent labourers as compared to them? – The wife is a very different person; she and her children are clean, and her cottage tidy. I have had very extensive opportunities of observing the difference in my visits; the difference is so striking to me, that, in passing along a row of cottages, I could tell, in nine instances out of ten, which were paupers' cottages and which were the cottages of the independent labourers.

Mr Brushfield of Spitalfields, London, examined:

Have you ever compared the condition of the able-bodied pauper with the condition of the independent labourer? – Yes. I have lately inquired into various cases of the labouring poor who receive parish relief; and, being perfectly acquainted with the cases of paupers generally, the contrast struck me forcibly. In the pauper's habitation you will find a strained show of misery and wretchedness; and those little articles of furniture which might, by the least exertion imaginable, wear an appearance of comfort are turned, as it were intentionally, the ugliest side outward; the children are dirty, and appear to be under no control; the clothes of both parents and children, in nine cases out of ten, are ragged but evidently are so for the lack of the least attempt to make them otherwise; for I have very rarely found the clothes of a pauper with a patch put or a seam made upon them since new;

their mode of living, in all cases that I have known (except and always making the distinction between the determined pauper and the infirm and deserving poor, which cases are but comparatively few), is most improvident. It is difficult to get to a knowledge of particulars in their cases; but whatever provisions I have found on visiting their habitations have been of the best quality; and my inquiries among tradesmen, as butchers, chandler's shop-keepers, &c., have all been answered with, 'They will not have anything but the best.'

In the habitation of the labouring man who receives no parish relief, you will find (I have done so), even in the poorest, an appearance of comfort; the articles of furniture, few and humble though they may be, have their best side seen, are arranged in something like order, and so as to produce the best appearance of which they are capable. The children appear under parental control; are sent to school (if of that age); their clothes you will find patched and taken care of so as to make them wear as long a time as possible; there is a sense of moral feeling and moral dignity easily discerned; they purchase such food, and at such seasons, and in such quantities, as the most economical would approve of.

Mr Isaac Willis, collector of the poor-rates in the parish of St Mary, Stratford-le-Bow, London:

Have you had occasion to observe the modes of living of those of the labouring classes who receive aid from the parish or from charities, and of those independent labourers who depend entirely on their own resources to provide for their families? – I have for many years, in collecting through my district.

Are the two classes externally distinguishable in their persons, houses, or behaviour? – Yes, they are. I can easily distinguish them, and I think they might be distinguished by any one who paid attention to them. The independent labourer is comparatively clean in his person, his wife and children are clean, and the children go to school; the house is in better order and more cleanly. Those who depend on parish relief or on benefactions, on the contrary, are dirty in their persons and slothful in their habits; the children are allowed to go about the streets in a vagrant condition. The industrious labourers get their children out to service early. The pauper and charity-fed people do not care what becomes of their children. The man who earns his penny is always a better man in every way than the man who begs it.

Mr Samuel Miller, assistant overseer of St Sepulchre's, London:

In the course of my visits to the residences of the labouring people, in our own and other parishes, I have seen the apartments of those who remained independent, though they had no apparent means of getting more than those who were receiving relief from the parish, or so much as out-door paupers. The difference in their appearance is most striking; I now, almost immediately on the sight of a room, can tell whether it is the room of a pauper or of an independent labourer. I have frequently said to the wife of an independent labourer, 'I can see, by the neatness and cleanness of your place, that you receive no relief from any parish.' 'No', they usually say, 'and I hope we never shall.' This is applicable not only to the paupers in the metropolis but, it may be stated, from all I have seen elsewhere, and heard, that it is equally applicable to other places. The quantity of relief given to the paupers makes no difference with them as to cleanliness or comfort; in many instances very much the contrary. More money only produces more drunkenness. We have had frequent instances of persons being deprived of parochial relief from misconduct or otherwise, or, as the officers call it, 'choked off the parish', during twelve months or more, and at the end of that time we have found them in a better condition than when they were receiving weekly relief.

The testimony, with relation to the superiority of the class of labourers who are deprived of the facilities of obtaining partial relief, is almost as striking and important. We shall advert to it in a subsequent part of the Report.

The following testimony of Mr Sleeth of Albany Road, Kent Road, is an instructive example of the tendency of pauperism to sap the foundations of industry, virtue, and happiness:

I have been a witness to the gradual ruin of a very deserving class of people, effected, as well as I can judge, by the superior temptations of parish allowance and idleness to those of independence with industry.

I was employed from 1819 to 1831 in a commercial house, of which the greater part of the business was the sale of home-made fabrics, chiefly of stockings. The demand for homespun articles is still very extensive amongst old people of all ranks, on account of their superior warmth and durability. The call for these goods when I first became acquainted with the business was very constant, and the supply abundant but not excessive. The competition of the factories had driven the spinners quite out of the market, and also the great bulk of the knitters; but of these latter, some of the most resolutely frugal and industrious persevered in working for the low reward which was to be got while the employment was breaking up. But after this period of change, which had taken place before the time at which my knowledge begins, the people who had persevered remained the only workers. In fact none were brought up to it, and none continued in it but those who had been long used to it, and of those only the most independent and exemplary. But they got the reward of their struggle in the monopoly of the supply, when all the most supine had ceased to contend with the progress of the factories.

The earnings of a family by knitting sometimes amounted to more than £20, and commonly from £12 to between £16 and £18, a very large sum, as everybody knows who knows the economy of a well managed cottage. These latter earnings were wholly additional to the ordinary labourer's earnings, as they never interfered with farm work, were frequent in parts of Sussex ten years ago, where the practice is unknown now except by some single superannuated old woman. The general shop of the village was, latterly, the medium between my employers and these poor people, who there received the materials and returned the made-up article, and could always receive the amount of their earnings at the same time. Usually they were partly taken out in goods, such as tea, soap, tapes, needles, &c., and sometimes in cash: they frequently made the dealer thus banker for some portion of their gains. Such was the occasional self-denial of these people that I know one family, of the name of Hinde, that received three several years' earnings in *cash*, during seven years that they were at work for us, amounting to above £43. This family consisted of a man past fifty, his sister older than himself, three orphan nieces, and one nephew. The history of this family is interesting. The man was and is an agricultural labourer; he speculated with his savings, purchasing the fruit or pigs of his neighbours, or their poultry, when they had a right of common, before they were fit for the market by advance of money on them, his neighbours tending them to maturity. He had a reputation of being very rich, and often lent some few guineas to needy farmers. *He found great difficulty in getting employment, it was refused him on account of his savings*; and bought a piece of ground to occupy himself on, but was afraid of farming. His sister was a bit of a shrew, but very notable, and the earnings by knitting were owing to her, for when she became bed-ridden the industry of the girls declined, and on her death ceased altogether; they quarrelled with their uncle; the boy, is now married and has a pauper family; one girl is married after having had a bastard, the other girl is in service in London, and is respectable. I consider these young people ruined solely by the example of their idle and dissolute half-pauper neighbours, who are never content to be haunted by the presence of more industrious or deserving characters, and spare no effort of argument or raillery to bring them to the common level – an event of itself too much to be feared, consisting of a change from care and labour to profligacy and idleness.

I should say I know 500 families who have so given up knitting for idleness and parish allowance, though their remuneration was constantly on the increase through the falling off of hands. In 1828 the quantity of these goods produced in the South became so small that we ceased to make any arrangements for them, and relied solely on the West of England, in parts where the parish allowance has not extended, and therefore where the motive to work continues unabated, yet at that time prices were more than double what could have been earned when this kind of industry was universal.

The allowance from the poor-rate was at the bottom of the whole, for competition had ceased, and it was generally allowed by the workers that equal industry would procure men more than *twice* the quantity of food or clothing that it would have done when the employment was general and prosperous. But the labour was continuous and irksome; even the cleanliness which was indispensable to putting the work out of hand in a proper state, the confinement to the house, perhaps the control of the old people, were in violent and constant contrast with the carelessness and idleness of those who could dispense with industry by relying on the parish. Pauper women are all gossips, the men all go to the ale-house; the knitters had little time for either, and they were assured that they debarred themselves for the good of the rich, and it was seen that no idleness or extravagance was attended with any alarming consequences against which the parish served as a shield.

I have every autumn been into the country, and have observed the gradual deterioration of these previously respectable families. The clothing was in great part made at home, and was sedulously well made.

Cleanliness was indispensable to the work, and the work itself was cleanly; and as it kept them much at home, it made comfort in that home more necessary than it is to those who loll their time away out of doors.

Besides, comfort and cleanliness are not the policy of those who apply to the parish; for the overseer always observes to those who are decent and tidy in their persons and houses, 'that they seem too comfortable to want', and mentions his suspicions of concealed savings.

I wish to be understood as speaking of the disappearance of these people all through, not as the result of competition with manufacturers, but as the consequence of the diminished industry of parties who had virtually a monopoly in their own hands, but who wanted motives to continue the industry necessary for its preservation.

I have to add that I regard the demoralization of these people as a further evil in the way of loss of a good example; for wherever they remained, in ever so small number, the superiority of their appearance was a model for their equals in grade, and formed a sort of *ton* for the rest, to which the parish officers and the gentry constantly pointed, and strove to make the general habit; but as they lost the characteristic standard fell, and those who had formerly been pointed out as patterns, are become undistinguishable from the rest. My observation is that the air of content and cheerfulness which formerly distinguished them has been displaced, in the very same individuals, by the common pauper appearance; that is, they look dirty, ill-fed, discontented, careless, and vicious.

Even the least contact with parochial assistance seems to be degrading. The following are extracts from the evidence of Mrs Barker of Hambledon, Bucks.; Mr Chappell, vestry clerk of St George's, Hanover Square; Mr Booker, assistant overseer of St Botolph-without-Bishopsgate; Mr Hobler, chief clerk in the Lord Mayor's Court; and Mr Brushfield of Spitalfields:

In the year 1824 or 1825 there were two labourers, who were reported to me as extremely industrious men, maintaining large families: neither of them had ever applied for parish relief. I thought it advisable that they should receive some mark of public approbation, and we gave them £1 a piece from the parish. Very shortly they both became applicants for relief, and have continued so ever since.

I can decidedly state, as the result of my experience, that when once a family has received relief, it is to be expected that their descendants, for some generations, will receive it also.

The change that is made in the character and habits of the poor by once receiving parochial relief, is quite remarkable; they are demoralized ever afterwards. I remember the case of a family named Wintle, consisting of a man, his wife, and five children. About two years ago, the father, mother, and two children, were very ill, and reduced to great distress, being obliged to sell all their little furniture for their subsistence; they were settled with us; and as we heard of their extreme distress, I went to them to offer relief; they, however, strenuously refused the aid. I reported this to the churchwarden, who determined to accompany me, and together we again pressed on the family the necessity of receiving relief; but still they refused, and we could not prevail upon them to accept our offer. We felt so much interested in the case, however, that we sent them 4s. in a parcel with a letter, desiring them to apply for more, if they continued ill: this they did, and from that time to this (now more than two years) I do not believe that they have been for three weeks off our books, although there has been little or no ill health in the family. Thus we effectually spoiled the habits acquired by their previous industry; and I have no hesitation in saying that, in nine cases out of ten, such is the constant effect of having once tasted of parish bounty. This applies as much to the young as to middle aged, and as much to the middle aged as to the old. I state it confidently, as the result of my experience, that if once a young lad gets a pair of shoes given him by the parish, he never afterwards lays by sufficient to buy a pair; so if we give to the fathers or mothers of children clothing or other assistance, they invariably apply again and again.

The regular applicants for relief are generally of one family; the disease is hereditary, and when once a family has applied for relief, they are pressed down for ever.

Whether in work or out of work, when they once become paupers, it can only be by a sort of miracle that they can be broken off; they have no care, no thought, no solicitude, on account of the future, except the old musty rent-roll of receipts or an old dirty indenture of apprenticeship, which are handed down from father to son with as much care as deeds of freehold property, and by which they pride themselves in the clear claims to the parish money and the workhouse. All the tricks and deceptions of which man is capable are resorted to; the vilest and most barefaced falsehoods are uttered, and all the worst characteristics of human nature are called into exercise, for the purpose of exciting a favourable feeling in their behalf; *their children are eye and ear witnesses to all this.* The child remembers his father's actions, and the hereditary pauper increases his ranks by instruction as well as by example. Their numbers will, as a matter of course, still increase while these laws exist in their present form.

The most striking examples, however, of the effects of pauperism are to be found in the report of Mr Codd, on the western division of the Metropolis. We will extract, from among many other passages equally striking, a further portion of the evidence of Mr Booker:

The deterioration in the character and habits of persons receiving parochial relief pervades their whole conduct; they become idle, reckless, and saucy; and if we take them into the house or place them at farm-houses, the younger learn from the older all their malpractices and are ready enough to follow them.

We have a good many young people upon our casual out-door poor list. We first receive them into the house, to endeavour to place them out in trades, or in service, or as apprentices; but they were so refractory and behaved so ill that the old people petitioned to be relieved from them: they would beat them or steal their victuals or sing indecent songs in the open yard, and so as to be heard by every one on the premises, and would annoy them in every way, besides doing everything they could to plague the master and mistress of the house, until we were obliged, in justice to the other inmates, to send them away to farmed houses, for which we paid 5s. per head per week besides clothes. At such houses, however, they were so disorderly and irregular that the owners refused to keep them and sent them back to us. We then sent them to other houses, and by constantly changing them from one to another, as they behaved ill, we got over a certain period of time. But at length most of them became so well known that no establishment of the kind in the metropolis would take them. We then tried them with employment out of the house, and used them to convey potatoes, coal, &c., to our infant establishment at Edmonton. This we were obliged to discontinue because some stole a part of the loads with which they were intrusted, and others made away with the whole and did not return to us for two or three weeks afterwards. For this conduct we took them, in some cases, before the magistrates, and got them committed to the tread-mill for seven or fourteen days; but this rather hardened them than did them any good. We then tried them at stone-breaking, but they broke their tools, almost as a matter of course; either on the first or second morning the hammers were brought in broken in the handles, by accident, as they alleged; but, as we well knew, by design. Our next course was to give them 2s. a week, at different periods in the week, with bread and cheese on the intervening days, leaving them to pursue their own course; but this we found left them upon the streets to prey upon the public, which they did so effectually that several of them were transported in a very short time afterwards, leaving their wives and families, where they had them, chargeable to the parish. The increase of depredations to which this plan gave rise was loudly complained of by the inhabitants of the neighbourhood and we were, therefore, obliged to give it up.

We are now employing the men as scavengers, and the women as cinder-sifters; but they constantly avoid working upon some excuse or another, although *we are actually obliged to pay the contractor 6s. a week for employing them, and to pay for their clothes besides.* These 6s. are paid by the contractor, at the rate of 1s. nightly, to the persons who have worked, and by us repaid to him; but the parties are not satisfied, and it is no uncommon thing for them to beset my house, soliciting me to send them to the compter; and if I refuse, they remain at the door and cannot be removed except by force. If they are taken before the magistrates and committed for short periods, they come to us again immediately that the period of their confinement is over, and behave worse than ever.

Whoever comes to us and swears before a magistrate that he has neither work nor money we are obliged to relieve, because we can neither give them work nor prove that they have constant employment; and paupers now understand the law, and also the practice of magistrates so well, from the many hours that they spend in police offices applying for summonses, &c., that they claim relief not at all as a matter of favour but as a matter of right.

The worst results, however, are still to be mentioned: in all ranks of society the great sources of happiness and virtue are the domestic affections, and this is particularly the case among those who have so few resources as the labouring classes. Now pauperism seems to be an engine for the purpose of disconnecting each member of a family from all the others; of reducing all to the state of domesticated animals, fed, lodged and provided for by the parish, without mutual dependence or mutual interest.

'The effect of allowance', says Mr Stuart, 'is to weaken, if not to destroy, all the ties of affection between parent and child. Whenever a lad comes to earn wages, or to receive parish relief on his own account' (and this we must recollect is at the age of fourteen),

although he may continue to lodge with his parents, he does not throw his money into a common purse, and board with them, but buys his own loaf and piece of bacon, which he devours alone. The most disgraceful quarrels arise from mutual accusations of theft; and as the child knows that he has been nurtured at the expense of the parish, he has no filial attachment to his parents. The circumstances of the pauper stand in an inverted relation to those of every other rank in society. Instead of a family being a source of care, anxiety, and expense, for which he hopes to be rewarded by the filial return of assistance and support when they grow up, there is no period in his life in which he tastes less of solicitude, or in which he has the means of obtaining all the necessaries of life in greater abundance; but as he is always sure of maintenance, it is in general the practice to enjoy life when he can, and no thought is taken for the morrow. Those parents who are thoroughly degraded and demoralized by the effects of 'allowance', not only take no means to train up their children to habits of industry, but do their utmost to prevent their obtaining employment, lest it should come to the knowledge of the parish officers, and be laid hold of for the purpose of taking away the allowance.

Mr Majendie states that at Thaxted mothers and children will not nurse each other in sickness unless they are paid for it. Mr Power mentions the following circumstance as having occurred at Over, Cambridgeshire, a few days before his visit:

A widow with two children had been in the receipt of 3s. a week from the parish: she was enabled by this allowance and her own earnings to live very comfortably. She married a butcher: the allowance was continued; but the butcher and his bride came to the overseer and said they were not going to keep those children for 3s. a week, and that if a further allowance was not made, *they should turn them out of doors*, and throw them on the parish altogether. The overseer resisted; the butcher appealed to the bench, who recommended him to make the best arrangement he could, as the parish was obliged to support the children.

'Those whose minds', say Messrs Wrottesley and Cameron,

have been moulded by the operation of the Poor Laws, appear not to have the slightest scruple in asking to be paid for the performance of those domestic duties which the most brutal savages are in general willing to render gratuitously to their own kindred. 'Why should I tend my sick and aged parents, when the parish is bound to do it? or if I do perform the service, why should I excuse the parish, which is bound to pay for it?

At Princes Risborough we turned over the minute book of the select vestry, and found the following entries:

'Samuel Simmons's wife applied to be allowed something for looking after her mother, who is confined to her bed; the mother now receives 3s. 6d. weekly. To be allowed an additional 6d. for a few weeks.'

'David Walker's wife applied to be allowed something for looking after her father and mother (old Stevens and his wife), now ill, who receive 6s. weekly. To be allowed 1s. weekly.'

'Mary Lacy applies for something for waiting on her mother, now ill. Left to the governor.'

'Elizabeth Prime applies to have something allowed for her sister looking after her father, now ill. Left to the governor.'

'At the time of my journey', says Mr Cowell,

the acquaintance I had with the practical operation of the Poor Laws led me to suppose that the pressure of the sum annually raised upon the rate-payers, and its progressive increase, constituted the main inconvenience of the Poor Law system. The experience of a very few weeks served to convince me that this evil, however great, sinks into insignificance when compared with the dreadful effects which the system produces on the morals and happiness of the lower orders. It is as difficult to convey to the mind of the reader a true and faithful impression of the intensity and malignancy of the evil in this point of view, as it is by any description, however vivid, to give an adequate idea of the horrors of a shipwreck or a pestilence. A person must converse with paupers – must enter workhouses, and examine the inmates – must attend at the parish pay-table, before he can form a just conception of the moral debasement which is the offspring of the present system; he must hear the pauper threaten to abandon his wife and family unless more money is allowed him – threaten to abandon an aged bed-ridden mother, to turn her out of his house and lay her down at the overseer's door unless he is paid for giving her shelter; he must hear parents threatening to follow the same course with regard to their sick children; he must see mothers coming to receive the reward of their daughters' ignominy, and witness women in cottages quietly pointing out, without even the question being asked, which are their children by their husband, and which by other men previous to marriage; and when he finds that he can scarcely step into a town or parish in any county without meeting with some instance or other of this character, he will no longer consider the pecuniary pressure on the rate-payer as the first in the class of evils which the Poor Laws have entailed upon the community.

[CHARACTER OF PERSONS WHO DISTRIBUTE AND AWARD RELIEF]

═══════

HAVING given this outline of the maladministration of the laws for the relief of the poor, and of the causes which have induced large classes of persons to be favourable to that maladministration, we will now consider how far the character of the persons by whom relief is awarded and distributed is likely to be favourable or unfavourable to its due administration.

The persons by whom relief is actually distributed are the overseers.

The persons by whom it is awarded are the overseers, the vestry, either general or select, and the magistrates.

We will examine separately the motives likely to affect the conduct of each of these classes of functionaries.

I

THE OVERSEERS

As the law now stands the overseers are to make, assess, collect, and distribute the fund for the relief of the poor. They are to decide, in the first instance, what amount of money is wanted, what persons are to pay it, and in what proportions; they are to enforce payment of it from those persons, and they are to dole it out to those whom they think proper objects of relief, so as to satisfy what they think the necessities of those objects. Where a select vestry exists, they are desired by the 59 Geo III, c. 12 [1818] to conform to the directions of that vestry; but as the Act does not put an end to their responsibility, or enact any penalty for their non-conformance, this clause, though productive of important results in practice, appears to want legal sanction.

2

[*Annual overseers*]

The office is annual, and sometimes lasts only six or four, or even three months, it being in some places the practice to appoint two or three, or even four every year, each of whom serves for only half a year or four months, or only three. The persons appointed are in general farmers in country places, and shopkeepers or manufacturers in towns.

If they refuse or neglect to serve, they may be indicted or fined, but they receive no remuneration for serving.

Such agents must often be prevented, by their other avocations, from giving the time necessary to the vigilant and effectual performance of their duties; neither diligence nor zeal are to be expected from persons on whom a disagreeable and unpaid office has been forced, and whose functions cease by the time that they have begun to acquire a knowledge of them; and even when zealous and diligent, they must often fail from want of experience and skill. To these sources of maladministration may be added the danger of the parochial fund being misapplied either in the way of actual embezzlement, or, what is more frequent, through jobbing or partiality and favouritism, or through the desire of general popularity, or through the fear of general unpopularity, or of the hostility of particular individuals.

The only checks, then, on their profusion or partiality, or fraud, are the share which they bear as ratepayers in the burthen, and the necessity of annually submitting their accounts to the vestry, and having them allowed by the magistrates.

With respect to the former check, it is to be observed, first, that the increase or diminution of the rates of the whole parish, which one overseer can effect during his year, or half-year, or three months of office, is in general so small, and his own individual share of that increase or diminution so trifling as to be an insufficient motive for making any real sacrifice or encountering any real danger; and secondly, that if, as an immediate employer of labour, he is interested in keeping down its price, he may gain, or think that he gains, more by the reduction of wages than he loses by the rise of rates. With respect to the latter check – that arising from the necessity of having the accounts passed – it is to be observed, that no form is prescribed for keeping these accounts, that sometimes they are merely entered on loose paper, and that in most cases they consist of a mere day-book of receipt and expenditure without any statement of the grounds on which relief has been afforded, and often without stating even the names of the persons relieved. Such accounts afford clues by which a person devoting himself to their investigation might in time ascertain the mode in which the fund had been administered, but on a cursory examination, they tell nothing; and we shall see that they do receive only a cursory examination from the vestry of which the overseers themselves form a part, and are then passed, as a matter of course by the justices.

On the other hand, if the overseers refuse relief, or grant less than the applicant thinks himself entitled to, they may be summoned before the justices to defend themselves against the charge of inhumanity and oppression; and if they do not comply with the magistrates' order, they are punishable by indictment or fine; and, unhappily, the applicant who has been refused relief has frequently recourse to a much more summary remedy than the interference of the magistrates. The tribunal which enforces it sits, not at the petty sessions, but at the beershop; – it compels obedience, not by summons and distress, but by violence and conflagration. The most painful and the most formidable portion of our evidence consists of the proof, that in many districts the principal obstacle to improvement is the well-founded dread of these atrocities.

The following extracts from the evidence will, perhaps, be more convincing than our general statement of its result:

As a body, I found annual overseers wholly incompetent to discharge the duties of their office, either from the interference of private occupations, or from a want of experience and skill; but most frequently from both these causes. Their object is to get through the year with as little unpopularity and trouble as possible: their successors, therefore, have frequently to complain of demands left unsettled, and rates uncollected, either from carelessness or a desire to gain the trifling popularity of having called for fewer assessments than usual. In rural districts the overseers are farmers; in towns generally shopkeepers;

and in villages usually one of each of those classes. The superiority of salaried assistant-overseers is admitted wherever they exist, and in nearly all the instances where a select vestry has fallen into disuetude, the assistant-overseer has been retained. In short, so bad is the annual system considered, that an enactment was frequently proposed for compelling all parishes to appoint and remunerate permanent overseers, to be removable in case of unfitness or misconduct.

SLAUGHAM.

Population ... 740 | Expenditure ... £1,706.

The above large sum of money is expended principally in orders on the village shops for flour, clothes, butter, cheese, &c.; the tradesmen serve the office of overseer by turns; the two last could neither read nor write.

With the exception of two or three instances in great towns, the overseers are tradesmen, shopkeepers, and farmers, who complained universally of the vexatious demands on their time.

The circumstances which were admitted to render the annual overseer inefficient were change, difference of opinion in a successor or a colleague, and the appointment of persons who supply the poor with goods, and thus have a direct interest in giving them money from the poor-rate. The relief that should be afforded to the industrious classes, by exonerating them from the heavy burden of the duties of the compulsory overseer, is worthy of consideration. I met with one instance of a respectable farmer who had been overseer ten times in sixteen years, because there was only one other person in the hamlet qualified to serve: and I cannot convey an idea of the dismay of another who, in the midst of harvest, when occupied in carrying wheat and watching every cloud that passed, was called away by some parochial duty.

There are six overseers annually appointed; and it has been the practice – a very injurious one, in my belief – that each overseer should take the duty of relieving the poor for one month by turns: the consequence is that all the evils which attach to the ordinary cases of overseers acting for a year – namely, their necessary ignorance of the parties with whom they have to deal, and their inability to give up sufficient time to become acquainted with them – are aggravated in a six-fold degree. When I state to the Commissioners what occurred to myself last month, the second month I took the duty, it will be seen how impossible it is that an overseer should know all that he ought to know about the parties whom he relieves.

In that month I relieved, with sums under 2s. 6d. each, 472 persons, whose families amounted in the aggregate to 1,097; this relief amounted to £101 13s. In sums of above 2s. 6d. each I distributed £67 13s. 10½d. within the same period. This money was issued entirely at my own discretion; the parties were very nearly all the same persons that I relieved in the first month of my duty, when I saw them for the first time in my life; most of these parties were therefore relieved by me on the first occasion, upon evidence little better than that afforded by their own statements; and this must be the case with all other overseers annually appointed. It is a general complaint among overseers, at least among those who accept the office with the object of duly applying the parish funds, that it is impossible for them to do the duties assigned to them effectually.

Besides the casual relief issued as above-mentioned, upon my sole responsibility, and without control, there were paid in the same month of December £361 12s. 6d. in weekly pensions, and £122 1s. 6d. for bastards.

We have no checks upon the payments made by our overseers either to the weekly casuals, or to the mere casual poor. In the course of my long experience I have known many overseers, men in trade or otherwise, who have been obliged to leave the management of the parochial fund, so far at least as regards the payments made to the casual poor, to their wives, children, or shopmen. It is a very common remark with overseers. 'Well you have imposed a very unpleasant duty on me, and I shall endeavour to get through it with as much comfort to myself as possible.' Another objection is that they are sometimes taken from poor neighbourhoods, in which case it commonly occurs that some of their customers are among the paupers who apply to them for relief.

I am one of the three annual overseers, who each take four months of duty. I am a tradesman, and I cannot give much time to inquiry; besides, as I am only employed four months I cannot learn anything of the habits and characters of the people.

I would take from the annual overseers the administration of relief; first, because they are appointed for a year, and in many instances divide their time with their brother overseers, so as to restrict their periods of active service even to two or three months; and it is therefore quite impossible that they should acquire any adequate knowledge of the paupers with whom they have to do, and by whom they are in consequence imposed upon to a lamentable extent; next, because they are honorary officers who are generally dependent on other employments for their support, and whose whole time and attention cannot be given to the performance of their duties, even for those short periods during which they undertake to transact them; they therefore either neglect them, devolve them upon others, or perform them unwillingly; and lastly, because they are members of the parochial boards by which their conduct and accounts are, for the most part, to be canvassed and passed, and there is therefore only a very imperfect appeal as to their proceedings, either as regards the parish or the paupers.

I consider a great portion of the evils now found to exist in the operation of the Poor Laws may be ascribed to the discretionary power placed in individual irresponsible hands, and that the present laws might be rendered tolerable, and in some degrees beneficial, if such power was taken from the hands of individuals and vested in a public board. My reasons for such an opinion are that as the office of church-warden or overseer is generally filled by a tradesman (in the metropolitan parishes at least), frequently a retail tradesman, who is perhaps entirely dependent on the neighbourhood immediately around him for success in his business, it would be matter of wonderment in the mind of any man conversant at all with the world and human nature, if, in some cases at least, the funds which such persons have the right of disposing of with impunity are not dispensed at the dictation of other motives than the desire of relieving the distressed; if partiality towards particular individuals is not frequently found directing the hand which holds the parish purse; and if the funds are not often bestowed from motives of self-interest, on most improper and undeserving objects belonging to the same religious society. I look upon the tradesman that fills the office of overseer as holding a place of temptation to serve his own interests, to show partiality to his own circle of favourites; and I am sure no man ever filled the office that was more just, upright, and impartial than the discretionary powers appended to the office would lead men acquainted with mankind and social life to suppose or expect him to be. I say this much from personal proofs of its operation on a tradesman, being myself a tradesman. When I served the office of overseer I was incessantly importuned by persons that I knew had no need of it for assistance, or a 'trifle', as they would say, or a pair of shoes, or some article of clothing, with this universally used argument in favour of their claim, 'I have *dealt* with you a many years, never lay out a farthing any where else, and I never *did* have anything from the parish; I *know* you can do it if you like, and it is nothing out of *your* pocket'; and they give pretty broad hints that if you do *not* comply with their requests, they will never lay out another farthing with *you*. I lost many customers by my non-compliance with their importunities, and I am certain that every overseer similarly situated must feel the same inconvenience which I felt. Sometimes persons on whom you are in some way dependent apply to you in behalf of some of *their* favourites, and you are placed in a very awkward predicament as to how to act. You do not wish to offend your friend, and you do not wish to do wrongfully with the parish money. Here stands the balance of the matter; which of the two impressions kick the beam? By adopting one plan, you wrong the parish, and are an unworthy steward; by adopting the other, you perhaps sacrifice your best prospects in life, and injure your family.

Lewes is divided into seven parishes. There are twenty-one overseers of all the different trades, and five poor-houses. The overseers are chosen from so low a class of petty tradesmen, that it is notorious that they use the balance of parish money in their hands to carry on their own businesses; being little removed above the paupers, they are not able to resist them, and there is the constant temptation to lavish relief supplied on the articles in which they deal. Jobbing of all sorts seems to prevail. Mechanics threaten to assault the officers if their demands are not acceded to. A select vestry has been tried in one parish; it was upset by the journeymen mechanics, who assembled in an overwhelming number; the same party objects to assistant overseers.

In Portsmouth there is no paid assistant. The overseers collect the rates. The situation, though of no emolument, is generally canvassed for by the tradesmen.

The present and late overseers of Great Grimsby stated that they were aware of the bad state of the parish, but offered, as an excuse, that they were all retail tradesmen, and dependent on the lower orders for the principal part of their custom; and that as they were totally unsupported by the authorities or the respectable part of the community, it might prove their ruin if they acted so as to acquire a character for harshness in the administration of the Poor Laws.

BREDE.

Population ... 1,046 | Rental ... £2,035 | Expenditure £2,606

The overseer says that most of the relief is altogether unnecessary, but he is convinced that, if an abatement were attempted, his life would not be safe; he looks to the farmers for support, which they dare not give, considering their lives and property would be in danger.

The tone assumed by the paupers towards those who dispense relief is generally very insolent, and often assumes even a more fearful character. At Great Gransden, the overseer's wife told me that, two days before my visit there, two paupers came to her husband demanding an increase of allowance; he refused them, showing at the same time that they had the full allowance sanctioned by the magistrates' scale;

they swore, and threatened he should repent of it; and such was their violence that she called them back and prevailed on her husband to make them further allowance. Mr Faircloth, by a stricter system of relief, and affording more employment, reduced the rates at Croydon; he became unpopular among the labourers, and after the harvest they gathered in a riotous body about his thrashing machine and broke it to pieces. At Guilden Morden, in the same neighbourhood, a burning took place of Mr Butterfield's stacks, to the amount of £1,500 damage. Mr Butterfield was overseer, and the magistrates have committed, on strong circumstantial evidence, a man to whom he had denied relief, because he refused to work for it. I have found, and it is not to be wondered at, that the apprehension of this dreadful and easily-perpetrated mischief has very generally affected the minds of the rural parish officers, making the power of the paupers over the funds provided for their relief almost absolute, as regards any discretion on the part of the overseer.

The overseers are chiefly farmers, and continue in office only during the time prescribed by law, being desirous of getting rid, as speedily as possible, of an office in which they are exposed to unceasing importunity, and live in constant terror of having the threats of violence, which are uttered against them by the discontented, carried into execution. The destruction of property by fire has now become so common, that where men want resolution to be the ministers of their own vengeance, wretches are to be found who, for a trifling reward, will execute it for them. The insurance offices have been obliged to use extreme caution in insuring the property of any one who has once suffered from fire, as it is evident that he must, in some way, have made himself obnoxious. Cases are to be met with where a farmer has been unable to renew his insurance. In consequence of this melancholy state of society in those parts of the country where fires have been frequent, instead of the well-stocked farm-yard, the farmer is obliged, in prudence, to place his stacks at a sufficient distance to prevent the fire from communicating, in order to diminish the loss to which every one is exposed.

Further evidence can scarcely be wanted; but if it is required it will be found in abundance in our Appendix. But if there were no such evidence, if the results of the experiment were not known, what could have been expected from functionaries almost always reluctant, unless indeed when their object is fraud; who neither come to their office with knowledge, nor retain it long enough to acquire knowledge; who have little time, and still less motive, for attention to its duties; on whom every temptation to misconduct has been accumulated; who have to give or to refuse public money to their own workmen, dependants, customers, debtors, relations, friends, and neighbours; who are exposed to every form of solicitation and threat; who are rewarded for profusion by ease and popularity, and punished for economy by labour, odium, and danger to their properties, and even their persons?

2

Assistant overseers

The 59 Geo. III, c. 12 [1818] authorized the appointment of paid and permanent overseers to act as the assistants of the annual overseers. It appears by the returns of 1831 that they were then employed by not less than 3,249 parishes. And the reports of the Assistant Commissioners are unanimous as to their general utility.

'I perceive no difference', says Mr Okeden, 'in the management of the poor in towns and villages, except that where there is an assistant overseer the management is the best.'

'Considerable saving', says Mr Maclean, 'has been effected in those parishes which have adopted the plan of paying and retaining permanently, though subject to annual re-election, an assistant overseer. I have invariably found these persons very intelligent, zealous, and, when properly encouraged and looked after, useful and economical to a parish.'

Captain Chapman states that in the district investigated by him (Cornwall, Devonshire, and parts of Somersetshire and Wiltshire):

Assistant overseers had been appointed in most of the larger parishes, and were found so much superior to the annual overseer as to be much on the increase. I only met with one instance in which the assistant overseer has been discontinued, viz., at Ashburton, where there had been great want of unanimity among the rate-payers; and the select vestry had also been discontinued, after having been adopted many years. The result was stated to be great difficulty in finding persons qualified to act as overseers, and an immediate increase in the poor-rate.

Two instances came under my notice in large towns, where the assistant overseers had been suspected of embezzlement, and removed;

but they had been replaced by others, and thus gave proof of the conviction of the parishioners of the superiority of the paid over the annual overseer.

Some instances occurred, in which the assistant overseers had received the thanks of the vestry for their exertions; and a few, in which they had received a gratuity in addition to their salaries.

The assistant overseers were invariably intelligent, attentive, zealous, possessing great knowledge of the laws, and thus preventing litigation and saving expense. I found them frequently made the referee and oracle by ordinary overseers of the surrounding parishes. In St Austell and Exeter this was strikingly brought before me; on market-days the overseers apply in every difficulty to the assistant overseer at St Austell, and in the same manner to the assistant treasurer in Exeter. Their efficiency, activity, and intelligence, when compared with those of the annual overseer, were so superior as to lead one to consider the introduction of the paid overseer the greatest improvement in the management of the poor, and that its universal adoption is one of the first steps towards any important amendment.

A similar opinion as to the necessity of appointing a paid overseer is expressed by Mr Codd, by Messrs Cameron and Wrottesley, Mr Majendie, Mr Power, Mr Moylan, Captain Pringle, Mr Stuart, Mr Richardson, Mr Tweedy, Mr Everett, Mr Lewis, Mr Walcott.

It is to be observed, however, that under the statute, the adoption, the nomination, the continuance, and the salary of an assistant overseer depend on the vestry, and that the vestry, not the law, is 'to determine and specify the duties to be by him executed and performed'. A more perfect state of subserviency can scarcely exist. Whatever may be the vigilance and impartiality of an officer so appointed and paid, he cannot prevent the grossest extravagance or jobbing on the part of those who are in fact his masters, the vestry and the annual overseers; he may refuse his aid, but cannot interpose the slightest resistance. No refusal on his part can indeed be expected; it must be made at the risk of his place, and for the purpose of diminishing rates to which his contribution, if he contribute at all, must be trifling; nor could a profuse or corrupt vestry find any difficulty in selecting a willing instrument for their purposes. The testimonies which we have cited in favour of the assistant overseers, prove, however, that this is seldom the case; and it probably may be accounted for by the circumstance, that in the worst parishes an assistant overseer is not appointed. The adoption of such an officer may generally be considered a symptom of a desire, on the part of the rate-payers, for improvement. It follows, indeed, that those parishes in which the services of a strict and uncorrupt officer are most wanted are precisely those in which such an officer is the least likely to be appointed or continued. This is the necessary imperfection of the permissive legislation of the 59 Geo. III, a statute which appears, from all our inquiries, to have been so useful where it has been adopted, that we cannot but regret that its adoption should depend on the will of a body so constituted as a vestry.

II
VESTRIES

VESTRIES are either open, composed of all the rate-payers who choose to attend; or representative, appointed by virtue of a local Act, or under the 59 Geo. III, c. 12 [1818]; or self-appointed, either by prescription or a local Act.

1
Open vestries

The legal powers of an open vestry are subject to the doubt and obscurity which seem to be peculiarly attendant on our Poor-Law legislation. The 43 Elizabeth [1601] vests the whole power and imposes the whole responsibility on the overseers; and though the 3 & 4 Will. & Mary, c. 11, s. 11 [1692], by directing the parishioners to meet yearly in vestry, in order to make a list of the persons whom *they* shall *allow* to receive collection, and the 9 Geo. I, c. 7, s. 1 [1723], by forbidding a justice to order relief until oath has been made by the pauper that he has applied to the parishioners, assembled in vestry, or to two of the overseers, and has been refused, appear to imply in the vestry an authority as to giving and refusing relief equal or even superior to that of the overseer; yet as these Statutes do not sanction the overseers in giving the relief which has been ordered by the vestry, or indemnify them for refusing what the vestry will not allow, and as they give to the vestry no power either to raise or to distribute the parochial funds, it is very difficult to say what is the legal authority as to matters of relief of an open vestry, or whether such a body has now in fact, on such matters, any legal authority at all. It appears, however, both from the reports of the Assistant Commissioners and from the answers to numbers 33, 34, and 35 of the printed queries, that almost everywhere the practical influence of the vestry is very great; that it forms, in fact, the ruling authority of the parish, a sort of council of government, of which the overseers are members, and generally the most influential members, but voting among the others and submitting to be controlled by the majority.

The vestry consists exclusively of the rate-payers, that is, of the actual occupiers of lands and houses; the owner, unless an occupier, not having, except in the few cases in which he is rated under the 59 Geo. III, c. 12 [1818], a right even to be present. If we were now framing a system of Poor Laws, and it were proposed that a great part of the principal contributors to the fund for the relief of the poor should be excluded from all share in its management, and even from all power of objecting to its administration, and that the control should vest in an irresponsible body, many of whom should have little interest on its permanent diminution, what jobbing profusion and malversation would be anticipated from such an arrangement! But such is the existing system. We have seen how slight, in ordinary cases, is the interest of the majority of the rate-payers in the permanent reduction of rates. And yet this check, such as it is, is the only one to which vestries are subject. In every other respect they form the most irresponsible bodies that ever were entrusted with the performance of public duties, or the distribution of public money. They render no account; no record need be kept of the names of the persons present, or of their speeches or their votes; they are not amenable, whatever be the profusion or malversation which they have sanctioned, or ordered, or turned to their own advantage. On the other hand, they have all the motives for maladministration which we have ascribed to the overseers. Each vestryman, so far as he is an immediate employer of labour, is interested in keeping down the rate of wages, and in throwing part of their payment on others, and, above all on the principal object of parochial fraud, the tithe-owner; if he is the owner of cottages, he endeavours to get their rent paid by the parish; if he keeps a shop, he struggles to get allowance for his customers or debtors; if he deals in articles used in the workhouse, he tries to increase the workhouse consumption; if he is in humble circumstances, his own relations or friends may be among the applicants; and, since the unhappy events of 1830, he feels that any attempt to reduce the parochial expenditure may endanger his property and person.

We shall proceed to illustrate these views by some passages from the evidence contained in the Appendix. Mr Majendie states generally, in the outset of his report from East Sussex, East Surrey, Kent, and Essex, that the bad constitution of parish vestries, particularly when in the hands of small farmers, where there is no resident proprietor, and where the clergyman takes no part, seems to be the cause of the bad condition of the worst parishes which he visited. Among the parishes, the state of which confirms this remark, are:

Lindfield, in which the 'Jobbing in the supply of the workhouse was once carried to the fullest extent. The farmers sent in all the different articles, corn, pork, fuel, &c., and charged their own price; they sent favourite labourers for relief, which was paid to them in produce; they hired cottages with their farms, and underlet them to their labourers at £6 and £7, which was paid out of the parish purse; thus some farmers – what with rents and the supply of the workhouse – paid all their rates, and had money besides to receive from the parish; high rates furnished an irresistible argument against the rents of the proprietor, who, if absent himself, and not represented by an agent, his own tenant acting in collusion against him, found his property wasted away by a conspiracy which he had no means of detecting. A gentleman of considerable estate, with the assistance of an occupier who was a man of education and intelligence, determined to put a stop to this: they attended every vestry; they cleared off the debts, and reduced the rates from 15s. to 6s. 6d. in the pound.

Marden, formerly one of the most prosperous parishes in Kent, in which the rates are now more than £2 per head on the whole population, being about four times the average expenditure throughout England, in consequence of the opposition to tithes on the part of the farmers, and their determination to throw on the lessee of the great tithes part of the payment of wages; and Great Hawkesley, in which, while a dispute concerning tithes continued, the rates amounted to £1,800 a year, a principal farmer hired the tithes, and made an arrangement with the occupiers, and they then fell to £1,000.

'Sometimes', says Mr Power,

we shall find the lessee of a term, or the small capitalist, ground to the earth by the immediate pressure of the rates and bearing, perhaps, more than his share of the parochial ruin, complaining, but helpless; and sometimes we shall find the substantial farmer, though paying enormous sums yearly in the support of a stagnant labouring population around him, apparently indifferent (particularly when a yearly tenant) to that circumstance, and seeming, in fact, to feel that he finds his account in the Poor Laws and their mischievous operation. He views the poor-rates in the light of a deduction from his rent, and usually he has good grounds for that consideration; and in estimating the amount of that deduction, it is seldom taken into account by a considerate landlord that a supply of cheap labour, expeditious harvests, excellent roads, and other advantages are derived by the farmer from the very source in respect of which he claims his deduction. Accordingly, we hear this class of persons constantly complaining, not of the poor-rates, but of the insufficient price of corn; they would pay their poor-rates with pleasure, they say, and their rent too, could they only get a fair price for their wheat; and I believe them. But little interest or exertion in reduction of the rates can be expected from such a class of persons when administering relief.

Captain Pringle states that:

The persons who sway the vestries would, from what I have observed in many instances, be averse to any measures that would render the labourer independent of parish assistance, which, by keeping him to its confines, retains him always at their command when wanted for urgent work.

In nearly all the agricultural parishes it will be found that by indirect modes the householders pay a portion of the wages of farm labourers;

clothes, shoes, payment of rents, allowances for children, are, when such subjects are brought forward in vestries, not allowed to be a payment of wages; and I have heard it observed. Why should the farmers keep their labourers all the year, to save the gentlemen and householders from poor-rates?

Mr Stuart states that:

The small size of the parishes in Suffolk renders the administration of the poor fund by the parochial authorities liable to many abuses, and to much individual hardship. The administration being vested almost exclusively in those who are the sole employers of labour, offers temptations to them to pervert it to their own advantage, by making it an instrument for reducing wages, or throwing part of that charge off their own shoulders on others. As each parish forms a small and separate society, the paupers are able to urge their demands with more frequency and violence on their immediate neighbours, which subjects the parish officers to the influence of fear or favouritism. When a farmer is about to quit his occupation, he gives the least possible cultivation to the land, which throws the men usually employed on the farm on the parish for support, to the loss of those who are to remain. When any individual chooses to quarrel with the parson, he gratifies his spite by having the tithes rated, and then pays off all his labourers who have settlements in the parish, and hires men from other parishes, for the purpose of being revenged by the heavy contribution which will fall on the parson, although it is to his own hurt and that of all his neighbours. I visited a parish in which one or two farmers conspired together in this way, in order to force the clergyman to abate his tithes, although his demand was considered reasonable by the majority of the occupiers. The dispute was accommodated within six months by the mediation of the principal landlord, but it cost the parish an extra 2s. 6d. rate, which the clergyman paid for those who did not enter into the conspiracy. In another parish, where a similar state of things had existed for a series of years (owing to the spite of the principal farmers), after the parties had nearly ruined each other, they came to terms, and the expenditure fell from a fluctuating amount of from £700 to £1,000 a year, to from £350 to £400.

And he adds, on the other hand,

That in the large parishes it is seldom that a sufficient unanimity exists in the vestry meetings to enable them to form any plan which may promote the general welfare of the parish. There are so many petty and conflicting interests to be accommodated that these meetings are scenes of angry contention and violent debate, which end in nothing and disgust the respectable portion of the inhabitants, who resign themselves to endure the evils which they cannot cure. The occupier being the direct payer of the rates, he imagines that they ought to be entirely under his dominion, and views with jealousy the interference of any other party; as, however, they ultimately fall on the proprietor and are often used as an argument for a reduction of rent, it seems but just that the landlord should be admitted to some control over them. In my attempts to ascertain the causes of the difference of expenditure in one part of the country, as compared with another, it has frequently been assigned to me as one reason that many of the occupiers of land being proprietors as well, it was quite contrary to their interests to allow the corruption which prevailed where the tenant has an unlimited control. I have been told that meetings of vestry have been held when the rates have been diminishing for the purpose of considering whether they were not getting too low.

'The members of vestries', says Captain Chapman,

in the rural parishes generally, consisted of farmers and tradesmen, on whom, in consequence of the diminished number of resident gentry, the administration of the Poor Laws devolves more and more, in proportion as the Continent and cities absorb the more educated classes. A great proportion of the rate-payers, and those who take an active part in the vestry, are persons who have only a temporary interest in the parish, and who are thus naturally averse to incur any extra expense from which they might not receive benefit, although productive of great ultimate good. In most parishes there are also a proportion to whom the poor-rate is a convenience who employ the smallest possible number of steady labourers, and depend upon the parish to supply the additional demand which they require periodically.

'Where everybody', says Mr Everett,

complains of the amount and burthen of the poor-rates, it might be expected that any plan which promised with any chance of success to diminish the burthen, only require to be known to be adopted. In practice, however, it is found to be otherwise; and those parishes which are the most heavily burthened are generally the least ready to listen to any suggestions for improving their condition, or to adopt any different system of management from the one they have been accustomed to. It cannot fail to be remarked, however, that in those parishes in which the poor-rates have been reduced under an improved system of management, the new system has originated either with the clergyman or some resident proprietor of the parish, and not with the tenants or principal rate-payers, who are frequently the greatest opponents of any change of management. In most agricultural parishes the entire management of the poor is entrusted to those of the farmers who are the principal occupiers of the land, and whose interest in the parish, and consequently in the poor-rates, is limited by the probable duration of their tenancy, and who, though the largest immediate payers of the rates, are no more the ultimate payers of these impost than they are of tithes. It cannot be wondered at the measures for reducing the amount of the poor-rates, which have been tried with success in particular parishes, and which in all probability would be attended with the desired effect in other parishes similarly situated, are not more frequently adopted, if it is a fact that the persons who have the control of the expenditure of the poor-rates have not only not the greatest, but no material interests in the reduction.

'I shall not here attempt', says Mr Day,

to investigate how far the magistrates have merited the censures that have been bestowed upon them: but I will take upon myself to say that whatever blame attaches (and much somewhere, I fear, there is) is to be visited in at least equal degrees on parish officers and parish vestries. I was present at a vestry where a material alteration in the management of the parish was proposed. It met, as I had anticipated, with opposition, and an extended discussion ensued. In the course of it a friend of mine, a magistrate of considerable experience, and also a practical farmer, said to one of the principal renting occupiers in the parish, 'Why, Mr Spencer, you know perfectly well, as a man of business, if you will have the candour to avow it, that the tenantry are interested in *high nominal expenditure.*' To my surprise he did avow it, and replied, 'I admit, sir, that is perfectly true.' In short, both from my own experience, and from what I have known in other instances, I am satisfied in the long run that however an individual may succeed in stemming pauperism for a time, he will generally ultimately be beaten. There are few who will long endure the bear-garden of a parish vestry. And to point out one amongst many of the motives that influence these meetings, I shall mention only two parishes in this county, Hurstmonceux and Pulborough, where the whole labour has been thrown upon the rates, for the *avowed* purpose of fighting the parson.

The whole subject is explained, with the clearness and force which are to be found only when a witness is detailing the results of his own experience, in the following evidence:

Examination of Mr John Mann of Eastbourne.

How long have you been a parishioner of this parish? – I have lived in this parish thirty-five years, and I have been a member of the select vestry fourteen years.

Have you been a frequent attendant at the vestry? – I very seldom miss attending.

How long have you farmed land in the parish? – About twenty years.

Of whom do you hold your land? – The land which I farm is my own.

Of what class are the majority of persons attending the vestry? – Chiefly the smaller farmers. A few tradesmen do attend occasionally.

Do any of the landowners or of the gentry attend? – No. Now and then a steward will attend.

Would the attendance of the proprietors be liked by the small farmers? – No; I am convinced that it would not be liked by the farmers.

Are you, from your habits of intercourse with the farmers of this district, well acquainted with their sentiments? – Yes, I am.

To what do you ascribe the fact, if fact it be, that the attempts to procure additional labour for the paupers in this parish, and to obtain a more efficient management and a considerable reduction of the poor's rates, have been generally coldly received or thwarted, or openly opposed and defeated? Take time to consider your answer – I know that the farmers would sooner have high rates and low rents, than high rents and low rates; that, I believe, is the general feeling. The farmers like that their men should be paid from the poor-book.

If the farmers had the option of paying 75 per cent in poor's rates, and 25 per cent in rent, or 75 per cent in rent and 25 per cent in poor's rates, which do you believe they would prefer? – The low rents and the high rates, undoubtedly.

Have you ever heard them state this sentiment openly? – Yes, openly in the vestry.

Have you heard them declare this since 1830? – Yes, and before that time too.

How low do you think the farmers would be willing to have the rates reduced? – I do not believe they would be willing or care much to have them reduced much more than they have been; the great farmers in particular I do not think want them reduced. Whilst the rates are as they are, they can always get what hands they want extra, and as soon as it rains they can turn them all on to the parish again;

and besides that, they can make the shopkeepers, the lodging-house keepers, and other persons pay a proportion of the wages of the men they turn off. Sometimes they have taken men off the parish for half a day, and have made the parish pay for the other half of the day.

Do the farmers consider that they have a permanent interest in the land? – No: there they have not; they hold mostly from year to year, and hardly consider themselves as more than birds of passage.

Do they not see, as a result of this system, the total pauperization of the whole of the labouring population, and the total destruction of all property, unless some strong measures be taken to save it? – They feel no danger; as soon as they find that they are losing money, they can go. I have no doubt this is their feeling. Their whole course of conduct shows it, though they do not express as much.

2

Representative vestries

The 59 George III, c. 12, s. 1 [1818], authorizes the inhabitants of any parish, in vestry assembled, to elect not more than twenty or less than five substantial householders, who, together with the minister, churchwardens, and overseers, after having been appointed by a magistrate, are to form the select vestry of the parish; they are directed to meet every fourteen days, or oftener, and to inquire into and determine the proper objects of relief, and the nature and amount of the relief to be given. The overseers are desired to conform to their directions; and where such a vestry exists, the magistrates are forbidden to order relief until it has been proved to the satisfaction of two justices that the applicant is in want, and has been refused adequate relief by the select vestry, or that the select vestry has not assembled as directed by the act. 'Provided always', adds the act, in its usual spirit of qualification, 'that it shall be lawful for any justice to make an order for relief in any case of urgent necessity to be specified in such order.' A subsequent clause directs them to keep minutes of their proceedings, which are to be laid before all the inhabitants in general vestry assembled, twice in every year.

The act seems to be deficient in not defining the relative powers of the select vestry and the overseers. Though the overseers are directed to conform to the directions of the vestry, yet if they refuse, as is sometimes the case, the vestry appears to have no power of compelling their obedience. The attendance of the different members is purely voluntary, and the act does not expressly require it to be recorded; and there appears reason to suspect that the frequency of the meetings directed by the act (once every fourteen days or oftener) is in some places injurious. The return from Shenley, Herts., to question 33 of the rural queries, states that 'The select vestry, being bound to meet too often, has been abolished. It worked well for some years; then attendance grew remiss, except by a very few. It was a call to paupers from an ale-house for relief. The monthly vestry suffices.'

'It was a very general opinion', says Captain Chapman, 'that frequent meetings of the vestry only tended to encourage applications, and to increase dependence on the poor-rate. In St Thomas the Apostle, which is under Gilbert's Act, the vestry meets only monthly; and the experiment has been tried of occasionally omitting to do so, and was found to diminish the number of applicants.'

In South Petherwin the select vestry meets every fortnight; but it was thought there would be less pauperism if it met once a month, as a number of idle and worthless people always attend, whether they want anything or not, on the chance of getting something. In proof of this, it had been found that the demand for clothing, which was issued every fortnight, was materially on the increase; the vestry limited such applications to a quarterly meeting; the demand diminished; and there was a saving of full £50 per annum, or one third of the expenditure. The vestry meets at two o'clock, which was considered a very important arrangement, not only as regards the poor, but the members of the vestry. When they met at five o'clock in the evening, it was a scene of noise and confusion; those within, noisy and quarrelsome, those without, rebellious and insubordinate.

Notwithstanding these defects, we feel bound by the general result of our evidence to express our concurrence in the third Resolution of the House of Commons' Committee on Vestries, 'That the Acts under which the rate-payers are empowered to elect a committee for the management of their parochial concerns, have proved highly beneficial.' But after admitting the superiority of select over open vestries, we are inclined to believe that that superiority arises principally from their comparative freedom from magisterial interference, the presence of the clergyman, and the regular minutes kept of their proceedings. They are selected from the same persons who form the open vestry, and are subject, therefore, to the same corrupting influences. They are equally free from responsibility for the abuses which they may have permitted or continued, or even introduced. The act gives no remedy against them, and it would be absurd to suppose that they could be checked by the fear of not being re-elected to a gratuitous, troublesome, and invidious office. In fact, when we consider the constituency by which they are elected, it appears probable that a profuse or mischievously directed administration must often be what that constituency would approve, and that attempts to prevent the payments of wages out of rates, to rate cottages, or even to prevent the parish from being surety to the cottage landlord, to reduce the allowances of the customers to the village shop or the beer-house, to diminish the profit arising from the workhouse expenditure, or to incure any present expenditure for future purposes, must in many places expose a select vestryman to immediate unpopularity, and ultimately prevent his re-election. In places where a constituency, actuated by such motive, predominates, a select vestry, though it may be an improvement, is not likely to be a great improvement over an open one.

Mr Wilson has furnished a list of the select vestry of Morpeth in 1832. Out of the twenty persons composing it, one is a brewer, two are brewers' clerks, five are publicans, two beer-shop keepers, and one a porter-seller; so that eleven, or the majority of the whole number, are interested in the sale of beer; and the mother of one, the wife of another, and the uncle, aunt, and cousins of a third are paupers. We cannot wonder to find it stated that the better class of vestrymen retired in disgust from the interested clamour of their colleagues. It appears from Mr Power's report, that a similarly constituted body was elected at St Andrew-the-less, Cambridge, where the small rate-payers assembled in great numbers, called a low mechanic to the chair, and nominated persons whose appointment the magistrates refused to sign. More frequently, however, where the small rate-payers form the majority in value, the open vestry refuses to appoint a representative body. Such has been the case at Knaresborough, at Lewes, and in other places mentioned in the reports. On the other hand, where the majority in value is composed of any class having a peculiar interest, they have the power of forming themselves into a select vestry for the purpose of favouring that interest. Mr Majendie states that at Eastbourne, to the condition of which we have had so often to refer, the farmers constitute the select vestry, and are often tenants-at-will.

The following extract from Mr Maclean's report from Surrey and Sussex gives a general view of the difficulties which in that district oppose the introduction or continuance, and diminish the utility, of the representative vestries.

In many parishes the system of a select vestry has, after an experiment of a year or two, or sometimes of a few months, been abandoned; and the cause of their being so is not to be ascribed so much to any defect in themselves, or in the Act under which they are established, as to the remissness of the members in their attendance. Many were abandoned at the time of the riotous proceedings in the winter of 1830–31, when the lawless and outrageous meetings of the agricultural labourers, and in some instances their attacks upon the vestry, produced an intimidation and fear of consequences which paralysed the exertions of some, and disinclined other members to incur the odium, or expose themselves to the vengeance openly threatened against the persons or property of those whom the rioters chose to consider active in the administration of the parochial funds.

The unpopularity of an extra rate, or of any unavoidable expense, is visited upon the heads of the members of the select vestry; and as these increase with the distress of the parish, the accumulated odium disgusts and drives from their offices, and generally from an interference in parochial matters, those who, from situation, time, or intelligence, are best calculated to inquire into the condition and relieve the wants of the poor.

In other places select vestries became unpopular, as their establishment, and their being in the hands of the higher class of rate-payers, cut off from many those opportunities for jobbing and favouritism which had been considered in some degree a return for the amount paid by them in rate, and had been justified by usage.

After the determination of a select, and a return to an open vestry, I invariably found the latter state of the parish which had made the exchange worse than the former. The causes of the discontinuance of a select vestry being as stated above, the consequence is obvious, i.e. a withdrawal on the part of all the respectable rate-payers of their time and attention from the concerns of the parish, and a triumphant recurrence to the old and pernicious system, which has been abandoned on account of its glaring abuses, and inadequacy to do justice between those who pay, and those who receive the rates.

In the parish of Epsom a select vestry was established in 1823, which has continued down to the present year; and very material advantage has arisen to the inhabitants, both from the reduction which was effected in the scale of expenditure, the number of applications to the parish, and the general conduct of the town-class of parishioners. This year, however, in their report, the select vestry express, as their 'decided opinion, which every year's experience has strengthened, that the select vestry system is the best possible mode of conducting the management of the poor and the poor-rates; but, at the same time, they consider that from want of support from the parishioners, an efficient select vestry cannot be formed.'

We regret to add, that the general result of these causes has been to diminish the number of select vestries, and that in an increasing ratio. The number for the last six years stands thus:

In the year 1827	...	...	...	...	2,868
1828	...	...	...	...	2,823
1829	...	...	...	...	2,736
1830	...	...	...	...	2,725
1831	...	...	...	...	2,535
1832	...	...	...	...	2,391

3
Self-appointed vestries

The worst constituted vestries appear, as might be expected, to be those which are self-elected. Some of them are exposed to all the temptations to misconduct which affect open or representative vestries, and all are free from the control, such as it is, of a constituency; their maladministration also, whether arising from error or corruption, is more likely to become permanent. The system of an open or a representative vestry is always liable to exposure and interruption from new members, whose interests, or opinions, or principles prevent their sanctioning the existing abuses; but in a self-elected body, abuses are apt to become settled traditionary rules; all candidates who are supposed to be opposed to them being carefully rejected. It is a great misfortune that the same name, that of select vestries, has been applied both to representative and to self-constituted vestries, and that the adoption of the former is often prevented by the odium which not unjustly adheres to the latter. Both are, in fact, select vestries; but the difference in the modes of selection occasions representative vestries to be beneficial, and self-elected vestries to be mischievous.

III

MAGISTRATES

WE have seen that the early statutes of Elizabeth gave extensive powers to the justices. The 5 Elizabeth [1563] enabled them to tax an obstinate person according to their good discretion. The 14 Elizabeth [1572] directed them to select the objects of relief, to tax all the inhabitants in their divisions, and to appoint collectors to make delivery of the contributions according to the discretion of the justices. This discretionary power, however, did not long continue. The 39 Elizabeth, c. 3 [1597], and the 43 Elizabeth, c. 2 [1601], which in this respect, as in most others, merely repeats the 39 Elizabeth, after having directed the justices to appoint overseers, impose on the overseers the whole business of raising and distributing relief, and give to the justices no further authority than that which is implied by the direction that the overseers, in certain parts of their duty shall, act 'by and with the consent of two or more justices': a direction which appears to give to the justices only a negative authority – an authority to forbid, but not to command. Nearly a century elapsed before their power was enlarged; and it may be a question whether the 3 and 4 Will. and Mary, c. 11 [1692], which is the foundation of their present power to order relief, was intended to produce any such result. The object of that statute was to check parochial profusion. It recites, in words which we might now adopt as a part of this Report,

That many inconveniences do daily arise by reason of the unlimited power of the overseers, who do frequently, upon frivolous pretences, but chiefly for their own private ends, give relief to what persons and number they think fit; which persons being entered on the collection bill, become a great charge on the parish, notwithstanding the occasion or pretence of their receiving collection often ceases, by which means the rates are daily increased, contrary to the true intent of the Statute made in the 43d year of the reign of Her Majesty Queen Elizabeth, intituled 'An Act for the Relief of the Poor.'

'For remedy of which, and for preventing like abuses in future', it enacts,

That books be kept in every parish wherein the names of all such persons as receive collection shall be registered, with the day when they were first admitted to have relief, and the occasion which brought them under that *necessity*; and that yearly, in Easter week, the parishioners shall meet in vestry, before whom the book shall be produced; and all persons receiving collection called over, and the reasons for their taking relief examined; and a new list made of such persons as *they* shall think fit to *allow* to receive collection; and that no other person shall receive collection, but by *authority* under the hand of one justice of peace residing within such parish, or if none be there dwelling, in the parts near or next adjoining, or by *order* of the justices in quarter-sessions, except in cases of pestilential disease.

If the framers of the act had intended to make in the law the enormous change which these few words 'but by the authority under the hand of one justice' effected, if they had intended to vest in a single justice not necessarily resident within the parish, or acquainted with its concerns, the power to order the overseer to distribute, as the justice might think fit, the property of the rate-payers, it can scarcely be supposed that they would have introduced an enactment of such importance by way of exception at the end of a clause, or prefixed to it so irrelevant a preamble. The real meaning of these words seems to have been the same as that of the similar words in the 43 Elizabeth (the statute to which the 3 William and Mary had previously referred), 'by and with the consent of two justices'. The overseers were not to relieve any but those whom the vestry had thought fit to allow to receive collection, except under the authority of a justice, that is, when authorized by him. The act gives a single justice no power to do more than to sanction the conduct of the overseer; to protect him in

acting, but not, according even to the words, and much less according to the spirit, to order him to act. The power to *order* is given
to the justices in quarter-sessions, and to them alone. This construction appears to us to be supported by the 8 and 9 Will. c.
30 [1697]; that act, 'To the end that the money raised *only for the
relief of such as are as well impotent as poor*, may not be misapplied and
consumed by the idle, sturdy, and disorderly beggars', enacts that

every person, who, after the 1st September, 1697, shall be upon the
collection, and receive relief of any parish, and the wife and children
of any such person cohabiting in the same house, (such child only
excepted as shall be *by the churchwardens and overseers of the poor permitted to live at home,* in order to have the care of and attend an impotent and helpless parent), shall wear on the shoulder a large roman P,
together with the first letter of the name of the parish whereof such
person is an inhabitant; and if such person neglect or refuse, it shall be
lawful for any justice of the county, city, or liberty where such offence
shall be committed, to punish such offender by ordering his or her
relief, or usual allowance, or the collection, to be abridged, suspended,
or withdrawn.

It will be observed that the act considers the question whether
the child of a pauper shall or shall not be permitted to live at home
as a question to be decided by the overseers, and that the power
which it gives to the justice is to order not that relief shall be given,
but that it shall be abridged, suspended, or withdrawn. But though
this seems to be the natural interpretation of the 3 Will. and Mary,
c. 11, a different construction was applied to it. This appears
from the preamble of the next Act on the subject, the 9 Geo. I,
c. 7 [1723]; that act recites,

That under colour of the proviso in the 3 and 4 Will. and Mary, many
persons have applied to some justices of peace, without the knowledge
of any officers of the parish, and thereby upon untrue suggestions, and
sometimes upon false or frivolous pretences, have obtained relief which
hath greatly contributed to the increase of the parish rates. [For remedy
whereof it enacts:] That no justice of the peace shall order relief to
any poor person until oath be made before such justice of some matter,
which he shall judge to be a reasonable cause or ground for having
such relief, and that the same person had, by himself or some other,
applied for relief to the parishioners of the parish, at some vestry or

other public meeting of the said parishioners, or to two of the overseers of the poor of such parish, and was by them refused to be relieved, and until such justice hath summoned two of the overseers of
the poor to show cause why such relief should not be given, and the
person so summoned hath been heard or made default to appear before
such justice. [And, further] that the person whom any such justice
of peace shall think fit to order to be relieved, shall be entered in such
book or books so to be kept by the parish, as one of those who is to
receive collection, as long as the cause for such relief continues, and
no longer.

The history of the Poor Laws abounds with instances of a
legislation which has been worse than unsuccessful, which has
not merely failed in effecting its purposes, but has been active in
producing effects which were directly opposed to them, has
created whatever it was intended to prevent, and fostered whatever it was intended to discourage. Thus the 3 and 4 Will. and
Mary, which was passed to check the profusion of overseers, to
enable the parishioners to decide whom *they* should think fit
and *allow* to receive relief, was construed as authorizing the justices
to order relief to those who applied to them without the knowledge of the parish officers; and the act which was passed to remedy
this abuse enabled the justice, on the pauper's statement of some
matter which the justice should judge to be a reasonable cause or
ground for relief, to summon the overseers to show cause why relief
should not be given, and to order such relief as *he* should think fit.
An order against which there is no appeal.

One clause in the 9 Geo. I was, however, efficient in promoting
the objects of the act – that which enabled parishes to purchase
or hire, or unite in purchasing or hiring, a workhouse, and to
contract for the maintenance there of their poor, and enacted that
any persons who should refuse to be lodged in such houses should
not be entitled to receive collection or relief. An enactment which,
while it was in operation, appears to have checked the increase of
pauperism, and in many instances to have occasioned its positive
diminution.

But towards the end of the last century, a period arrived when
the accidents of the seasons and other causes occasioned a rise in
the price of the necessaries of life. If things had been left to take

their course, the consequences in England would have been what they were in Scotland, and what they were with us in those occupations which, from their requiring skill, raise the workman above the region of parish relief. Wages would have risen to meet the depreciation of money, and the labourer would have earned the same or nearly the same amount of raw produce, and a larger amount of manufactured commodities.

But things were not left to take their own course. Unhappily no knowledge is so rare as the knowledge when to do nothing. It requires an acquaintance with general principles, a confidence in their truth, and a patience of the gradual process by which obstacles are steadily but slowly surmounted, which are among the last acquisitions of political science and experience. Under the 3 and 4 Will. and Mary, and the 9 Geo. I, or under the 5 Eliz. c. 4, empowering the justices to fix the rate of wages, it appeared that the existing difficulties might be instantly got rid of. The latter statute appeared to enable a forced rise of wages, the former statutes appeared to enable relief to be ordered if wages should remain insufficient. Each plan was proposed. Sir Frederic Eden's account of the mode in which the latter plan was adopted is so instructive, that we will venture to quote it.

Instead of an advance in wages, proportioned to the increased demand for labour, the labourer has received a considerable part of that portion of his employer's capital which was destined for his maintenance, in the form of poor's rate (the very worst that it could assume), instead of being paid it as the fair, well earned recompense of equivalent labour. This is a deplorable evil, which has fallen heavier on the poor than on the rich; and it has been considerably aggravated by the very injudicious steps which have been adopted for administering relief to those whom the pressure of the late scarcity had incapacitated from supporting themselves and families in the way to which they had been accustomed. Many instances might be adduced of the ill effects of the indiscriminating charity of individuals, and of the no less ill effects of the discriminating interference of magistrates and parish officers; but, that I may not swell this work to too great a length, I shall content myself with offering a short statement (which was obligingly communicated to me by a gentleman who himself served the office of overseer in his own parish) of the proceedings which took place in a single county, for the relief of the poor last year.

The very great price of the necessaries of life, but more particularly of bread-corn, during the whole of last year, produced numberless extraordinary demands for parochial assistance. In many parishes in the county of Berks., relief from the poor's rates was granted, not only to the infirm and impotent, but to the able-bodied and industrious, who had very few of them ever applied to the parish for relief, and then only during temporary illness or disability. There was no doubt but that the circumstances of the times required an increase in the income of the labourers in husbandry, who, in this country at least, compose the most numerous body of those liable to want assistance from the parish. But there existed a difference of opinion respecting the mode of making such increase. In order to apply some adequate remedy to the evil, a meeting of the magistrates for the county was held about Easter, 1795, when the following plans were submitted to their consideration:

First, that the magistrates should fix the lowest price to be given for labour, as they were empowered to do by 5 Eliz. c. 4; and secondly, that they should act with uniformity in the relief of the impotent and infirm poor, by a table of universal practice, corresponding with the supposed necessities of each family. The first plan was rejected, by a considerable majority, but the second was adopted, and the following table was published as the rule for the information of magistrates and overseers:

Had political regulations not interfered, the demand for labour would have raised its price, not only in a ratio merely adequate to the wants of the labourer, but even beyond it; and that price would have been advanced by the individual who employed him, instead of being a general tax on those who are liable to be rated, and who are not all employers of labourers. The capital which employs labour has increased; the demand of labour would consequently increase; it did increase, for the situation of the labouring poor in Berks. was never better than during the last hard winter; but they received these advanced wages in the way most prejudicial to their moral interests; they received it as charity, as the extorted charity of others, and not as the result of their own well-exerted industry; and it was paid them, not by their immediate employers, but by those who were, in many instances, not the employers of any labour.

We directed our Assistant Commissioners to inquire in every parish in which they found the relief of the able-bodied existing, at what period, and from what causes, it was supposed to have

This shows, at one view, what should be the weekly income of the industrious poor, as settled by the Magistrates for the county of Berks., at a meeting held at Speenhamland, 6 May 1795.

When the gallon loaf is	Income should be for a man.	For a single woman.	For a man and his wife.	With one child.	With two children.	With three children.	With four children.	With five children.	With six children.	With seven children.
s. d.	s. d.	s. d.	s. d.	s. d.	s. d.	s. d.	s. d.	s. d.	s. d.	s. d.
1 0	3 0	2 0	4 6	6 0	7 6	9 0	10 6	12 0	13 6	15 0
1 1	3 3	2 1	4 10	6 5	8 0	9 7	11 2	12 9	14 4	15 11
1 2	3 6	2 2	5 2	6 10	8 6	10 2	11 10	13 6	15 2	16 10
1 3	3 9	2 3	5 6	7 3	9 0	10 9	12 6	14 3	16 0	17 9
1 4	4 0	2 4	5 10	7 8	9 6	11 4	13 2	15 0	16 10	18 8
1 5	4 0	2 5	5 11	7 10	9 9	11 8	13 7	15 6	17 5	19 4
1 6	4 0	2 6	6 3	8 5	10 3	12 3	14 3	16 3	18 3	20 3
1 7	4 3	2 7	6 4	8 10	10 6	12 7	14 8	16 9	18 10	20 11
1 8	4 6	2 8	6 8	8 3	11 0	13 2	15 4	17 6	19 8	21 10
1 9	4 6	2 9	6 9	8 10	11 3	13 6	15 9	18 0	20 3	22 6
1 10	4 9	2 10	7 1	9 5	12 9	14 1	16 5	18 9	21 1	23 5
1 11	4 9	2 11	7 2	9 7	12 0	14 5	16 10	19 3	21 8	24 1
2 0	5 0	3 0	7 6	10 0	12 6	15 0	17 6	20 0	22 6	25 0

arisen. We insert the following extracts from Mr Maclean's report from Sussex, and Mr Villiers's from Warwickshire and Worcestershire, which confirm Sir Frederic Eden's narrative:

'I found', says Mr Maclean,

great difficulty in ascertaining accurately the period at which the system of relieving able-bodied men, on account of their families, originated; but this difficulty, as relates to the western part of the county of Sussex, was removed by the kindness of Mr Woods, who stated to me that as well as he could recollect after so distant a time, the system of parochial relief, on account of the dearness of bread, commenced after the high prices of 1795. It was then only occasional till the still higher prices of 1800 and 1801, when the magistrates of the bench of Chichester recommended (instead of advancing wages in proportion to the times) the various parishes to make certain allowances, in consideration of the higher prices of corn. This mode was very generally acted upon; but being attended with some difficulties, a paper was drawn up and calculated by one of the influential magistrates of the day, and having been approved of by others, was circulated and recommended to the parish officers for their guidance.

1804-5. The annexed table is intended to show the exact difference which the advance in the price of flour makes to the poor, when it exceeds 1s. 4d. per gallon, and what sum is required for their relief, so as to enable them to have it at all times at that price.

From the following calculation, viz., a man, his wife, and two children are supposed to consume three gallons of flour per week, which, when flour is at

	s.	d.
2s. per gallon, would cost them	6	0
Three gallons of flour, at 1s. 4d. is	4	0
The difference of cost in this case would be ...	2	0

which in a family of four persons, as above-mentioned, would make 6d. per head per week, or 2s. per head per month, and the same difference, be the number in the family what it may.

'In obedience', says Mr Villiers,

to the instructions, I made inquiry into the origin, in these counties, of the system of applying the parish rates in aid of wages; and I found the period usually referred to was during the years of scarcity towards the close of the last century. In Warwickshire, the year 1797 was mentioned as the date of its commencement in that county, and the scales of relief

MONTHLY AMOUNT OF A FAMILY.

Price of FLOUR per gallon. (s. d.)	Amount weekly per head. (s. d.)	One. (s. d.)	Two. (s. d.)	Three. (s. d.)	Four. (s. d.)	Five. (s. d.)	Six. (£ s. d.)	Seven. (£ s. d.)	Eight. (£ s. d.)	Nine. (£ s. d.)	Ten. (£ s. d.)	Eleven. (£ s. d.)	Twelve. (£ s. d.)
1 5	0 0¾	0 3	0 6	0 9	1 0	1 3	0 1 6	0 1 9	0 2 0	0 2 3	0 2 6	0 2 9	0 3 0
1 6	0 1½	0 6	1 0	1 6	2 0	2 6	0 3 0	0 3 6	0 4 0	0 4 6	0 5 0	0 5 6	0 6 0
1 7	0 2¼	0 9	1 6	2 3	3 0	3 9	0 4 6	0 5 3	0 6 0	0 6 9	0 7 6	0 8 3	0 9 0
1 8	0 3	1 0	2 0	3 0	4 0	5 0	0 6 0	0 7 0	0 8 0	0 9 0	0 10 0	0 11 0	0 12 0
1 9	0 3¾	1 3	2 6	3 9	5 0	6 3	0 7 6	0 8 9	0 10 0	0 11 3	0 12 6	0 13 9	0 15 0
1 10	0 4½	1 6	3 0	4 6	6 0	7 6	0 9 0	0 10 6	0 12 0	0 13 6	0 15 0	0 16 6	0 18 0
1 11	0 5¼	1 9	3 6	5 3	7 0	8 9	0 10 6	0 12 3	0 14 0	0 15 9	0 17 6	0 19 3	1 1 0
2 0	0 6	2 0	4 0	6 0	8 0	10 0	0 12 0	0 14 0	0 16 0	0 18 0	1 0 0	1 2 0	1 4 0
2 1	0 6¾	2 3	4 6	6 9	9 0	11 3	0 13 6	0 15 9	0 18 0	1 0 3	1 2 6	1 4 9	1 7 0
2 2	0 7½	2 6	5 0	7 6	10 0	12 6	0 15 0	0 17 6	1 0 0	1 2 6	1 5 0	1 7 6	1 10 0
2 3	0 8¼	2 9	5 6	8 3	11 0	13 9	0 16 6	0 19 3	1 2 0	1 4 9	1 7 6	1 10 3	1 13 0
2 4	0 9	3 0	6 0	9 0	12 0	15 0	0 18 0	1 1 0	1 4 0	1 7 0	1 10 0	1 13 0	1 16 0
2 5	0 9¾	3 3	6 6	9 9	13 0	16 3	0 19 6	1 2 9	1 6 0	1 9 3	1 12 6	1 15 9	1 19 0
2 6	0 10½	3 6	7 0	10 6	14 0	17 6	1 1 0	1 4 6	1 8 0	1 11 6	1 15 0	1 18 6	2 2 0

giving it authority were published in each of these counties previously
to the year 1800. It was apprehended by many at that time that either
the wages of labour would rise to a height from which it would be
difficult to reduce them when the cause for it had ceased, or that during
the high prices the labourers might have had to undergo privations to
which it would be unsafe to expose them. To meet the emergency
of the time, various schemes are said to have been adopted, such as
weekly distributions of flour, providing families with clothes, or maintaining entirely a portion of their families, until at length the practice
became general, and a right distinctly admitted by the magistrates was
claimed by the labourer to parish relief, on the ground of inadequate
wages and number in family. I was informed that the consequences of
the system were not wholly unforeseen at the time, as affording a
probable inducement to early marriages and large families; but at this
period there was but little apprehension on that ground. A prevalent
opinion, supported by high authority, that population was in itself a
source of wealth, precluded all alarm. The demands for the public
service were thought to ensure a sufficient draught for any surplus
people; and it was deemed wise by many persons at this time to present
the Poor Laws to the lower classes, as an institution for their advantage,
peculiar to this country; and to encourage an opinion among them,
that by this means their own share in the property of the kingdom
was recognized; and to these notions, which were prevalent at that
time, must be ascribed the spirit in which the Poor Laws have been
administered for thirty years past. The Rev. Mr Broomfield, of
Napton, in Warwickshire, stated to me, that he remembered that in
the year 1797, when a meeting was called in that parish, to take into
consideration the best means of supporting the labourers during the
high prices, and that a regular distribution of flour by the parish, in aid
of wages, had been agreed upon, his father, who was then the incumbent of the same living, warned the meeting of the system they were
introducing, reminding them of the feeling which then existed among
the poor with regard to being supported by the parish, and the probable
result of confounding in their mind all distinction between alms and
wages, saying, that if their pride upon this subject was once destroyed,
the Poor Laws would become a most formidable engine directed
against the morals and the property of the country; a prediction, the
fulfilment of which, Mr. Broomfield lamented to say, he had long since
survived.

The following extract from the evidence delivered by Mr La-
coast, of Chertsey, before the House of Commons' Poor Law

Committee, in 1817, shows the introduction of the system into a parish at a somewhat later period:

The magistrates have been rather more liberal to our poor than in the neighbouring parishes, and that has brought people into the parish; they have endeavoured and obtained settlements. We have had several instances where a man has refused a house at £8 a year, and taken one at £10 not so good, for the purpose of making himself a parishioner.

Do any of the labourers who are earning the wages you have stated, (from 12s. to 15s. a week) procure relief in money from the overseers? – Yes.

On what ground do they obtain such relief? – We had a scale sent by the magistrates to the overseers and the committee, desiring that we would allow every man, woman, and child that there were in family, to make up their wages equal to two quartern loaves per head per week, all at 3s. a week as nearly as possible. We thought that the poor people, many of them, were allowed too much money, and the committee conceived that there was not a distinction made between the labourers who worked from day-light to dark, and the men who worked for 12s. a week only, for seven or eight hours a day, and we made an alteration according as we thought they deserved it: to some we gave more than the magistrates ordered, and some less; and we received an order the next morning, that the money should be made up immediately to those who received less.

When was the scale by which the paupers are paid, first fixed? – I should think about four months since.

Can you state at all the effect that it had? – I know an instance myself where a man was at work and earned 18s. a week, and another man who lived next door to him was at work and had 12s.; and after the scale was settled by the magistrates, the (first) man did not go to work in the usual way, but worked easier, and the money was made up by the parish.

Has there not been a committee appointed to carry those orders of the magistrates into execution? – It is an open committee of the whole parish; no select committee.

There was a wish expressed by the magistrates, that some of the most respectable of the inhabitants should form a committee? – Yes; and I went down with some of the larger renters of the parish, and made an alteration, and reduced some and added to others: but the magistrates ordered that they should have so much per head, whether they worked or not.

Is the scale you speak of used in other parishes besides yours? – I believe not.

Framed for your parish specially? – I believe the magistrates framed it for the whole hundred, but the other parishes refused to comply with it, and have not done it. Some of the magistrates that attend our bench did not agree with the scale, but were overruled by the majority; therefore when the overseer of Thorp applied to the magistrate there, he did not compel them to give that sum, but left it to the discretion of the overseer. The men in our parish are impudent, and will not work, and they tell us so.

It is probable that the allowance system was encouraged, and perhaps suggested, by the 33 Geo. III, c. 8 [1793], which ordered that if a militia-man, when called out and ordered to march, should leave a family unable to support themselves, the overseers of the poor of the parish where such family should dwell, should, by order of the justice of the peace, out of the rates for the relief of the poor of such parish, pay to such family a weekly allowance according to the usual price of labour in husbandry in the place by the following rate: a sum not exceeding one day's labour, nor less than 1s. for the wife, and a similar sum for each child under ten years old; and it must have been facilitated by the 33 Geo. III, c. 55, which enabled the justices at petty sessions to fine the overseers for disobedience to the orders of any justice or justices.

The clause of the 9 Geo. I, c. 7, prohibiting relief to those who refused to enter the workhouse, was, however, an obstacle; to remove it, the 36 Geo. III, c. 23 [1796] was passed. That act, after reciting the clause in question, proceeds thus:

And whereas the said provisions contained in the Act above-mentioned has been found to have been, and to be, inconvenient and oppressive, inasmuch as it often prevents an industrious poor person from receiving such occasional relief as is best suited to the peculiar case of such poor persons; and inasmuch as in certain cases it holds out conditions of relief, injurious to the comfort, and domestic situation, and happiness of such poor persons.

And then repeals the clause forbidding relief to those who should refuse to enter the workhouse, and proceeds more directly to its object by the following provision:

And be it further enacted, that it shall be lawful for any of his Majesty's justice or justices of the peace for any county, city, town, or place, usually acting in and for the district wherein the same shall be situated, at his or their just and proper discretion, to direct and order collection and relief to any industrious poor person; and he should be entitled to ask and receive such relief at his home or house, in any parish, town, township, or place, notwithstanding any contract shall have been, or shall be made, for lodging, keeping, maintaining, and employing poor persons in a house for such purpose hired or purchased; and the overseers for such parish, town, township, or place, are required and directed to obey and perform such order for relief given by any justice or justices as aforesaid.

Those who are irritated by the pressure of the evils which allowance to the able-bodied has produced, and by the apprehension of the still greater evils which it may be expected to produce, are sometimes inclined to attribute the most childish folly, or the most profligate dishonesty, to those who could aid in establishing such a system. But we must not judge them according to the knowledge which we have acquired in the dear-bought experience of forty years. It is clear that when the magistrates assembled at Speenhamland in 1795, 'to settle the weekly income of the industrious poor', public opinion sanctioned their attempt. This is shown by the 36 Geo. III, c. 23, which was passed a few months after, and may be considered the great and fatal deviation from our previous policy. The 43 Elizabeth never contemplated, as objects of relief, industrious persons. It made no promises of comfort or happiness; it directed that those having no means, and using no daily trade of life to get their living by, should be set to work, and that the impotent should receive necessary relief. These were unalluring offers – they held out nothing but work and necessary relief, and those only to the impotent, and to persons who must always form a small minority in any tolerably regulated society – that is, persons having no property, and using no daily trade. The able-bodied industrious labourer was carefully excluded, and relief, therefore, as Mr Pitt (in the speech introducing his Poor Bill in 1796) complained, became a ground for opprobrium and contempt. They were precise offers; the question whether a person using no trade had been set to work, or one unable to work had received necessary relief, were matters of fact. The engagements of the 43 Elizabeth, were, perhaps, dangerous engagements; but they were engagements which, for a hundred years, were performed apparently without substantial injury to the morals and industry of the labourers, or to the general prosperity of the country. And whatever may be the objections in principle to the power given to the magistrates, or assumed by them under the 3 and 4 Will. and Mary, and 9 Geo. I, it does not seem to have produced much practical evil, while the 9 Geo. I was in force. Parochial relief appears to have been given chiefly through the workhouses, and not to have been extended to many besides the impotent. The duty of the magistrate was tolerably plain: if the applicant fell within the classes pointed out by the 43 Elizabeth as objects of relief, that is, if he had no property, used no ordinary and daily trade to get his living by, or was lame, impotent, old, blind, or otherwise not able to work, he could direct him to be admitted into the workhouse, and if he was included in the first class, set to work by the parish officers; or, if included in the second class, supplied with necessary relief. Relief was considered a burthen to the payers, and a degradation to the receivers (and to be marked as such by a badge), a remedy for unexpected calamity, and a mitigation of the punishment inflicted by nature on extravagance and improvidence, but no part of the ordinary fund for the support of labour. Public opinion sanctioned the magistrate in a sparing exercise of his power, and he had, in fact, no motive for undue interference. The paupers were a small disreputable minority, whose resentment was not to be feared, and whose favour was of no value; all other classes were anxious to diminish the number of applicants, and to reduce the expense of their maintenance.

The 36 Geo. III removed all these fences; it recognized, as objects of relief, industrious persons, and enabled the magistrate, at his just and proper discretion, to order it to be given in a way which should not be injurious to their comfort, domestic situation and happiness. Mr Pitt's bill went still further; it admitted, within the pale of pauperism, not only the industrious labourer, but the person with property, and enabled him, when possessed of land, not only to retain it while an applicant for relief, but to be supplied, at the expense of the parish, with a cow. It is true, that this bill was dropped, but as it was not an individual, but a government measure, it may be cited as evidence of the general feeling on the subject.

When allowance to the able-bodied, in aid of their wages, had once been introduced, when it had been found to be an expedient by which the expenditure in wages could be reduced, and profits and rents could be raised, when the paupers became numerous in most districts, and in some places formed the majority and even the large majority of the peasantry; when their clamours for allowance were favoured by the farmers, and apparently justified by the rise in the price of the necessaries of life, who can be surprised if the magistrates were led, in some places to connive at, in others to sanction, and in still more to promote a practice, the evil of which had not then been experienced, which seemed so plausible in itself, and which so many persons combined to favour? Who can wonder that, thus urged and encouraged, they should have fancied themselves entitled to settle the weekly income of the labourers; and who can wonder at any amount of evil that has followed so preposterous an attempt?

We have seen that one of the first effects of the power thus assumed by the magistrates was the publication of scales of relief – a practice which still continues. The publication of these scales has been much complained of, but we think rather unreasonably. It is true that the evils of the system recommended or enforced by the scales, cannot be exaggerated; and it is true that the publication of a scale is an acknowledgement of the system, which shows how little those who publish it are aware of the consequences of their conduct. But the evil resides in the practice, not in the scale, which is its almost inevitable consequence. When a magistrate takes on himself 'to regulate the incomes of the industrious poor' within his jurisdiction, he of course frames to himself some standard by which to regulate them: if he does not, all must be favour or caprice; of course also the magistrates of the district or the division must be anxious to make their individual standards correspond, or, in other words, to agree on a scale. It need not, indeed, be published, but no one can doubt that though unpublished, the paupers soon find it out, and the only difference is that it is traditionary instead of written – the common law of the district instead of a code.

The following answer by the Rev. John Oldham, rector of Stondon Massey, in the county of Essex, to question 39 of our queries for rural districts, is an instructive account of the enactment and repeal of a scale:

An order issued from the poor bench at Epping, in 1801, directing allowances to be made in proportion to the number in family (borrowed, probably, from Pitt's Poor Bill of 1797). Not then acting as magistrate, but from a wish to facilitate the execution of the order, I formed a scale of allowances according to it, beginning with one up to ten in family, and taking the quartern loaf from 6d. up to 2s.; showing the amount of money to be made up between such extremes. I had it printed, and sent one or more copies to each parish of the division. I was thanked for the trouble I had taken, and the scale was adopted and acted upon, not merely in our division, but probably in different parts of the country. It was, however, soon discovered that the paupers and labourers, having got to the knowledge of it, availed themselves of the opportunity of claiming under it what they were willing to consider a regular pension. The evil was felt very sensibly, and a meeting called of all the magistrates in the division, which I attended; this, I think, was in 1806, and the meeting determined unanimously to call in, as far as possible, all copies of the scale, and to make no further use of it; it was, in fact, suppressed, and no longer referred to. In consequence, many applicants expressed great disappointment and ill-humour, but the magistrates were firm, and nothing is said of it.

The evils of the scale system are so generally admitted that we think it sufficient to quote the following statement of them by Mr Okeden, himself a magistrate of great experience, contained in his report from that part of Oxfordshire which lies west of the great canal.

About twenty-four years ago the payment of head-money, by a scale, was introduced into all these divisions, and continues in full operation, with all its varieties of roundsmen, billet system, &c. &c. The magistrates decide on the sum which is, in their opinion, necessary for the support of a man and his wife and children, and, by a scale, order the overseers to make up the man's low wages to that sum from the parish. This scale system is so complete, that the history of one of the parishes is, in fact, the history of all. I will, therefore, lay before you a general statement of the working of this scale process throughout the western divisions of the county of Oxford.

There is a trifling variation of the scale in some districts, but so small as hardly to deserve notice. One system, therefore, pervades all the districts, and all the parishes are governed precisely in the same form, only varying at times from the better or worse management of the overseers. The results of this system (of its illegality I need not speak) are now become apparent. The first and most prominent is that from neglect of single men, and the lower place to which they have been and are forced in the scale, a series of early marriages has ensued, for the avowed purpose of increasing income, until a generation of superfluous labourers has risen up, all demanding work or pay from the scale. If this system continues, in ten years more another generation will be hastening on. The present race, which this illegal perversion of the Poor Laws has created, are playing the game of cunning with the magistrates and overseers; give them ten years, and they will convert it into the dreadful game of force. My humble opinion is that if some measure be not adopted to arrest the progress of the evil, a fearful and bloody contest *must* ensue.

But besides the first result of this scale system, namely, the creation of a generation of superfluous labourers, two others accompany it: one is the equalization of industry and idleness, the other that of honesty and dishonesty. I asked every overseer of the 104 parishes, the condition of which I investigated, whether the due regard was paid to character and industry in the granting of relief. Every one openly and shamelessly avowed that no attention was paid to either, but that *all* were relieved according to the scale. I put the strongest possible case, that of a man who, by repeated thefts and rogueries, had actually flung himself out of employ, so that no farmer would permit him to enter his premises; the answer was still the same, 'We should relieve him and his family from the scale.' The odium of this part of the scale process the overseers seem inclined to fling on the magistrates, and, I believe, with reason.

So much for the placing honesty and knavery on a level. With regard to the equalization of industry and idleness, when the honest, industrious labourer sees by his side, on the road or in the field, a notoriously lazy fellow dawdling over his work, what must be the consequence? He reasons the case over in his mind, finds that his idle companion, with the deduction of only twopence per day, receives as much as himself, and of course he relaxes in his work; and indifference and laziness succeed to vigour and industry; the industry of the labourers is everywhere decidedly diminished; agricultural capital is on the wane; the poor regard the allowance as a right, and it is called sometimes 'the county allowance', sometimes 'the Government allowance', sometimes 'the Act of Parliament allowance', and always '*our income*'.

But though the scale is the worst form in which the influence of magistrates can be exerted, great evils arise from their interference even when less systematically exercised. In the first place, the very mode in which their jurisdiction is enforced seems intended to destroy all vigilance and economy on the part of those who administer relief, and all sense of degradation or shame on the part of those who receive it. The overseer is summoned, perhaps, six or seven miles from his business, or his farm, to defend himself before the tribunal of his immediate superiors against a charge of avarice or cruelty. He seldom has any opportunity to support his defence by evidence; the pleadings generally consist of the pauper's assertions on the one side, and the overseer's on the other. The magistrate may admit or reject the evidence of either party at his pleasure; may humiliate the overseer in the pauper's presence with whatever reproof he may think that his frugality deserves, and finally pronounces a decree, against which, however unsupported by the facts of the case or mischievous in principle, there is no appeal. It must be remembered too that the pauper has often the choice of his tribunal. The clause of the 3 & 4 William and Mary, c. 11, which confined the jurisdiction to a justice of the peace residing within the parish, or, if none be there dwelling, in the parts near or next adjoining, was disregarded at the unfortunate period to which we have referred. The 36 George III, c. 23, gives its discretionary powers to any of his Majesty's justice or justices of the peace for any county, city, town, or place, usually acting in or for the district wherein the same shall be situated. And though the 59 George III, c. 12, s. 5 [1818], has required the concurrence of two justices to an order for relief, yet this restriction, as is the case with many other wisely intended clauses in the act, is neutralized by a proviso enabling one justice to make an order in case of emergency: an emergency of which *he* is the judge. All the overseers of a district are therefore at the mercy of any two magistrates, and to a considerable degree at the mercy of any one. The pauper may select those magistrates whom misdirected benevolence, or desire of popularity, or timidity, leads to be profuse distributors of other people's property and bring forward his charges against the overseer, secure of obtaining a verdict. He appears in the character of an injured man dragging his oppressor to justice. If he fails, he loses nothing; if he succeeds, he obtains triumph and reward. And yet we find persons expressing grave regret that the parochial fund is wasted, that relief is claimed as a right, and that pauperism has ceased to be disgraceful. The subject of regret is either that the existing system is suffered to continue, or that such is the constitution of human nature, that a vigilant administration of public money is not to be expected from those on whom we have heaped every motive to extravagance and every obstacle against economy; that what the magistrate awards is considered a right, and that the exercise of an acknowledged right is not felt a degradation.

Most of our preceding remarks apply not to the magistrates personally, but to the jurisdiction exercised by them respecting relief, and would be applicable to any tribunal invested with similar powers; to any tribunal, in short, which should be empowered to enforce charity and liberality by summons and fine. But supposing that such a power ought to exist, there are strong grounds for thinking that the present magistrates are not the best persons to be intrusted with it. In the first place, they are men of fortune, unacquainted with the domestic economy of the applicants for relief, and as unfit from their own associations 'to settle what ought to be the weekly incomes of the industrious poor', as the industrious poor would be to regulate the weekly expenditure of the magistrates.

The following passages from Mr Chadwick's and Mr Villiers's reports, and which are corroborated by all our evidence, show how loosely and imperfectly the means of the independent labourers has usually been inquired into, and how little is really known of their wants by those who order relief.

'I have endeavoured', says Mr Chadwick,

to ascertain from several of the magistrates who are advocates for the allowance system or for the regulation of wages, in what way the labouring man within their districts expends for his maintenance the sum which they have declared to be the minimum expenditure, to sustain life. Some of these gentlemen admitted that they did not know; others stated that they laid it down as a general rule, that a labouring man must have bread and meat; but whether three or four loaves of bread, whether a pound or a pound and a half of meat, constituted the least quantity requisite as food for a given period, none of them could state. Several promised to make inquiries on the subject, when I asked them how they could safely set aside the decisions of the parish officers, or determine with due precision what was the minimum allowance of money for the labouring man's subsistence, unless they knew how many commodities were absolute necessaries for him, and the exact quantity and the price of each.

Whilst complaining of the effects of the beer-shops established under Mr Goulburn's Act, the same magistrates frequently stated that habits of drunkenness prevailed with the whole of the labourers within their districts, and that these labourers were accustomed to carouse, during one or two days in the week, gambling and indulging in the most vicious habits. Having previously received evidence that so large a proportion of the agricultural poor-rate is expended in aid of wages, I have been startled by the declarations that the habits of dissipation have become so prevalent. In answer to further inquiries, I received assurances that the habit is *general*; that there are few, if any, exceptions. I again asked whether the exceptions are formed of those who received parochial relief, and I was assured (and satisfactory evidence was adduced to me to prove the fact), that the agricultural labourers receiving poor's rates in aid of wages, are to be found at the beer-shops as frequently, at least, as the independent labourers. The questions which appeared to me naturally to follow are: Do you consider beer or gin a necessary of life to the paupers? – if it be admitted that beer is a necessary of life to the independent labourers, at all events the quantity required for intoxication can hardly be necessary. Ought you not, then, to ascertain and deduct the amount of money spent in drunken revelry? As it must be presumed that a man pays for the beer he drinks at the beer-shops (which beer is not deemed absolutely necessary for his subsistence), is it not clear that you have not arrived at the minimum allowance? If, for example, you order wages to be made up to a man to the amount of 9s. a week, and you find that he gets drunk one or two days in the week, and that his excess of drink costs him 2s. a week, since he actually lives on 7s. a week, does he not prove, by so living, that 7s. is all that he really requires?

It was observed by Colonel Page, one of his Majesty's deputy-lieutenants for Berks., in his communications with me, that the magistrates, from their ignorance of the habits of the labouring classes, are extremely unfit judges as to the amount of relief to be administered. 'To a gentleman,' said he, 'a shilling appears an extremely small sum, but it often procures two, or even three days' subsistence to a labouring man;

and hence the most benevolent men commonly make the most profuse and injurious allowances.'

The witnesses, who have had much experience in maintaining considerable numbers, attest the correctness of the rule – that by adding rent and 20 per cent as the retailer's profit on commodities, an estimate may be made of the expense at which a single person may live, in the same manner that a number are kept in a workhouse, or in a community of any sort, where the commodities are purchased at wholesale prices. Thus, if at any place, as at Gosport workhouse, the able-bodied paupers are clothed and fed better than most labouring men, at an expense of 2s. 6d. per head, allowing 6d. for the retailer's profit, and 1s. for rent, the allowance to enable an out-door pauper to live in the same manner would be 4s. per week. If the allowances in aid of wages are tried by this rule, it will be found that a large proportion of them are in error, to the extent of 100 per cent. I have found none that were in error less than about 20 per cent.

'In the parish of Hanley Castle, in the Pershore hundred of Worcestershire, and in the neighbourhood,' says Mr Villiers,

having heard much complaint of the magisterial interference, I visited the gentleman who was said to be the senior magistrate of the district, and inquired of him, upon what principle he ordered relief to be granted to the able-bodied labourers. He informed me that he considered that every labourer was entitled to claim a certain sum per week for every child born after the third. Upon further asking him if he considered that to be the proper and legitimate construction of the statute of Elizabeth, he stated that he did so entirely, and that he thought that when a man had four children, he might fairly be considered within the meaning of the Act as 'impotent', which he further explained by saying that he considered it impossible for any labouring man to support four children. Having been previously informed of the fact, I inquired of him if he was not aware that a man living in his own parish was at that time maintaining his wife and five children, independently of all relief. He said that he was not aware of any such case, and should think it extraordinary if there was. He then referred to a farmer residing in his parish to ascertain the truth. The farmer assured him that the fact was as I had stated it; that the man referred to was a regular labourer, peculiarly industrious, but that he was not earning more than the average wages of the division, which was considered about 10s. a week for the man, paid by the day, or 12s. or 14s. by the piece.

In answer to our question whether a labouring family can save, a great majority of the respondents state positively that they cannot. About half the respondents from Devonshire made no answer to the query. W. J. Coppard, the minister of Plympton, St Mary's, says, 'A *few* have trifling sums in the savings bank.' The other respondents either express a strong doubt whether anything could be saved by a labouring man, or declare positively that he could lay by nothing; yet we find, from the returns of the deposits in the Exeter savings' bank, upwards of £70,000 saved, under all obstacles, by two thousand labourers, or by one out of every ten heads of agricultural labourers' families in the same county.

The following are the statements of some of the respondents (clergymen and gentlemen serving parochial offices in the metropolis) to queries 35, 36, 37, 38 – What can a family earn, and whether they can live on these earnings, and lay by anything?

The answer from Chiswick states that a family *might* earn £49 per annum, on which they might live, but could not save. From St Anne and Agnes, and St Leonard, Foster-Lane, family might earn £60; could not live on it. From St Botolph-without Aldersgate, family earn £63 18s., on which they might subsist, but could save nothing. From Mile End, New Town, and St Mary Somerset, city of London, family might earn £65, on which they might live, but could not save anything. From St Leonard Eastcheap, family might earn £78; could not save, and cannot ascertain whether they could live upon it. From St James's, Westminster, man might earn £78, besides material assistance from his wife and children; might live on wholesome food, but cannot attempt to say whether they could save. From Holy Trinity the Less, family might earn £93; might live on spare diet; could not save anything. Mr Baker, the coroner and vestry clerk of St Anne's, Limehouse, states that a family might earn £100, on which they could live, but *not* save. The return from Hammersmith declares that a family might earn £49 8s., which would give them wholesome food, and that they might and *do* save.

The variations in the several returns above quoted exhibit the uncertainty and the wide variations of the impressions on which relief is administered, and the utter want of any standard of reference. Each gentleman, from the one who at Chiswick declares that forty-nine pounds is the sum on which a family could only live, to the gentleman who pronounces that one hundred pounds per annum only suffices for the bare subsistence of a labouring man's family, which is higher than the actual incomes of hundreds of families of professional men, would doubtless in his respective district fix the condition of the pauper agreeably to his impression of the means of subsistence required. This variation is not greater than the actual variations of the nature and amount of relief administered to the same classes within the same district. It is a remarkable and important fact that it is found that at the boards of guardians, or other parochial boards for the administration of relief, those members who are distinguished for the greatest strictness, which others decry as harshness, in the administration of relief, are commonly persons who have themselves risen from the ranks of labouring men. This strictness, which is usually exhibited where there is no connection or acquaintanceship to bias them, appears to arise from the better knowledge which they possess of the real wants of the applicants, and of the nature of the means of satisfying them.

Secondly, the magistrate, even if he have a general knowledge of the subject, seldom has and seldom can acquire a knowledge of the individual facts on which he has to decide. A pauper claims 3s. on the ground that his family consists of five persons, and that he has earned during the last week only 7s. The overseers believe that he has, in fact, earned more, or that he might have earned more if he had thought fit to exert himself, or that the lowness of his acknowledged earnings is the result of a collusion between him and his employer, in order to throw part of his wages on the parish. The vestry agrees in opinion with the overseer, and the pauper appeals to the magistrate. If questions like these, so difficult of proof, and the two latter matters of opinion not of perception, are to be decided, it must be by a tribunal acquainted with the habits and character of the applicant and of his employers, capable of collecting and weighing many minute indicia of evidence, and ready to undergo so tedious and unsatisfactory a task. Can it be expected that it will be performed, or even undertaken by the magistrates, who give a few hours a week to the affairs of twenty parishes, who live at a distance from the scene of the dispute, and know little more than the names of the parties to it, and perhaps not even so much? In fact, the appeal is made from those who are acquainted with the general nature of the subject to be inquired into, to those who are ignorant of it; from those who either know the facts, or have the power to ascertain them, so far as they are capable of being ascertained, to those who have no previous knowledge of the matter, no interest in diligent investigation, and no means to render that investigation successful.

We have selected from the vast body of evidence contained in the Appendix respecting the prevalence and effects of magisterial interference, the following passages, not as peculiarly striking, but because they illustrate most of the remarks which we have made.

Mr Majendie states that in his district:

The opinion of many of the most experienced magistrates themselves coincides with that expressed by occupiers and overseers, that the over liberality of magistrates in granting relief has been a principal cause of the high rates, and of the dependence of labourers on the parish. In many instances they have adopted a dictatorial tone to the parish overseers, which has induced men of respectability to avoid the office, and when harsh observations have been made in presence of the pauper, the authority of the officer is destroyed. Though the mischief of this proceeding has been apparent, and a more cautious plan has been adopted, still there are many complaints of magisterial interference, particularly in those districts where a scale of allowance is adopted; overseers represent that they give relief to a greater extent than they think requisite, from a conviction derived from experience, that such relief would be ordered on application to the bench. In some districts where the magistrates represent that they have discontinued a fixed scale, and decide each case according to its merits, the overseers still act under the impression that such a scale exists. A magistrate whose opinion is looked up to with much respect expressed to me his feeling that deciding in cases of applications for relief was the most unsatisfactory and painful of his duties; on the one hand, injudicious liberality might be a great injustice to the rate-payers; on the other, the denial of relief might be an act of cruelty to the applicant, who, in periods when the low wages of farmers and bad state of agriculture cause many to be out of work, might be reduced to severe distress. Great part of the mischief has been effected by the magistrate acting singly in his own house. A gentleman of property first starting in that office, without experience in the employment of labour, or the character of labourērs, is easily imposed upon by their false representations; and should he obtain the character of the poor man's friend, he becomes in fact their greatest enemy, and may throw a spell over the industry of a whole district. Both in Kent and Sussex I have heard that paupers threaten application to some individual magistrate.

'At Over', says Mr Power, 'a village not far from Cottenham',

I found a person of great judgement and experience in Mr Robinson, the principal farmer in that place. He is now serving the office of overseer for the fourth time. At present there are forty men and more upon the parish; the average during eight months is twenty-five. Part of this arises from farmers living at Willingham and Swavesey, occupying about one fifth of Over parish; these persons employ none but Willingham and Swavesey labourers; it arises also in part from the growing indifference to private employment generated by the system of parish relief. A man with a wife and four children is entitled to 10s. and more from the parish for doing nothing; by working hard in private employ he could only earn 12s., and the difference probably he would require in additional sustenance for himself; consequently all motive to seek work vanishes. Coming into office this year, Mr Robinson found twelve married men on the box, some of the best men in the parish; he knew they could get work if they chose at that time; he set them to work digging a piece of land of his own at 3d. a rod; they earned that week only about 7s. 6d. each, though they might have earned 12s.; and the next week they disappeared to a man. He complains bitterly of the obstruction given to these exertions by the decisions of the magistrates; they are always against him, and he regrets some unpleasant words spoken to him very lately by one of the bench. On one occasion he had refused payment of their money to some men who would not keep their proper hours of work upon the road; they complained to the bench at Cambridge, and beat him as usual, and returned to Over, wearing favours in their hats and button-holes; and in the evening a body of them collected in front of his house, and shouted in triumph.

Mr Robinson's evidence having brought me once more to the subject of the magistracy, I will take the opportunity of saying that one disastrous effect of the general maladministration is to prevent many gentlemen, the most eligible in respect of understanding and ability, from joining the body, or from acting with them in the general business of the petty sessions. I could mention, were it not perhaps invidious, the names of several persons whom I know to have been so influenced, and whose services have been lost to the side of good sense and propriety. Another cause of monopoly of the parochial business in the most objectionable hands is the power which the paupers have of choosing their own tribunal. It was said by a farmer the other day, of a most excellent and benevolent gentleman in this county, 'We', (meaning the parish) 'could afford to give him £100 a year, sir, if he would consent not to act.' Another anecdote communicated to me at Gamlingay is also pretty much to the point. The overseer there told me that a few days ago he had a difference with several of the paupers about their parish pay, when they summoned him before a magistrate who lives about six miles off. On the day of their attendance there, something prevented the case being heard, and they all returned to Gamlingay together. In passing the house of another magistrate, about two miles from home, the overseer said, 'Now, my lads, here we are close by; I'll give you a pint of beer each if you'll come and have it settled at once, without giving me any more trouble about it.' The proposal was rejected without hesitation. I merely mention this to show that paupers have their preferences, and that they consider it important to abide by them.

I shall only make one more observation on this subject. It is in vain for the magistrate to represent the difficulty of his situation in cases where he sees the pauper does not deserve relief, but where it is also clear that he is in destitute circumstances. 'True,' say they, 'the man is a bad character, and he ought to have saved his money; but then you know, overseer, he must not starve.' There is no difficulty in the situation whatever; the overseer requires neither magistrate nor ghost to tell him that the man must not starve; he has human feelings like the magistrate, and he is also liable to be indicted for cruelty in the discharge of his office; therefore why not let him use his discretion, and abide the consequences? particularly when, after all and in spite of the order of relief, he may still misuse the man at the peril only of the like punishment. It remains, however, to be observed, that were parish officers left to their own discretion, there would probably be found very few who, like Mr Robinson, would apply themselves with zeal and vigilance to the reduction of the parish expenses; the greater part have seemed to me but too happy to waive the trouble of a strict adminis-tration, and to shift from themselves to the magistracy the heavy re-sponsibility of the parochial extravagance and ruin. Resistance to the demands of the bold and turbulent is seldom attempted, on the plea that the magistrates cannot be depended on for their support in such cases; while, on the other hand, the true objects of the charity, the helpless and impotent, are sometimes so harshly treated as to justify that interference by the magistrate in their behalf, which makes the overseer's excuse in the former cases. By the joint operation of these two ill-assorted functions, mischief is progressing with a fearful rapidity.

In 'the case of appeals to individual magistrates,' says Captain Chapman,

I found that the usual course of proceeding was to send the applicant back with a note to the overseer, desiring that the matter might be inquired into, and, if not satisfactorily arranged, that both parties would attend at the house of the magistrate at a time named.

This, the most mild mode of exercising the power vested in the magistrates, was open to the objections of being influenced by the peculiar views of each individual, of reducing the inquiry into a statement on the part of the pauper, and a counter statement on the part of the overseer, and of thus tending to render the decision of the vestry of no avail. The result of this course was generally conclusive, so that instances of summonses were very rare.

In the cases which were brought before the petty sessions which I attended, great pains were taken by the magistrates to get at the truth; but here again the question degenerated into a statement and counter statement, unsupported by any evidence or document, so that the bench, with every desire to do justice, had not the power to do so. The leaning in the spectators was decidedly in favour of the pauper; the magistrates considered themselves as the protectors of the poor, and whatever were the demerits or merits of the case, that they were equally bound to prevent the parties from starving; the overseers were looked upon as almost devoid of the feelings of humanity, and the tendency was still more decidedly to render the decisions of the vestry of no avail. Every appeal gained by the pauper was looked upon as a triumph over the overseers and vestry, and this feeling, in some cases, was participated in by the labouring classes in general. At St Petherton, near Taunton, for instance, I was informed that on a recent occasion a pauper, who had gained his point, returned throwing his hat into the air, hurraing and cheering, and that he was joined by many others, who conducted him in triumph to his home; but cases in which this feeling was so decidedly expressed are, I believe, of rare occurrence, although its existence was universally complained of by the overseers.

The effect upon the vestries, I was led to believe, was to cause many respectable persons to refrain from attending, and to have even caused many select vestries to have been given up; the members leaving the overseers to 'fight it out with the pauper and magistrates'

The duty which has been thus imposed upon the magistracy appeared to place them in a situation of peculiar difficulty. In almost every parish a proportion of idle and worthless are to be found who are a constant source of trouble and of complaints; whatever may be their character, the magistrate has no power to punish unless a regular complaint is made by the overseers for the special purpose, and whatever may have been their previous earnings, he must prevent the pauper from starving. In the rural districts, where there are no workhouses, there are no means of control, and the only resource is work, or, where the family is numerous, pecuniary assistance in addition. If the industrious, by any chance beyond their control, are reduced to the necessity of applying for relief, the only means of marking a distinction in character is by making a difference in the amount of relief; this leads to all the inconveniences of difference in opinion, and places the magistrates not only in collision with the vestry, but in an invidious and false position as regards each other.

In most cases a sum, considered as a minimum on which a person can live (1s. 6d. per week), is the guide in ordering relief; but although a bench may have agreed upon this, they have no security that each individual member will adhere to it; so that the efforts of the experienced and the decision of the bench may be frustrated by the views of a mistaken, weak, or a designing man. This was frequently complained of, and thus forcibly expressed by a magistrate of long standing and experience:

Great difficulties in the administration of the Poor Laws arise out of the power which one magistrate has of ordering relief arbitrarily; and one good effect of the Select Vestry Act is, that it limits the application for relief and the complaint of the pauper to two justices; for let a man's intentions be ever so good, he is subject to passions, and often errs when he acts alone; but where a second magistrate is present, his conduct and judgement will be more cautious and deliberate. The effect of this I have remarked even in men of the best intentions; but in the case of unprincipled or popularity-hunting magistrates, or of a weak and over-liberal dispenser of his neighbour's money, the evil of intrusting the power of giving relief at all to one magistrate is most apparent.

'If two or ten magistrates of a division agree to act in unison or with vigour on the subject of relief to the poor, more especially the idle and dissolute poor, and one black sheep in that division, one popularity-hunter, chooses, he may thwart and destroy the effect of their endeavours, and perhaps they may get their stacks burnt about them for their hard-heartedness, or rather, I should say, integrity and principle.

'I have often been threatened by paupers, to whom I have refused relief, that they would go to a neighbouring justice who was always kind to the poor; and I have had occasion to write to that justice on the subject, and to endeavour to stop his interference after I had refused relief. This is one of the crying evils of the Poor Laws.'

The greatest evil of which I am aware, is the facility with which every plan of the vestry or overseer is brought into question on the complaint of the pauper, who selects a kind and often inconsiderately liberal magistrate as his patron.

These extracts apply to country parishes. In towns and, above all, in the metropolis, the number of cases which require investigation, and the difficulty of obtaining information where everybody is lost in the general crowd, renders the jurisdiction of the magistrates with respect to relief still more objectionable. The evidence, of which the following is an extract, was collected by Mr Chadwick, respecting the district within the jurisdiction of the Worship Street office; and its value is much increased by its having been subsequently read over to Mr Benett, the magistrate principally complained of, and his replies and comments being inserted.

Evidence of Mr Heritage, chief clerk of the Magistrates at Worship Street.

With regard to applications for summonses against parish officers for refusing to grant relief, I may state that summonses are granted indiscriminately upon application at our office. When the parish officers attend upon the summonses relief is ordered almost as indiscriminately. We have constantly fine, hale, hearty-looking young men applying for relief.

I have known an officer sent with as many as twenty paupers in a day, with an order to see them relieved. It was not sufficient that the officer left the paupers with the overseer; he was enjoined by Mr Benett to see them relieved, and if there was no overseer to be found, he was directed to relieve them out of his own pocket, the magistrate promising that he would undertake that the overseer should reimburse him the next day. This has been a practice for several years; it has occurred most frequently on Saturdays. Now the parish officers frequently attend, to render these steps unnecessary.

Mr Benett: This is generally on the Saturday night, when the overseer has neglected to attend; of course, it would not be done when the overseer is present.

Today three hearty young women, from eighteen to twenty years of age, applied for relief; summonses were granted them without any inquiry. I mentioned this case to Mr Twyford, but he seemed to think we had no discretion.

The Act now allows only one magistrate to interfere in cases of 'urgent necessity'; but they deem all cases to be of urgent necessity, for the summonses are uniformly ordered by one magistrate.

Examination of Mr John Othen, office-keeper at the Public Office, Worship Street.
[Has been in office eighteen or nineteen years.]

I generally have to make out the summonses granted at the instance of paupers against parish officers who have refused them relief. Of late years the applicants have greatly increased in number as well as badness of character; in badness of character particularly.

I should think that there are, upon an average, thirty paupers receiving summonses daily. A very large proportion of these paupers are Irish, in St Luke's parish especially. I think that there are more females amongst the applicants. I see the same characters constantly; from their dress and deportment I know a large proportion of them to be prostitutes. Every day we have a proportion of not less than ten of this description amongst the applicants from the various parishes. They invariably have summonses when they apply, and say that the overseers have refused to give them relief. Their cant name for the parish money is 'their reg'lars'; this is 6d. a day for each person, male or female; this is the allowance which the magistrates stipulate that they should have from the parish.

Amongst the males who apply for relief are a number of able and hearty young fellows, who are vagabonds at large, and who will not work so long as they can get a sixpence from the parish. Their general object is the allowance of 6d. a day. I believe that there are many of these men who make out their living by petty depredation.

We have had it happen that after their cases have been heard and relief has been ordered to them, but when it has not been quite so much as expected, they have threatened to 'serve out the overseer', and the paupers have waited outside the office in clusters, each encouraging the others, and waiting for their respective parish officers. If the beadle happens to be in waiting, he conducts the overseer home; but where the beadle has not been present, the overseer has applied to the magistrate for protection, and an officer has accompanied him home. In some instances, however, the beadle is not sufficient, and additional protection is required. The magistrates have so little knowledge of people of this class of life, that they cannot see what is seen by us who know more of them.

Mr Benett: That is natural enough. The magistrates can hardly be expected to know so much of this class of persons as those who mix with them, and converse with them, and overhear them.

In cases where the parish officer suspects that the applicant, being a strong hearty man, might obtain employment, or that he has employment or means of subsistence, is it usual for the magistrate to postpone the case, to give the parish officers an opportunity of investigating the case? – No. The magistrate says, 'This man swears he is in want of subsistence, and you must give him relief; if you hereafter find out that he has the means of subsistence, bring him before us, and we will punish him.'

Mr Benett: This relief is only for the exigency of the moment, and not permanent. This relief is never permanent, but only day by day, as the exigency occurs.

In the great majority of cases, the oath of the pauper is conclusive.

It frequently, constantly occurs that the applicants for relief inquire who is sitting. If it is one magistrate, they will say, 'We will go away, we shall get nothing.' If another sits, they say, 'Oh, that will do; we will stay.' They make themselves acquainted with the character of particular magistrates, and their decisions, and know them well. It is the class of paupers who come the most frequently, the young and able-bodied, who make this application. It is with the most humane magistrate that the worst class of paupers succeed best. I have known them go away, when they found that this magistrate was not in the way.

Examination of Mr John Coste, relieving overseer of St Leonard, Shoreditch.

In consequence of the practice which one magistrate (Mr Benett) has pursued at Worship Street Police-office, I do believe that if that magistrate had the undivided control, it would be impossible for our parishioners to pay the rates.

Mr Benett: My practice is invariably this. When the pauper applies for relief, the first question put to him is, 'Do you live in the parish?' The second question is, 'Have you asked the overseer for relief, and been refused?' If the answers are in the affirmative, I grant a summons. If the overseer does not appear to the summons, and the pauper applies again, I ask if he has given the overseer the summons. If the answer is again in the affirmative, I grant a second summons, with a recommendation in the margin that immediate relief may be given to the pauper: it is only a recommendation. If the second summons is not attended to, and the pauper applies the *third* time, I ask him if has given the second summons to the overseer, and if the answer is still in the affirmative, I send an order of 6d. a day for an adult, and 3d. a day for a child, for seven days, the Act of the 59 Geo. III, c. 12, s. 5, empowering me to make an order for fourteen days, or until the next petty sessions, where there is no select vestry. The order is served on the overseer by one of the officers of the establishment, who keeps a copy. This is my *general* practice; but in case of urgent distress, I send a summons, with the recommendation of 'immediate relief' in the margin, by an officer, and also on the Saturday night, when the overseer does not appear to a previous summons.

His practice is, without swearing the parties as to whether they have applied for relief, to grant summonses to all who choose to apply for them, and who choose to say that they are in need.

Mr Benett: That is true, and that practice must be continued. The pauper must have his case heard.

There is usually the following *nota bene* affixed to these summonses:

(N.B. It is requested by the sitting Magistrate that this pauper may be immediately relieved.

(Signed with the Magistrate's initials.)   ...   *W.B.*)

Mr Benett: This is the second summons, except in a case of urgent distress, and then an officer is sent with the summons, to explain the nature of the case to the overseer, who can appear before the magistrate, if he chooses to object, it not being an order. It is generally a mere matter of form for the pauper to say he has had no victuals that day, when the *nota bene* is at once attached.

Mr Benett: The recommendation is not an order, and the overseer can answer that *nota bene* if he likes, he not having answered the summons. It is, in fact, a caution to him, equivalent to saying that, 'if you do not appear, and show cause why you do not relieve the pauper, an order will be granted.'

It is very rare that any investigation into the real case of the pauper is made before this order is given.

Mr Benett: Who is to be examined; the pauper alone, who will make good his own case, or the overseer, who refuses to appear and state his case before the magistrates, which refusal has occasioned the order to be made? The examination of forty or fifty paupers would consume from three to four hours, at three or five minutes each person, which at the office of Worship Street, where there are occasionally upwards of seventy persons committed for trial in a month, and where the great variety of other business presses so severely on the magistrates' time, that the office is frequently kept open until six o'clock in the evening, and the business resumed again at seven in the evening.

Since June 1831, I have received from the magistrates of this office about 590 summonses. Of these there were from

Mr Benett ...	240	To the summonses of each	109	
Mr Twyford	179	of these magistrates were	46	*nota benes.*
Mr Broughton	167	attached	27	

In the year 1827, I had as many as fifty names on one summons, on one day, from Mr Benett, and I venture to say, that of these above thirty were bad characters, prostitutes and thieves, who ought not to be relieved at all.

Mr Benett: This is a proof of the justice of my complaint of the immense masses of paupers brought from the parish of Shoreditch before the magistrates of Worship Street. Many of these paupers ought to have been relieved without the intervention of the magistrates. In this instance, he says that thirty of the fifty were bad characters, who ought not to have been relieved. Why were not the twenty who were *not* bad characters relieved without the intervention of the magistrates; and were the cases of the thirty individuals objected to inquired into by the officer before the cases were brought before the magistrate? I do not think that the character of a pauper, if he is in distress, can be taken into consideration; for the Poor Laws were not established as a reward for good conduct, but as a provision for the person in immediate distress, and a person just discharged from the house of correction, or a prostitute, is as much entitled to relief as the most respectable pauper in the parish, because the principle of the English Poor Law is that no one shall starve; therefore the magistrates are obliged to order relief to bad characters as well as good if they are incapable of supporting themselves. If you refuse to persons who are bad characters relief when they are in immediate distress, the collective result must be very injurious to the best interests of society.

All this troop, about fifty persons, came to my door, with an officer at the head of them, demanding immediate relief on the magistrate's order. I said, 'No I cannot think of letting the parish be robbed in this way; I shall attend the summons this night at the office.' I did attend, and stated to Mr Benett that I should insist on the whole of those fifty cases being gone into separately before I gave any money.

Mr Benett: To examine into these cases of fifty paupers, at five minutes per case, would take four hours and ten minutes, which is impossible to be done, and *unnecessary*, inasmuch as it was the duty of the overseer to have inquired into the cases himself, and relieved the deserving, and rejected the undeserving.

He said he was not going to have a vestry-room made of his office. I then handed him up the summons, and said, 'That is your signature, and I am come to answer it.' He then went into two or three of the cases. I think the first or second of these cases was that of a lad named Perkins. One of the officers told me that he knew that this Perkins had been at work that week, and had earned 8s. or 10s. This was proved. I then asked Mr Benett whether such a lad as this ought to have had a summons and an order for immediate relief.

Mr Benett: It being Saturday night, and the overseer having neglected to inquire into the cases, it would not do to risk the chance of rejecting really distressed persons, and forcing them to go without relief through the Sunday, or starving until the succeeding Monday.

Mr Benett said no; but that he had no means of inquiring into the cases. The lad was certainly discharged without relief. This lad has since been transported. I had no specific information, and had no means then of obtaining any with respect to the rest, and Mr Benett having gone through about half a dozen of these cases, I then said to him, seeing him getting very angry at the prospect of a long detention, 'I will take the rest of them into the house.'

Mr Benett: It is the usual practice which prevails now for the overseers to attend at the office on a Saturday night, I may almost say with masses of paupers. I have known a hundred, for I have had them counted. I have then said to the overseer words to this effect: 'There must be a great many distressed persons deserving of relief in this number; take them out, and relieve those who are deserving of relief, and bring back those whom you object to, and I will hear them separately'; and this has been frequently done by Mr Coste. On these occasions I have sat at the office till ten and eleven o'clock at night. From the refusal of the overseers to relieve the paupers, and from their inattention to the summonses, such inconveniences constantly occur on a Saturday night.

Myself and the beadle then went away, followed by the train of paupers, for on Saturday nights I find it necessary to take one or two beadles with me for personal security. The paupers used excessively bad language to us, and as they passed by-streets on the road to the workhouse, they slunk away, until at the workhouse, I think, we had only ten or a dozen, who chose to come in and accept the bread, for the want of which they declared to the magistrate they were starving at the time they first applied for immediate relief.

Mr Benett: This is very probable; but how is the magistrate to help that, if, upon the investigation in the office, the pauper succeeds in his imposition? It is the duty of the overseer to inquire into the cases of the paupers, and he might come prepared with the evidence to prove the fraud.

We frequently make the experiment of taking the applicants into the house with much the same results; but it by no means follows that when they are willing to go into the house they are deserving characters. They frequently get a magistrate's order to get into the house –

Mr Benett: This cannot be; the magistrate has by law no power to order the parties into the house.

– But are no recommendations given which the overseers may call orders?

Perhaps he means by an order, a recommendation. We often recommend the overseer to admit the parties into the house, but the law gives us no power to order.

– for the purpose of getting clothed, and then escaping with the clothes; and very commonly, when they escape with their clothes, they sell them.

Observations of W. Benett, Esq.

From the injurious practice of the overseers of some of the parishes in the district of Worship Street, and particularly of the parish of Shoreditch, of refusing to relieve their poor, many of whom are deserving characters and in immediate distress, without the intervention of the magistrates, great numbers of their paupers apply daily at the office for summonses; if they are asked whether they have been to the overseer, such reports are frequently made by them of the answers of one of them to the applications, and so offensive, as far as they regard the magistrates that they are often obliged to check them in their replies; and this completely puts an end to all confidence of the magistrates in that overseer, who once gave such an answer to an officer of the establishment who was sent with a pauper and an order for immediate relief, which was not obeyed.

I have known an instance of another overseer of Shoreditch, appearing before me at the office at Worship Street, and in the presence of 105 paupers, who were counted, when I remonstrated with him, and desired him to relieve such as were in real distress, and bring those he objected to before me, declaring that he cared not for me or the law, and that he would not relieve one of them. I then proceeded to make an order in each individual case, when he stepped forward, and as each order was made, said, 'I will relieve him', (or 'her'), and so continued throughout the whole number, converting by these means the magistrate into a relieving overseer, and the office into a vestry-room, and I did not finish this painful and unnecessary task till 11 o'clock that night.

No one can read Mr Benett's evidence without being convinced of the excellence of his intentions; and our following remarks are directed not against him individually, but against the system, of which he is one among many administrators. It appears that he considers every adult within his district entitled, merely on his own showing, to 6d. a day from the public, unless the overseer can show cause to the contrary. The 59 Geo III, c. 12 [1818], em-powers a single magistrate, in case of emergency and urgent dis-tress, to order such relief as the case may require, stating in his order the circumstances of the case. The Act throws on the magis-trate the *onus probandi*; he is not only to ascertain that the party is in urgent distress, but he is to state in his order the circumstances of the case; that is, the nature of the urgent distress which has been proved to him. His practice, and it appears from other parts of the evidence to be a common practice, is to throw on the overseer the *onus probandi*; not to require the applicant to prove that he is in urgent distress, but the overseer to prove that he is not. The overseer, generally a person fully occupied by his own concerns, is to show this on a day's notice, with respect perhaps to fifty persons, scattered among the hundreds of thousands of this metropolis. 'His practice', says the overseer of St Leonard's, 'is to grant summonses to all who choose to apply for them, and who choose to say they are in need.' 'That is true,' replies Mr Benett, 'and that practice must be continued.' 'It is very rare', says the overseer, 'that any investigation into the real case of the pauper is made before the order is given.' 'The examination', replies Mr Benett, 'of forty or fifty paupers would consume from three to four hours at three or five minutes each person.' This might be a ground for altering the law, and for enabling a justice to order relief without inquiring whether it is such as the case may require, and without stating in his order the circumstances of the case, or it might be a ground for the magistrate's refusing to interfere, and leaving the overseer to exercise the discretion which the law throws upon him; a discretion, for the excercise of which he alone is responsible; but while the law remains unchanged, it is no ground for ordering the applicant relief without investigation, on the plea that, if the overseer thereafter finds that he had the means of subsistence, the magistrate will punish him; punishment of which we do not find a single example. 'I stated', says the overseer, 'that I should insist on the whole of the cases being gone into before I gave any money.' Mr Benett – 'To examine into these cases of fifty paupers, at five minutes per case, would take four hours and ten minutes; which is impossible to be done.' To examine into them satisfactorily would probably have taken fifty or a hundred hours; and there cannot be a clearer proof of the necessity of returning to the words and the spirit of the law. When the 3 & 4 Will. and Mary, c. 11 [1692], enacted that no person should receive relief except those whom the vestry should think fit and allow, but by authority of a justice of the peace; when the 9 Geo. I, c. 7 [1723], enacted that no justice should order relief until oath should be made before him of some matter which he should judge to be a reasonable ground; when the 59 Geo. III, c. 12, s. 5, directed that in every order the special cause for granting the relief thereby ordered should be expressly stated; and when the liability of the overseer to an indictment for not affording necessary relief without a previous order was carefully continued and not a single act *requires* the justice to make an order, who can doubt that the power given to the justice was a power to be regulated by a sound discretion, to be enforced only when he was convinced that the balance of evil was on the side of non-interference, and convinced by a careful examination of the facts of the case – an examination so complete as to enable him to state them in his order?

The unquestionable fact that sufficient inquiry cannot be made when fifty cases are to be decided on in an evening proves only that the Legislature did not intend that the jurisdiction of the justice should form part of the routine of the administration of the Poor Laws. It was to be excercised *in case of emergency*. If its exercise is to be habitual, every populous parish must have its peculiar magistrate, as well as its peculiar overseers. On no other grounds can we explain why the justices are required to take into consideration the character and conduct of the applicant; a duty which is not enforced on the overseer. The justices are at liberty to interfere or not. The overseer has no such discretion. If he has suffered a man to starve, it is no defence that the applicant starved only because such was his character and conduct that he could obtain no work and he was unsuccessful in stealing. As he is not to be influenced by the character of the applicant, he is not directed to ascertain it.

The magistrates are to take it into consideration. For what purpose? That they may order to persons of good character more relief than is strictly necessary? Whatever may be the errors of our pauper legislation, it has stopped short of this. Necessary relief is all that the justices can order to the most meritorious applicant. How, then, are they to deal with the undeserving? Are they to consider their conduct, and then act precisely as if they had not considered it? The only conceivable construction of the Act is that if they think the character and conduct of the applicant such as to render their interference inexpedient, they are to leave the matter in the hands of the overseer. The whole of the evidence shows how little this has been understood.

Our Appendix contains many complaints of the conduct of magistrates. It is to be observed, that much of this is *ex parte* evidence, which the persons complained of had no opportunity of contradicting or explaining, and that the overseers, from whom it was principally derived, may be supposed to have been anxious that the blame of maladministration should rest on any persons but themselves. It must be acknowledged, however, that in so large a body as the magistracy of England and Wales, invested with powers so extensive and so uncontrolled, cases of misconduct must from time to time arise. Admitting, as we are anxious to admit, the general integrity and intelligence of the magistracy, and the importance of their services in the administration of justice, we yet cannot doubt that there are to be found among more than two thousand persons some exceptions to the general character. But we believe these exceptions to be rare, and that in a great majority of instances – so great as to form the general rule – the magistrates have exercised the powers delegated to them by the

Poor Laws – not wisely, indeed, or beneficially, but still with benevolent and honest intentions, and that the mischief which they have
done was not the result of self-interest or partiality, or timidity or
negligence, but was, in part, the necessary consequence of their
social position, and of the jurisdiction which was confided to them,
and in part arose from the errors respecting the nature of pauperism
and relief which prevailed among all classes at the time when the
allowance system and the scale were first introduced, and still
appear to prevail among the majority. Under the influence of such
opinions even good intentions may become mischievous. A more
dangerous instrument cannot be conceived than a public officer,
supported and impelled by benevolent sympathies, armed with power
from which there is no appeal, and misapprehending the consequences of its exercise.

*

We have now given a brief outline of the most striking points
in the present maladministration of the laws for the relief of the
poor, and of the principal causes to which we attribute it. We
have endeavoured to account for it by the immediate gain which
large classes have hoped to obtain, and in many cases have actually
obtained from the maladministration, and from the constitution
and character of the authorities by whom parochial relief is distributed and awarded. There remains, however, one source of evil
which has been alluded to in our previous remarks, but never
distinctly stated; and that is the evil which has arisen, and is arising,
from the law which throws the burthen of relieving the pauper
in the first place on those who occupy property in the district in
which he is said to be *settled*. We will preface our account of them
by a short history of the Law of Settlement.

SETTLEMENT

THE 43 Eliz. c. 2 [1601], contains no definition of settlement; but we have seen that in a long train of legislation, a person had been considered settled in the parish in which he was born, or in which he had dwelled or been principally conversant for the preceding three years; or under the 39 Eliz. c. 4 [1597], in the case of vagabonds, whose place of birth could not be ascertained, for one year. So that until the 13 & 14 Car. II, c. 12 [1662], there seem to have been only two statutory grounds of settlement, birth and residence, first for three years, and afterwards in some cases for one.

The 13 & 14 Car. II, c. 12, after reciting that 'the necessity, number, and continual increase of the poor, not only within the cities of London and Westminster, but also throughout the whole kingdom of England and Dominion of Wales is very great, and exceedingly burthensome; and that by reason of some defects in the law, poor people are not restrained from going from one parish to another, and, therefore, do endeavour to settle themselves in those parishes where there is the best stock, the largest commons or wastes to build cottages, and the most woods for them to burn and destroy; and when they have consumed it, then to another parish, and at last become rogues and vagabonds, to the great discouragement of parishes to provide stocks, where it is liable to be devoured by strangers', enacts:

That it shall be lawful upon complaint made by the churchwardens or overseers of the poor of any parish, to any justice of peace within forty days after such person or persons coming so to settle as aforesaid in any tenement under the yearly value of £10, for any two justices of the peace whereof one to be of the quorum of the division where any person or persons that are likely to be chargeable to the parish shall come to inhabit, by their warrant to remove and convey such person or persons to such parish where he or they were last legally settled, either as a native, householder, sojourner, apprentice, or servant, for the space of forty days at the least, unless he or they give sufficient security for the discharge of the said parish, to be allowed by the said justices.

Never was such important legislation effected by means of exceptions, qualification, and hints, and seldom have any laws been so pertinaciously adhered to after the principal, and in some cases the only, reasons for their introduction had ceased. The direct purpose of the act stripped of all that qualifies it, is to enable the justices, on complaint of the churchwardens or overseers, to remove any newcomer from a parish, though not applying for relief, if they think or profess to think that he is likely to become chargeable. Such a power, however, was even then felt to require some restriction. It was required, therefore, that it should be exercised within the first forty days after the arrival of the new settler, and persons settling in a tenement of the yearly value of £10, a sum equal, according to the present value of money to more than £50, were directly excepted. Forty days' residence, without removal, or occupying a tenement of £10 annual value, gave, therefore, a right to remain, or, as it is now called, a settlement, and the direction that persons should be removed to the place where they were *last* legally settled as natives, householders, apprentices, servants, or even sojourners, for forty days made also forty days' residence a means, not only of acquiring a settlement, but also a means of losing any previous settlement, and established birth as a settlement, where no other had been acquired. To these the common law added estate, or property in land, because no person ought to be removed from his estate, and marriage in the case of a woman, and parentage in the case of a legitimate child, on the ground that a wife must not be separated from her husband, or a child, until emancipated, from its parents; and the 3 & 4 Will. and Mary, c. 11, s. 6 [1692] added serving an annual public office, and contributing to the public taxes of a parish.

The object of all the subsequent acts on this subject has been to restrict these modes of acquiring a settlement. First by enacting that except in cases of persons serving offices, or paying parochial taxes, unmarried persons without children hired for a year, and apprentices, the forty days' residence, shall be accounted only from the delivery of a notice in writing to the overseers, which they are bound to read in church and register: secondly, by preventing residence from conferring a settlement on persons bringing a certificate from the overseers of their previous parish, acknowledging them to be settled there: thirdly, by declaring that hiring shall not confer a settlement unless the person hired shall continue in the same service a year: fourthly, by enacting that the *purchase* of an estate for less than £30 shall not confer a settlement: fifthly, by preventing a settlement from being gained by payment of taxes in respect of tenements of less annual value than £10, a restriction which has virtually repealed this head of settlement: sixthly, by a series of acts, all endeavouring to explain and define the circumstances under which renting a tenement shall confer settlement.

In the meantime, however, the circumstances under which apprenticeship, hiring and service, estate, renting a tenement, and serving an office, had been held to confer a settlement had changed. We have seen that they were introduced as qualifications and restrictions on the power given by the 13 & 14 Car. II of removing all newcomers whom the overseers chose to consider likely to become chargeable. This power was put an end to by the 35 Geo. III, c. 101 (1795), which enacts that no poor person shall be removed until he shall become actually chargeable; a change so imperiously demanded, not only by expediency, but by justice, that it is difficult to conceive how the arbitrary enactment of the 13 & 14 Car. II could have been tolerated so long.

It might have been expected that the grounds of settlement which were established when the power of removal was given would have been reconsidered when that power was taken away. This, however, appears not to have been done, for it cannot be supposed that, if attention had been called to the subject, they would all have been allowed to continue. The consequence has been that in this instance, as in many others, like a patient who continues the use of remedies after the disease has ceased, we are suffering under laws of which the grounds have long been removed.

The reply to our printed question – 'Can you suggest any and what alteration in the settlement laws?' almost always contains a protestation against settlement by hiring and service. As the demand for agricultural labour varies with the seasons, it is of great importance to the labourer that he should be engaged by the year. When hired for any shorter period he is in danger of being out of work during the winter months, at the very time when his wants are greatest. It is of the greatest importance, also, to the farmer that the persons on whose conduct his own welfare so much depends should have the local knowledge and skill, and the attachment to his person and his interests, which only long continuance in the same service can produce. Accordingly we find that where things are left to take their natural course the agricultural labourer is generally hired by the year and often passes his whole life on the same farm. But instead of things being left to their natural course, the employer has always to consider how his interests may be affected if he allows a labourer to obtain a new settlement, and the labourer, what may be the consequence to himself, of losing his previous one. If the farmer, either from being a proprietor or a lessee, or a tenant-at-will, with the prospect of continuance, is interested in preventing settlements, he effects it either, firstly, by employing no non-parishioners; or, secondly, by hiring all his non-parishioners for periods less than a year; or, thirdly, by preventing those whom he hires from sleeping in his own parish. The first plan, when generally adopted in a district, distributes the labourers, not according to the real demand for labour, but to the accidental divisions of parishes. The second plan is sometimes used as a mere evasion, the labourer being hired for fifty-one weeks, or for 364 days, or some other period less than a year, but practically retained without intermission from year to year. In this case, however, the only protection against settlement is evidence that the contract between the parties, almost always a verbal one, was for less than a year. The danger that this evidence may be lost, or wilfully suppressed, or falsified, has occasioned it to be more usual to let the service, as well as the hiring, be for less than a year; an interval of a few days being interposed, after which a new contract is made and a new service begins. This interval, however, is almost always spent by the labourer in idleness, and often in debauchery, to the injury of both parties; and even if it be not so spent, the constant recurrence of a separation and a new agreement destroys the intimacy and security of the connection, and has a tendency to introduce the still worse practice of hiring by the season, the month, the week, or even the day; a practice which many of our most experienced informants describe as most mischievous to the character and happiness of the agricultural labourers. On the other hand, the labourer, if he thinks his parish a *good* one, that is, one in which public or private relief is profusely distributed, is averse to endanger his existing settlement, by leaving it. With that general and vague idea of the law on the subject which floats in the minds of those who have picked it up by hearsay, he is aware that there are many means by which a settlement may be lost as soon as a man has left his parish, though he is not precisely aware what they are, or how they are to be evaded; while he stays, however, he is safe. The land, to use his own expression, is to maintain him, and it is not his business to inquire whether he is wanted elsewhere, or whether he is an incumbrance where he is.

The Rev. R. R. Bailey, chaplain to the Tower, who has had extensive opportunities of observing the operation of the Poor Laws in the rural districts, was asked –

Can you give any instances within your own knowledge of the operation of the existing law of settlement? – I was requested by Colonel Bogson, Kesgrove House, to furnish him with a farming bailiff. I found a man in all respects qualified for his situation; he was working at 9s. a week in the parish where I lived. The man was not encumbered by a family, and he thankfully accepted my offer; the situation was, in point of emolument, and comfort, and station, a considerable advance; his advantages would have been doubled. In about a week he altered his mind, and declined the situation, in consequence, as I understood, of his fearing to remove from what was considered a good parish to a bad one, the parish to which it was proposed to remove him being connected with a hundred house, in which there is more strict management. I was requested by a poor man, whom I respected, to find a situation for his son, in London: the son was a strong young man, working at that time at about 8s. a week: I eventually succeeded in getting him a good situation of one guinea per week, in London, where his labour would have been much less than it was in the country; but when the period arrived at which he was expected in London, he was not forthcoming. It appeared he had altered his mind, and determined not to take the place; as I understood, his reason for refusing to accept it arose from a reluctance to endanger his settlement in his parish. Such are the instances which are continually presented to my observation with respect to the operation of the present system of settlement.

'Among our present modes of conferring a settlement', says Mr Russell, in the replies to which we have already adverted,

that by hiring and service is incomparably the most pernicious; it tells the poor man that he shall encounter a prohibitory duty in every market in which he attempts to dispose of the only commodity he must live by selling; it shuts the door against the most respectable and advantageous employment in which a servant can engage; by abridging the term, it impairs the strength of the connection between him and his master; and it not only drives the servant from his place, but often betrays him, during the interval between his being discharged from one house and hired at another, into bad company, dissipation and vice.

There seems, indeed, good reason to suppose that the influx of Irish labourers into London is mainly attributable to the disinclination of the labourers in the neighbouring country to quit their existing settlements. 'As far as my experience goes', says Mr Tyler, the rector of St Giles, 'I think it probable that the Irish labourers obtain employment here to the extent to which they do, in consequence of the English labourers being kept in their parishes by the present mode of administering the law, and the effects of the present law of settlement.'

'I found', says Mr Chadwick, 'that in nearly every parish I examined, where bodies of Irish labourers are located, the evidence as to the cause of their location was of the following tenor:

Mr Joseph Whittle, one of the guardians of the poor and overseer of the poor, in the parish of Christchurch, Spitalfields, stated –

In our parish it is a very rare thing to find any labouring men working for less than 12s. a week: indeed, the average rate of wages throughout the year is not less than from 15s. to 20s. a week. A man could not be obtained to work job-work at less than 3s. a day.

Are there many Irish labourers in the parish? – Yes; there is a great proportion of them, and especially about Spitalfields market.

Do they usually receive the average wages you mention? – Yes, they do.

Why are English labourers not employed; or why are Irish labourers preferred? – Because English labourers are not to be had for love or money to perform the labour. Thousands of instances may be given, where the labourers will not stir for fear of losing their parishes. I think the law of settlement is the great means of keeping the English labourers confined to their parishes; it appears to them to be like running a vay from their heir-looms, or their freeholds. I am sure, from my own knowledge of the Whitechapel and other adjacent parishes, that there are not enough of English labourers to be had for such wages to perform the labour.

'Mr T. H. Holland, sometime vestry clerk of Bermondsey, stated:

There are great numbers of Irishmen employed in our parish; but they are only employed because English labourers cannot be got to do the same work for the same wages.

And what sort of wages are those? – Not less than from 10s. to 15s. a week. An English labourer might live upon this. But English labourers would have more wages, if they were to be had for the work, because they are worth more. I have heard a saying amongst the employers of these labourers, that an Irishman must always have his master over him. An English labourer does not require so much superintendence.

Why is it that, in your district, the English labourers have not taken the employment? – I fear that the facility of obtaining parochial relief indisposes them to exert themselves or seek about to procure employment, or to take the labour which is given to the Irish.'

The third plan, that of preventing the unsettled labourer from sleeping within the parish, accounts for the frequent occurrence in the most pauperized districts of small parishes with very low or almost nominal rates. When a parish is in the hands of only one proprietor, or of proprietors so few in number as to be able to act, and to compel their tenants to act in unison, and adjoins to parishes in which property is much divided, they may pull down every cottage as it becomes vacant, and prevent the building of new ones. By a small immediate outlay they may enable and induce a considerable portion of those who have settlements in their parish to obtain settlements in the adjoining parishes; by hiring their labourers for periods less than a year, they may prevent the acquisition of new settlements in their own. They may thus depopulate their own estates, and cultivate them by means of the surplus population of the surrounding district. Against such conduct as this a parish in which the property is much divided, and that is the case in all towns, has no defence. Small master bricklayers and carpenters, and retired tradesmen with trifling accumulations, find cottages and houses inhabited by the poor a most lucrative investment. They must exercise, indeed, great vigilance and occasional harshness; they must be ready to wring their rents from their tenants, or to extort them from the overseer, by constantly threatening, and sometimes effecting distresses and executions; and as no educated person could bear to seize the small property of the poor, or to turn whole families into the streets, those who seek a profit by providing accommodation for the labouring classes are generally persons whose habits have rendered them not merely indifferent to the general prosperity of the parish, but anxious to promote the pauperism that creates the demand for their crowded and unhealthy habitations. On this point, as in many other, the evidence of the Rev. H. Millman of Reading, is very valuable.

'I have now', says Mr Millman,

between ten and twenty families residing together, who belong to one parish, and, though working for the farmer of their own parish, are obliged to reside in mine, at the distance of two, three, or four miles from their work, and whose cottages have been almost literally pulled down over their heads. Even when cottages are not destroyed none are built where the population increases. Many, again, are bribed by presents in actual money, or by promises of advantage, to seek their fortunes in the town. There are always plenty of speculative builders ready to run up cottages, which spring up around us like mushrooms. More than one has told me that, when they made a request for a cottage, the answer was, 'there are plenty in Reading'. I feel convinced, that if the present pressure long continues, that system of demolishing cottages in small parishes, and wherever the landlords can combine for the purpose, will become a general system, and the inevitable consequence will be, to crowd still more those parishes which are already overcrowded, and to force a large portion of the village population into the provincial towns.

The instances of similar practices on the part of the manufacturers are comparatively few; but we cannot hope that so obvious a source of profit will long be overlooked. If the present system continues, we may expect to see manufactories erected on one side of a parochial boundary, and cottages for the work people on the other; so that all the allowances to the labourers, all the casualties to which they are subject, and the great casualty of the failure of the manufactory, may fall exclusively on that parish in which the master manufacturer owns, perhaps, nothing but the three or four acres which he has covered with his cottages.

The evils arising from settlement by apprenticeship, though less than those produced by hiring and service, are still very considerable. In the first place, it leads to a shameful abuse of the trust reposed in the parish officers who have to bind out apprentices, a trust of which the importance cannot well be exaggerated, since the whole welfare of the child may depend on its faithful execution.

Mr Henderson states that in some towns in Lancashire (and Lancashire ranks high among the best administered counties) 'the practice pursued systematically is to bind the parish apprentices into out townships in order to shift the settlement, so that the binding parish may be rid of them. When he inquired how they turned out, the answer was, "we have nothing to do with them afterwards".' This evil is much promoted in many parishes by charitable endowments, for the purpose of apprenticing children. The premium supplied by the charity affords an easy mode of tempting an out-parishioner to take the children, and it is to be feared that in many cases the parish officers inquire no further; they have changed the child's settlement, and if he is ruined in consequence, his new parish must maintain him.

'The object of overseers', says Mr Single of Mile End Old Town,

is to get rid of the boy, to find a master in another parish. They seldom take any trouble to inquire into the character of the master who applies for one, nor ever make any inquiry about the lad after he is gone; they have got him off the parish, and they think they have gained something; but, as other parishes do the same, nothing is gained: we have only placed ours on some other parish, and in return have got another one placed on ours. I have known many instances where the masters having obtained the first part of the premium, then turned them adrift. It is a very rare instance now for a respectable, or even a decent tradesman, to take a parish apprentice, consequently the poor boys get badly used, and badly brought up.

Another evil of settlement by apprenticeship is the influence which it allows to mere accident. An apprentice is settled finally in the parish where he sleeps the last night in his condition of apprentice, provided he has slept there either continuously or at different times, though with intervals even of years, for forty days in the whole. In the meantime he carries with him, wherever he goes, a contingent right of settlement, and may in fact gain as many settlements as there are periods of forty days in the period of his apprenticeship; each fresh settlement suspending all the previous ones, subject to their revival, if his last night is spent in any parish in which he has slept as an apprentice for thirty-nine days. Bitter complaints are made of this grievance by the rate-payers of towns having ports, or situated on the banks of navigable rivers.

The following is an extract from a memorial addressed to us by the overseers and select vestry of South Shields:

That the township of South Shields is a narrow piece of ground, bounded on one side by the river Tyne, and on the other by the township of Westoe, and that it consists of docks, manufactories, shops, and houses, which houses are occupied, for the most part, by the working classes.

That the township of South Shields becomes excessively burthened with 'sailor poor', so much so that of 1,500 paupers at present receiving relief, 75 per cent belong to that class.

That, as the law at present stands, the settlement of a seaman is purely a matter of chance, depending on the direction and force of the wind, the state of the weather, the manner in which a ship lies moored, and other circumstances purely casual; and that in by far the greater part of the applications made to this vestry by seamen, the settlement cannot be ascertained, and the difficulty is still much greater when the application is made by the widow.

That all parishes and townships bordering on navigable rivers are more or less affected by the same circumstances.

'The following case of hardship, from this cause', says Mr Maclean, was represented to me by a gentleman resident in and occupying nearly the whole of Itchenor, a small parish at the western extremity of the county of Sussex. This parish is divided from that of Bosham by a small arm of the sea running up to the port of Chichester. It is the practice of vessels belonging to the above port to unload their cargoes at Itchenor, and consequently to moor the vessels there. It not unfrequently happens that articles of apprenticeship expire during the time that a vessel is moored there, and consequently the apprentice gains a settlement, as he has probably, during the term of his apprenticeship, slept the requisite number of nights at Itchenor. The allowing a settlement to be gained by the passing of forty (not consecutive) nights off Itchenor is one grievance, but there is another in this case: the channel divides Itchenor from Bosham, and as the cable is long enough to allow the vessel to swing across to the Bosham side, according as the wind may blow, if a man will swear the ship was lying at Itchenor, and the parish officer is unable to prove to the contrary, he will be sent home on an order by the magistrates, and so obtain a settlement. The father of the present occupier tried the point and lost it, as the post to which the vessel was moored was on the Itchenor, and not on the Bosham side of the water. The appeal, I understand, was allowed. The parish of Itchenor derives no benefit from vessels unloading or taking on board their cargoes. It is considered that more than half of the persons having settlements in this parish have obtained them in the above manner; and it is impossible to say how many other persons may have acquired settlements, or how soon, and with what families they may come home. From the above cause the expenditure has increased one third within the last few years.

Nearly the same objections apply to settlement by hiring and service, the servant being settled where he slept the last night before his discharge, provided he has slept there during the course of his service, though at different periods, for thirty-nine days in one year. Years may elapse between the occurrence of the last of these important sleepings, and their consequences to the parish in which they occurred. A man applies to a London parish for relief for himself, his wife, and their six children. He states that he was born in Suffolk, and at the age of fifteen apprenticed to a person in the parish of A.; that disliking his treatment, he absconded at the end of the first two months; that his master, satisfied with having received the premium, made no inquiry about him; that he came to London, and has lived there for the last thirty years, always hired by the day, or the week, or the job. On this statement he and his wife and family are sent to parish A.; parish A., however, endeavours to show that he did not go to London immediately after he ran away from his master, but was hired for a year as a gentleman's groom, and discharged at the end of his year's service at B., a small watering-place in Wales, where his master had been spending six weeks. To B., therefore, the pauper with his wife and family are again removed, subject to still further removal, if B. can show that the gentleman with a groom, who is said to have staid six weeks at the hotel, thirty-one years ago, in fact staid there for only five weeks and a half, or that though six weeks elapsed between his arrival and final departure, yet that during three days he was absent with his groom on a visit, or that though he kept his groom for a year, he did not hire him for a year, or that he discharged him a day before the year ended, or a day before the forty days of residence ended, or can adduce any other fact, however apparently trifling, of equal legal force. And it is on absurdities like these that the question depends, whether parish A. or parish B., neither of which has any real connection with the pauper, neither of which could by any vigilance have prevented his acquiring a settlement, is to support him and his family, and perhaps his children's children, for ever.

It is no slight aggravation of these evils that they may arise not merely from accident, but from fraud. 'Settlement, by hiring and service', says Mr Maclean, 'may be converted into a most prolific instrument of fraud upon parishes: e.g., an individual assessed to a large amount in the parish of A., and to a small amount in the adjoining one of B. wishing to relieve the burdens of parish A., takes into his service at a yearly hiring in the parish of B., parishioners of A.; these he employs for one year, and then discharges, to be a permanent burden on B., and is again at liberty to take others, and act by them in a similar manner.'

The case supposed by Mr Maclean is described by Mr Cowell as actually occurring in Ely.

A proprietor possessing nearly the whole of a parish at some distance from Ely, as we were told, hired a farm in Ely, which he manages by a bailiff; he sends his own parishioners to work on it. To these persons his bailiff gives settlements in Ely, by hiring, and at the end of the year they are turned off upon Trinity parish in Ely, and their places supplied by fresh immigration from the mother parish. The proprietor may have had very different motives from those attributed to him by our examinants, and this circumstance is not mentioned for the purpose of casting any reflection on him (we do not know his name, nor what account of the transaction he himself might give), but in order to point out the temptations which 'settlement by hiring and service' throws in the way of persons even of station and education. In the case of Great Shelford, are not the landowners, who daily see their property slowly but surely passing away from them, under a strong temptation to save themselves from ruin by hiring a couple of farms for seven years in two distinct parishes, and bribing their supernumerary families to take service there? And this is clearly possible by the existing law.

'Many settlements', says Mr Everett, 'have been obtained in Saint Andrew-the-Less, Cambridge, by persons who have rented houses of £10 yearly value; the rent for which has been in reality paid by other parties or parishes collusively, for the purpose of getting rid of troublesome parishioners, and fixing them in the parish of Saint Andrew-the-Less.'

'I have been told', says Mr Maclean, 'that some parishes have arrangements with brokers and other persons in large towns, who are in the habit of letting small tenements, under which the broker or other person receives a premium upon each pauper of whom he so relieves a parish.'

Settlement by estate is a still easier mode of fraud than settlement by renting a tenement, as the slightest interest in land, if acquired gratuitously, even the last six months of a hovel let at 5s. a year, confers a settlement. Mr Majendie mentions the case of an Irishman, to whom, for the express purpose of fixing him and his wife and family in a Sussex parish, his father-in-law conveyed some land. He now receives in consequence a fixed weekly allowance of 11s. 6d. from the parish.

Settlement by marriage seems to be a fertile source of fraud.

'It is the usual custom', says Mr Brushfield of Spitalfields,

when single women are pregnant, for them, as a matter of course, to make application to the parish officers for relief. The parish officers inquire as to her settlement. She belongs to their parish; but they find that the father of the child is single, and belongs to another parish, and acting for the benefit of their own local circumscribed boundary, they immediately begin a sort of negociation for the purpose of marrying the father and the mother previous to the birth of the child. Such negociations frequently succeed, and so by removing the burthen from the shoulders of their parish altogether, a comparatively light burthen, they inflict on a neighbouring parish a heavy load, and on society a perpetually increasing evil. To such sources may be attributed, as I conceive, a very great portion of that misery, immorality, want of care and affection for their offspring, attachment to home, respect for themselves, and for domestic economy, which are so prevalent among the labouring classes of society. That such negociations are anticipated in many cases by the parties is very evident, for on the first application to the parish officers, the young woman is ready with 'He's willing to marry me *if he could afford it* and he does not belong to you' (viz., your parish).

'Marriages', says Mr Mott of Lambeth,

are frequently made up by parish officers, in order to throw the charges on other parishes. To evade the odium and avoid publicity, the arrangement is often made by some pretended disinterested person, and the money repaid by the overseers; but the beadles are commonly employed to effect the arrangement. The following case occurred last week. A young man, named Charles Brockley, belonging to some parish in Hertfordshire, applied to the overseers of Lambeth, offering to marry a young woman named Sarah Isles, an inmate of Lambeth workhouse (a most determined drunkard). The overseers bargained with him for two guineas, and agreed to pay, in addition, the marriage fees. Monday, 22nd April, one guinea was advanced to buy Isles some clothes; a gown was purchased, and Isles had it to make. Wednesday, 29th April, was appointed for the marriage. The gown was made by Thursday, and on Friday morning *Isles pledged it for one shilling*. On the Monday morning she related the circumstance to Mr Drouet, with a mixture of pretended regret and laughter, imploring him to lend her a shilling to get the gown out of pawn, otherwise she could not be married. This was done. A person was sent to accompany them to church, and, upon the completion of the marriage, paid the fees and gave the husband the remaining guinea. Such marriages are very common. In cases where young women are likely to inflict a burden upon parishes, being pregnant, the reputed fathers are frequently induced by such arrangements to marry the girl, and thereby throw the burden of the young woman and her offspring upon another parish. During some inquiries I made, a beadle, in a *small district* of one parish, assured me he had alone effected fifty marriages of this description in the course of a few years, and that the aggregate of such marriages in that parish in one year was very considerable.

To these evils must be added the perjury and falsehood which seem peculiarly incidental to these inquiries. Though the English law has assumed that the minutest interest overbalances in every man and on every occasion, both the love of truth and the fear of punishment, inasmuch as it has declared that a witness who has anything, however trifling, to gain or lose by the decision, is unfit, not merely to be fully trusted, but even to be heard,* it yet admits, and necessarily admits, the evidence of the proprietor on points which are to decide whether his property is or is not to support an additional burden, and that of the pauper, when the question is as to the place where he is to be fixed during the remainder of his life. It admits this questionable evidence where it cannot possibly be verified or contradicted. Settlements are claimed by hiring and service under masters who have long been dead, under apprenticeship when the indentures are lost or destroyed, by renting a tenement when houses have been pulled down. And they are rebutted or supported by narratives of conversations which occurred, perhaps, twenty years before, and which were not of a nature to dwell on the memories of those who profess to report them. We cannot better characterize the evidence on which the justices have to decide in matters of settlement, than by saying, that it is almost as unsatisfactory as that which guides them in matters of relief.

These evils arise almost exclusively from the heads of settlement which were introduced in consequence of the 13 & 14 Car. II [1662], and might be almost entirely removed if those heads of settlement were put an end to. But there are others greater and more extensive, which arise from the mere existence of a law of settlement, whatever that law may be, which increase in intensity in proportion as the limits of the district which has to support what are called its own poor are restricted, and could be miti-

* Since this passage was written the law on this point has been materially improved by the 3 & 4 Will. IV, c. 42, s. 26 and 27.

gated only by its extension, and removed only by its entire abolition.

As soon as it was established by practice, whether legally or not we will not inquire, that all the persons having settlements in a parish must be supported, either paid for working or paid for being idle, it became the interest of every parish having more parishioners than could be profitably employed to apportion among the applicants the fund for the subsistence of the labouring classes, in such a manner as to give to all a subsistence, and if possible to none more than a subsistence; to treat them, in short, like slaves or cattle. Everyone who endures the painful task of going through this Report must be struck and, if the subject is new to him, astonished by the cases which we have cited, in which those men who have accumulated any property are found to be refused employment, to be denied even the privilege of working for hire, until their savings have been wasted in idleness; by the difference in the remuneration obtained from the same master in return for the same exertion by the married and single; and by the studied attempts by means of mutual compacts among the farmers and by rating strangers and excusing parishioners, to drive all who have no settlement from the parish. But all these are the natural results of the parochial system and cannot be got rid of, unless we are willing either to refuse parochial relief to the able-bodied and their families, or to distribute the burden affording that relief over districts so large as to prevent any individual from feeling that its immediate pressure on himself can be increased or alleviated by his own conduct.

BASTARDY

ONE subject remains to be considered, which, notwithstanding its importance, we have placed at the end of this portion of our Report, as it is a branch of the Poor Laws distinguished from the rest both as to the principles on which it is founded and the evils which it has produced. This comprehends the support of illegitimate children, the relief afforded to their mothers, and the attempts to obtain the repayment of the expense from their supposed fathers.

By the first act on this subject, the 18 Eliz., c. 3, s. 2 [1576],

concerning bastards begotten and born out of lawful matrimony (an offence against God's law and man's law) the said bastards being now left to be kept at the charges of the parish where they be born, to the great burden of the same parish, and in defrauding of the relief of the impotent and aged, *true poor of the same parish*, and to evil example and encouragement of lewd life, it is enacted, that two justices of the peace, upon examination of the cause and circumstance, shall, by their discretion take order as well for the punishment of the mother and reputed father, as also for the better relief of every such parish in part or in all; and for the keeping of every such child, by charging such mother or reputed father with the payment of money weekly, or other sustentation, for the relief of such child in such wise as they shall think convenient: and if after the same order by them subscribed under their hands, the said persons, viz., mother or reputed father, upon notice thereof, shall not, for their part, observe and perform the said order, every such party so making default to be committed to gaol, there to remain, except he, she, or they shall put in sufficient surety to perform the said order, or else personally to appear at the next general sessions of the peace, and also to abide such order as the justices of the peace then and there shall take in that behalf.

The object of this act was merely to force the parents to support their child – a duty which appears to have been previously performed for them by the parish. Its failure may be inferred from the next act on the subject, the 7 Jac. I, c. 4, s. 7 [1609], which 'because great charge ariseth upon many places within this realm by reason of bastardy, besides the great dishonour of Almighty God, enacts that every lewd woman which shall have any bastard which may be chargeable to the parish shall be committed to the house of correction, there to be punished and set on work, during the term of one whole year; and if she shall eftsoons offend again shall be committed to the said house of correction as aforesaid, and there remain until she can put in good sureties for her good behaviour, not to offend so again' – a sentence which, if executed, must often have been imprisonment for life. The 50 Geo. III, c. 51, s. 2 [1810], repeals this power, and enables the justices to sentence the woman to imprisonment for any period not less than six weeks, or more than one year.

It appears, by the 13 & 14 Car. II. c. 11, s. 19, that the previous acts were defeated by the parents' running away out of the parish and sometimes out of the country, leaving their children on the charge of the parish where they were born. The act, therefore, enables the churchwardens and overseers for the poor of such parish where any bastard child shall be born, to take so much of the goods and chattels, and receive so much of the annual rent or profits of the lands of such putative father or mother as shall be ordered by any two justices of the peace for or towards the discharge of the parish for the bringing up and providing for such child.

By the 6 Geo. II, c. 31 [1732], and the 49 Geo. III, c. 68 [1809] (by which the former act is repealed and then re-enacted with some variatios), it is ennacted, 'That if any single woman declare herself to be pregnant, and charge any person with being the father, it shall be lawful for any justice of the division, on the application of the overseers, or of any substantial householder, to issue his warrant for the immediate apprehending such person, and he is required to commit such person to gaol, unless he shall give security to indemnify the parish, or enter into a recognizance, with sufficient surety to appear at the quarter sessions, and to perform the order to be then made':

'It seems', says Mr Nolan, the principal text writer on the subject, that proceedings under this statute may be altogether *ex parte*. No summons need issue to bring the person accused before the justice;

and it appears unnecessary that he should be present at the woman's examination. When the reputed father is brought by warrant before the justice, the magistrate has no power to examine into the merits of the case, but is bound by the express terms of the statute to commit him to the common gaol or house of correction, unless he gives security, or enters into a recognizance with sufficient surety.

If there were no other objections to these laws than that they place at the mercy of any abandoned woman every man who is not rich enough to give security or find sureties, that they expose him to be dragged without previous summons, on a charge made in his absence, before a tribunal which has no power to examine into the merits of the case; if these were their only faults, we should still feel it our duty to urge their immediate abolition. What can be conceived more revolting than a law which not only authorizes but compels the oppression thus detailed by Captain Chapman:

At Exeter, an apprentice under eighteen years of age was recently committed to the house of correction for want of security. It was admitted that there was no chance of his absconding, but the overseers said he had been brought for punishment. The woman stated that she was only three months gone with child; and thus the boy is taken from his work, is confined five or six months among persons of all classes, and probably ruined for ever, on the oath of a person with whom he was not confronted, and with whom he denied having had any intercourse.

The overseers, it seems, said that 'he had been brought for punishment'. For what was he punished? For having committed the act with which he was charged? That act was an offence not punished by the English law. Whether punishable or not, he denied having committed it; and the tribunal which sentenced him, though competent to punish, was not competent even to hear his defence; he was punished simply for his youth, poverty, and friendlessness, for not being able to give security or find sureties; and his punishment was five or six months' imprisonment – a punishment severe even to hardened criminals, but absolutely ruinous to a boy of eighteen.

But these are not the only, they are not even the principal, objections to the enactments of which we have stated the substance.

The mode in which they oppress the innocent, revolting as it is, is far less mischievous to society than that by which they punish the guilty. Without recurring to the proceedings which may take place during the mother's pregnancy, we will consider those which follow the birth of an illegitimate child. The mother, as a matter of course, requires the parish to support her child. The overseers apply to the magistrates, who make an order that the woman, and the man whom she swears to be the father, shall each pay to the parish a weekly sum for the child's support. The sum charged on the woman is scarcely ever exacted, as she is supposed to earn it by nursing the child. If the man, on demand, refuse to pay the sum charged on him he may be imprisoned three months, and so from time to time while the order remains in force. Whatever is received from the man is paid over by the parish to the woman, and in almost every case the parish pays to the woman the sum, whatever it may be, that has been *charged* on the man, whether paid by him or not. The sum charged on the man varies from 7s. or 8s. a week to 1s. The average is about 3s. or 2s. 6d. in towns, and 2s. in the country; but generally higher if he is in good circumstances. In most cases the sum is as great, in many it is greater, than that for which a child can be put out to nurse, or than that which would be allowed by the parish if it were legitimate and its father dead. To the woman, therefore, a single illegitimate child is seldom any expense, and two or three are a source of positive profit. To the man, indeed, it is a burden unless, as is frequently, perhaps we might say most frequently, the case, he avoids it by flying to some part of the country where he is unknown, or so distant from the scene of his delinquency as to make the expense of endeavouring to enforce payment a sufficient motive to leave him unmolested. Still more frequently, however, as soon as he finds that the evil of becoming the father of a bastard is otherwise inevitable, he avoids it by marrying the woman during her pregnancy – a marriage of which we may estimate the consequences, when we consider that it is founded, not on affection, not on esteem, not on the prospect of providing for a family, but on fear on one side, and vice on both.

We will support these statements and inferences by the following passages from the evidence:

First, with respect to the pecuniary indemnity, and in many, and those the most aggravated cases, the pecuniary benefit offered to the woman for her incontinency.

Colonel A'Court, J.P., Castleman's, near Maidenhead, Berks., June, 1832.

The certainty of women obtaining care and provision for themselves during pregnancy and birth of children born in bastardy, as well as parish allowance for the maintenance of their children so born, tends to remove those checks to irregular intercourse which might otherwise operate were they in such cases left more dependent upon the honour and ability of the men to support them in such difficulties. No restraint is now imposed by necessity of circumstances to influence women to observe caution or forbearance, or even decent scruples, in their choice. Middle-aged women will sometimes unblushingly swear mere lads to be the fathers of their bastard children; lads whom they have perhaps enticed to the commission of the offence. I have seldom observed any diffidence in women in passing through the forms prescribed by the laws for the affiliation of bastards; but I have witnessed a disposition on their parts to persuade the magistrates to order the weekly payment by the men as heavy as possible, which being invariably paid by the parish to the woman, she considers as a sort of pension to herself.

John Kirkham, Assistant Overseer, Louth, Lincolnshire, has had six parishes at a time under his charge.

With respect to the women, in the course of my personal acquaintance with those parishes I have had to manage, as well as from extensive inquiry, I find there are numbers in most parishes who have from two to four children, receiving different sums of money with each according to the ability of the putative father; so that the sum the woman receives with the whole of the children, and what the mother can earn, enables them to live as comfortably, or indeed more so, than most families in the neighbourhood. It may be truly said, that the money she receives is more than sufficient to repay her for the loss her misconduct has occasioned her, and it really becomes a source of emolument and is looked upon by others as an encouragement to vice. Many of those escape punishment of any sort, and if some of them go to the house of correction for twelve months, it appears to have very little effect either upon them or upon the morals of others.

John Dodgson, Roanstrees, parish of Bewcastle, Cumberland.

We, at this time, in our parish, are supporting two bastard children whose mothers have landed property of their own, and would not marry the fathers of their children. The daughters of some farmers, and even land-owners, have bastard children, who keep their daughters and children with them, and regularly keep back their poor-rate to meet the parish allowance for their daughters' bastards. We have no doubt the same grievance exists in many other parishes.

Edward Tregaskis, vestry clerk, Penryn St Gluvias, Cornwall.

We know and are satisfied from long and serious observation and facts occurring that continued illicit intercourse has, in almost all cases, originated with the females; many of whom, under our knowledge, in this and neighbouring parishes, do resort to it as a source of support, taking advantage of the kindness of the provisions for the nurture of the offspring from their own known inability to contribute, and thus receive the fixed weekly allowances from the parish officers; and a deliberate repetition of offence gives them in this manner a right to claim the allowances, which, when added together according to the number of their children generally with them, is sufficient in many cases to afford support.

'At Totness', says Captain Chapman,

the sum ordered upon putative fathers varies from 1s. 3d. to 2s. 6d., according to means; the whole is given to the mother, whether paid to the parish or not, the order being considered as an order upon the parish itself; one case of a person having absconded some years ago, on whom an order was made for 2s. 6d., the parish continued to pay the full amount. In addition to the allowance the mothers receive clothing.

A widow, with a legitimate child, would in no instance receive more than 1s. 6d. per week.

It was a matter of general notoriety that such persons receive money from those with whom they may have had intercourse, to induce them not to affiliate upon them, but to swear to some poor man who is frequently paid, and from whom nothing can be recovered. At Liskeard, the assistant overseer informed me that a person of respectability had within a few days paid an allowance or composition for a bastard, and lamented that he had been such a fool as to refuse to give the mother a small sum, which she had asked for, and then would have sworn to some other person. Instances of such arrangements are said to be very common. In garrisons in particular, it is a common practice to swear the child to a soldier, from whom nothing can be recovered, and who can only be sent to the tread-wheel for a short time. Indeed, so general is the system of compromise that it was the opinion of the most experienced parochial officers, that from ignorance and wilful perjury combined *nine bastards in ten are falsely sworn in towns*. But I heard of no instance of punishment for perjury, and believe that they are of very rare occurrence.

'In some districts', says Mr Majendie,

the custom prevails of overseers paying over to the mother of a bastard the sum directed by the order of maintenance, whether it be recovered from the father or not, and this comes under the denomination of 'pay' in pauper language. The sum allowed to the mother of a bastard is generally greater than that given to the mother of a legitimate child; indeed, the whole treatment of the former is a direct encouragement to vice. If a young woman gets into trouble. she is probably taken into a workhouse, where she is better lodged and fed than at any period of her former life, and maintained perhaps for a year in perfect idleness; it is not wonderful, then, that she comes back under the same circumstances; hence the bastardy debt sometimes amounts to £500 or £600 in agricultural parishes; not more than one fifth of the expense is recovered from the fathers, and that subject to the deduction of heavy law expenses.

In Croydon the number of bastards in the house is twelve, out of the house eighty-eight, amounting to a hundred; the vicinity of London is considered a cause of this large number. The total annual expense is, on an average, £500, of which about one fifth is recovered from the fathers; the order of maintenance is from 2s. to 3s. per week, according to the circumstances of the father, and is paid to the mother whether received from the father or not; to the mother of a legitimate child, if in distress, the weekly allowance is 2s.: thus the mother of a bastard is, at all events, as well provided for, and it may be better.

'The administration of the laws on bastards', says Captain Pringle,

are the cause of great evils, without appearing to have almost any redeeming quality.

The allowance made to the mother for the support of her child, and secured to her by the parish in case of the putative father failing to pay the amount awarded, is an encouragement to the offence; it places such women in a better situation than many married women, whatever may be the number of children.

The system of making the allowance vary from 1s. up to 5s. per week, according to the circumstances of the putative father, is an inducement to false swearing. It appears even to be a cause of leading the parish officer to encourage the woman to pick out a 'good man', for the latter can easily be made to pay; whilst servants, labourers, and mechanics often escape; so that from one half to one third is never recovered from the father, and, consequently, comes as a charge on the parish.

Parish aid has a tendency to remove all shame: thus, in Cumberland, the daughters of farmers sometimes claim such allowance, or it is claimed by their fathers, and deducted out of their payment of poor-rates.

Mr Tweedy:

Snaith, Yorkshire. The usual order on the father has been 2s. per week, and the same on a second or third child; but now the magistrates seem determined to allow no more than 1s. 6d. If a woman has 2s. a week allowed for each child, she may save something on having a third child. There is one instance in Carleton of a woman who is now receiving 4s. for two children, and is about to have a third; and she said, if she had a third, she could live as well as anybody.

Mr Cowell:

Swaffham, Norfolk. A woman in a neighbouring parish had five illegitimate children, for which she was allowed 10s. per week, and 6s. for herself. She is now in the receipt of 18s. per week, the produce of successful bastardy adventures.

My informant in this and the following instance was Mr Sewell, clerk to the magistrates at Swaffham.

A woman of Swaffham was reproached by the magistrate, Mr Young, with the burdens she had brought upon the parish upon the occasion of her appearing before him to present the parish with her seventh bastard. She replied, 'I am not going to be disappointed in my company with men to save the parish.' This women now receives 14s. a week for her seven bastards, being 2s. a head for each. Mr Sewell informed me that had she been a widow with seven legitimate children, she would not have received so much by 4s. or 5s. a week, according to their scale of allowance to widows. A bastard child is thus about 25 per cent more valuable to a parent than a legitimate one. The premium upon want of chastity, perjury, and extortion, is here very obvious; and Mr Sewell informed me that it is considered a good speculation to marry a woman who can bring a fortune of one or two bastards to her husband.

Holbeach, Lincolnshire. Informants, the overseer and master of the workhouse.

Many illegitimate children – ten or twelve every year; bastards increasing; order from 1s. to 2s. 6d., and above – *depends on the circumstances of the father.*

An unmarried girl, upon leaving the workhouse after her fourth confinement, said to the master, 'Well, if I have the good luck to have another child, I shall draw a good sum from the parish; and with what I can earn myself, shall be better off than any married woman in the parish'; and the master added that she had met with the good luck she hoped for, as she told him a short time before I was at Holbeach that she was five months gone with child.

I asked him what she had for each child. He answered, 2s.; and that women, in that neighbourhood, could easily earn 5s. a week all the year through. Thus she will have 15s. a week.

Mr W. Sefton, collector of the poor-rates of Lambeth.

I have had the care of the bastardy accounts of the parish for seven years; and I am of opinion that the crime has greatly increased in our parish within that period, far more than in the proportion in which the population has increased.

In cases where the children are affiliated, we pay over to the mothers all the sums we receive from the fathers under the order of the magistrates; and they vary from 2s. to 7s. a week; indeed, I know one case in which 8s. was awarded by the magistrates, and that sum has been paying for several years, and is still paid to the mother, who is now married and living respectably.

Mr George Chadwin, vestry clerk, and Mr James Unwin, overseer, of St Mary, Battersea.

We have many illegitimate children; and we think that the numbers have increased of late years. If a young woman has two or three bastard children, and receives 2s. 6d. a week for each, it is a little fortune to them. As soon as the children can run about, they can be taken into infant schools for 2d. a week, and kept from nine in the morning till five in the evening; so that the mothers can get their living by work, or waste their time in idleness.

'In Sunderland', says Mr Wilson,

the witnesses dwelt on the shocking inequality established in the bastard's favour over the legitimate child. A respectable widow would actually receive less for her children than a prostitute for the offspring of promiscuous concubinage; and when the overseers endeavour to correct this sort of regimen, the first question asked them by the magistrates when summoned before them, without allowing them time to explain the reasons of their conduct, is, 'Why don't you pay the sum named in the order?' and this in the girl's presence, who is thus encouraged to claim *her rights*. Witness mentioned a case within his own personal cognizance of a young woman of four-and-twenty, with four bastard children; she is receiving 1s. 6d. weekly for each of them. She told him herself, that *if she had one more, she should be very comfortable.* Witness added, 'They don't in reality keep the children; they let them run wild, and enjoy themselves with the money.'

Secondly, as to its tendency to promote her marriage.

Charles Sawyer, Esq., J.P., Bray, Berks.

In the case of poor people, the magistrates of the Maidenhead division of the county of Berks. order the father of the bastard to pay 2s. a week for the maintenance of the child; and it sometimes happens that if a woman has two or more bastard children she is considered a good object of marriage on account of these weekly payments; and thus marriages are contracted which are in the end productive of misery to the parties and of injury to the community, by becoming the source of a disorderly and profligate population.

'The charge of bastardies', says Mr Power,

is accompanied by a very large share of mischievous and immoral consequences. The disgrace, such as it is, is the only punishment which awaits the mother; the other difficulties affect neither her nor her relations. The usual allowance of 2s. *guaranteed by the parish*, makes an illegitimate child a less incumbrance, almost by half, than a legitimate one. But the most active inducement to incontinence in the female, is the prospect of all being cured by a forced marriage, the usual consequence of a state of pregnancy in country parishes. Accordingly, it is found, and the fact is so flagrant as to make a part of all testimony on this subject, that the female in very many cases becomes the corruptor; and boys, much under the age of twenty, are continually converted by this process into husbands. At Girton, a small village about four miles from Cambridge (population 330 in 1831), I was told that twelve marriages had taken place within the parish during the last year, and that all the parties were very young. It is difficult to say whether the Bastardy Laws, or the system of relief, have the greatest effect in the promotion of those early marriages.

'Bastardy', says Mr Villiers,

leads to marriage. At Bulkington, in Warwickshire, Mr Warner
stated that he had lately questioned the clergymen of the parish as to
the proportion of pregnant women among the poor whom he married,
and his reply was, 'Not less than nineteen out of every twenty.' Having
repeated this statement to the clergyman at Beckenhill, in the same
county, he said that it precisely corresponded with his experience in
his own parish.

At Nuneaton the solicitor to the parish, Mr Greenaway, stated
that his house looked into the churchyard; that he was in the habit
purposely of watching the persons resorting to the church for marriage,
and that he could confidently say that seventeen out of every twenty of
the female poor who went there to be married were far advanced in
pregnancy.

'Where early marriages are complained of,' says Mr Richardson,

that is everywhere, I have also been told that the women, as they
feel no disgrace either in their own eyes or in those of others at becoming the mothers of bastards, have still less reluctance in allowing
the claims of a husband to anticipate the marriage ceremony, in fact
they are almost always with child when they come to the church. I
heard from the brother of a clergyman living at a parish which I had
not time to visit that his brother, being anxious to reform the morals
of his parish, had preached for some years with great vigour and plain-
ness of speech against this custom, and had offered rewards to any
woman whose first child was not born within a given time. It was
only given once, and even then it turned out that the clergyman had
been deceived. This parish, I believe, was a very bad one, for the
corruption had extended there to rather a higher grade of society than
the common labourers; but so far as they are concerned, the experiment might be repeated with the same ill success in all the pauperized
villages in the country.

'In the parish of Midhurst', says Mr Maclean,

there has been no increase of chargeable bastards, but a great increase
of marriages to prevent it; and these, though not compulsory on the
part of the parish, take place under the impression, that it is better for
them to receive an allowance for a legitimate, than to be liable to a
weekly payment for an illegitimate child.

In the parish of Cranley, with a population of 1,350, the number of bastards chargeable does not average one in the year, as the man marries the woman as soon as she is with child, in the expectation of being better off. The order is generally 2s. on the father, and nothing on the mother.

Several clergymen told me that four fifths of the women are with child, and frequently near their confinement at the time of their marriage, and that this want of chastity may be attributed in a great measure to the law of bastardy, which secures to the woman either a husband or a weekly allowance for the support of the child.

'Bastardy', says Mr Walcott, is a growing evil in Wales.

The laws on this subject were universally condemned, not only as inefficient to indemnify the parish and repress the mischief, but as operating directly to cause its increase. I found that in practice, so far from punishing the female, they intercept one of the punishments naturally consequential on the offence, the burthen of supporting a child; they hold out to her, if not a pecuniary reward, in many instances, the powerful aid of parish officers in obtaining a husband; they effect, and often by the most shameful practices, marriages which ought to have been discountenanced; they encourage perjury on the woman's part, to the injury and disgrace of innocent persons; they convert into vagrants and dissolute characters many of the industrious; and worse than all, they tend to induce the crime of abortion, from the interest they give the man in preventing a birth which presents the alternative of a prison or (to him) a heavy weekly expense. Instances were mentioned to me of applications to medical practitioners, by males, for drugs for this purpose.

A detail of all the instances adduced to exemplify the operation of these laws would be tedious, but on the subject of improper marriages it may be observed that where the female is of a different parish to the male, the officers of her parish, upon default in payment under the order of maintenance (to use the expression of one of my informants) sometimes 'takes the woman in one hand and a warrant in the other, and gives the man the option of going to church, or to gaol'. An aggravated case of this sort was related to me by a clergyman, where a man to whom a child had been affiliated by a woman of loose character, in order to avoid the imprisonment with which he was threatened, consented to marry her; but lest he should change his mind and abscond before a special licence was obtained, he was kept under lock and key, and ultimately led handcuffed to the church-door. As soon as the ceremony was over he quitted the neighbourhood. The object, however, was gained in the transfer of the female's settlement to another parish.

One gentleman stated that in forty-nine out of every fifty marriages that he had been called on to perform in his parish amongst the lower orders, the female was either with child or had had one, and many affirmed this of nineteen out of twenty cases.

The remedy which the majority of witnesses thought would meet most, if not all, of the present evils would be to repeal the bastardy laws, and to make it unnecessary for parishes to interfere with illegitimate children, except they were orphans or deserted.

The application of such a remedy to a first offence in North Wales may perhaps seem too harsh from the appearance of hardship in punishing one whose fall a national custom may have greatly contributed to effect. But for a second or subsequent offence this could not be urged; and on the whole, I think the plan might be beneficially adopted. The natural consequences of misconduct would then be its punishment, and the motives for prudence on the woman's part rendered as powerful as they could now be made.

I met with a striking instance which proves that the female in these cases is generally the party most to blame; and that any remedy, to be effectual, must act chiefly with reference to her. In 1823 the then overseer of the parish of Machynlleth, who was represented to be of a strict and resolute character, made known his determination to punish every single woman offending in this way, and he kept his word; the consequence was, that in the two years succeeding his year of office, not one case of bastardy occurred in the parish; but in the third year, when the terror of his reign had somewhat abated, the evil recommenced with one case and, no punishment following, gradually increased to its former level.

Desertion of children, with infanticide, were objections sometimes urged against the plan; but the great majority of clergymen, magistrates, and others whom I examined on the subject thought that the former would not be more frequent than at present; and that abortion and infanticide would be less frequent not only from there being fewer cases to give rise to them but because the man who in most instances is now the first to suggest these crimes, especially that of abortion, and to assist in their execution, would no longer have an interest in doing so; and the female left to herself, from maternal feelings and natural timidity, would seldom attempt the destruction of her offspring. The repeal of the present laws would likewise deprive the man of a plea of great weight with the female, namely, that if she is likely to become a mother, he shall be compelled to marry her or go to prison.

We will conclude this picture by the following extract from the evidence delivered by Mr Simeon before the House of Lords' Committee on Poor Laws in 1831, pp. 361, 362.

The Bastardy Laws proceed upon the principle of indemnifying the parish by throwing the onus of the bastard upon the father. Now I rather believe that we shall never be able to check the birth of bastard children by throwing the onus upon the man; and I feel strongly convinced that until the law of this country is assimilated to the law of nature and to the law of every other country, by throwing the onus more upon the females, the getting of bastard children will never be checked. Your Lordships are aware that when a man has the misfortune to have a bastard child sworn to him, he is brought before a magistrate. The magistrates are placed in this predicament; they say to the man, 'Will you marry this woman, will you support the child, or will you go to prison?' The man very naturally says, 'I cannot support the child, for I have not got the means; out of 3s. 6d. a week, it is impossible to give 2s. a week, and I am exceedingly unwilling to go to Oxford gaol, and, therefore, of the three evils I will choose the least, and marry the woman, although it is probable that the child is not mine.' Your Lordships are aware that when a bastard child is sworn to a man, the magistrates will not go into the question, whether the woman has had any connection with any other man. The consequence is that a woman of dissolute character may pitch upon any unfortunate young man whom she has inveigled into her net, and swear that child to him; and the effect of the law, as it now stands, will be to oblige the man to marry her. The consequence is that the parish, instead of keeping one bastard child, has to keep half a dozen legitimate children, the result of the marriage. As far as regards the females the case is infinitely worse. You say to a woman, 'As long as you continue virtuous and modest you have no chance of getting a husband because, in the present state of things, the men are cautious about marrying; but if you will be intimate with any person you please, the law will oblige him to marry you.' You thus secure to her what every woman looks upon as the greatest prize – a husband. You thus make the vice of the woman the means of getting that which she is anxious to get; and I feel convinced that three fourths of the women that now have bastard children would not be seduced, if it were not for the certainty that the law would oblige the man to marry.

Is it not an unlawful act on the part of the magistrates? – The magistrates do not put it in so many words; but the man comes before the magistrate knowing perfectly well that such and such will be the case; and the magistrate would never venture to say to the man 'if you do not marry the girl I will send you to prison': but the man knows that will be the case. For myself I am so convinced of the iniquity of the Bastardy Laws, that I have always refrained from acting upon them in my own house, and send the cases to the petty sessions.

What alterations can you suggest in the Bastardy Laws? – By refusing to give any order upon the father for support, or upon the parish even. I would throw the onus entirely upon the woman. I know of many instances in which the mothers have themselves been instrumental in having their daughters seduced for the express purpose of getting rid of the onus of supporting them, and saddling them upon any unfortunate young man of the neighbourhood whom they could get to the house. Now as long as their consent can meet with that result it will invariably be continued, and the population must go on increasing.

Do you then attribute the rapid increase of the population very much to the effect of the Bastardy Laws in forcing early marriages? – Almost entirely.

The objects of these laws appear to be two: the diminution of the crime; and the indemnity of the parish when it has occurred. Of these the first is, of course, the most important. Unhappily both the attention of the legislature and the efforts of those who administer the law have been principally directed to the second; and with the usual fate of pauper legislation and pauper administration, the indemnity of the parish has not been effected, though every other object has been sacrificed to it. The guidance of nature has been neglected, the task of resistance has been thrown upon the man instead of the woman; marriages in which the least fault is improvidence, have been not only promoted but compelled; every possible inducement has been held out to perjury and profligacy, simply to save parishes from expense, and the direct effect has been, in all probability, to double or quadruple that expense – the indirect effect to augment it still more. As far as we can judge from our returns, it appears that not one half of the money paid by parishes to the mothers of bastards is recovered from the putative fathers, and that the portion so recovered is generally recovered at an enormous expense; on the other hand, whenever an unmarried female becomes pregnant in a parish of which she is not a parishioner, a new and artificial expense is created by her removal to her place of legal settlement. Captain Pringle states that in a Cumberland parish the clergyman told him that in one year to seven legitimate children he had baptized nine bastards, almost all of them the children of women who had been out at service out of the parish, and removed thither to lie in; one from Suffolk at great expense. It may be added that in many, perhaps the majority of these cases, the women, if allowed to remain unremoved, would have earned their own and their children's support.

'There are many cases', says Mr Wilson, in his report from Durham,

of mothers of bastard children, who would struggle on for years without applying for parish relief. So soon, however (as my informant, Mr Hall of Wickham, expressed it), as the ice is once broken, so soon as the overseer has once spoken to the female, all shame and reluctance are at an end and she ever after comes to demand the allowance, which she regards as her right. In evidence of the expediency of the parish abstaining from interference, and leaving the offence to be attended with its natural consequences, witness mentioned three cases in which relief had never been asked. In two of these the women had secreted themselves before birth of the child, in order to avoid removal; in the third, she had clandestinely returned after removal; in all three, the mothers had struggled on without aid from the parish.

When we add to these sources of expense the profuseness of the allowances to the mothers in compliance with the order on the father, not half of which is, as we have seen, recovered, the tendency to vice which the hope of those allowances creates, and the number of illegitimate births, and the still greater number of legitimate births which are the consequence, it is impossible to doubt that even the saving for which all these evils have been let loose has not been effected. Even among the laws which we have had to examine, those which respect bastardy appear to be pre-eminently unwise.

Before we quit this subject we must advert to one class of illegitimate births mentioned in the evidence as productive of great and growing inconvenience. It appears that the Irish in the capital and in large towns, either with a view to effect the consequences which we are going to state, or from ignorance or negligence, are frequently married by Roman Catholic priests alone. These marriages satisfy the conscience of the wife, and while the family requires no relief their invalidity is unknown or unattended to. But as soon as the man becomes chargeable and the parish proceeds to remove him and his family, he shows that he is not legally married, and his children claim settlements on the parishes in which they were born. A magistrate who has sat for only a very few months informs us that as many as a dozen of these cases have come under his notice in a single day.

[LEGISLATIVE MEASURES CONSIDERED BUT NOT RECOMMENDED]

WE have now reported the result of our inquiry into the practical operation of the Laws for the Relief of the Poor, and into the mode in which those laws are administered; and we proceed to the performance of the remaining part of our duty, that of reporting what alterations, amendments, or improvements may be beneficially made in the said laws, or in the mode of administering them, and how the same may be best carried into effect.

We shall preface this part of our Report by a short statement of the principal amendments which have been suggested to us and to which we cannot add our recommendation.

I
[NATIONAL CHARGE]

MANY persons, for whose opinion we have a great respect, have proposed that the relief of the poor should be made a national instead of a parochial charge, and be both provided and administered under the direction of the government.

The advantages of making it a national charge would be great and immediate.

It would put an end to settlements. With settlements would go removals, labour-rates, and all the other restrictions and prohibitions by which each agricultural parish is endeavouring to prevent a free trade in labour and to insulate itself by a conventional cordon as impassable to the unsettled workman as Bishop Berkeley's wall of brass. There would be no longer a motive for preferring in employment the men with large families to those with small, the married to the unmarried, the destitute to those who have saved, the careless and improvident to the industrious and enterprising. We should no longer have these local congestions of a surplus, and, therefore, a half-employed dissolute population, *ascripta glebae*, some driven not by the hope of reward but by the fear of punishment to useless occupation, and others fed on condition of being idle; character would again be of some value to a labouring man. Another advantage much smaller than the first, but still considerable, would be the diminution of expense; a considerable sum would be instantly saved in litigation and removals, and we might hope to save a still larger sum by substituting the systematic management of contractors and removable officers for the careless and often corrupt jobbing of uneducated, unpaid, and irresponsible individuals.

It may be added that there is no change that would have so numerous and so ardent a body of supporters; all the heavily burdened parishes, and all those which, though still in a tolerable state, foresee from the annual increase of their expenditure the ruin that is creeping on them, all the rate-payers who are hesitating between a voluntary exile from the homes to which they are attached, and remaining to witness vice and misery and encounter loss and perhaps danger, would hail with transport the prospect of such a relief. Other changes may be submitted to; this alone would have enthusiastic partisans.

Still admitting the force of all these arguments in favour of a national charge, we do not recommend one.

In the first place, it is objectionable in principle. To promise on the part of the government subsistence to all, to make the government the general insurer against misfortune, idleness, improvidence, and vice is a plan better perhaps than the parochial system as at present administered; but still a proposal which nothing but the certainty that a parochial system is unsusceptible of real improvement, and that a national system is the only alternative against immediate ruin, the only plank in the shipwreck, could induce us to embrace.

It is probable – indeed it is to be expected – that at first it would work well; that there would be a vigilant and uniform administration, a reduction of expenditure, a diminution of pauperism, an improvement of the industry and morality of the labourers, and an increase of agricultural profit and of rent. But in this case, as in many others, what was beneficial as a remedy might become fatal as a regimen. It is to be feared that in time the vigilance and economy, unstimulated by any private interest, would be relaxed; that the workhouses would be allowed to breed an hereditary workhouse population and would cease to be objects of terror; that the consequent difficulty of receiving in them all the applicants would occasion a recurrence to relief at home; that candidates for political power would bid for popularity by promising to be good to the poor; and that we should run through the same cycle as was experienced in the last century, which began by laws prohibiting relief without the sanction of the magistrates; commanding those relieved to wear badges, and denying relief out of the workhouse; and when by these restrictions the immediate pressure on the rates had been relieved, turned round, and by statutes, with preambles reciting the oppressiveness of the former enactments, not only undid all the good that had been done, but opened the flood-gates of the calamities which we are now experiencing. If we ought to be on our guard against the unforeseen effects of any untried institution, even when its obvious consequences appear to be beneficial, how much more is there to dread from one that in itself is obviously injurious, and is recommended only as less mischievous than what exists. If a national system had been adopted a hundred years ago, it is probable that our present situation would have been worse than we now find it; that the mischief would have been still more general, and the remedy still more difficult. Another objection is the difficulty of providing the necessary funds. In Guernsey, the poor are provided for by one general fund; but even in that island, one of the most flourishing parts of the empire, it is found necessary to provide for it by a general income tax of not less than three per cent. A property tax would be called for, for that purpose, in England. But all those who are domiciliated in Ireland and Scotland must be exempted from it, as respects their personal property. How should we be able to distinguish between the English, Irish, and Scotch funded property, even if the claim of fundholders to immunity from direct taxation were abandoned? And if funded property were exempted, how could we assess personal property of any other description?

If personal property is exempted, and the assessment confined to lands and houses, how bitter would be the complaints of those whose rates are now below what would then be the general average?

II

OCCUPATION OF LAND BY LABOURERS

THE plan which we have just been considering, aims at distributing more equally the existing burden, and applies both to the impotent and the able-bodied. Other schemes have been suggested, which propose to remove or diminish the burden created by the able-bodied: first, by emigration; secondly, by enabling them to become occupiers of land in England; thirdly, by enabling and compelling the present occupiers of land to employ more labourers in its cultivation. We shall defer the subject of emigration to a subsequent part of our Report, and now proceed to consider the probable effects of any legislative measures, for the purpose of enabling labourers to become occupiers of land.

We directed our Assistant Commissioners to inquire in each parish into the mode in which the occupation of land by labourers had been effected. The following are extracts from some of their reports on this subject.

Mr Okeden, after stating that there is scarcely a parish in Wiltshire or Dorsetshire in which the labourer has not the use of land, concludes his remarks on that subject in the following words:

The allotment of land to labourers divides itself into two chief points: first, as to that quantity of land just sufficient for the cultivation of a labourer and his family during their spare hours; and secondly, as to that larger quantity which requires to be worked by the assistance of others, or by the entire dedication of the labourer's time. The day is not long past, since in every industrious cottage family the wheel and the distaff, the shuttle and the knitting-needles were in full activity. At present, to compete with machinery would be a useless waste of time, money, and labour. We must however see if the hours formerly devoted to manufacture may not be profitably applied and habits of industry created. I cannot suggest any mode of doing so more profitable to the agricultural labourer and his family, than the cultivation of exactly that quantity of land which will occupy these hours as well as his own spare time. This quantity is calculated to be the one sixteenth part of an acre, or ten lug or rods, to each individual capable of work.

To this, or to the system of renting of the farmer, and letting *him* manure and plough, and bring home the potatoe crop, I see no reasonable objection. It has sometimes struck those who have regarded the matter superficially, that the sum given for rent, viz., at the rate of £8 per acre, is enormous; but arithmetic will show us that the profit to the labourer is considerable. The general rent of land thus let is £8 per acre.

The farmer's expenses and profits are as under:

	£	s.	d.
Rent paid his landlord, for the acre	1	10	0
Two ploughings	1	6	0
Twelve loads of manure	1	16	0
Tithe	0	10	0
Rates	0	3	0
	£5	5	0
Profit to the farmer upon, let at £8 per acre	2	15	0
	£8	0	0

The labourer's expenses and profits are:

	£	s.	d.
To rent	£8	0	0
Labour in setting crop, and housing when brought home	3	0	0
Five sacks of seed potatoes	1	12	6
	£12	12	6

Per contra:

	£	s.	d.
Fifty sacks of potatoes, at 6s. 6d. per sack ...	£16	5	0
Small potatoes, for pigs	1	0	0
	£17	5	0

	£	s.	d.
Value received in potatoes	£17	5	0
Expenses as stated	12	12	6
Net profit to labourer, on the acre	£4	12	6

If this system of allotment be pursued, one of its benefits is the finding manure for the labourer; the family must cultivate the garden so as to gain a large supply of vegetables for themselves, and of food, at least, for one pig.

The allotment of larger portions of land than ten rods to an individual, has this evil – if the labourer cultivates it himself with only the aid of his family, he over-forces his strength, and brings to his employer's labour a body exhausted by his struggle.

This I have witnessed, and of this I have heard frequent complaints.

But, let us consider a still more enlarged allotment, one which will occupy the *whole* time of the man and his family to obtain support. The labourer then becomes a petty farmer, without capital, working land inadequately manured and half cultivated, and yielding, of course, insufficient crops as the return of fruitless exertions. Nor is this the only evil of the large allotments; a hovel perhaps is erected on the land, and marriage and children follow. In a few years more, the new generation will want land, and demand will follow demand, until a cottier population similar to that of Ireland is spread over the country, and misery and pauperism are every where increased.

'Of the acquisition of land by labourers', says Mr Majendie, 'the effect is invariably beneficial';

their character and conduct seem immediately raised by having means of exerting themselves in some other mode in addition to the uncertain demand for labour. It is contrary to the principles of human nature that labourers should be happy and contented when they are turned off at short notice to the parish-roads or gravel-pit, or degraded by what they term convict-labour; while land immediately before their eyes is passing out of cultivation.

There is no class in society whose feelings and opinions are so much known to each other as the labourers; it can be no secret to them that the crops which may be raised by their exertions on small plots of land are infinitely greater than those produced by ordinary cultivation. The denial of land to them will constantly produce an increase of ill-feeling on their part. It is to the proprietors that they must look for this boon; and it seems probable that nothing can more effectually tend to restore the good feeling which formerly prevailed between the different classes of society than the allotment system under prudent regulations.

In the minds of many occupiers there exists considerable prejudice on this subject; they are afraid of making labourers independent; and some look with an evil eye to a supposed diminution of their profits by introducing a new class of producers. The favourable reports which are made from all quarters will, it is hoped, diminish these prejudices. The system of cottage allotments is one of the most effectual modes of doing away with the noxious practice of allowance according to the number of children; many instances have occurred in which labourers have preferred retaining their land without relief, rather than give it up and return to parish pay, which in money would be at least an equivalent. Other instances of good feeling have occurred of labourers to whom land had been allotted, making a voluntary relinquishment of weekly relief. It is generally considered that a quarter of an acre can be cultivated by a labourer with a family at his leisure time, still making his dependence on regular farming employ. The danger of giving a further stimulus to population does not seem to attach to small allotments; on the contrary, the tendency to reckless improvidence in marriage seems rather to be checked by placing before the labourers something to look forward to beyond the resource of daily labour for a master. Extraordinary instances of accumulation of capital from small beginnings are reported, and the mere circumstance of enabling a labourer to sell so many days' labour to himself diminishes the demand either on the farmers or the parish purse.

The following practice may be worthy of notice. A farmer gives up to a labourer a portion of a field for a single crop of potatoes, dividing the produce with him. The farmer has the advantage of spade culture without expense; the labourer has a stimulus to exertion, an interest in the soil; and this plan steers clear of any danger of the introduction of the cottier system by a permanent subdivision of the land.*

Mr Walcott, in his report from North Wales, states that

A few leases for lives are occasionally met with, chiefly in Montgomeryshire, which have been granted by the lords of manors with from five to fifteen acres of land; not enough to make the tenants farmers, and too much to permit them to be labourers. On comparing the condition of these small freeholders with that of labourers, who have only just sufficient land to occupy their leisure time, the result is greatly in favour of the latter. My own observation was confirmed by the testimony of others. Mr Davies, the rector of Aberhavesp, stated that in

---

* 'This practice is mentioned as a very common one in France, by M. de Chateauvieux, in his excellent Essay on the Condition of the Labouring Classes in France, which he has kindly enabled me to present to the Board.'

his 'neighbourhood, several persons had obtained leases for lives of a few acres of land which had been recently enclosed, and that the majority of them are now actually in a worse condition than paupers. They trust solely to the produce of the land, and if there is a bad season, or they are improvident, which is often the case, in the consumption of a short crop, they are reduced to a dreadful condition as the possession of the land operates against their obtaining parochial relief.'

The quantity of land which a labourer can beneficially occupy without interfering with his ordinary labour is admitted, with scarcely an exception, to be about one quarter of an acre, and certainly not more than half an acre. I examined, on this subject, several small farmers who from working on their own land as labourers were the best judges of the matter; and in giving the testimony of one or two, I in effect give that of all. A farmer of the parish of Guildsfield, in Montgomeryshire, stated that a labourer could not do justice to his master and the land if he had more than half an acre, and that he must be a very industrious and good workman, and be assisted by his wife and family, to work up even that quantity, which he thought was too much. He added that if he wanted a labourer, and two men, equally strong and equally skilful, were to apply, one of whom had a quarter of an acre, and the other one or two acres of land, he should without hesitation prefer the former. A farmer in Kerry likewise stated that if a labourer had more than a quarter of an acre he is not a valuable servant, since he is apt to curtail the time which belongs to his master in order to attend his own land; this, he said, he had found to be the case. The Rev. Mr Jones of Treiorworth, in Anglesea, says on this point that he is the owner of several cottages let to labourers, and he finds that he has committed an error in giving to each half an acre as they rely too much on the land, to their own detriment.

Over the greater part of North Wales the labourers are permitted, on payment of so much a bushel, either in money or in kind, to plant as many potatoes as they may need on the fallow land of the farmer, who, in most instances, manures and prepares it ready for use. If the labourer finds manure, which is sometimes the case where a pig is kept, he has the use of the land without any charge. The plan is advantageous to both parties; the labourer obtains a crop at a cheaper rate than if he rented in the usual way and manured the land, and the farmer, besides the remuneration in money, produce, or manure, has his ground carefully cleaned and better fitted to receive a crop, after the potatoes are reaped, than if it had continued fallow.

Where a labourer was possessed of a small portion of land, sufficient, and not more than sufficient, to occupy his leisure time and furnish his children with employment, I found a striking improvement in the general condition of the whole family. The children were early and practically taught the beneficial effects of industry, and the man appeared to be more contented with his lot, and had less inducement to keep loose company. From what I witnessed, therefore, I cannot too strongly recommend that every facility should be granted to encourage the occupation of land to this extent by the labouring classes. The measure was warmly advocated by all classes, and is universally popular.

Mr Power, in his report from Cambridgeshire, states that:

Allotment of small portions of land to labourers for the purpose of employing their leisure hours, giving them a feeling of dependence on their own exertions and bettering their condition by increased sustenance and comforts, is beginning, much to the credit of the land-owners, to be very generally adopted in this county. Of the excellent effects of this practice, I am provided with testimony from many quarters; but as separate details would present few varieties of circumstance, it will be sufficient to say generally with regard to the objects above specified, that they have been invariably realized, to a greater or less degree, in all instances which have come within my observation. Those cases in which I have found those effects combined also with a reduction of parochial expenditure, distinctly assignable to the adoption of this practice, I regret to say are not many; but the universal increase of rates from various causes, may have frequently prevented a demonstration of this effect, where actually existing. That the effect ought to exist universally, and that it would, under a strict system of relief, I have no doubt, from the representations made of the considerable profits which the rent leaves in the hands of the occupiers of these small allotments. This is confirmed by the regularity with which the rents are paid, and the anxiety of the labourers to obtain occupations or additions to them, in parishes where the experiment has been tried. Under the present state of things these advantages, which certainly are most desirable as accessions to the comforts of the labourer, are little looked upon by himself as a means of keeping him from the necessity of parish relief, when for a season unemployed, or when visited by the infirmities of sickness or age. Much of this is due to the habit of not saving, at this time too generally established by the Poor Laws.

The farmers object very generally to the introduction of allotments. They are jealous of such deductions from their holdings; they have to go farther for their manure; and they object to the increased independence of the labourers. As to the first, if the allotment system is regarded in its proper light, namely, as a cheap charity on the part of the landlord, there seems little reason to apprehend its trenching materially on the large farms; for the instant it should change its character and be viewed as a source of rent, those influences which have caused the absorption of small farms into large ones, will check the breaking up of the latter into small ones again. As to the increased independence of the labourers, there is no doubt that leisure hours will not always be sufficient, and that absence of half-days and days must occasionally not only deduct from the market of labour, but place the allotment occupier on a better footing as to the terms of the contract with his employers. But who does not exult in this, who considers at what advantage the farmer has the labourer during the greater portion of the year, and remembers how little, during the times of dear bread, wages kept their due proportion to the price of corn; and reflects that pauperism, in its present aggravated shape, almost dates from that period of immense farming profits?

I regret, however, to say, that in several cases I have found these considerations operating to the exclusion of allotments; at the same time it must be added, in justice to the class, that in some instances, after a successful introduction of the system, these prejudices have yielded to humanity and good sense.

'The principal cases of allotments of land', says Captain Chapman, 'which came under my observation were at Wells, West Looe, St Germains, Warminster, Frome, Westbury, Trowbridge, Shepton Mallet, and Bradford.'

At Wells, fifty acres are now granted by the Lord Bishop of Bath and Wells to 203 persons, in quantities varying from one-twelfth to half of an acre, at a rent of 12s. 6d. the quarter of an acre. Of these persons not above ten are unmarried, and many are widows. The average of each family being taken at five, upwards of a thousand persons are thus benefited.

The conditions are that no lot shall exceed half an acre; that the land shall be tithe and tax free; that the holders shall pay their rents regularly, and previous to the crop being dug up, unless the agent shall allow a part to be removed (not exceeding the half) for the purpose of paying the rent; that the land shall be kept properly manured; that no damage shall be done to the walls or fences round the land; and by way of encouragement, the sum of 2s. 6d. annually is allowed to each on punctually paying his rent, and who has not broken any of the above conditions (thus reducing the rent to 10s. the quarter acre); and the Bishop also annually gives premiums to those occupants who produce the largest quantity of potatoes on the same portion of land. The tenure is considered as secured during the life-time of the Bishop and during good conduct.

No stipulation is made against the receipt of parochial relief, but the result has been to the same effect, as only three of the number actually receive such relief; two of whom are infirm persons who would otherwise be in the workhouse, and the third, also infirm, belongs to Bristol; twenty-nine names were pointed out of persons who formerly had received relief, but had discontinued it since they had got land. Many Dissenters have allotments.

The system was commenced in 1826, with three pieces amounting to thirty acres, which were given in lots to 109 families; a fourth portion was added in 1831, and a fifth has been given in 1832, but has not yet been brought under cultivation, making the whole amount to fifty acres.

The land, which was previously worked out, is much improved and the crops very abundant.

The following is an account, on an average of six years, of the profits of a quarter of an acre. (Furnished by the agent.)

					£	s.	d.
Rent for a quarter of an acre	...	...	...		0	12	6
Digging ...	...	...	...	...	0	8	0
Manure ...	...	...	...	...	0	10	0
Seed ...	...	...	...	...	0	3	0
Planting ...	...	...	...	...	0	4	0
Hoeing, &c. ...	...	...	...	...	0	8	0
Digging and hauling ...	...	...	...	0	10	0

	£	s.	d.
Supposing the man to hire and pay for everything	£2	15	6

Produce:

				£	s.	d.
Twenty sacks potatoes ...	...	...	...	£4	10	0*
Other vegetables ...	...	...	...	1	0	0

	£	s.	d.
	£5	10	0
Less, Labour, &c. as above	2	15	6

	£	s.	d.
Clear Profit, supposing man to hire and pay for everything ... ... }	£2	14	6

	£	s.	d.
If all be done by the man	£4	4	6

* It will be observed that Captain Chapman states the amount of produce

The opinion expressed by the agent was that a man who works for a farmer for twelve hours, from six to six, with the help of his wife and family, can manage half an acre, supposing it half potatoes, keep a pig, and support his family; and that a mechanic can do more.

The continued increase in the demand for allotments is the best proof of the advantage derived from them.

There is a general improvement in the character of the occupiers, who are represented as becoming more industrious and diligent, and as never frequenting those pests, the beer-houses. Frequently they have been known to work by candle-light.

Not a single instance has occurred in which any one thus holding land has been taken before a magistrate for any complaint.

The rents are collected without difficulty; and, as a proof of the good feeling produced, the pheasants in the adjoining wood, so far from having been destroyed, as was foretold by some, have been most carefully preserved; and at the time of the Bristol riots, the occupiers offered to come to the defence of the Bishop's palace.

This is, however, a very peculiar case, as few instances can occur in which land situated so close to a town, and of such quality, can be procured on terms so favourable to the holders. The nature of the soil, which is clay, is also peculiarly favourable, as ashes, which are easily procured in a town, form the best manure. Under these circumstances, subsequent inquiries lead me to believe that the land is let considerably below its value.

The amount of the allotments to which a person can do justice is, therefore, larger than under ordinary circumstances. But even here it will be seen that the quantity in no case exceeds the half acre.

The favourable effects of this measure, which were admitted by all, have most deservedly directed attention to the subject; and the system has not only been followed up on the Mendip hills by the Bishop, but I was led to believe is very extensively adopted in other parts of the county, the extent of the allotments being generally regulated on the same principle as those at Wells.

West Looe – Within the last five years a portion of a common belonging to the borough, and which, from time immemorial, had been waste, was enclosed; it amounted to about twenty-two acres, and was let in acres, half and quarter acres, in no case more than one acre. The price was fixed from 20s. to 15s. per acre; the distribution was made by lot. In the first instance it was confined to the poor belong-

---

per acre higher than Mr Okeden, but the price of a given quantity of produce lower. Mr Okeden's estimates of prices appear to us much too high.

ing to the borough of West Looe. The only conditions were that the land should be properly cultivated; the rent paid annually to a committee, or, in default, the occupier to give up possession. The money to be applied to the poor-rate.

The result of this experiment was such as to induce the committee to enclose another portion of about the same extent, which was let to any of the poor residents in the town, without consideration as to their being parishioners.

The rent of the first portion has been punctually paid, but that of the second was not due.

The effect on the poor-rate has been a diminution from 10s. in the pound to 3s; but the moral effect upon the poor is beyond calculation, the population being principally seafaring men who, in bad weather, had no occupation, and who idled about, a dead weight upon the poor-rate; but who have now occupation, and are happy, contented, and laborious.

I went over the land, and found it in excellent condition; the men can pick up sea-weed and procure lime on easy terms, so that they can do justice to a larger portion of land than under ordinary circumstances.

The borough only contains a hundred acres, and the population is only 593.

St Germains – Allotments have been made under Lord St Germains, in no case exceeding thirty perches, but without limit as to quantity; this is, however, found to be as much as a man with a family can do justice to. The land is good, and celebrated for its potatoes. The price paid is 6d. per perch, but an annual dinner, with premiums, more than absorbs the whole. Even this small quantity requires occasional assistance in hauling, lime, &c.

In Cornwall, the miners have a practice of purchasing from three to six acres of rough land, on three lives, but they are a distinct class, having great advantages over the ordinary labourer, so as to form an exception to the rule; but even they frequently find the quantity too great, as may be seen from the following extract from a pamphlet by Dr Carlyon, a magistrate of Truro, 1827:

'Above all, no industrious cottager should be allowed to remain unprovided with such a spot of ground as he is capable of cultivating at leisure hours; and from one eighth to a quarter of an acre will generally be better than more; for without the aid of a lucky start in mining, or some other piece of good fortune productive of means beyond the proceeds of daily labour, no poor man should attempt to cope with several acres, especially of a coarse description. After years of hard strug-

gling, a severe winter, sooner or later, will arrive, and find him ill-pro-
vided for the maintenance of his little stock, and a petition, such as may
be seen perpetually in circulation, will soon inform the humane and
charitable that the loss of a horse or of a cow has brought him to great
distress. Besides, when there is too much to be done at home the labourer
will seldom be worthy of his hire elsewhere; so that, whether we have
regard to the interests of the labourer himself, or of his employer, or of
the parish, with reference to the poor-rate, in which he lives, it will
equally, I believe, be found that he cannot be placed better for the maintenance of a family than where the produce of a well-cultivated garden
goes to help out the earnings of regular daily labour.

'There may be something very captivating with cursory observers in
the praiseworthy efforts of a poor miner who contrives to erect a cottage
for himself on a dreary common, and to enclose acre after acre, full of
quartz stones, which must be removed at infinite pains before cultivation
can begin: yet judging from the usual results, I am persuaded that such
attempts should not be encouraged; and with respect to cottagers generally, and miners in particular, that they should confine themselves to
gardens, and lay up their little savings in some neighbouring savings'
bank.'

Agricultural labourers generally have gardens; those in steady
employ have about one sixteenth to one twelfth of an acre, given rent-
free, for a crop of potatoes; others rent a piece of ground, for the crop
at 6d. the pole if they find manure, and for 1s. if the farmer finds it.

The value of a crop of a quarter acre thus held was estimated at
S. Petherwin at £3, for which the labourer would pay 20s., and have a
clear gain of 40s.; but it was stated that if the labourer had the money
to lay out, he might buy a larger quantity of potatoes for the same
sum.

This plan is considered by the farmers as more advantageous than
that of allotments.

The same system of renting prevails in Devonshire and parts of
Somerset.

In the latter county, as previously mentioned, the influence of the
example of the Bishop of Bath and Wells is causing the plan of allotments to be adopted very extensively; but in consequence of illness, I
was unable to return to that district as I had proposed.

Warminster – Twenty acres have been many years let to the poor,
in lots from twenty to fifty poles at 4½d. the pole, on condition solely
of the rent being punctually paid. But this is never considered at the
pay-table. Many have held their lots for several years. Twenty acres
in addition were recently taken by the parish, and offered, rent free, on

condition that all claim to parochial relief should be forfeited; but no one would take it on these terms.

The opinion expressed at Warminster, by a gentleman of great experience, was that the quantity of land occupied by any labourer should be sufficient to supply his wants, but *not* to furnish any quantity for sale; for this purpose a quarter of an acre would, in general, be ample.

Frome – The letting of gardens to the poor was an experiment on a small scale. In 1820 the Marquis of Bath granted about six acres of excellent pasture land in Frome. It was divided into small portions to the poor, seed being given them, on the condition of their relinquishing some a part, and in some cases all parish pay. Industrious persons were selected, and neither rent, poor-rates, or tithes were paid. The letting was for one year. No manure was wanted. All went on pretty well the first year, under careful management. In the second year various complaints were heard. It was said the poor robbed each other. Some of them demanded their pay as before. Some refused to cultivate the ground, alleging that the very small portion of time at their command would be consumed in going to and from the gardens. Finally it was relinquished as of no advantage to the parish or the paupers.

Westbury – Allotments of land have been tried for twenty years past in this neighbourhood, labourers generally giving 6d. per perch, free of all tithes, &c., for land manured by themselves, and 1s. per perch, when manured and ploughed fit to receive the seed, and the crop carted home. Labourers have also received land from the parish; but when they conceive that they have worked out their rent by abstaining from the parochial allowance to the same extent, they consider themselves entitled to full relief again.

The following is a statement for the year 1831–2 of the land thus let by the parish of Westbury:

Dr.	£	s.	d.	Cr.	£	s.	d.
One year's rent to Michaelmas, 1831	50	0	0	Rent of pasture, being part not occupied by poor	14	0	0
One year's land tax ...	2	7	3	Rent of potato land ...	47	17	0
,, poor-rate ...	2	11	0	Rent of barn ...	0	11	8
,, tithe ...	7	0	0				
Seed potatoes ...	6	1	0		£62	8	8
				Loss to parish ...	5	10	7
	£67	19	3		£67	19	3

Bradford – Forty acres in four portions, situated in different parts of the parish, were taken by the parish, and let in lots for spade husbandry at from a half to a quarter of an acre. In three cases they were cultivated on account of the parish; the fourth was given up to occupants; but they have been abandoned with the exception of one portion, which is about to be given up.

The failure here is attributed to the want of an overlooker. No effect was produced upon the poor-rates.

Shepton Mallett – Thirty-two acres are rented by the parish at £5 per acre, which have let in portions from a quarter to one acre at the same price. The parish pay rent and taxes. Portions have been hitherto taken by persons of a superior class, but only twelve acres are at present let. No effect has been produced upon the poor-rate, so that it is in contemplation to give the whole up, when the term for which it was taken expires. It was considered beneficial to the poor, by making them more comfortable, and by keeping prices down.

Trowbridge – Seven acres of land were hired by the parish three years ago, and were given out in lots from thirty to forty perches, or more if required, free of rent, tools being found; no conditions were made. The people appeared very indifferent about it, and did not take much trouble to cultivate it. They sold the crops, and then came, as before, to the pay-table.

The experiment is considered a total failure, and is about to be abandoned.

As far as I am enabled to judge, the effect of allotments, when made by the parish, is not likely to be beneficial, because the land is taken with suspicion and distrust, and because it rarely happens that it is attended to, and steadily looked after, either by the parish or by the poor; but when made by individuals, allotments are thankfully received, and have a most beneficial effect upon both the character and condition of the poor. They form, in fact, the natural resource against those inequalities in agricultural labour which are almost inevitable.

It appears, however, far preferable for the labourer to hire a small portion of fresh land every year, from which he can reckon upon a crop with some degree of certainty, than to have a larger portion of poor land, on which both his time and labour may be thrown away; and to be important so to regulate the quantity as to be sufficient to supply his wants, but not to send him to market with his crop.

Both of these conditions appear to result from a practice previously mentioned, and which is very general in the west of England, but particularly in Cornwall, of letting land at 6d. the pole, the labourer finding manure; or (in some cases) of dividing the crop, on the same condition. The quantity of land is thus limited by the supply of manure, and the farmer has it in his power to give whatever quantity he pleases; the poor man and the farmer are both benefited, and a degree of kindly feeling created instead of jealousy and distrust.

The portion of land thus rented very rarely, if ever, exceeds a quarter of an acre, and confirms the opinion generally expressed that the average quantity of land to which an agricultural labourer can do justice, under ordinary circumstances, and at the same time fulfil his duty to his employers does not exceed a quarter of an acre.

A large body of testimony to the same effect is to be found in the Appendix, particularly in the reports of Mr Stuart, Mr Everett, Mr Lewis, Mr Maclean, and Mr Tweedy, and in the evidence taken before the House of Lords' Committee on Poor Laws, in 1830 and 1831, especially that of Mr De Maimbray, Mr Pollen, the Bishop of Bath and Wells, and Mr Estcourt.

The general results seem to be, firstly, that the extent of land which a labourer can beneficially occupy is small – seldom exceeding, even when his family is large, half an acre. Such an amount appears to be the utmost which he can cultivate, and continue to rely on his wages as his regular and main support. And if he ceases to rely on his wages; if he becomes, in fact, a petty farmer before he has accumulated a capital sufficient to meet, not merely the current expenses, but the casualties of that hazardous trade; if he has to encounter the accidents of the seasons, instead of feeling them at second-hand after their force has been broken on the higher classes, his ultimate ruin seems to be almost certain. The following statement by Mr Day, respecting the effects of large allotments at Rotherfield, Sussex, is very instructive:

I shall here insert part of a series of questions proposed a few years since to the parish officers of Rotherfield by a gentleman in this neighbourhood, together with the answers returned by them.

'Q. 11. Have the inclosures and system of cottage-building on Crowborough materially contributed to increase the pauper population of Rotherfield? – Yes, very much. "Resolved, at a vestry meeting, February 22, 1827, that in consequence of the increasing evil daily arising from huts and small tenements erected in this parish, we are determined to object to all grants and admittances in this parish requested in future by any person or persons whomsoever.

Signed by the churchwardens, overseers, and several inhabitants."

'Q. 12. When were they first allowed to be made? – In a slight degree upwards of a hundred years, but at the fullest extent about eight years ago.

'Q. 13. By whom? – The Earl of Abergavenny.

'Q. 14. Upon what terms? – In consideration that the person should pay 5s. per acre quit rent, and after two years to receive no relief from the parish: if he did, to give up his land to the said Earl. The consequence has been, that the occupier has been obliged to sell his land, thereby bringing other families into the parish, and himself ultimately has become a pauper.'

I believe the facts at present are much stronger than as represented in these answers. The evil has now become so great that the parish buys up the allotments as they are offered for sale, to prevent a succession of families from becoming pauperized on them. The language of the resolution of the vestry uses the word 'huts'. They are, however, very decent and indeed good, cottages, built of stone found on the spot, with slated roofs. The allotments vary in size, generally about four acres, but some as large as ten or twelve.

Secondly, that where the system of letting land to labourers has been introduced and carried on by individuals, it has generally been beneficial; and on the other hand, that where it has been managed by parish officers, it has seldom succeeded.

The causes of this difference are well pointed out by Captain Chapman, in the passage which we have cited. Under the unhappy system which has prevalied for the last forty years, charity has been converted from a bond of union into a sort of discord. The applicant for relief has been trained to consider the distributors of that relief, the very persons who are to minister to his necessities, as his enemies. He views even their gifts with suspicion, and distrusts still more their attempts to bargain with him. He neither brings to any contract with them the cheerfulness, nor performs his part with the activity and perseverance which would be necessary to the success of the undertaking, even if all that is to be done on their part were wisely and diligently executed. The overseers, on the other hand, anxious to escape with as little trouble as possible from the thankless office that has been forced on them, are likely to bestow little care on the selection of tenants, or in the framing of rules, and still less on enforcing their observance. It cannot, therefore, be matter of surprise that undertakings which succeed where each party co-operates, should, under opposite circumstances, fail.

Thirdly, that the occupation of land by the labouring classes may be made, and in fact is made, beneficial to the lessor as well as to the occupier. This appears to us the most important result of our inquiries on this subject.

If letting land to the poor, though beneficial to the occupier, required a sacrifice on the part of the lessor, it is clear that it could not prevail extensively, unless it were effected at the expense of the public. And that, if such a system were adopted, as the land applicable to that purpose, or indeed to any other purpose, is limited, and the number of applicants is rapidly augmenting, every year would increase the difficulty of supplying fresh allotments and diminish their efficiency in reducing the increasing mass of pauperism, until the arrival of a crisis when it would be necessary either to give up the system, resume the land, and clear it as we could of its inhabitants, or abandon the whole country to a helpless and desperate population. Still the immediate advantages of allotments are so great that if there were no other mode of supplying them, we think it might be worth while, as a temporary measure, as a means of smoothing the road to improvement, to propose some general plan for providing them. And in that case, it would be necessary to collect the fullest possible information as to the quantity which ought to be awarded to each family, or each member of a family, the terms as to rent, taxes, mode of cultivation, and other points which ought to be imposed on the lessees, and the assistance in stock, manure, seed, or otherwise, which ought to be supplied to them; and it would be necessary to inquire far more diligently than has yet been done into the amount and the situation of the land which might be thus employed, into the means of keeping up, for a time at least, the supply of allotments, and into the mode by which the population bred up on them could be disposed of.

But since it appears that the land may be let to labourers on profitable terms, the necessity for any public inquiry on these points seems to be at an end. A practice which is beneficial to both parties, and is known to be so, may be left to the care of their own self-interest. The evidence shows that it is rapidly extending;

and we have **no** doubt that as its utility is perceived it will spread still more rapidly; and that experience will show, if it has not already shown, on what mutual stipulations it can be best effected. It would, probably, be facilitated by some legislative provisions respecting settlement, rates, tithe, and ejectment. The two first we shall advert to in the course of this Report. As to the two last, tithes and ejectment, though we think it probable that in time the liability of small allotments to tithes would be found dangerous, and that the lessors' present legal remedies would prove too expensive and dilatory, we do not think it necessary that this Commission should propose any alteration. Both subjects have been already brought before Parliament, and we have no doubt that they will be considered with reference, among other things, to the occupation of land by labourers.

III
LABOUR-RATE

WE now proceed to a third scheme for removing or diminishing the burthen created by the able-bodied – namely, that which proposes to effect it by compelling the rate-payers to provide employment, at a given rate of wages, for those labourers who are, or profess to be, unable to procure it for themselves. The mode by which this is effected, we have already designated as the Labour-Rate System. Under this system each rate-payer is required either to employ and pay at a certain rate a certain number of labourers, or to pay to the overseer the wages of those whom he makes default in employing and paying.

Before the 2 & 3 Will. IV, c. 96 [1832], was passed, such an agreement was not binding on those who refused to accede to it; any one rate-payer, therefore, who would not employ or pay for his proportion of labourers was able to set the rest at defiance, and profit by the immediate diminution of rate without bearing his share of the cost.

This difficulty was attempted to be removed by the first clause of that act, which enacts, 'that when a majority of three-fourths of the rate-payers of any parish, the votes being taken according to the provisions of the 58 Geo. III, c. 69, shall come to any agreement, solely for the purpose of employing or relieving the poor of such parish, such agreement, when approved of by a majority of the justices at petty sessions, shall be binding on the contributors to the poor-rates of such parish, for any period not exceeding six months, therein specified.'

Clauses follow, declaring that the act does not sanction the custom of paying labourers less than the comon rate of wages, and making up the deficiency from the poor-rates; that it shall not be lawful to employ any part of the poor-rates of one parish in the employment of persons in any other parish, and confining its operation to those parishes in which the rate exceeds 5s. in the pound. But as no penalty is imposed on disobedience to the agreements thus declared to be binding, the act has contributed to the increase of labour-rates, rather by the sanction which it gives to them, than by the actual force of its enactments.

The agreements generally set forth that the labour-rate is made 'for the better employment of the poor'; and go on to state that all or certain of the rate-payers shall employ labourers in proportion to their assessment or acreage, or to some other standard.

Considerable difference exists, varying almost with each parish adopting the system, as to the classes of rate-payers who are to furnish employment, as to the degree in which it is to be furnished by each class, and as to the working men who are to be considered within the agreement.

One of the three following plans is generally adopted as regards the rate-payers who are to find employment.

The principal, as being by far the most common, is –

That each rate-payer shall employ labourers in proportion to his assessment to the poor's rates.

This plan is almost exclusively adopted in Surrey and in Sussex, besides being very frequently found in every other county in which labour-rates are instituted.

The next most frequently used is –

That the occupiers of land shall share among themselves the whole of the agricultural labour (including the surplus).

This plan is almost exclusively followed in Buckinghamshire, but occurs rarely in any other county.

The third and least common plan of all is —

That the occupiers of land shall be compelled to employ a fixed number of labourers, according to acreage or rental; and then, in common with the tradesmen and other rate-payers, to employ, according to their respective rental, a share of the surplus labourers.

This plan is only adopted in five parishes with the labour-rates of which we are acquainted; viz., in Aylesbury, Bucks.; Farnham and Frensham, Surrey; and Downton and Westbury, Wiltshire.

Although the three plans stated include the principal bases of the agreements, each separate agreement differs in its details from almost every other agreement, though based on the same common plan, as much as each separate plan differs from the other two. Thus it may truly be said that scarcely two agreements are in all their provisions the same. The details in which consist the differences in the various agreements are:

The amount of assessment, or the number of acres rendering it incumbent to employ a labourer.

The deduction to be made on the assessments on trade, on houses below a certain rental, on mills, malt-houses, &c., or on occupations under a given number of acres.

The time for which each rate is made.

The amount of the rate.

The mode in which the return of labourers employed is to be made.

The wages to be paid to the labourers.

The description of work people to be considered and allowed for as labourers, and particularly whether farmers working on their own farms, or their sons, and how many, are to be considered labourers.

Yet among modifications as numerous as the parishes resorting to the system, not a single instance will be found in which classes of individuals do not complain of the peculiar severity with which the labour-rate affects them. The practice seems to be not a sharing in fair proportions of the burthen amongst all, but a shifting of the burthen from one class to some other.

Under the first plan, either the whole surplus labour is cast upon trade, and the whole of the agriculturists share the advantage; or the larger agriculturists, or those whose proportion of arable land is large, cast the weight upon the small occupier, the occupier of grass land, the occupier, who alone or with his sons can do all the labour his farm requires, and the tradespeople and householders. In some cases a strong desire has been shown to place it upon the tithes, and were it not for the number of compositions, it is probable that such instances would have been frequent.

At Stebbing, in Essex, which is under the first plan, the farmers generally are gainers at the expense of trade. The following are replies of the tradespeople.

I have not an acre of land, nor any employment whereby I can employ an agricultural labourer. The effect is as follows:

Old System.	£	s.	d.	New System.	£	s.	d.
1 Year's poor-rate	21	0	0	1 Year's charge for labour	20	0	10
				1 Year's poor-rate	13	10	0
					£33	10	10
				Deduct old system	21	0	0
				Annual loss	£12	10	10

As I have no profitable employment for agricultural labour, the system has the effect of raising my contributions to the poor from 11s. 8d. to 18s. 6d. in the pound, which I contend is severe and unjust.

As a proof that it works well for the farmer, and that it does not impose upon him too much labour, the first rate we had, which was a six weeks' rate, was worked out in four weeks, with the exception of about £15, and the subsequent rate was over-worked by almost every farmer.

Thomas Jasper.

It has a very injurious effect on me, as it charges me for labour which I cannot find, unless I stand still myself in order to have a man to do the work which I can do myself; which I do not hesitate to say is unjust. I am a publican, and have a small garden, which is all the business I have. I am principally concerned in the beer-trade which in a country place like this is very small; so that I have plenty of time to attend to the concerns of business, without the incumbrance of an agricultural labourer; and I consider that all the money that I pay for labour-rate is as though so much money was given away.

Thomas King, victualler,
assessed to the poor at £6.

It affects me in a small trade, and occupier of about two acres of land, rated £2 10s.; trade rated £9 10s. My trade, on the labour-rate, is taken at £5, which, if I had not the two acres of land, it would be most oppressive, and much worse than the old custom of paying at times sixty or eighty unemployed poor out of the poor-rates.

In my humble opinion, the labour-rate only ought to be on the land, as I could on my two acres employ double; and I think a man ought to be paid so that he could support himself by his own labour, not to have half from his employer and half from the parish.

The trade would then have a plenty to do to pay the necessitous poor-rates, loaded as the trade is with taxation.

Edward Taylor, shopkeeper,
assessed to the poor at £12 12s. 6d.

To me it proves an evil, because I have but little land, not so much as I can cultivate with my own spade; and then I am obliged to have a man so many days in the labour-rate, or pay so much money as the labour-rate amounts to, though I have not work for myself.

Jeroboam Ffitch, gardener and beer-shop-keeper,
assessed to the poor at £2 10s.

I am obliged to have an errand lad, by whom I easily work out the labour-rate. But supposing I was inclined to take an apprentice of any respectable individual not belonging to the parish, or not a pauper of the parish, the labour-rate would then have a very injurious effect upon me, as I should be compelled to pay the charge for labour without an opportunity of working it out, and the consequence would be that my payments for the relief of the poor would be considerably increased, which I consider would be unjust. I consider that the labour-rate has had a beneficial effect upon the morals of the poor, as well as upon the agricultural interest; but the contrary is to be said as it regards several tradesmen who reside in this parish.

Robert Monk, glazier, &c.
assessed to the poor at £3.

The following two being able to work out their rate are benefited:

It has been to me beneficial; as it saves in the poor-rate assessment 4½d. in the pound in six weeks, and does not cost me so much for the labour-rate as I paid for errands, &c., before to idlers who are now better employed. I and a person similarly situated to myself now employ a boy at 2s. per week, which is more than our labour-rate amounts to, but less than what we paid before.

Elisha Mumford, harness-maker,
assessed to the poor at £3.

It has benefited me, and all others in a similar situation; as we now get work done for our money, which before we had to pay to support from fifty to sixty men in idleness or useless employ.

W. Messent, victualler,
assessed to the poor at £7.

Four farmers do not speak decidedly in favour, but their leanings are favourable; a fifth is likewise favourable, provided a slight alteration be made giving an allowance to grass farmers. A sixth, John Tarbert, objects decidedly, because he can himself do all the work his land requires, and is therefore precisely in the situation of a tradesman; the labour is of no use to him. M. Choppin and Wm. Thurgood, the one being allowed to return himself, and the other his son, being thus clear of the rate, are benefited.

I for myself, holding 121 acres of land, which gives to me six and half labourers, and having one-third meadow, of course not requiring the labour, I find myself inconvenienced, and beg to recommend a distinction to be made; such as giving about one man to forty acres on the pasture instead of apportioning it altogether, as three parts of the year there can be nothing done but what would be injurious to crops upon pasture. The law undergoing a few modifications, I am of opinion, will tend to a great general good, in giving employment on the land to the idle and dissolute, as also putting the land into a better state of cultivation. As regards rate-payers in towns and villages, there are but few but have gardens that can dispense with the allotment of one man for one or two days, as their assessments are in general very low.

Henry Clarke, farmer,
assessed to the poor at £126 4s. 6d.

I do not consider mine any criterion, on account of the land being in a very bad state of cultivation. I have felt myself under the neces-

sity of employing more than twice the number of labourers than I shall
be able to find employment for two or three years hence; but as my
residence is in Stebbing, although my occupation is much larger several
miles distant, doubtless I shall be able to employ as many or more
labourers than will be allotted to me. I approve of the labour-rate,
because it keeps the principal part of the labourers' bodies and minds
employed, and tends to make them better subjects than their parents,
who have been for years unemployed otherwise than at parish work.

I believe I may say the labour-rate is a system almost universally
approved of in this parish. I know of only one person who objects
to it; that is Thomas Jasper.

J. Budge.

I certainly think it a general benefit to the farmer and labourer, if
it was put on a right foundation; but as it now stands it presses heavily
upon me, and all others in the same situation, in a most ruinous
manner. I am a small landholder and cannot get a livelihood except
I put my hand to the plough; but if the law was so made as to allow
all small landholders to be returned as labourers, it would be the most
beneficial Act that ever passed; for it cannot be supposed a small
holder can employ the same number of men as the great holder,
except he and his sons are allowed to work out their proportion of the
rate.

John Tarbert, farmer,
assessed to the poor at £42 10s.

It has done me good, as it is a saving to me of 6s. in the year. As I
am a small landholder, the parish allow me to return my son a half a
man, and that is more than covers my labour-rate.

M. Choppin, gardener,
assessed to the poor at £2 10s.

It has done me good, as it has taken a great many men out of the
road, and those who were supported in idleness, which has reduced
the poor-rate. The parish allowed me to be returned to labour-rate
half a man, which is as much as I require; if the law was made for
us small holders to be returned as this parish has allowed them to be,
it would benefit all small holders like myself; and if to the contrary, it
would be most ruinous. The labourers feel themselves better satisfied
than when they had to go to the overseer for their money, as it makes
them more independent.

William Thurgood,
assessed to the poor at £12 12s.

The parish of Henfield, Sussex, also under the first plan, is an instance of the large farmers deriving advantage, whilst the small farmer, the occupier of grass land, and the tradespeople, are oppressed.

The following are some of the letters received from the tradespeople and small farmers.

I am a carpenter in a small way, but do it all myself, not wanting a man. I have also about five acres of meadow land, which only requires a labourer in the summer time, when the labour-rate is not required; therefore I cannot work out my labour-rate in the winter months. I must say I have never paid so much any year to the poor as last year, being nearly as much again in proportion as the large farmers, 18s. 6d. in the pound to their 10s. A few years back, many of the farmers in our parish paid their labourers half the amount due to them for labour, and sent them to the poor-book for the other half; and I must say that this labour-rate seems intended to act upon the same principle.

Arthur Brooke.

I am a gunsmith, but do all the work myself; I have not any garden or any means of employing a labourer. If myself and many of my neighbours who cannot and, having no use for a husbandry man, ought not to pay for labour we do not want; if such is to be the case, many of those who now contribute towards the support of the poor would soon become receivers, by belonging to that class of persons. I cannot think it right that I should pay 18s. 6d. in the pound, while the farmers are paying only 10s. in the pound.

Peter Ward.

Being a shoemaker in a small line of business, without any land to employ a labourer on, it has done a hurt to me, having been rated to pay after the rate of 18s. 6d. where the farmers have paid only 10s. I consider that a person without land has no right to be reckoned to pay towards a labour-rate.

Richard Ware.

I am convinced that myself and every one not using land must feel the inconvenience of paying money for labour to the farmers, that they may apply it towards the wages of the men they employ: the farmers in this parish last year paid only 10s. in the pound, while I paid 18s. 6d. They may well exclaim that never was any plan adopted that worked so well, when one farmer in this parish acknowledged that he paid £40 less last year for labour than he ever did before. And with whose money was it paid? Why, it was taken out of the pockets of the inhabitants, who could not employ labourers. Would it be at all reasonable for householders, tradesmen, &c., to call a meeting, to say, 'Our rents are due, we have contributed towards paying your men their wages; now, in return, you must assist us in paying our rents'?

James Wattsford.

I am compelled to contribute to the poor-rate, in alleviation of the opulent farmer. The churchwardens, as well as the overseers, of the parish are composed of opulent farmers and millers; therefore it is their interest to uphold and support a labour-rate because they alone are benefited, to the great injury of very many tradesmen, shopkeepers, and others who have no opportunity of employing any surplus labour, and which labour they, the farmers, cannot dispense with; it is a fact well known here, they, the farmers, have discharged their usual labourers that they might employ the surplus labourers, and deduct their wages from their labour-rate; added to which, the farmers have deducted from their labour-rate for their sons, as part and parcel of their families; and one large farmer in the parish has acknowledged, that his poor-rate cost him £40 less on account of the labour-rate.

The plain fact is the opulent farmers, who can best afford, have paid 10s. on the pound, while the dependent tradesmen and shop-keepers have paid 18s. 6d. for the same time.

W. Williams.

I consider it would have been a decided injury to me, but that I happen to be in partnership with my father and brother, as surgeons, and using at the same time about twenty acres of arable and meadow land; and, therefore, our servants happening to belong to this parish, we were allowed to work, or rather outset for them, according to the labour scale, which otherwise would not have been permitted. Of course, to all persons who had the means of working out their rate in lieu of paying money (by the employment of the parochial labourers), it must be said to have been a decided advantage; whilst to all the small occupiers of houses, rated for that species of property only, the whole of whom are either small mechanics just able to live by their own individual industry, or widows living on a small income, or little tradesmen, it was a very great and unequal impost inasmuch as they had to contribute 4s. in the pound more under the labour-rate system than they ever did before under the old one; whilst to those who worked their rate, such as the large and moderately large farmer, it was a benefit of 8s. 6d. in the pound.

Nelson Smith Morgan.

Large farmers in our parish were quite elated with the labour-rate; they exclaimed in raptures, 'the best thing that ever was done'. Why? They paid, in the same period of time, 10s. in the pound, while the shopkeeper, small tradesman, and various householders, not employing a man of any description, nor wanting them, had to pay, under the labour-rate, 18s. 6d. in the pound; and with much difficulty it was prevented being carried on two months after Lady-tide. Some of them declared they would have it all the summer.

John Hicks.

Mine is a small farm, and most part of it is marsh land, and in the winter it is frequently under water; that being the case, I have not sufficient employment to enable me to work out the rate. It is the large farmers that receive the benefit from it, as the regular labourers they are in the habit of employing work out the whole of their rate; consequently they pay nothing towards it, and my rate goes to their benefit at my loss; so you see in this case and many others, it acts unequally.

T. L. W. Dennett.

It operates, in my opinion, much in favour of the great farmer, and against the little one. The great farmer, always having a set of regular workmen in his employ, will always outset the labour-rate; whereas the little farmer is compelled to do the greatest part of the labour himself, for which no allowance is made from the rates; and the tradesmen, I think, are nearly in a similar situation, not having the power of working out the rate, but at a great loss, as many of the great farmers pay little or nothing and the little farmer and trades-people nearly the whole of the rate.

John Dennett.

I am a householder, and occupy a small grass farm, and only employ a labourer occasionally, and have been enabled to work out nearly all my rate; therefore I do not consider myself hurt or injured by it.

When the labour-rate was first proposed in this parish, I voted against it for this reason; that all the labour population of the parish being put into the rate, consequently the rate falls very unequally on the rate-payers, namely, the householders, little farmers and trades-men, as many have not employed extra labourers to work out their rate.

And I am also of opinion that the great land occupiers, by placing their regular workmen, whom they must necessarily employ, in the rate, are reaping the benefit of the same at the expense of the other classes.

L. D. Smith.

The rates seem to have been enforced even to the injury of the labourer, who is striving to keep from pauperism.

John King says –

I am a gardener; having no land of my own, I go to work for any person who will employ me; I keep no person to assist me whatever; therefore I have no chance of working out my labour-rate. Now I have desired my neighbour to say that this labour-rate is an injury to every one except the large farmer.

At Pulborough in Sussex, the labour-rate, also on the first plan, threw the principal burthen on the tithes. The following is the effect as stated by the incumbent, the Rev. J. Austen:

The parish of Pulborough is thus rated in round numbers to the poor-rate; land, £4,000; glebe and tithes, £1,050; houses, £950: £6,000.

By the first resolution one man is to be taken for every
£30 rating, 30s. £1,050 for glebe and tithes   ...   35 men
By the second resolution, 1s. in the pound is to be paid
every six weeks – 1,051 shillings; this divided by six
gives 175 shillings weekly, which will pay at 10s. each   17½ men

52½ men

The glebe and tithes must employ or pay, as all the houses
and ratings under £30 are exempt from the first resolution; there would still be sixty men left on the highways,
of whom the tithes and glebe would pay one sixth   ...   10 men

The rectory would thus pay   ...   .   62½ men

Besides the common poor-rate of 8s. in the pound.
Sixty-two men, at 10s. each, weekly – £31 and for a whole year, £1,612, and £420 for the common poor-rate; in the whole, £2,032.

The Rev. J. Calvert of Whatfield, Suffolk, speaking of Cosford Hundred, in which that parish is situated, says —

It is almost superfluous to state the temptation which is thrown in the way of occupiers of land, to combine against the tithe-owner. One instance of this I conceive to have taken place in the parish of Layham; and another is likely to occur in a parish where the tithes belong to a lay impropriator.

The clergymen of other parishes within this hundred have, on account of their compositions in lieu of tithes, been exempted from any causes of complaint; I, for one, am a gainer in the diminished rates which I have to pay this year.

The Rev. T. S. Hodges of Little Waltham states —

I cannot conceal from myself the fact that were the labour-rate a permanent measure, it would very materially affect the value of tithe property, and in fact be a tax upon it to that amount; inasmuch as at present the clergyman's income arises from a tenth of the produce of the land, free of the cost of producing it, whereas the labour-rate would inflict upon him one-tenth of the whole labour of the parish: the hardship would be greater, as he alone would be unable to employ the labour imposed upon him, unless during the harvest-work the law not allowing him (a law advisable rather to restrain than to enlarge) to occupy more than fifty acres beyond his glebe.

Many expressions will be found in the replies evincing the desire of the farmers to establish a labour-rate, for the express purpose of reaching the tithes.

Mr Wm Venton, a farmer at Lenham, Kent, says —

I objected, upon the ground that the labour-rate did not embrace all assessable property, *and most particularly the tithe*, which, as it now stands, is a very great check upon employing a superabundant number of labourers.

The attempt to throw the weight of pauperism upon particular classes has been as successful under the second plan, under which the agriculturists divide the whole labour amongst themselves, as it has been under the first plan.

The tradespeople, not being assessed to the labour-rate under the second plan, will in no instance be found to complain; if, indeed, they are not as extensively benefited as particular classes of the agriculturists, they are at least slightly benefited by a reduction of the poors' rates consequent upon a portion of the receivers having been withdrawn from the parish pay table.

Under this plan in the parish of Great Kimble, we find the large occupiers of arable land casting the burthen on the grass farmers and on small arable farmers, who with their children can perform the requisite labour. The distribution in this parish is made according to assessment; a double injustice to grass land, which requires least labour, and on that very account pays the highest rent, and is subject to the highest assessment. If the distribution of labourers had been by the acre, the grass farmer would have received as many labourers as the arable farmer, whilst he has employment for only half the number; by the distribution according to rental he is compelled to take twice the number of labourers allotted to the farmer occupying an equal quantity of arable land, he therefore receives four times as many labourers in proportion to his wants. The following are answers received from Great Kimble:

I cannot like the name of a labour-rate, as I know I cannot get a living with it. I have got a living for a large family without it for fifty years, on a small farm of sixty-one acres. I know that a labour-rate will soon ruin small farmers like myself, if the grass land is to take the same quantity of labourers as the arable land. There must be twice the work on arable land as on grass, therefore they ought to have twice the labourers. Grass in our parish is taxed higher than the arable, therefore with a labour-rate they will have more men, and not so much work.

If there is a labour-rate allowed by Act of Parliament, I hope it will be only for the winter half-year; for I know the large farmers would like to have their harvest done by the parish. And if there is a labour-rate allowed, I ask to be allowed my sons as labourers on the farm, according to the scale in the parish, without being beholden to the overseers, to allow just who they may think proper, as was the case last winter. If renting farmers like myself are not allowed to count their sons, I ask the Commissioners, how are they to live? If it be possible, I beg the labour-rate will be done away with, and still let us be free.

John Plested.

The labour-rate is to me very injurious, as it compels me to take men which I have no employ for. I occupy only forty-nine acres of grass land, and have two sons, and not got half work enough for ourselves, while I am compelled to take a man and a boy; the boy's pay I about save by paying less poor-rates; the man's wages is all loss to me; therefore it injures me 8s. per week.

I consider the arable farmer ought to take double the men as grass farmers do, to make it on a fair scale. If there is a labour-rate allowed, I hope there will be a fair difference made between arable land and grass land, and I hope all renting farmers will be allowed to count their sons as labourers on their father's farms, according to the scale in the parish, without being beholden to the overseer to allow just whom he thinks proper. I do not ask for them to be allowed as do not work; if sons are not allowed, it must soon ruin men like myself with families. The labour-rate will undoubtedly soon ruin small concerns; the inclosures have ruined three parts of the little farms, and the labour-rate will soon ruin the remaining few farms.

Edmund Callam.

I occupy seven acres of grass land, and have not half work enough for myself; therefore the labour-rate compels me to pay for other men's labour which cannot do without them.

John Hughes.

I have only six acres of grass land, and have two sons. The labour-rate wrongs me very much, as I cannot get any employ for my sons, as my neighbours will not employ my sons, as they cannot be allowed by the overseer.

Therefore while there is a labour-rate, we three are obligated to live on our little and have a boy to do our work for us; without this rate we could get a little work at times.

John Langstone.

Princes Risborough, likewise under the second plan, affords an instance of the occupiers of rich soil making an acreage disposition of the labourers equally upon lands of all qualities, although the parish includes a large tract of sheep-walk. By this means of course the burthen is thrown upon two or three sheep-walk occupiers, who, with the occupiers of all other qualities of land, are compelled to receive one man to thirty-five acres. The degree of injury thus inflicted in Princes Risborough may be judged of by the fact that in the parish of Westbury, Wiltshire, only one man is allotted to 400 acres of sheep-walk, whilst one man is given to every thirty acres of arable land, and one to every fifty acres of meadow.

The following is an extract from the letter of J. Grace, occupier of 600 acres of sheep-walk in Princes Risborough.

The parish of Risborough contains about 5,000 acres, part of which is very good land, and a part very bad; the occupiers of the good land are more numerous than those of the poor land. Myself and another hold nearly 600 acres each of nearly the worst land in the parish: you may therefore easily see that we are out-voted in the select vestry, who agreed that the labour-rate should be levied, not by value, but by acreage; thus making land, now occupied, a considerable extent of it, as sheep-walk, and consequently producing no labour at all: what is not so applied is of poor quality, and cannot produce so much, and require so much labour as the best land, which produces a larger bulk of corn and straw. I therefore considered this mode of levying the labour-rate very unfair, and with others in the same situation objected to it; but we were out-voted by the rest of the select vestry, who were occupiers of good land, and would not consent to a fair allowance.

In this parish the little farmers league with the large farmers; it is not the large farmer shifting the burthen upon the small farmer, but the occupiers of rich land, both the large occupiers and the small occupiers casting the burthen upon a few occupiers of extensive sheep-walk.

Even under the third plan, on the face of which great fairness appears, the same system of burthen-shifting will be found to prevail. At Farnham, in Surrey, where the third plan was used during the last year, and is now in use, two provisions formed the basis of the agreement. The first —

That for every thirty acres of *pasture wood and arable land* and for every six acres of hop ground, the occupier shall find constant employ for one man, before he will be permitted to work out his portion of the above rate.

Here no allowance is made for the smaller quantity of labour required for pasture and for woodlands; no exemption is made of the small holder occupying less than twenty acres of land, exempted in many parishes on the express ground that he is *bona fide* a labourer, and capable of performing all the labour that his little holding requires. No mention is made of the sons of the small farmer who, with himself, are more than sufficient for working his farm. Thus, then, we find that under the terms of the agreement, a large share of the burthen may be cast upon the holder of meadow, the holder of woodland, the holder of less than twenty acres with or without sons, or the small holder with two or three sons.

The second provision enacts –

That all persons who are assessed to this rate, and are not occupiers of land, may participate in the benefit of the rate *by making terms with the occupiers of land to work out their rate for them.*

Under this provision, a further burthen is necessarily cast upon traders. It appears that the agriculturists generally worked out the rate for those not holding land, at one half of the wages awarded by the parish. Mr Paiu, an extensive grower of hops in that parish, says –

Rate-payers who had no land were allowed to get their portion of the labour-rate worked out by any farmer who had previously complied with the terms of the agreement, *and it has generally been done at one half. Every* such rate-payer might have had his rate thus worked out if he had chosen; very many have done so, amongst others, the proprietors of the large and small tithes, and thereby have directly effected a saving of half the amount.

Thus the trade portion of the surplus labourers is awarded to the large agriculturists at half wages, trade bearing the other half. This agreement, in fact, partakes of the unfairness of the first plan, as oppressing the tradespeople, and of the unfairness of the second as oppressing the small agriculturists and the owners of meadow land.

The following is the statement of a rate-payer:

When the labour-rate was first introduced, I had hoped it would have been beneficial to all parties; but if it is to be continued as it is now acted upon in this parish, it will increase rather than diminish pauperism. Almost every person in the town now has something to do with the pauper labourer; he must either keep a man in idleness, or send him to work upon some farm, and pay half his wages. Such a system as this is both monstrous and disgraceful on the part of the farmers, and, if continued, will make the men worse instead of better, because there is no hope of their being freed from the thraldom of pauperism.

The labour-rate was adopted because, as the farmers would have it, there was more labourers than could possibly be employed upon the land. Now, supposing there was thirty men too many, the fair proportion would be to allot twenty to the farmers, and ten to the town; the town people would have taken the ten, and employed them the best way they could; but the farmers now turn round and say, 'No, we can employ ten in addition to our twenty, if you will pay half the amount of their wages; and if you will not agree to that, you must pay the whole amount of the labour-rate assessed upon you.' What can be more convincing than this, that here is not a man too many? I intend, when another labour-rate is proposed, to make a strong objection to such shameful proceedings as this.

William Mellersh.

The Farnham labour-rate, however, appears to have been among the most successful experiments of the kind, which may probably be attributed to the following clause, and to the fairness with which the arbitrators have performed their duty.

Sixth. That Messrs J. M. Paine, Charles Knight, J. Lidbetter, George Smith, and William West, be, and are hereby appointed, arbitrators to determine in case any dispute should arise between the parish officers and the parties who apply to work out their rate; and likewise that they be, and are hereby appointed, to make such alteration in the application of that part of the second resolution which relates to the quantity of land upon which a labourer must be constantly employed, as they may consider just and reasonable, in order to obviate any particular grievance which may arise from its strict and literal enforcement, and that the decision of any three of such arbitrators shall be final and conclusive.

But what can be said in favour of a legislation which depends for its success on the impartiality of persons empowered to decide on matters in which they themselves have a strong and immediate pecuniary interest, which enables three persons out of a population of 5,858, to make a decision which shall be final and conclusive as to the quantity of land upon which a labourer must be constantly employed: which enables them to decide, as they appear to have done, that the sons of farmers are labourers, but that gardeners, grooms, or assessed servants are not?

In an adjoining parish, Frensham, the third plan was also tried; but instead of each occupier of land being compelled to take labourers according to his acreage, as at Farnham, he was compelled to take one man for every £20 assessment; and in this parish no restriction was placed upon those who did not hold land as to the disposal of their share of the surplus labour. Against this agreement no complaints were made by the trades-people. The small farmers having sons who work as labourers upon their farms seem numerous in this parish, and upon them the burthen appears to have fallen. The following are statements made by that class:

I have sons (eight) enough to do the whole work on my farm (about sixty acres), and to be compelled to pay for labour, the consequence would be, I must bring my own children in idleness to employ and pay others; and in that case it must be injurious; and in all cases of small farmers, if the farmer cannot do the labour without hiring (when there is a family) it is impossible in the present state of things for that man to live and pay his way.

William Mayhew.

The resolutions of the parish exclude the sons of farmers above one from working out the labour-rate, although they be actually employed as labourers by their parents. I have three sons, and am under the necessity of sending them to work as labourers. It therefore places on me two more labourers than it does on many of my neighbours, who hold an equal farm with me and have no family. Such proceedings are very injurious to the working farmers who have a family, and would on me and all others so situated, I think, end in ruin.

Stephen Baker.

It will be a great good to the great rich farmers; no doubt they sing, 'O, be joyful!' that all others not of like caste are obliged to help pay their labourers. But to all little farmers and others, it will be a great evil and tax; I know two or three little farmers who have sons grown up, and do all their business; now, is it not a hard case they should be obliged to hire a labourer or two to work out their rate, or pay 25 per cent more than their opulent neighbours pay, as a full rate is made, and 25 per cent deducted on such persons as work out the whole rate?

Since this labour-rate has been in operation, the poor-rates have been the same as usual. I have paid since October last three 5s. rates in the pound, and perhaps another will be brought forward before next October.

James Keet.

It may be assumed that there are not any grass farmers in this parish, as no complaint is made by any such person. Had there been such, the injury to them would, as we have seen, have been great, labourers being forced on them on the precise ground that they do not want them.

The parish is thus described by Mr Mason:

The parish of Frensham is an agricultural parish. The land is of a very similar quality throughout, and there is scarcely a rate-payer who is not in the occupation of land, or otherwise in a situation to give employment. These circumstances afford peculiar means of equalizing the burthen, and yet success was not obtained.

The agreement at Downton, in Wiltshire, is also under the third plan; the labourers being apportioned according to assessment. The following is the statement of Mr R. H. Hooper, a select vestryman of that parish:

There ought to be a difference between a farm that is chiefly of arable and one with a large proportion of meadow land, as those occupying the former admit that both with their quota of regular and freemen, they have barely sufficient, while those occupying the latter state that they have considerably more than they can find work for: it can be accounted for only in this way; the meadow lands, standing three times as high on the rate as arable land, are in consequence obliged to employ three times the number of regular labourers, although they do not want so many, as there is no ploughing, sowing, carting manure, or threshing required on meadow land.

It is evident from this that the burthen rests upon the grass farmer, and no doubt also on the small arable farmer who by himself or with his sons can perform the labour which his farm requires.

Great oppression upon an individual rate-payer, or upon a class of rate-payers, may likewise be exercised by the overseers determining by whom each labourer shall be employed. Mr Griffin of Send and Ripley says –

A few days ago I hired a strong, healthy, middle-aged labourer, at 10s. per week; the next day, a little old man came and told me the overseer had sent him instead of the man I had agreed with.

We might continue to illustrate the unfairness with which the system is conducted, until we had exhausted the parishes from which we have received information on the subject: for in each parish the surplus labourers are thrown chiefly upon one class by a combination amongst the other classes. The small occupier, who, by himself or with his children, is able to perform the labour necessary to his little farm, will however, in the great majority of cases, be found to be the severest sufferer, whether the labour-rate be upon the first plan, the second or the third. The only small occupiers who seem content are those without sons, and whose farms are sufficiently extensive to require their own time in superintendence. This class will invariably be found to prefer the system, and the reason is admitted by themselves; viz., that they save in poor-rate, and do not receive under the labour-rate more persons than are sufficient to do their work. In some instances they state that they do not receive under the labour-rate as many labourers as they previously employed.

It may perhaps appear strange that perpetrating, as they usually do, such serious injury upon the largest portion of the rate-payers, labour-rates should have been so extensively adopted. The explanation is that the large farmers are benefited, and that in an agricultural parish they command a majority in vestry.

Mr Bullen of Kelvedon, Essex, says –

There was no occasion in this parish, nor would it have been done but for a junto of powerful landholders, putting down opposition by exempting a sufficient number to give themselves the means of a majority.

Unfortunately, the power is often vested in the very class which has the least inducement to make a good use of it – those who hope to find in paupers an abundant supply of cheap labour. The Rev. R. Johnson of Lavenham, Suffolk, says –

I am told that language to the following effect has been made use of in this neighbourhood, i.e. , 'The more men unemployed the better, and the higher the poor-rates the better for us; the landlords must reduce their rents in proportion, and we shall be benefited by employing men at such wages as we choose to give them.'

The small farmer who, by himself or with his sons, can perform all the labour he requires, gains nothing by the real or apparent cheapness, for he employs none. The tradesman too is similarly situated; he must lose by pauperism, and, unlike the farmer, to whom local connection is of no importance, is tied to the spot, and must bear all the evils which belong to the parish, for to leave it would be to leave his bread. He is likewise very frequently a small proprietor, owning his house and a few acres of land.

In many cases the large occupiers have been enabled to carry the plan by intimidation. A rate-payer in a parish in Surrey, whose name and residence, from fear of injury to him, are suppressed says –

I am bound by the overseers or guardians of the parish (who have influence over trade) not to vote against a labourer's rate, or to lose their work or custom.

Again, Mr Hicks of Henfield, says –

There are very many small farmers in this parish, who, *from fear of losing their little farms, or of offending their more wealthy neighbours,* or from not understanding how the labour-rate would operate, consented to give it a trial. The result has been that several have proved the expenses 25 per cent more than before the existence of a labour-rate. *There are smiths, coopers, harness-makers, &c., who, from fear of offending, abstained from making their objections.*

In many instances, after having tried the system for a year or two, a majority of the rate-payers have succeeded in discontinuing it. So strong, however, is the apparent promise of a labour-rate, that even those who complain bitterly of its oppressive nature, according to the plan adopted in their own parishes, conclude with admiration of the principle, 'provided it can be carried into operation with an equal pressure upon all'. No one, however, has yet pointed out any means for effecting the desired 'equal pressure', which means have not been tried in some other parish, and there proved ineffectual.

A bill was introduced into Parliament during the last Session for amending the 2 & 3 Will. IV, c. 96 [1832]. The principal object of this bill was to enforce the adoption of the third plan, that by which each occupier is compelled to employ men in proportion to his acreage (reference being had to the description of cultivation), before he is considered as taking a share of the surplus labourers. The intention of the bill, however, as to the equalization of the burthen would probably have been defeated by the wide discretion which it gave to the rate-payers, under the provision

That every occupier should take one able-bodied labourer for so many acres of arable land *as may be determined by the majority afore-said of the rate-payers in vestry assembled* to require one such labourer for the proper cultivation of the same, regard being had to the description and quality of the land; and also that every such occupier shall employ one able-bodied labourer for so many acres of grass land, one for so many acres of wood land, and one for so many acres of hop ground, in his occupation *as shall respectively be determined by the majority as aforesaid*, before he shall be permitted to claim any exemption from the payment of his proportion of the said rate, or derive any benefit or assistance therefrom.

Under this provision, the arable farmers, if the majority of votes, might make the grass land, the wood land, and the down land take the same amount of labour as the arable land; or the farmers, generally combining against trade, might vote that after the farmer should have received one man, or even less, to every hundred acres, the remaining labourers should be considered surplus, and be distributed amongst the rate-payers generally, according to assessment.

A plan for remedying all unfairness in the distribution of the labourers has been proposed in a circular letter issued by Mr Hillyard, the President of the Northamptonshire Farming and Grazing Society.

Mr Hillyard's scheme resembles the first plan, that generally used in Surrey and Sussex. It proposes to obviate the objections to an assessment distribution by a graduated scale, intended, of course, to represent the exact proportion of demand for profitable labour possessed by each of the rate-payers. But the data upon which the calculations are founded appear to be arbitrary. Mr Hillyard says, 'Occupiers of houses above £5 to be rated at one third of the amount of the poor-rate.' Such houses then ought to have as much real demand for the one third allotted to them, as arable land has for the three thirds. But the assertion is wholly unsustained. The proposition may appear liberal, but it appears so only because to rate householders in the same sum as landholders would be the height of injustice. Again, he proposes that 'Occupiers of pasture or woodland be rated at one half of the amount of the poor-rate.' Grass land is generally rated twice as high per acre as arable, and therefore, if burdened with labourers in proportion to one half of its assessment, would be bound to employ as many labourers per acre as arable, though requiring only half as many. Again, 'Occupiers of land, one half or more of which is pasture, the remainder arable land, to be rated at three fourths of the amount of the poor's-rate.' Supposing the pasture to exceed one half, in the degree that it exceeded the half, the burthen would increase in unfairness. Lastly, 'No land to be deemed pasture that has not been constantly in grass for seven years and upwards.' This is a proposition for a seven years' injustice. If legalized, it would act almost as a prohibition of laying down land.

A nearer approximation towards preventing the oppression of any class of rate-payers would be to ascertain the average number of labourers required by each mode of cultivation, and then to enact that one man be employed by –

—— acres of arable land,
—— acres of pasture,
—— acres of down,
—— acres of hops,
—— acres of woodland,

and for smaller or larger quantities of land in proportion.

That the owners of water meadow should be exempt during the time their lands are under water.

That every farmer should take one man for every —— horses,

		—— oxen, cows, &c.,
____	—	—— sheep,
____	—	—— pigs.

That farmers and their sons who work as labourers should be acknowledged as such, and allowed for accordingly.

And that after this apportionment had been made, the remaining labourers should be apportioned amongst the employers of labour in proportion to their assessment to the poor's rate.

This would be as near perhaps as a statute could reach; all further adjustment must be left to the parishioners themselves. And yet there remains abundant room for disagreement and oppression. Between the farmers, as to the quality of arable land; is land that requires little labour in its cultivation to be burthened, and that which requires much to be comparatively exempt? Again, what shall be considered pasture or meadow land, is land laid down for grass to be charged as arable, and if not, how can a farmer be prevented from pretending that his land is laid down when he intends to plough it at the recurrence of the season? Who shall determine where down land ceases and meadow begins? Who shall determine when water meadow is in a fit state to admit labour upon it? What shall constitute 'working as a labourer'? Is the farmer who works one day in the year as such to be exempt, or is the man who can prove that he worked twelve hours a day during a whole year, with the exception of a few days, to be denied his claim to be reckoned a labourer because he did not work those few days? Again, as between the farmers and the rate-payers generally. The farmers may vote all the arable land in the parish inferior, and requiring a less quantity of labour; they may vote the pasture to be down land, or a species of poor marsh, or unfit to bear labour; they may vote that all farmers and their sons have performed the labour necessary to include them as agricultural labourers, and such occurrences might follow as are described in the following communication from Mr Griffin of Send and Ripley:

Farmers having any number of sons were allowed to rate them as labourers out of this rate, so that we have now yeomanry paupers, hunting, shooting, and riding about the country, enjoying themselves on labourers' allowances.

With the utmost care of the Legislature, most of these means of oppression must remain open. The Legislature cannot arrange the detail requisite for every parish even for one year, and on the details depends the working of the general provisions.

Even were it possible to prevent injustice between the rate-payers of the same parish, it would be impossible to prevent injustice between parish and parish. In almost every labour-rate which we have seen, a provision exists expressly prohibiting employment to labourers who have not a settlement. Indeed, many persons avow their object to be the expulsion of non-parishioners. At Thorney Abbey, Cambridge, the number of labourers remaining in the parish gives only one man to sixty acres.

Mr John Pask says –

The labour-rate has done good, by excluding strangers from the parish at a period of the year when they were not wanted, and by giving employment to the labourers belonging to the parish.

Mr William Stanford of Henfield, Sussex, states –

There are some parishes who speak highly of a labour-rate, viz., such parishes as have not enough of their own poor to do all the labour within their parish; although they may have had several of their own out of employ, occasioned by some farmers employing out-parishioners; but by confining their resolutions in the labour-rate to their own parishioners, those who employ men belonging to other parishes are compelled to discharge them.

The parishes from which the least dissatisfaction is expressed will generally be found to be of this class. Polstead, in Suffolk, is an example; in that parish the resident parishioners amount only to three and a fraction for each hundred acres. Lemer is another instance, and so is Nuthurst, in Sussex.

Mr J. W. Smith of Nuthurst says –

We have about 2,600 acres of land in the parish, and but 85 labourers *belonging to it*, which is not sufficient to do the work.

But those parishes whose labourers have sought employment elsewhere, and are driven back, make loud complaints.

Mr Newman of Crawley, in Sussex, complains of the evil thus inflicted upon his parish: he says –

There has been no labour-rate in the parish of Crawley, in consequence of there not being sufficient agricultural land to employ half the labourers; and I am sorry to say, owing to the labour-rate in the adjoining parishes, our labourers have been sent home and we have been compelled to support them in comparative idleness ever since the above rate was adopted, and must continue to do so under the present system.

The advantage thus unfairly gained, however, has in many cases been of short duration.

Mr William Stanford of West Grinstead, Sussex, says —

As soon as we could arrange, a rate was made for the better employment of the poor in this parish, and continued in force until the 15th of April last, and certainly enabled us to get through the first part of the winter with less men out of employ than we otherwise should have done. After Christmas, we began to feel the effect of other parishes adopting a labour-rate, and confining themselves to their own parishioners, in consequence of which several labourers came home, and, although men of good characters, had no chance of finding employment but on the parish account.

A still more serious injury appears to be caused to parishes not having a labour-rate, when a portion of its occupiers hold land in a labour-rate parish. To make room for the labourers imposed on them by that parish, they discharge their own parishioners, preferring, of course, a smaller burden in the form of a poor-rate, to a greater one in that of a labour-rate.

The following communication from Mr Glascock, churchwarden of Castle Hedingham, Essex, will show the extent of evil to that parish from the practice.

The labour-rate was not adopted in this parish, although it has been tried in all the surrounding parishes except Little Yeldham, and is now in force in Great Yeldham, Gestingthorpe, and Great Maplestead. The result has been that in these parishes there has been no demand for the labourers of this parish; that some of our labourers who were employed by farmers holding land in this and one of the labour-rate parishes have been discharged; and that farmers whose principal occupations are in the labour-rate parish have employed in our parish the labourers of the other parish to our prejudice, so that, as is truly observed by Mr Stubbins, overseer of this parish, the surplus labour of other parishes has been thrown upon Castle Hedingham. The facts from which you will draw your conclusion are these: Mr —'s principal labourers in this parish are from Great and Little Yeldham; Mr —, on 114 acres in this parish, has but two men belonging to this parish, the rest are all from Gestingthorpe, whom

under the labour-rate he is obliged to employ; Mr — has discharged
one man; he had discharged two belonging to this parish, alleging
that he must employ a certain number of Gestingthorpe men, and he
has not work for all, and a Gestingthorpe man is now actually residing
in this parish and having work in this parish. Mr — is also obliged to
employ Gestingthorpe men. Mr — has been also called upon to employ
one Yeldham man.

A witness residing in Hurstpierpoint, in Sussex, occupying land
in that and in two adjoining parishes, in the former of which only
has the labour-rate been adopted, admits that he has pursued
this course. He says, speaking of Hurstpierpoint, the labour-
rate parish,

I hold thirty-three acres of land in the parish, half arable and half
meadow; also I have about 450 acres in two adjoining parishes, and I
employ some labourers in those parishes out of this parish, because
they are not very full of paupers. In neither of those parishes (which are
Albourne, a small parish, and Woodmancoat, a larger one) has the
labour-rate been employed.

Having thus shown the operation of the labour-rate system on
the rate-payers, we will now consider its effects on the labourers:
effects of far greater importance, both as applying to a much
more numerous class, and as influencing not only their prosperity
but their morals.

There appears to be no doubt that the adoption of a labour-
rate has, in many instances, produced an immediate improvement in the condition and character of a portion of the labourers
within its operation.

It must be remembered, that working on the roads and in the
gravel-pits is considered by the labourers as wholly useless, and
therefore only inflicted upon them to gratify the malice of the
overseers; in some cases, perhaps, of the rate-payers generally.
And this opinion is no doubt often strengthened by the incautious
and petulant remarks of an overseer who feels himself surrounded
by difficulties in the performance of his office and, being an
uneducated man, has not perceived that the vicious, as the victims
of ignorance, are truly objects of compassion, and therefore
deserving of all the lenity which is compatible with their own

good, and the good of society. Considering themselves the victims of persecution, it is not wonderful that ignorant men should thus be impressed with vindictive feelings towards the rest of society, and become thoroughly vicious. Under such circumstances almost any alternative would prove to be, and would by them be considered, an improvement in their condition. A feeling of contentment is thus created which no doubt exhibits itself in more moral conduct, and in increased industry.

John Boxall, a labourer, at Frensham, Surrey, says –

It has completely allayed that feeling of discontent which was so general a short time ago, by the improved mode of employment it has given to a great number of us. The value of our labour is all we want.

Mr John Marchant of Hurstpierpoint, Sussex, says –

When they work for the parish in such numbers, they corrupt each other (being chiefly the worst labourers), but when divided amongst the occupiers of lands and houses, they become better men in every sense.

Mr Morgan of Henfield says –

I believe *we all agree* that the peace and morality of the lower orders were much improved during its continuance.

Mr Long of Farnham says –

From the circumstance of no young men having been brought before the magistrates for any disobedience or misdemeanour, it may be inferred that they have become even steadier under their improved condition.

Mr Hooper of Downton, Wiltshire, says –

Previous to its employment, large numbers of men were congregated together, either at the gravel-pits, the roads, or some other public work, badly paid, not overlooked, and, consequently, daily becoming more indolent, discontented, and insolent; but by distributing them to the different farms, these evils were got rid of.

The Rev. Richard Blunden of Alton, Hampshire, says –

I have no doubt the labour-rate, dismissing the pecuniary saving from our view, has been very advantageous both to the morals and the comfort of the labourers in this parish, and would have been much more so was it not for the pernicious operation of the present beer bill. In reference to the morals of the labourers, it disperses them from their consultations in the gravel-pit and on the road, where was concocted the means by which they might rob the preserves of game, hen-roosts of their inmates, and gardens of vegetables.

Another circumstance may likewise account for the change in the state of mind of this portion of the labourers; they generally obtain increased wages.

B. Pease, Holywell –

Agricultural labourers receive a benefit from the labour-rate, as they are employed and paid better than they would be when they are employed at parish work.

J. Cranfield, Holywell –

As it respects agricultural labourers, they receive a benefit from the working of the rate; for they are employed, and paid better than they would be were they on the parish.

W. H. Paine, Farnham –

The labourer now finds little difficulty in procuring work, and generally gets better wages than before.

But this partial improvement appears to be dearly purchased. We have seen that the first act of a labour-rate is to expel every unsettled labourer. No matter how long he may have been a steady and faithful servant; no matter how good a workman. He is not a parishioner, and however much he may be attached to his employer, and to the spot, he must give up his employment and go where he is not known, and where none but parish work may be found him.

Mr Robert Aichison of Westbury, Wilts., says –

An effect of the system has been severely felt in our part of this parish (which is almost exclusively an agricultural district, and remarkable for the sobriety and good behaviour of the labourers), namely, that it has obliged several of my farming neighbours to discharge workmen of approved character and tried fidelity (some of whom had been brought up on their estates from their youth), simply because they did not happen to have a settlement here, and take in their places men less qualified and not so trustworthy. With some of these persons I have had opportunities of conversing, and have felt much pained to observe the sad consequences of the breaking up of that mutual attachment which had for so many years subsisted between their masters and themselves.

Mr Lacy of Farnham, Surrey, speaking of out-parishioners, says –

There are cases where good labourers and old servants have received their discharge.

Mr Clapson of Hellingley, Sussex –

I employ two men who do not belong to this parish, and if I were forced to employ my proportion of those who belong to this parish, I must of necessity discharge the two above mentioned. This case is very common in this neighbourhood, and I have no doubt but the labour-rate would cause the removal of many of the best workmen in the country.

The Rev. F. Calvert of Whatfield, Suffolk –

Labourers being able to obtain employment only in the parishes to which they belong are often obliged by a labour-rate to leave situations in which they may have maintained themselves by industry many years in order to remove to their own parishes, where they must, in all probability, become paupers.

H. Barker of Henfield, Sussex –

The labour-rate has had this effect; those who have had their servants for years in their employ in our parish have sent them home to their parishes, because they would employ those belonging to the parish.

Mr Stanford of West Grinstead, Surrey –

The adoption of any plan that will, in its effect, remove good and industrious workmen from their present employers, and send them home to their own already burthened parishes, must be attended with the worst of consequences, that of destroying the morals and principles of the men, and bringing utter ruin on the parishes.

Mr Hicks of Henfield, Sussex –

It is very plain that such a bill may have the effect of cruelly injuring the industrious labourer under a kind but distant master, by sending both him and his family home to their parish; and whatever parish might hereafter become burthened with poor, the labourers would have no hope of distant employment, because the universal cry would be, 'We have a labour-rate, and it obliges us to employ or pay (exclusively) our own parishioners, whether they are good workpeople or bad.' It surely must be an error to attempt to remedy surplus agricultural labour by driving men home to their parishes by indirect means, and then compelling the farmers to employ them through parish vestries and bench boards of agriculture.

It has been customary in Sussex to hold out rewards to labourers who could bring up their families without parochial relief; but such a system as the labour-rate would entirely prevent so desirable an object; they would soon become slaves instead of free.

The following are the replies of four labourers residing at Ifield, Sussex, but not belonging to that parish.

It is an injury to the labouring classes in general, as the farmer and the gentleman are alone benefited by it, and not the labourer. In particular, people situated like myself, out of their own parish, are driven from their work and their homes to their parish, and are wholly dependent on the overseers for employment when, but for that, they might be earning a comfortable living, with a very little assistance. This has been the case with many families since the labour-rate commenced, and should it continue, the injury will be great to many an industrious labourer.

James Edwards.

I inform you, as a labourer, that if a labour-rate had taken place in this parish as proposed, it would have been an injury to me. I inform you that I am an out-parishioner, and nothing to depend upon but my daily labour. Not belonging to the parish, I find it difficult to get employ, and, in addition to being out of employ, I have the rate myself to pay, and the system in its present form will certainly injure me.

William Razzle.

I do not belong to this parish, therefore I cannot say anything in the behalf of the labour-rate, as it appears that it prevents all outparishioners getting a day's work, so that it is a harm.

Richard Smith.

I am afraid the labour-rate is of no good to me, as I do not belong to the parish; I am afraid it will throw me out of work and drive me home to my parish for employment, and I think it of little use for out-dwellers.

James Stradwick.

But the evil to the labouring population is not confined to the non-parishioners. The ultimate effect of a labour-rate, or, in other words, of a measure which forces individuals to employ labourers at a given rate of wages, must be to destroy the distinction between pauperism and independence. Our inquiries have convinced us that it is only by keeping these things separated, and separated by as broad and as distinct a demarcation as possible, and by making relief in all cases less agreeable than wages, that anything deserving the name of improvement can be hoped for. But under the labour-rate system relief and wages are confounded. The wages partake of relief, and the relief partakes of wages. The labourer is employed, not because he is a good workman, but because he is a parishioner. He receives a certain sum, not because it is the fair value of his labour, but because it is what the vestry has ordered to be paid. Good conduct, diligence, skill, all become valueless. Can it be supposed that they will be preserved? We deplore the misconception of the labourers in thinking that wages are not a matter of contract but of right; that any diminution of their comforts occasioned by an increase of their numbers, without an equal increase of the fund for their subsistence, is an evil to be remedied, not by themselves, but by the magistrates; not an error, or even a misfortune, but an injustice. But can we more effectually maintain this state of feeling than by proclaiming that, at the expense of the landlord, the tithe-owner, the small farmer, and the shopkeeper, all the labourers of the parish are to be kept at the ordinary wages, or nearly the ordinary wages of the district, in a state free from anxiety, restriction, or degradation, however great their numbers, however little their diligence, or however reckless their profligacy or their improvidence?

The following is the labour-rate scale of wages used at Princes Risborough:

Each able-bodied labourer above 25 years of age, 8s. weekly.

from 20 to 25	,,	7s.
Lads from 18 to 20	,,	5s.
from 16 to 18	,,	4s.
from 14 to 16	,,	3s.
from 12 to 14	,,	2s. 6d.
from 10 to 12	,,	2s.

The scale used at Farnham, Surrey, is curious, as showing that a youth of seventeen, and a man above seventy-five, are held equally capable.

Boys from 12 to 15 years old, 2s. 6d. per week.		
from 15 to 18	,,	5s.
from 18 to 21	,,	7s. 6d.
Men		10s.
from 65 to 75	,,	7s. 6d.
Above 75	,,	5s.

It is true that these are *minimum* scales, but we know the tendency of the *minimum* to become a *maximum*.

In some parishes in Suffolk an attempt is made to pay each labourer according to his comparative value, and consequently the labourers are divided into classes, each class having a separate rate of wages. At Polstead, in Suffolk, the labourers are classed at 9s., 8s., 7s., and 6s. per week; boys at 5s., 4s., 3s., and 2s. It is, however, probable that these classes have reference to age, and number in family, rather than to the comparative value of the labourer's work. The following is the list circulated amongst the rate-payers at Polstead:

That the following labourers be entitled, when so employed, to the respective wages as under-mentioned:

Men at 9s. per week. (Here follow about 80 names.)

Labourers	...	at 8s. per week	...	...	5 names.
Labourers	...	at 7s. per week	...	...	7 names.
Labourers	...	at 6s. per week	...	...	7 names.
Boys ...	...	at 5s. per week	...	...	5 names.
Boys ...	...	at 4s. per week	...	...	7 names.
Boys ...	...	at 3s. per week	...	...	14 names.
Boys ...	...	at 2s. per week	...	...	6 names.

The following are opinions expressed by rate-payers as to the probable effect of the labour-rate upon the habits and morals of the independent labourers. Mr Joseph Sexton of Westbury, Wilts., says –

One evil connected with the labour-rate is omitted, I believe, by all; that its operations bring many industrious labourers on the parish, who otherwise never would have been paupers. Every kind of labour is done in some way or other by the stem-men, and consequently there is nothing left for the usual labourer, and there is no alternative but for him to go to the parish for relief: thus the independent labourer becomes a pauper. There are many instances of this nature in the parish from the plan last year.

Another evil is, the plan throws out of employ many who come on the rates; and it is impossible to prevent this unless all men would act conscientiously. As soon as the stem-system commences, immediately farmers do not want so many regular labourers; these are consequently paid off and placed on the stem. I met with a case this week to illustrate this fact: an industrious young man who had been a soldier, and married a wife abroad, was discharged; he returned to his parish (Westbury), but did not apply for relief. His wife who is a respectable woman, with himself, slept on straw; they endured the greatest privation rather than go to the parish. At length he got regular employ at 9s. per week. He now became comfortable; he furnished his house, and everything was going on well till the stem commenced, when he was informed he could not be employed any longer; and he could not get labour till he consented to be stemmed at 3s. per week, for which he labours about three days. He is now off the parish again by his industry, but he told me the stem was £4 out of his pocket, last year, only for labour.

The consequences are injurious; when once a person is registered on the parish book, he loses his independence, and generally is not anxious to return to labour. The stem is finished; the work is all done; he then goes to the overseer and demands his allowance; the parish is burthened; the man is degraded; he forms associations with other paupers; idleness and corruption of morals go together; family ties are broken; misery enters the family, and a great deal of the parish money goes to the beer-shop. Thus the number of paupers are increased, the rates are increased, and we are all involved in greater expenses, with less trade to support them.

The Rev. F. Calvert of Whatfield, Suffolk –

Piece-work must be generally discontinued where farmers have so many labourers quartered upon them that they have not employment enough to supply their increased number of hands with piece-work, nor sufficient capital to pay the increased weekly wages if they could find such work for them.

A consequent diminution of the industry of all labourers. A gentleman who is a neighbour of mine, and one of the principal occupiers in the hundred, tells me that it is his opinion there would not be found, under the operation of a labour-rate continued two or three years, a single industrious man in the whole neighbourhood.

Single men obtaining constant work under a labour-rate, in whom habits of improvidence have already been fixed by the existing system of pauperism, spend the greatest part of their increased earnings at beer-houses.

Mr Brand of Kelvedon, Essex –

I believe it has done harm to the rate-payers by making the labourers less laborious, by giving them less encouragement and more cause for discontent, by not giving an adequate compensation to the industrious man, and assuring the idle a certainty of employment.

Mr Meade of Princes Risborough, Bucks. –

But it is not advisable that all the labourers be paid their wages by the labour-rate, as many employers wish: such a proceeding will render the men all paupers, and destroy the little respectability and independence that yet remains; and at the same time gradually deprive the proprietors of the soil of all rent whatsoever, as to Cholesbury.

Mr J. Grace of the same parish –

The effect of a labour-rate would be good, as far as regards the profitable employment of the labourers, instead of congregating together as they now do on the roads; but for no other purpose do I think it desirable, or likely to improve the condition of the labouring class; because it holds out no stimulus to encourage the working sort, but puts them on a level with the idle, who will never move from the parish as long as they can demand a certain income from it.

Mr Hooper of Downton, Wiltshire –

They never try to get employment, but now look constantly to the regulator, and are little desirous to please. The labourer is aware that he is a pauper; that when he has served one master a few days or weeks he shall be sent to another, and so changing from master to master he acquires no interest with any.

Mr Goodman of Thorney Abbey, Cambridge –

It has made my labourers, who belong to this parish, regardless of civility and of giving satisfaction in their work, and been the cause of their not remaining so stationary and attached to the place where they have had employment during the winter as they otherwise would be; they knowing and saying it is not now necessary, as it used to be, for them to care about pleasing their master by staying with him during harvest, as when the winter sets in, he, or some other farmer in the parish, must find them constant work at not less than 10s. per week; and the consequence is that most of my labourers belonging to this parish whom I employ in the winter leave me in the months of May, June, and July, and the chief part of my harvest-work is done by strangers, who know nothing of my ways, and I nothing of their characters, which, to say the least of, is to me very objectionable.

Mr Hennant of Thorney Abbey, Cambridge –

If I complain of the little work done, or its being ill done, the reply is (interlarded with the grossest blackguardism), 'Oh, we don't care a —; if you don't like it as it is, you may do your work yourself; for if you discharge us, you must keep us, or have others of the same sort in our stead.'

Mr Stephen Cadby of Westbury, Wilts. –

The greatest evil, in my opinion, is the spirit of laziness and insubordination that it creates; if you remonstrate with these men, they abuse or injure, certain, however their conduct, they shall receive their money.

Mr John Harris of the same parish –

Knowing they must receive a certain sum per week, they seldom come to work till seven o'clock, and generally leave by four, and if you remonstrate with them, you only get abuse.

While such are often the effects of a labour-rate on the industry of the labourers, it is equally unfavourable to their frugality and independence. We have already dwelt on the oppression of refusing employment to the labourer who has saved any property. Under the system which we are now considering, the possession of property, or even the mere abstinence from pauperism, becomes sometimes a ground for further taxation.

The following are the replies of some working men who are assessed to the labour-rate:

Those of Ifield, Sussex, say –

> I have built a small cottage on the waste land given me by the lord of the manor, and I have not employment at all times at my trade, that is, bottoming sieves and chairs, and rake-making; *and when I am out of employ, the farmers will not employ me, because I have got the cottage.* Therefore, to send me a man for me to employ, I think an imposition. I pay the highway tax, poor tax, and tithe, which taxes were quite as high when the labour-rate prevailed.
>
> William Lidbettor.

> I am a journeyman bricklayer, and when the labour-rate came into operation last winter, I was myself out of employment; it therefore cannot be supposed that I had any thing to set a man to work at, as the large farmers in this neighbourhood can at any time of the year employ the labourers who are out of work to advantage. I myself, as well as others, are of opinion that the labour-rate should be chargeable only on the farmers, and not on cottagers such as myself.
>
> James Still.

> To persons situated like myself, it is an injury to us, as we have men sent us and we have no employment for them. I employ no men, and I work at farming work myself, and only hire a small cottage; therefore the money for labour is paid out of our own pockets, nearly useless. It appears that the poor-book in our parish has been quite as high all the same.
>
> Thomas Elsey.

Those of Boddicot, Oxfordshire, say –

> As to myself, in the winter I have not work half my time, and have nothing for a labourer to do, and it is a grievous thing for me, and it has done a deal of harm to us poor house-dwellers; many of us can scarce get our living.
>
> Joseph Lovell, painter.

A labour-rate will do me an injury, as I am a labourer, and receiving no more than 9s. per week, with an infirm wife, sometimes not able to wait on herself. My cottage and garden contain five poles only; my rent £3; and each rate 2s.; therefore I have no employment for a labourer.

> The mark ✕ of John Adkins, labourer,
> assessed at £1 10s.

I am a poor labourer, and receiving no more than 10s. per week to support myself, wife, and two children, and occupy a small cottage, with a garden but a few yards square, and have nothing for a labourer to do. My poor rate is 2s.; therefore a labour-rate would be an injury to me, and in the shape of a double poor-rate.

> John Stanley.

It will do me an injury, as I am a poor labourer, and receiving no more than 10s. per week for my labour, and that to support myself, wife, and three children, and to pay a rent of £4 per annum for my cottage, with a small garden, containing altogether, by admeasurement, eight poles. My poor-rate is 1s. 3d. each rate. A labour-rate would be a double poor-rate, as I have nothing for a labourer to do. Thus it will be seen, that a poor-rate considerably distresses me in attempting to pay it, and am worse in circumstances than many that receive parish support.

> John Adkins, jun. maltman.

Samuel Barnett of Westbury, Wilts., says –

I feel myself much aggrieved by it. I rent a small quantity of land, 4½ acres, for which I have paid last year nine grants and a half of poor's rates, at 7s. 3d. per grant. This, Sir, is exclusive of rent and every other tax. These men are sent to me when I want labour myself, and one of them I offered half his week's wages of 8s. to go about his business; but he refused it, and I was compelled to find him employ at a serious loss to myself; because, as he was a clothworker, and I an agricultural labourer, he did not understand his work.

Thomas Mercer of Hurstpierpoint, says –

I think it pressed very hard. I am a labouring man in agriculture, and have nothing to depend on for support but my labour. I am charged with poor-rates which I can ill afford to pay, and I was also charged to the labour-rate, and hired a man to outset my quota, although at the same time I was out of employ myself.

A further objection to a permanent labour-rate system is the great additional difficulty which it will create in the already arduous task of Poor Law amendment. When the direct employers of labour have for some time been sanctioned by the Legislature in extorting from others the payment of a part of the wages of their labourers, when the best class of labourers, those who are not settled in the place of their employment, have disappeared, when what now remains of repugnance to relief or of degradation in accepting it has been destroyed by its being merged in wages, when all the labourers have been converted into a semi-servile populac , without fear but without hope, where can we look for the materials of improvement?

On these grounds, we believe that the labour-rate system, or any other system of forced employment by individuals at a compulsory rate of wages, if it ever become extensive and permanent, will purchase at the expense of enormous and lasting mischief and injustice whatever immediate advantage it affords.

Our preceding remarks apply principally to agricultural parishes, to which, as we have already stated, labour-rates have as yet been confined. But a manufacturer has as much inducement to tax the rest of the parish for his own benefit as a farmer; in fact, he has a much greater inducement. As an extensive employer of labourers, his advantage over the farmer is as great, or still greater, than that of the farmer over the rest of the community. If we suppose there to be in the same parish a clergyman, a farmer, and a manufacturer, each rated at £200 a year, it is probable that the manufacturer would be found to employ at least a hundred men, the farmer about ten, and the clergyman two. In such a case, the gain to the manufacturer from a labour-rate would be ten times as great as to the farmer. We see therefore no reason for hoping that, if labour-rates become more frequent, they will continue to be confined to the agricultural districts.

It is true that although some of the objections which we have stated apply to all the labour-rates which we have seen, a rate might be framed which should be free from many of them. The rate might apply only to the occupiers of land, leaving out houses and tithes. It might be assessed on the land, not according to acreage or rent, but according to the real demand of the occupier for labour arable being taxed more heavily than pasture, and pasture than wood. A distribution of this last kind is made in the Lenham rate. And lastly, the distinction between those having and those not having settlements in the parish might be given up. But, in the first place, a labour-rate so qualified as this would scarcely ever be adopted; and, secondly, the worst ingredient of the system would continue. The line between the pauper and the independent labourer would be *pro tanto* obliterated; and we do not believe that a country in which that distinction has been completely effaced, and every man, whatever be his conduct or his character, ensured a *comfortable* subsistence, can retain its prosperity, or even its civilization.

REMEDIAL MEASURES

THE most pressing of the evils which we have described are those connected with the relief of the able-bodied. They are the evils, therefore, for which we shall first propose remedies.

If we believed the evils stated in the previous part of the Report, or evils resembling or even approaching them, to be necessarily incidental to the compulsory relief of the able-bodied, we should not hesitate in recommending its entire abolition. But we do not believe these evils to be its necessary consequences. We believe that under strict regulations, adequately enforced, such relief may be afforded safely and even beneficially.

In all extensive communities, circumstances will occur in which an individual, by the failure of his means of subsistence, will be exposed to the danger of perishing. To refuse relief, and at the same time to punish mendicity when it cannot be proved that the offender could have obtained subsistence by labour, is repugnant to the common sentiments of mankind; it is repugnant to them to punish even depredation, apparently committed as the only resource against want.

In all extensive civilized communities, therefore, the occurrence of extreme necessity is prevented by alms-giving, by public institutions supported by endowments or voluntary contributions, or by a provision partly voluntary and partly compulsory, or by a provision entirely compulsory, which may exclude the pretext of mendicancy.

But in no part of Europe except England has it been thought fit that the provision, whether compulsory or voluntary, should be applied to more than the relief of *indigence*, the state of a person unable to labour, or unable to obtain, in return for his labour, the means of subsistence. It has never been deemed expedient that the provision should extend to the relief of *poverty*; that is, the state of one who, in order to obtain a mere subsistence, is forced to have recourse to labour.

From the evidence collected under this Commission, we are induced to believe that a compulsory provision for the relief of the indigent can be generally administered on a sound and well-defined principle; and that under the operation of this principle, the assurance that no one need perish from want may be rendered more complete than at present, and the mendicant and vagrant repressed by disarming them of their weapon – the plea of impending starvation.

It may be assumed that in the administration of relief the public is warranted in imposing such conditions on the individual relief as are conducive to the benefit either of the individual himself, or of the country at large, at whose expense he is to be relieved.

[PRINCIPLE OF ADMINISTERING RELIEF TO THE INDIGENT]

THE first and most essential of all conditions, a principle which we find universally admitted, even by those whose practice is at variance with it, is that his situation on the whole shall not be made really or apparently so eligible as the situation of the independent labourer of the lowest class. Throughout the evidence it is shown that in proportion as the condition of any pauper class is elevated above the condition of independent labourers, the condition of the independent class is depressed; their industry is impaired, their employment becomes unsteady, and its remuneration in wages is diminished. Such persons, therefore, are under the strongest inducements to quit the less eligible class of labourers and enter the more eligible class of paupers. The converse is the effect when the pauper class is placed in its proper position, below the condition of the independent labourer. Every penny bestowed that tends to render the condition of the pauper more eligible than that of the independent labourer, is a bounty on indolence and vice. We have found that as the poor's rates are at present administered, they operate as bounties of this description, to the amount of several millions annually.

The standard, therefore, to which reference must be made in fixing the condition of those who are to be maintained by the public, is the condition of those who are maintained by their own exertions. But the evidence shows how loosely and imperfectly the situation of the independent labourer has been inquired into, and how little is really known of it by those who award or distribute relief. It shows also that so little has their situation been made a standard for the supply of commodities, that the diet of the workhouse almost always exceeds that of the cottage, and the diet of the gaol is generally more profuse than even that of the workhouse. It shows also that this standard has been so little referred to in the exaction of labour that commonly the work required from the pauper is inferior to that performed by the labourers and servants of those who have prescribed it: so much and so generally inferior as to create a prevalent notion among the agricultural paupers that they have a right to be exempted from the amount of work which is performed and indeed sought for by the independent labourer.

We can state, as the result of the extensive inquiries made under this Commission into the circumstances of the labouring classes, that the agricultural labourers when in employment, in common with the other classes of labourer throughout the country, have greatly advanced in condition; that their wages will now produce to them more of the necessaries and comforts of life than at any former period. These results appear to be confirmed by the evidence collected by the Committees of the House of Commons appointed to inquire into the condition of the agricultural and manufacturing classes, and also by that collected by the Factory Commissioners. No body of men save money whilst they are in want of what they deem absolute necessaries. No common man will put by a shilling whilst he is in need of a loaf, or will save whilst he has a pressing want unsatisfied. The circumstance of there being nearly fourteen millions in the savings banks, and the fact that, according to the last returns, upwards of 29,000 of the depositors were agricultural labourers who, there is reason to believe, are usually the heads of families, and also the fact of the reduction of the general average of mortality, justify the conclusion, that a condition worse than that of the independent agricultural labourer, may nevertheless be a condition above that in which the great body of English labourers have lived in times that have always

been considered prosperous. Even if the condition of the independent labourer were to remain as it now is, and the pauper were to
be reduced avowedly below that condition, he might still be
adequately supplied with the necessaries of life.

But it will be seen that the process of dispauperizing the able-
bodied is in its ultimate effects a process which elevates the condition of the great mass of society.

In all the instances which we have met with, where parishes
have been dispauperized, the effect appears to have been produced by the practical application of the principle which we have
set forth as the main principle of a good Poor-Law administration,
namely, the restoration of the pauper to a position below that of
the independent labourer.

The principle adopted in the parish of Cookham, Berks., is thus
stated:

As regards the able-bodied labourers who apply for relief, giving
them hard work at low wages by the piece, and exacting more work at
a lower price than is paid for any other labour in the parish. In short,
to adopt the maxim of Mr Whately, to let the labourer find that the
parish is the hardest taskmaster and the worst paymaster he can find,
and thus induce him to make his application to the parish his last and
not his first resource.

In Swallowfield, Berks., labour was given 'a little below the
farmers' prices'.

The principle adopted by the Marquis of Salisbury, in Hatfield,
Herts., is set forth in the following rules:

All persons, except women, employed by the parish, under the
age of fifty, shall be employed in task-work. The value of the work
done by them shall be calculated at *five sixths* of the common rate of
wages for such work. Persons above the age of fifty may be employed
in such work as is not capable of being measured, but the wages of
their labour shall be *one sixth* below the common rate of wages.

The rule adopted in the parish of Welwyn adjacent to Hatfield
is that –

When employment is found for an able-bodied labourer who is
willing to work, but unable to find it, he shall be as much as possible
employed in task or piece-work, and at wages below what are usually

given, so as to make him desirous of finding work elsewhere, rather than of applying to the overseer.

In the parish of St Mary, Nottingham, the principle adopted is thus stated:

First, steadily refusing to make up wages. Secondly, invariably taking every applicant for relief and the whole of his family, however large, entirely on the parish, and setting him to work of some sort or other, without any view to profit, or to any principle but that it should be more irksome than ordinary labour.

The principle adopted by Mr Lowe, at Bingham, was also that of 'rendering it more irksome to gain a livelihood by parish relief than by industry'.

The principle adopted by Mr Baker, in the parish of Uley, in Gloucestershire, is thus stated by him:

To provide for those who are able to work, *the necessaries of life*, but *nothing more*, to keep them closely to work, and in all respects under such restrictions, that though no man who was *really in want* would hesitate a moment to comply with them, yet that he would submit to them no longer than he could help; that he would rather do his utmost *to find work* by which he could support himself than accept parish pay.

All labour is irksome to those who are unaccustomed to labour; and what is generally meant by the expression 'rendering the pauper's situation irksome', is rendering it laborious. But it is not by means of labour alone that the principle is applicable, nor does it imply that the food or comforts of the pauper should approach the lowest point at which existence may be maintained. Although the workhouse food be more ample in quantity and better in quality than that of which the labourer's family partakes, and the house in other respects superior to the cottage, yet the strict discipline of well-regulated workhouses, and in particular the restrictions to which the inmates are subject in respect to the use of acknowledged luxuries, such as fermented liquors and tobacco, are intolerable to the indolent and disorderly, while to the aged, the feeble and other proper objects of relief, the regularity and discipline render the workhouse a place of comparative comfort.

The measures adopted at Southwell are thus stated by Mr Cowell, on the authority of the governor of the workhouse:

All the orders were —

1. To separate the men and women. 2. To prevent any from going out or seeing visitors, and to make them keep regular hours. 3. To prevent smoking. 4. To disallow beer. 5. To find them work. 6. To treat and feed them well.

If they misbehaved themselves very grossly, I had authority to imprison them in a solitary cell with the consent of the overseer. But never since I have been governor have I had occasion to imprison but one person, a woman, who was a violent idiot. To the violent turbulent young paupers who came in, swearing they would beat the parish, I gave bones or stones to break in the yard — had a hammer made on purpose.

But it appears that in others of the dispauperized parishes, the course adopted was simply refusing all relief, except in the workhouses. In the parish of Llangaddock, in Brecon, it is stated —

We placed the parish under Mr Sturges Bourne's Act; we made a small poor-house out of some houses adjoining one another, borrowing £300 upon the security of the rates. All persons applying for relief were compelled to move into the poor-house or go without.

In the parish of Leckhamstead, Berks., the means are described to have been —

1. By the establishment, in the autumn of 1827, of a poor-house for the maintenance of the aged and infirm, and for the employment of children, we have reduced the expenses of the parish about one third.

2. By adhering strictly to the Statute of 43 Elizabeth, and by setting all the children that required relief to work, feeding and lodging them in the poor-house, we have done away entirely with the bread system, or head allowance, now totally unknown in this parish; and the alteration induces our poor to look out for employment for themselves and children, which before they did not trouble themselves about.

It is to be observed that, although they are variously stated, all these modes of relief, whether by paying wages lower than the ordinary rate in return for out-door labour, or by maintenance in the workhouse, imply that the condition of the independent labourer is taken as a standard, and the condition of the pauper purposely kept below it; and that these objects seem to have been effected with little real severity in any point, and least of all in that of food. In some instances a low diet was prescribed *in terrorem*, but there appears to have been scarcely ever a rigid enforcement of the rule; and in general the paupers within the workhouse enjoyed a diet profuse compared with that of the independent labourers of the same district.

In the course of an investigation induced by the fact already noticed, that wherever any members of vestries, or of boards of parish officers were distinguished by strictness in the administration of relief, these members were generally persons who had themselves risen from the labouring classes; it appeared that the principle which we have set forth for the administration of the poor's rates (and to which we shall frequently refer in subsequent passages of this Report) is generally adopted by the labouring classes themselves, as the only safe principle for the government of their friendly societies. Mr Tidd Pratt was examined on this point. Under the 10 Geo. IV, c. 56 [1829], which was brought into Parliament at the instance and with the concurrence of delegates from the friendly societies, composed of the labouring classes throughout the country, he has examined and certified about three thousand sets of regulations for different societies, all of which, with the exception of about two per cent, were framed by the members. He was asked, 'In these institutions, is the condition of a member receiving relief, or living without work, ever allowed to be as eligible on the whole, as the condition of a member living by his work?' He answered –

In most cases the allowances made by the societies are so adjusted as to make it the interest of every member not to receive relief from the society so long as he can earn his usual wages. The average allowance which they make is about one third of what a member can earn. Thus, if the average earnings of the members of a benefit society were £1 4s. a week, the allowance in the case of sickness would be, on an average of the whole time of the sickness, about 8s. a week. During the last session Mr Slaney brought in a Bill for the purpose of sanctioning the formation of societies for the relief of members when out of employment. At his instance I made inquiries amongst some of the most intelligent and respectable of the labouring classes as to what should be the extent of allowance to those who were out of work. I suggested to the parties that one half the usual wages might be a proper allowance. The unanimous reply of all the operatives with whom I conversed on the subject was, that an allowance of one third would be ample, and that more than that would only induce the members to continue on the society rather than endeavour to find work.

[EFFECTS OF PROPOSED ADMINISTRATION ON ABLE-BODIED PAUPERS]

WE now solicit attention to the various classes of effects produced by the application of this principle, though less strictly, to the administration of the poor's rates.

The first immediate effects produced in Cookham were the conversion of the able-bodied paupers into independent labourers, and the reduction of the parochial expenditure.

'About sixty-three heads of families which were formerly constantly on the parish at once disappeared from the poor-books.'

In the course of Mr Whately's examination he was asked:

Did the change of system drive any of the parishioners into other parishes? – Certainly not. Not a single family of parishioners of the labouring class has removed; and what is more remarkable is that although the allowance formerly given to parishioners living at a distance was discontinued, none were brought home.

Do you mean that not one family of parishioners of the labouring class has removed from the parish since the change of system? – I do. Of course I do not mean to state that the youth of both sexes are not encouraged to look out for suitable services wherever they may be found; and many have done themselves and their friends credit by doing so, who under the old system of relief might have had their efforts paralysed, and have continued through life a burden both to themselves and their friends.

The money payments were reduced from £2,608 to less than half the amount. During the first eight years of the operation of the new system £15,000 was saved as compared with the expenditure of the eight years preceding.

In Swallowfield, the annual rates were reduced from 6s. 8d. to

3s. 4d. in the pound. All able-bodied labourers left the work-house, and the total number of able-bodied claimants was diminished one half.

Among the effects produced at Leckhamstead, it is stated that forty-three able-bodied labourers were formerly chargeable to the parish, and that three only are now chargeable. In answer to further inquiries Mr Brickwell, who effected the change, states that —

The forty have mostly found employment within this parish; there may be four or five employed generally in the adjoining parish of Lillingstone Lovell, where they have not a sufficient number of labourers for their ordinary work, and at some periods of the year others obtain work in the neighbourhood. Since the change of our system the farmers are more inclined to employ labourers; previously they would leave all the work that could by means be put off until some rounds-men came to their turn, or until they could get men at reduced wages, the parish making up the remainder; now the case is different, that inducement for protracting their work is done away with, and there is a more regular supply of labour; the men find it much easier to obtain work at fair wages; none are driven out of the parish by our improved system; but we do observe a greater desire and anxiety to obtain work amongst the labourers than was formerly the case.

In this parish it appears that the total population is not more than 499, and that seventy-seven of these are labourers employed in agriculture. The population was, in 1801, 346; in 1811, 397; in 1821, 519. During the five years preceding the change, the total expenditure was £4,172; during the five years subsequent it was £3,000.

In Hatfield also, the able-bodied labourers found independent work within the parish. There appear indeed to have been no means of emigration. The master of the workhouse was asked:

Do the labourers ever go out of your parish to seek work? – No, they know it would be of no use; they are certain of it, as it is a general understanding in this part of the country that each parish shall employ its own poor.

The saving in money in this parish, during the ten years succeeding the alteration, as compared with the ten years preceding, was £14,000, the population having during that time increased by 378 persons.

In Welwyn, the results of the system were very soon perceived. The Rev. Mr Clutton states that —

Since the alteration, the labourers are less disposed to throw themselves out of work; not applying to the parish on every emergency; there are few new paupers. Some of those who had been on the parish as permanently sick for years have partially recovered, and have returned to work, supporting, or at least helping to support, themselves and their families. Several of the girls who came into the house when it was first opened have obtained respectable places, and have turned out well; but for the discipline and habits of the poor-house they would in all probability have been ruined.

In Southwell, the inmates of the workhouse dwindled from eighty in the first year to thirty and in the second to eleven. The total expenditure during the ten years preceding the change was £13,929; the total expenditure during the ten years succeeding, was £4,005.

In Bingham —

The inmates of the workhouse dropped from forty-five to twelve, all of them old, idiots, or infirm, to whom a workhouse is really a place of comfort. The number of persons relieved out of the workhouse dropped from seventy-eight to twenty-seven. The weekly pay from £6 to £1 16s. to pensioners, all of whom are old and blind, or crippled.

The expenditure in poor's rates was as follows:

1816 to 17	...	... £1,231	1823 to 24	...	... £365
1817 to 18	...	... 1,206	1824 to 25	...	... 431
1818 to 19	...	... 984*	1825 to 26	...	... 356
* New system began this year.			1826 to 27	...	... 345
			1827 to 28	...	... 360
1819 to 20	...	... 711	1828 to 29	...	... 334
1820 to 21	...	... 510	1829 to 30	...	... 388
1821 to 22	...	... 338	1830 to 31	...	... 370
1822 to 23	...	... 228	1831 to 32	...	... 449

In Turton, near Bolton, Lancashire, where a well-managed workhouse was introduced —

No sooner has this system been put into full operation in the house than the able-bodied, hereditary paupers began to disappear; the discipline was new to them – they disliked the restraint; they soon found that by persevering industry and a little management, they could live above pauperism; and they left us with their habits improved, to make their way in the world without parochial assistance.

Our poor-rates in 1790 were, upon a full valuation, nearly equal to nine per cent, and at some subsequent periods, viz., in 1816 and 1817, have been even more. After the establishment of our workhouse they began to decrease; for many years preceding the last, they have been very little more than five per cent, and last year they were less, although the population has become nearly double.

In Ilfracombe the overseer found that when 2d. a day less was given by the parish than by private persons, applications were no longer made to him by the able-bodied paupers. Not a single able-bodied man has been relieved since that time, and they are all in the employment of the farmers; the rate of wages being 1s. 4d. per diem, with an allowance for beer or cider.

In Uley, the burthens of the rate-payers were reduced more than one half; and Mr Baker, in speaking of the subsequent conversion of paupers into labourers, states –

That it is not so difficult for them to find work for themselves as it is generally believed to be, is proved from the shortness of the time that, with not above two or three exceptions, any able-bodied person has remained in the house; and by a list which has been made of more than a thousand persons who were on the parish books, and who now can be proved to be otherwise maintained, chiefly by their own exertions. The list shows what they used to receive, and for whom they now work. All who received parish pay before the workhouse was open are accounted for, excepting about eight or ten. Some few have left the parish, but not many. About 500 are now on the books, and most of those on reduced pay. I did not advise the introduction of the plan till I had read much and thought much, and till I had removed many doubts by private correspondence with those who had witnessed its beneficial effects for several years. Among these doubts the most important was, '*how, in the present scarcity of work, can those employ or support themselves who are now receiving parish pay?*' The answer was, 'You will be surprised to find how soon the impossibility will dwindle down to an improbability, the improbability to a distant hope, and that again to complete success.' I was also told that industry and frugality would increase, and that crime would become less; but I never was told, not had I the most distant hope, that the success would have been so complete. When it began the poor were idle, insolent, and in a state bordering upon riot; they openly acknowledged that they would rather live on the parish pay in idleness than work for full labourer's wages, and when hired, their behaviour was such that they could not be continued in work. Now all are glad to get work. I employed many of them in the winter of 1830, and in the spring I let them go; but I promised them work again in the next winter, for which they expressed more gratitude than I expected; but when the winter came very few claimed my promise, *they were in work which they had found for themselves*; and in this winter, up to this time (December 5th, 1832) only one person has asked me for work. There is one man at Uley whose character is, and ever has been, exceedingly bad and, his feet being inverted, he is lame. He was allowed parish pay till very lately; he applied for an increase of it; he asserted no one would employ him, and I believed him. At a vestry meeting, however, his pay was entirely taken off; he instantly found work for himself, and has lived by his labour ever since.

In no instance does the actual population of a parish appear to have been disturbed by these changes; no complaint has been made by adjacent parishes of the labourers of the dispauperized parishes having been driven in amongst them. The reason assigned by the witness at Hatfield for the labourers continuing in their own parish is applicable to most of the agricultural districts. Non-parishioners may gradually introduce themselves without exciting a murmur; but it appears that the Law of Settlement, and the present general administration of the Poor Laws, render the transference of bodies of the labouring population from parish to parish a matter of considerable difficulty. It is found less difficult to drive them into other parishes for residences, and even for settlements, than for labour; which last object arouses the immediate opposition of the settled labourers. It appears, however, that they had no need to seek labour in other parishes, as they found it on the best terms in their own parishes, as soon as motives to steady industry were re-imposed upon them. In some large town parishes the same principle of administration, with relation to able-bodied paupers, has been tried, and, as will appear from our subsequent quotations, found equally efficient in rendering them independent of parochial aid; but from the want of knowledge of the individual circumstances of the paupers, or the means of tracing them amidst a crowded population, the witnesses can seldom speak otherwise than on conjecture as to any further effects.

The evidence, however, which we have been able to obtain from towns resembles that afforded by the rural districts. Mr Gordon, a parish officer of All Saints, Poplar, one of the parishes in the metropolis where stricter management of the able-bodied paupers has been established, states –

I have lived thirty years in the parish, and being a cooper and ship-owner, employing in my own business between forty and fifty men, I am conversant with the condition of the labouring classes, and can state that the effect upon them in our district has been very beneficial. It has been beneficial in inducing them to rely more on their own resources than they did formerly. It has long struck me, that they contribute more regularly and largely to savings' banks and benefit societies; in fact, I know this to be the case as I am one of the trustees of the Poplar Savings' Bank. Now I have only one man working in my yard who does not contribute to a benefit society established amongst the men some years ago, at the instance of my brother; formerly, there were a great number of the men who did not contribute to it. Speaking of my own men, I can state they are much more steady in their work and more careful than formerly in not throwing themselves out of work.

The absorption of the able-bodied paupers, or, in other words, their conversion into independent labourers employed within the parish, and the reduction of the poor's rates, were immediately followed by an improvement in wages, so far as the amount of wages in a pauperized parish, confounded as they are with partial relief under the roundsman or billet or allowance or labour-rate system, can be compared with the amount of wages in the same parish after it has been dispauperized and the labourers paid by their employers.

At White Waltham, where the same system had been adopted, the wages of the labourers are stated to be 'rather better', although there were one hundred or one ninth more labourers in the parish in 1831 than in 1821, the year before the change took place.

In Cookham, the wages of the great body of the labourers were improved.

In Hatfield, the permanent overseer was asked, with respect to the independent labourers in the parish:

What effect has been produced on their wages? – The wages have improved somewhat; I cannot state exactly how much, but I believe the wages have improved by 1s. a week; they formerly got 9s. and 10s. a week, now they get about 11s. This, I think, is about the average of their wages here.

The Rev. F. J. Faithful, rector of Hatfield, J.P., examined.

Have the wages of the independent labourers been improved since the change of system of administration of the Poor Laws? – Decidedly so; and the wages are higher here than in any parish in the neighbourhood where a similar system has not been adopted.

In the adjacent parish of Welwyn, where the same system has been adopted, the wages of the independent labourers were improved.

In Swallowfield one of the first results of the change was that single independent labourers received better wages. One of the witnesses stated at the time of the visit of the Commissioner, that he had that day been seeking for a young man to hire, but that he had been obliged to go out of the parish for one; an event which he had never before known.

In Bingham, Southwell, and St Mary's, Nottingham, Mr Cowell made special inquiries as to the effect of the change upon the wages of labourers belonging to the classes receiving parochial relief, and found that in every instance there had been a striking improvement.

In Thurgarton, where wages have never been tampered with, and where no partial relief has been given during the last forty years, wages have remained steady in money, and advanced when estimated in kind. In the surrounding parishes which are pauperized, wages have been subject to mischievous fluctuations during the same period.

R. P. Garratt, the overseer of Downham Market, Norfolk, states that –

We began a change of system by invariably refusing relief in aid of wages. If the farmer would not give the labourers fair wages we took them wholly away and employed them for the parish, and we found very soon that, although it cost us much more at first, it soon had the effect of making the farmer pay his labourers fairly.

It must be added that the mere amount in money does not accurately represent the increase in wages. Beer, milk, potatoes, meat, flour, and other provisions, or the use of land, are so often allowed to the labourer, or furnished to him under the market price, as to form an important part of his means of subsistence; and these advantages are of course given to the best and steadiest workman. The Marquis of Salisbury states that at Cranborne, where he has successfully opposed the allowance system, the rate of wages is higher, if not in money, yet in value, if these privileges are to be taken into account, than in the neighbouring pauperized parishes.

Before the experiment was made, it might fairly have been anticipated that the discontinuance of parochial allowance would effect little or no improvement in wages unless a similar change were made in the neighbouring parishes. When a considerable proportion of the labourers who had been entirely dependent upon the parish were driven to rely on their own industry, it might have been anticipated that the wages of the entire body of labourers within the parish would have been injuriously affected by their competition. And this certainly would have been the case if they had added nothing to the fund out of which their wages came. That fund is, in fact, periodically consumed and reproduced by the labourer, assisted by the land and the farmer's capital, and, all other things remaining the same, the amount of that fund, and consequently his share of it, or, in other words, the amount of his wages, depends on his industry and skill. If all the labourers in a parish cease to work, they no longer produce any fund for their own subsistence, and must either starve or be supported, as they were at Cholesbury, by rates in aid. A single person who has no property and is supported without working bears the same relation to the labourers who do work as the parishioners of Cholesbury bore to the neighbouring parishes. He is supported by a sort of rate in aid on their industry. His conversion from a pauper, wholly or partially supported by the labour of others, into an independent labourer producing his own subsistence and, in addition to that, a profit to his employer, so far from injuring his fellow workmen, produces on them the same effects as the enabling the inhabitants of Cholesbury to support themselves has produced on the parishes which had to supply them with rates in aid. This has been perceived by some of our witnesses. A farmer of considerable intelligence who had resided in Cookham and observed the effects of the change in that parish declared his conviction that if such a change could be generally introduced the money saved in poor's rates would almost immediately be paid in wages. The withdrawal of relief in aid of wages appears to be succeeded by effects in the following order: first, the labourer becomes more steady and diligent; next, the more efficient labour makes the return to the farmer's capital larger, and the consequent increase of the fund for the employment of labour enables and induces the capitalist to give better wages.

The instances of the application of the same principle of administration in those of the manufacturing districts which are pauperized are comparatively scanty; but where they have occurred the effects are in general similar. The following answer to one of our queries from the parish of St Werburgh, Derby, by Mr Henry Mozley, affords an example of the operation of the discontinuance of allowances in aid of wages in a manufacturing district.

When I was overseer I refused to relieve able-bodied men working for other people, considering that, by relieving them I was injuring the respectable part of the poor (I mean those just above pauperism), by running down their wages. I found that some of the children in the workhouse were put out to the cotton and silk mills, and because they were workhouse children the manufacturers paid them less wages than were given to the children of independent work people, who, on applying for employment for their children at 2s. a week, were told, 'I only give that girl, who is older and bigger, 1s. 6d.'; I determined therefore to take them away from the mills, and that they should do something, or even nothing, in the house rather than injure the deserving poor. I am certain that for every 5s. loss that the parish sustained by this conduct is gained £5 by assisting the respectable poor, and by preventing them from requiring parish relief.

The next class of specific effects which have followed the application of the principle of keeping the condition of the pauper inferior to that of the independent labourer is that it has arrested the increase of population, which the evidence shows to be produced by the present state of the law and of its administration.

In the parish of Burghfield, Mr Samuel Cliff, the assistant overseer, states that he was –

convinced that the discontinuance of the allowance system had saved the parish from destruction; it did this by the immediate check which it gave to population. Whilst the allowance system went on, it was a common thing for young people to come to me for parish relief two or three days after they were married: nay, I have had them come to me just as they came out of church and apply to me for a loaf of bread to eat, and for a bed to lie on that night, and, moreover, for a house for them to live in. But this sort of marriages is now checked, and in a few years the parish will probably be brought about. If the former system had gone on, we should have been swallowed up in a short time.

Is your knowledge of the individuals resident in your parish such that you can state without doubt that there are persons in it, now single, who would, under the influence of the system of allowing rates in aid of wages, have married had the system been continued? – I have no doubt whatever that several of them would have married; I know them so well that I am sure of it.

In the report from Cookham, it is stated that 'some very striking consequences have resulted from the operation of the present system. In the eight years preceding the operation of the new system, the increase of population was very rapid; for the eight years subsequent there was, as compared with the eight years preceding, a positive diminution. Improvident marriages are less frequent.' In the report from Swallowfield, it is stated that 'the number of improvident marriages is diminished about one half'. In Bingham, the diminution of improvident marriages was about one half; and yet, in all these three parishes, illegitimate births, instead of having been promoted by the diminution of marriages, have been repressed still more effectually, and in the last, almost extinguished.

The master of the workhouse at Hatfield was asked:

What has been the effect, as regards marriages, of altering the system and paying according to the value of each man as a labourer, so far as that has been done? — I believe they think more before marriage. They would often formerly, as I have been informed, marry without having provided a home or a bed, or any thing, leaving all to the parish. I am not aware of any such marriages having taken place recently.

In the course of the examination of the manager of the poor in the parish of Great Farringdon (Berks.), to which we have already referred, in answer to the question — 'What has been the effect in respect of marriages?' — he answered,

It has been remarked that there are fewer marriages than in previous years; but the change has not, perhaps, been in operation a sufficient length of time to produce the full effect. During the last twelve months, however, we had only two cases of bastardy; whereas, the average, for the previous years, has been about six or seven. This alteration has been remarked as the result of the change of system.

The population of some of the dispauperized parishes has increased since the change of system; but generally in a diminished ratio as compared with the preceding rate of increase. The diminution was in the class of improvident and wretched marriages described by the witnesses above cited.

*

Whatever impels any class into courses of sustained industry must necessarily diminish crime; and we find that one characteristic of the dispauperized parishes is the comparative absence of crime. In Bingham, before the change of system took place, scarcely a night passed without mischief; and during the two years preceding 1818, seven men of the parish were transported for felonies; now there is scarcely any disorder in the place. In Uley and Southwell parishes crime has similarly ceased.

In almost every instance the content of the labourers increased with their industry.

The evidence on this subject, collected by the Commission, is confirmed by that taken in the last session by the House of Commons' Committee on the state of agriculture. We refer particularly to the following extracts from the evidence of Mr Smith Woolley, a land-agent and an occupier of land in the incorporation, so ably superintended by the Rev. Mr Becher.

How much have the poor-rates in your parish fallen? – including the roads, I think about one third, that is, from about £600 to £400.

What is the condition of the poor in your parish with the £400 a year expended upon them, compared with their condition when £600 was expended upon them? – Vastly improved in comfort and usefulness, as well as character.

Are they more happy and comfortable now? – Much more so; we endeavour to remove cause for complaint, and generally they are satisfied.

Has the gross produce in your parish, or in those fifty parishes to which you have referred, diminished or increased since your poor-rate fell? – As far as I can judge, increased; the employment of the labourers in draining and other improvements, has produced much effect, and the advantage is felt by the farmers more every year.

Even in these bad times the land has been permanently improved, and the gross produce increased under this system? – Most decidedly; in the last three seasons, indeed, our cold wet soils have suffered so much from continued rains that they have been very unproductive; but this has shown the advantage to be derived from draining, and more is done.

Have you any emigration? – Not to such an extent as to produce any effect.

Do all classes join in estimating the benefit of this system – the tenants and the labourers? – In the first instance there was strong prejudice in both parties, quite as much in the employer as the labourer; but they generally begin to see their mutual interest in it.

They were willing to incur the expense of the erection of the poorhouse? – There were objections, but not in many instances.

With respect to the introduction of the anti-pauper system of Mr Becher, not taking into consideration merely the expense of raising a workhouse, are there not other outgoings to be submitted to on the part of the farmer? – Yes; but they are more than repaid in the current year. The reduction in the poor-rates, of which I spoke, was when we paid fifty guineas to an overseer, and the instalments of the money borrowed to build the workhouse.

When in your parishes you (what you call) force people upon their own resources, to find the means of providing for themselves, you are in a country at no great distance from manufacturing towns, where there is considerable resource for persons so forced upon their own resources? – Not in ordinary times. I do not think we derive any benefit from them. In the very excited state of the lace trade, a few years ago, even labourers accustomed only to agricultural employment were engaged, but it was only temporary, and produced much more harm than good.

Do you think, from considering the poverty of the farmers, that they can afford paying those (i.e. high) wages for labour? – The question is, in what shape it shall be paid; certainly he can afford better to pay for labour for which he may expect a return, than in poor-rates, for which he can expect nothing but ruin.

[EFFECTS OF PROPOSED ADMINISTRATION ON NON-SETTLED PARISHIONERS]

THE general effects on the labouring population viewed collectively, as contrasted with their condition previous to their change, appear from the evidence to have been equally striking and important.

Mr Whately describes in the following passage the antecedent condition of his flock:

While the weekly wages of an agricultural labourer were still kept so very low that an industrious man could not subsist himself upon his earnings, this allowance of bread-money adapted itself to the circumstances of each particular family, without any reference at all to their moral qualities. The consequence was that all distinction between the frugal and the prodigal, the industrious and the idle, the prudent and the thoughtless, was destroyed at once. All were paupers alike. The most worthless were sure of something, while the prudent, the industrious, and the sober, with all their care and pains, obtained only something; and even that scanty pittance was doled out to them by the overseer. Like the Israelites in the Wilderness, 'They gathered some more, some less; yet he that gathered much had nothing over, and he that gathered little had no lack; they only gathered every man according to his eating.' Wages were no longer a matter of contract between the master and the workmen, but a right in the one, and a tax on the other; and by removing the motives for exertion, the labourer was rendered by this mischievous system, as far as was possible, totally unworthy of his hire. The moral and intellectual character of the good old English labourer (who in former times had boasted with honest pride that he never was beholden to a parish officer) was destroyed altogether; all habits of prudence, of self-respect, and of self-restraint, vanished; and since a family was a sure passport to a parish allowance, it is not to be wondered at that the most improvident marriages were the consequence of this most pernicious and most demoralizing system. Indeed, we have seen three generations of paupers (the father, the son, and the grandson), with their respective families at their heels, trooping to the overseer every Saturday for their weekly allowances; boys and girls marrying without having provided a bed to sleep upon or a roof to cover them: the parish was to provide everything. The most wretched hovels were converted into houses, the rents of which were charged to the parish account. In this village a carpenter's workshed has been divided into four tenements, for which the parish was charged five pounds a year apiece.

The following extracts from the examination of Mr Whately, and from Mr Chadwick's report, show the subsequent condition of the parish.

Is it observed that the personal condition of the labourers has in any respect changed since the change of system of administering the poor-rates? – Decidedly. A labourer, formerly a pauper, came to the vestry not long since to make inquiries respecting a house, in order to rent; when he had retired, one of the farmers exclaimed how neatly he was dressed, and how good his coat was; to which I answered, 'I can explain the reason of the change; it is, that there is no longer a bonus offered by the vestry for rags and dirt. You will remember when ragged clothes were kept by the poor for the express purpose of coming to the vestry in them; whereas the articles of clothing which we sell to the poor at prime cost, have every year, since the establishment of a select vestry, been required to be of an improved quality.'

Do you mean to state that they purchase more expensive articles? I do; the blankets I send for from Witney are required to be larger and of a better quality; and so of all other articles.

Do the labourers care to acknowledge to you that they wish to have the articles they purchase of a better quality? – Yes; and I find them less jealous of acknowledging their real condition than formerly; they now rather value themselves upon their respectability than, as formerly, attempt to impose and extort money by pretended destitution.

Is their food better or worse than formerly? – I think better. The labourers have a meal of meat once a day, and there is hardly a cottage that has not a supply of bacon on the rack.

Has their general moral conduct improved, so far as you, as a minister, have observed? – It decidedly has: and I state this as a magistrate as well as a minister.

Mr Chadwick mentions that Mr Russell, the magistrate of Swallowfield, stated 'that in riding through Cookham, he was so much struck with the appearance of comfort observable in the persons and residences of some of the labouring classes of that village, that he was led to make inquiries into the cause. The answers he received determined him to exert his influence to procure a similar change of system in Swallowfield.

'I visited', says Mr Chadwick, 'a large proportion of the cottages in the village of Cookham and some in Cookham Dean.'

Their internal cleanliness and comfort certainly corresponded with the condition of the exteriors, which had attracted the attention of Mr Russell. In company with Mr Whately I visited several of the residences of the labourers at their dinner-time, and I observed that in every instance meat formed part of the meal, which appeared to be ample, and was set forth in a very cleanly manner. One cottage in the village of Cookham, and the wife and family of the cottager, were most repulsively filthy and wretched in their appearance; and it was somewhat singular that this family was a pauper family, the head of which received an allowance in aid of his wages from an adjacent parish.

I noticed some very trim hedges and ornaments in the gardens of the labourers, and it was stated to me that nothing of that sort had been seen in those places before the parishes had been dispauperized. Mr Knapp, the assistant overseer, stated that the labourers were no longer afraid of having a good garden with vegetables and fruit in it; they were no longer 'afraid of having a pig', and no longer 'afraid of being tidy'. Before the changes took place he had been in public-houses, and had seen paupers drunk there, and heard them declare in the presence of the rate-payers, that they (the paupers) had had more strong drink than the rate-payers had, and *could* have it, and that the rate-payers could not help themselves.

During the agricultural riots there was no fire, no riots, no threatening letters in the parish. In the midst of a district which was peculiarly disturbed Cookham and White Waltham, where a similar system of Poor-Law administration was adopted, entirely escaped, although in Cookham there are several thrashing machines, and the only paper-mill had, at the time of the riots, been newly fitted with machinery.

At the time of my visit the deposits in the savings bank from the parishioners of Cookham amounted to about £7,000. A considerable number of the present contributors had been paupers chargeable to the parish at the time of the old system being discontinued. Mr Sawyer, the treasurer and constant attendant of the savings' bank, told me that the deposits from Cookham were greater than from any other part of the district comprehended by that bank. The average annual deposits from Cookham had risen from £310 to £682, and £39 3s. 8d. was collected in eight months from the children of the village. Three new schools had been opened at the instance of Mr Whately, and were maintained partly by the labourers themselves.

Mr Whately was asked:

Do you believe that the reduction of the poor's rates by the application of the new system would be as great throughout the country as it has been in your parish? – I have no reason to doubt it. I think one half or two thirds of the poor's rates might be saved; but judging from my experience in my own parish, I should say that even if no money were saved, the moral improvements and increased comforts of the community to be derived from such a system would more than compensate the trouble of the Legislature. I have often declared, both in public and private, that if all the money we have saved (which was upwards of £15,000 in the first eight years) had been thrown into the Thames, the parish at large would have been enriched by the acquisition of wealth by the improved nature of the labour of the late rate-receivers, independently of the moral improvement which has accompanied their improved frugality and industry.

Although the change in Hatfield was not so general, similar effects were perceived.

The Rev. F. J. Faithful examined.

I am decidedly of opinion that the moral benefits obtained are much greater, much more important than the pecuniary saving. Though as a minister I have every day much to lament, I am sure that I should have infinitely more to lament had the old system of maladministration continued. The most important effect of the new system is, first, in calling forth domestic sympathies and filial and paternal affections; and next, in creating provident habits (which is shown in the increase of deposits in the savings' banks). Under the old system, when a child was left an orphan it became, as of right, a pensioner to the parish and owed gratitude to no one. I constantly see children left orphans; and now, under the influence of our law that no one shall receive a pension out of the house, relations and friends come forward and support an orphan child, whom they would, without hesitation, throw upon the parish if they could do so. They do not like the idea of seeing in the workhouse a relation whom they would not mind having on the parish pension list, and they exert themselves to maintain the person. A child who owes its subsistence to relations owes a moral debt of gratitude to particular individuals, and is under moral securities for good character; but there is little gratitude to an abstract entity, the parish. What is singular is that we have scarcely any persons come to the workhouse now who are not persons of bad character.

Have the *personal* habits of your parishioners improved since the new system of parochial management has been introduced? – There has certainly been a very general improvement, and the advance was very considerable, until the most mischievous measure of licensing beer-shops came into operation.

Mr Paul Borser, who settled in the parish of Southwell in 1812 and became assistant overseer in 1813, gave the following evidence to Mr Cowell, with relation to the effects of the allowance system, and of its discontinuance:

At the time of his settling in the parish, the character of the labouring population was very bad, and it continued deteriorating till 1822; their habits grew more and more dissolute, and the average quality of their industry lower, while their demeanour got more and more turbulent and disorderly. Mr Borser gave me a great number of instances in proof of these general assertions, but I do not think it necessary to detail them; I was completely satisfied of the fact. The parish weekly pay-room, Mr Borser declares, was a constant scene of disorder, and violence; he, as overseer, was constantly threatened, and, on three occasions, was personally assaulted, for which the offenders were committed to the house of correction. The women were equally violent with the men; remembers a woman seizing a sum of money (5s.) on the pay-table, saying she would have it, and getting clear off with it. In general, the day following the weekly pay there were from eight to twelve cases before the petty sessions between paupers and himself; sometimes there might be only three, but has known as many as twenty. The behaviour of the paupers was frequently very violent in the justice-room. Has heard his predecessor say that he was constantly treated in a similar manner; and in general Mr Borser declares that the labouring population of the parish was a terror to the authorities, and that the burdens and troubles caused by them were annually increasing. Various plans and expedients were tried from 1813 to 1821 for remedying these evils, but nothing produced any benefit till the adoption of the new system. Since that time the character of the population, and their habits, have entirely changed, and their former state has gradually passed into one of order, happiness, and prudence.

The prudence and economy, the desire of having comfortable homes, exhibits itself in great variety of ways; for instance, many now keep pigs who did not and would not have done so before, because the fact of their being known to possess them would have precluded them from any claim on the parish; they are more anxious now to hire bits of garden ground for cultivation at odd hours; their cottages are better furnished; the men keep more at home, and are less at ale-houses; are more independent in their characters altogether. He knows that they bring up their children with a scorn of pauperism; does not believe that they would wish to change to their former state if they could; believes so because many of those who used to hate and revile him as overseer, are now quite changed, have saved money, and placed it in the savings' bank of which they know he is secretary, and never show any jealousy of his being acquainted with the amount of their savings.

It is noticed by Mr Faithful that scarcely any persons but those of bad character came into the workhouse. A similar result was also very strikingly exhibited at Cookham. Mr Baker of Uley states,

It has been said that many respectable poor persons are now starving in Uley from a dread of the workhouse. I know no such persons, but I have very lately heard of one woman who is in distress, and who said that if she took her family to it, they should all live much better than they now do, but the character of the inmates was so exceedingly bad, that she did not choose to be among them with her family.

These general statements are supported by many detailed examples.

Mr Cowell states that when the relief, though adequate, has been rendered ineligible,

New life, new energy is infused into the constitution of the pauper; he is aroused like one from sleep, his relation with all his neighbours, high and low, is changed; he surveys his former employers with new eyes. He begs a job — he will not take a denial — he discovers that every one wants something to be done. He desires to make up this man's hedges, to clear out another man's ditches, to grub stumps out of hedgerows for a third; nothing can escape his eye, and he is ready to turn his hand to anything.

In fact, the speed with which this method produces its ameliorating effects is one of its most remarkable characteristics. Mr Baker told me that one man, after having been in Uley workhouse *but a few hours*, was so disgusted that he begged permission to leave it instantly; and upon being told that the rules did not permit any one to quit the workhouse who did not make application before twelve o'clock in the day, displayed the greatest anxiety at the prospect of being kept in till that hour the next day, and pestered the governor with repeated requests to be permitted to depart in the interval. Yet this was a man pretending that he was starving for want of employment; and though he knew that he was secure of enjoying in the workhouse excellent food, lodging, and clothing, yet the prospect of restraint spurred him instantly to quit it and seek to maintain himself. But still more remarkable is the fact that the instant the system was put in action at Uley, the workhouse changed the whole of its inmates *three* times in *one* week.

In Southwell, the workhouse-keeper

only had occasion to try two with the bone plan. One said immediately, with sulky violence, that he would never break bones for the parish when he could go out and get something for breaking stones for others, and he went out next day. The other said it hurt his back to bend so much, and he would start the next day, which he did. A third had a hole to dig, which he liked so little that he went off the third day. He had been, for nine or ten years before, one of the most troublesome men in the parish, but he went off very quietly, saying that he did not complain of the victuals or accommodation, but if he was to work, would work for himself; he has never troubled the parish since, and now he gets his own living in a brick-yard, and by thrashing and other jobs, and has done so ever since.

In the report from Cookham, the following instance is given in respect to the change of system in discontinuing out-door relief by money payments:

The following case will serve as an example of the effects of the change of system, in respect to out-door relief by money payments: A man who went by the name of Webb was hanged for horse-stealing. He left a widow and several small children. The widow applied to the select vestry for relief the week after his execution. It was suspected they possessed resources which would enable them to provide for their own wants without parochial relief; and, in consequence of this suspicion, the vestry ordered them to come to the workhouse three times a week for such relief in kind as was deemed necessary. The woman begged to be allowed the money, or less money than the value of the bread, which was refused. The result was that she never applied, and she never received any relief whatever. In this case, as in almost all others, it would have been utterly impossible for the parish officers to have ascertained whether the pauper did or did not possess the suspected resources. Had relief, such as was requested, been readily granted, as it generally would, under the influence of the feelings of pity and from the impulse of blind benevolence, or from the love of popularity in appearing to yield to the demand for assistance in a case so deeply affecting the sympathies, or from a dread of unpopularity from the imputation of hard-heartedness 'towards poor children who could not be supposed to participate in their father's crime', or from the love of ease and the want of firmness to refuse, a *whole family* would have been placed as paupers or consumers of the labour of the industrious; the children of the woman would have been further demoralized, and rendered as miserable themselves as they were worthless and mischievous to others. The course of blind benevolence, but real cruelty, would have been productive of pain to this family, and the extra indulgence applied for would moreover have been injustice towards the children of the meritorious, to whom the rule was applied without relaxation. All the members of the family are well known to Mr Whately, in whose parish they reside, and they are in a satisfactory and thriving condition. So that in this case, which will apply to all others, the pauper would have had the relief of the exact kind and suitable (i.e., *bread* not *gin*), had it been absolutely necessary, but would be driven to her own resources, if she possessed any.

In a communication, dated in January last, Mr Whately states —

Nothing can be more prosperous than we are here. I am this moment returned from the vestry, which meets every fortnight, and where we talk of the state of Portugal, having nothing else to do there. I carried £15 to the savings' bank at Maidenhead a fortnight ago for a poor man who earns 12s. a week, and yesterday delivered ninety-three tons of coals to the poor, for the purchase of which they had subscribed last summer; I am to have for the use of the poor fourteen tons more. But that which gives me the greatest satisfaction is that the wife of a poor man (who was insane, and was about to be sent to St Luke's) told the overseer that if he would advance the money for her husband's expenses of admission, carriage to London, &c., she would repay him, for that she did not wish to trouble the parish. Pleased with this account, I went to the woman and gave her a guinea: it happened that before the man could be admitted at St Luke's he partially recovered the use of his reason, upon which his wife, with her duty, returned to me my guinea.

The following letter from Mr Russell of Swallowfield, in answer to one requesting from him a detailed account of the subsequent fortunes of those who in that parish had been refused out-door relief, is so curious and instructive that we venture to insert it notwithstanding its great length:

Swallowfield, November 5th, 1833.

A list of those men who, before we had a select vestry, were dependent principally upon parochial relief and who, since the establishment of the vestry, have supported themselves, would comprehend almost every labourer in the parish, except those who were in constant employment as carters, gardeners, or any other permanent capacity, and who consist, of course, of the men of the best character and steadiest habits. On examining the books, I have detected the following fifteen persons as instances of the improvement that has taken place under our new system, in the conduct and condition of the labourers. The whole population of the parish, according to the last return, is only 390; and of that number sixty-eight are agricultural labourers above the age of fourteen. The persons here mentioned, therefore, are nearly one fourth of the whole; and, taking into account only the married men to whom the inquiry principally relates, the proportion is still larger. It is necessary, however, to premise that in considering all statements upon this subject having reference to the county of Berks., it must be remembered that the system called 'make up', or 'bread money', prevails I believe universally, and that a man is not regarded as being 'upon the parish' if he only has his weekly earnings made up to the price of two gallon loaves for himself, and one for every other other member of his family.

Elijah Wheeler.	James Cordery.	James David.
John King.	Charles Cordery.	Richard Read.
William Oakley.	James Deane.	David Read.
Joseph Oakley.	George Cooper.	Richard Dance.
John Oakley.	James Davis.	Thomas Davis.

It is several years since Elijah Wheeler had any relief from the parish. I meet him frequently with his cart, and have reason to believe that his habits and condition are perfectly respectable. The house occupied by John King, and now used as a beer-house, with an acre and a half of ground adjoining it, belong to himself for a term, of which thirty-eight years are still unexpired; and he is, perhaps, on that account the strongest instance in the parish how much the facility of procuring relief has the effect of making men dependent upon it. But for the pernicious practice under the old system, of giving relief to almost everybody that asked for it, there is no reason why this man should have been more in want of assistance formerly than he is now. Until some sort of control was introduced into the parish by the select vestry, William Oakley was in the lowest possible state of idleness and misery. He never did any work at all; he was covered with rags and vermin; he had no fixed home, but slept under a hedge, or in any out-house to which he could get access. The clothes with which the parish occasionally supplied him were made away with for food or liquor; and, for some time, every attempt of the vestry to reclaim him was unavailing; by degrees, however, an amendment was wrought; and, although it would be too much to say that his reformation is complete, it is still greater than, under such circumstances, I could have expected. He now works steadily; he has no money but what he earns; he buys his own clothes, and keeps them; he sleeps at least with a roof over his head, and he has lost those reckless habits and that squalid appearance which before distinguished him from every other man in the parish. And for this change there is no other reason than the necessity of the case; he shifts for himself, because he is obliged to do so.

Joseph and John Oakley are the brothers of William, and though not so abject in their personal habits, they were hardly more respectable in character or conduct. Joseph is the only one of the three that is married. He has three children under eight years old. Formerly he lived upon the parish, and was always in want and idleness. John was, some years ago, in constant employ in my garden, but he absconded to avoid a warrant which was issued against him for theft, and was absent for some time. On his return he threw himself on the parish, and lived chiefly on the relief he obtained. Since the establishment of our vestry, a great improvement has taken place in both these brothers. Joseph has, for the last three years, been almost in constant employ with the same farmer. John works with different employers, and occasionally for the surveyor; and neither of them receive any relief out of the rates.

James Cordery is an instance of the dissolute habits into which ingenuity too often betrays persons in low life. By trade he is a hurdle-maker; he is also a carpenter, chair-mender, and tinker, and used to play the violoncello in church, and to teach the parish children to sing. But the more money he was able to earn, the more he was given to squander; he wasted his time at the alehouse and among prostitutes, and was never off the parish. Since the vestry refused to maintain him, he has had no difficulty in maintaining himself. He provided himself with a set of implements, and now lives in Reading, and earns an ample livelihood in grinding knives and mending pots and pans. With the exception of a fortnight last summer, when he was taken into the poor-house, in consequence of an attack of rheumatic gout, he has had no relief for the last four years; and instead of bringing up his children in their former idle habits, he is now endeavouring to apprentice one of his sons to a shoemaker.

Charles Cordery, no relation of the foregoing, is a married man with four children, of whom the eldest is under fifteen. He is so skilful and diligent a workman, that it must be his own fault if he is ever out of employ. Yet, under the former system, he was almost always dependent upon the parish; his wife and children were as idle and ragged as himself; and so bad was their character for pilfering and depredation, that they were successively turned out of every cottage that was occupied by them. At last they were absolutely without a roof to shelter them, and the vestry refused to support them any longer out of the rates. I was always disposed to think the man better than he appeared to be; and on his promise of amendment, I consented to place his family in a cottage belonging to my father, not-withstanding the remonstrance of the farmer on whose land it stood. Except in one instance, just after they had taken possession, I have had no complaint from their neighbours. The man is in constant work; his family seems to be in comfort; his rent is regularly paid; and his garden has been so well cultivated, that I am now enlarging it to such an extent as, I hope, will enable him to grow vegetables enough for his consumption.

James Deane is married and has three infant children. He has never borne a good character and was some time ago imprisoned for robbing his master's garden. He was formerly always idle, and a constant burden on the parish; but since the change of system intro-duced by the select vestry compelled him to depend on his own exer-tions, he has found work and supported his family. He occupies a cottage under the same roof as Charles Cordery; he is employed by the farmer on whose land it is situated; and at his request I have con-sented to make an addition to his garden, similar to that described in the case of his neighbour.

George Cooper, though he had advantages superior to most other men in the parish, was always as much in want of relief as any of them.

Until 1830 he had a cottage, with an acre of land, rent-free; he kept bees; he had an allowance from a gentleman in the parish, which produced him about £5 a year, for clearing and trimming a range of young hedges, which he did at unemployed intervals; and he was capable of draining, ditching, planting, and all the most profitable kinds of work; yet he seemed to be always in need, and was constantly applying to the parish for assistance. Since relief has been refused to him by the vestry, his cottage has been sold to a new landlord, and he has no facilities in procuring work that he had not before; yet he now not only supports himself, but pays his rent without complaint, and his children seem as much improved in their industry as he is himself.

James Davis has three children under ten years old. He is a good labourer, and understands draining, ditching, and all the better sorts of agricultural work; but before the affairs of the parish were under the management of a select vestry, he was constantly dependent upon relief. He is of a sullen, discontented temper, owing to which he lost a good place in a gentleman's garden; but he now supports himself and his family, and appears to have his full share of ordinary work.

James David is an elderly man with a grown-up family. By trade he is a thatcher; but he is also a carpenter, sawyer, and shoemaker; and can turn his hand to various jobs requiring dexterity. In his own trade alone he might always have found ample employment. There is but one other thatcher in the parish, and the work is more than he can get through; but David's dishonesty keeps pace with his skill, and nobody will trust him out of sight with their straw. He was always in want, and always on the parish; but since the vestry have peremptorily refused him relief, he has contrived to do without it. His condition is apparently better that it was, and, for nearly four years, we have had neither complaint nor application from him.

Richard and David Read are father and son. Richard is about fifty-six years old, and has seven children, of whom the youngest four still live with him. David's age is about thirty-four, and he has five children, of whom the oldest is under twelve. The loose character and habits of the whole of this family, of both sexes, have always been such as to exclude them from permanent, and therefore from the most advantageous and respectable, employment. But both the father and the son are remarkable for their skill and diligence as workmen, and the son is the strongest man in the parish. I happened to be one of the visiting justices of the gaol when he was committed for deserting his family; and on the occasion of a disturbance among the prisoners, I found that he had been chosen, by common consent, as the most powerful man within the walls. They both understand draining, ditching, planting, making roads and walks, levelling and laying out grounds, and every sort of agricultural and ornamental work requiring dexterity and neatness. They have both worked a good deal, and still are working for me, to my entire satisfaction in every respect; Richard as superintendent, and David in the same capacity, when his father has found an advantageous job elsewhere. Under the old system they both lived in habitual reliance on the parish, though Richard has a cottage rent-free for his life. David, by his own loose habits, actually reduced himself and his family to take shelter under a hedge, when he was put into a cottage taken for him by the parish, the overseers becoming responsible for the rent, which, however, he now pays regularly; and both the father and the son, though no essential amendment can be said to have taken place, either in their own propensities or those of their families, now support themselves and their children; and no application for relief has been made by either of them for a considerable time past. Richard Read's wife was the first person from whom I had a complaint of the distress occasioned to herself and her children by her husband's frequenting the new beer-houses. With him, and with most others in his condition, this evil is and must continue to be unabated, in spite of all that the local authorities can do to prevent it. The more I see of the effect of these houses, the more I am convinced that they have done and still are doing more to impoverish and corrupt the English labourer, than all the maladministration of the Poor Laws for the last fifty years put together.

Richard Dance is a widower, with four children, of whom the eldest is about sixteen. He was a soldier, and has a pension of 1s. a week. Neither his habits nor his skill as an agricultural labourer were improved by his being in the army, and notwithstanding his pension and the advantage of occupying a cottage belonging to the parish, for which he pays no rent, he used to be in constant want and the constant receipt of relief. Since the establishment of the vestry, he has been independent of the parish and is now free from those indications of distress which his appearance used to exhibit.

Thomas Davis is one of the most active young men and best labourers in the parish. He is able to perform every sort of agricultural work; but he has never borne a good character. He is a loose, blustering fellow, a loud and specious talker, and acts, upon occasion, as the spokesman for his brethren. At the time of the riots, in the winter of 1830, he was the only man in the parish who offered any objection to being sworn in as a special constable. He endeavoured to make terms for the compliance of the labourers, and was beginning to advocate the alleged grievances, but he was soon put down by the spirited interposition of a gentleman who was present. If his courage kept pace with his wishes, he might be a dangerous man; as it is, he is rather the instigator than the perpetrator of mischief. He has seven children, of whom the eldest is under fourteen, and until the establishment of the vestry was constantly dependent upon parochial relief. Since the change of the system, I have heard no complaint from him of his being in want, though he does not apply so much of his earnings as he ought to the support of his family. This is the man to whom I referred in one of my answers to the circular queries, as having, in November last year, been earning 15s. a week at thrashing. Some years ago he was allowed by the parish officer to build a cottage upon a piece of parish land, for which he was to pay a yearly rent of £1; but he seldom has paid it. He is as well able to do so as any other man in the parish; but having the parish for his landlord, he reckons upon their forbearance.

I referred the foregoing list to our assistant overseer, and this is the note with which he returned it to me: 'These men were working principally on the parish from April 1829 (the date of the assistant overseer's appointment) to December of the same year, when they were employed by ——; and from that time till the present we have never had any one on the parish for more than a month at a time, except in case of illness.'

The sum of this is that the labourers generally have the means of independent support within their reach, but that, except in a few instances of rare sobriety and providence, they will not of their own accord make the efforts necessary to command them. Of most of the men here described, I have said that they are good and diligent workmen. A want of ability and willingness to work, when work is given to them, is not among the faults of English labourers; and it cannot be expected that they will be at the trouble of finding work, if they can find support without it. They will not go in search of the meat of industry if they can sit down and eat the bread of idleness. If you maintain them in doing nothing, and put the key of the beer-house into their hand, what right have you to complain that they are idle and dissolute? A gentleman who has for many years farmed largely in this parish, told me that before the select vestry was established he frequently saw the labourers, in parties of twelve or fourteen, sauntering along the streams in pursuit of moorhens and, of course, poaching fish, when it was not the season to poach game. Their time, and the money they obtained from the overseer, were necessarily spent in drunkenness, dissipation, and pilfering.

The effect of the system to which this statement refers has been materially to reduce the amount of the poor's rate. In the year in which we established a select vestry (1829–30) our expenses were increased by various charges arising out of the change of system. In that year the rate was 6s. 8d. in the pound on the rack rent. The average rate of the three years preceding the change was 6s. 1d., but that of the three years subsequent to it has been only 4s. 5d.; nor has the benefit been confined to the payers. The condition of the poor has undergone a visible amendment. They are better fed and better clothed; they bear an appearance of greater ease and comfort, and they are more healthy than they were. When some exceptions were taken to our new regulations in 1829, I referred to the gentleman who contracts for the medical treatment of our poor, to know what effect the change had had upon their health. He told me that, under the old system, disease had become so prevalent in the parish, that he had made up his mind to relinquish the contract as no longer worth his holding; but that so great an improvement had taken place under the new system, that he abandoned his intention, and he has continued to attend the parish ever since. I repeated the same question to him yesterday, and his reply was, that although the parish had partaken of such disorders as had at various times been prevalent in the country, the improvement in the general health of the poor still continued relatively to what it had been before our change of system.

Even among the labourers themselves the change was productive of little discontent. What alarm they did show was when the select vestry was first talked of, and when they had an indistinct apprehension of unknown and indefinite changes, rather than when the new system had been actually put in force. One man only, James David, who is mentioned in the foregoing list, attempting any resistance. We proceeded against him, by complaint before the Bench, and he was sent to the tread-mill. Before the expiration of his sentence the parish officers solicited a remission of the remainder, and we have never since had occasion to resort to coercive measures. Our vestry was established in 1829. The agricultural disturbances took place in the following year. We were in the midst of the disorder, surrounded by the devastation committed by machine-breakers and incendiaries, yet there was neither a riot nor a fire in the parish, nor any single instance of malicious injury to property.

The important changes produced in the habits of the able-bodied paupers by means such as those displayed in the preceding extracts were in some instances aided by a measure which at first sight might appear calculated to become an obstacle and a means of producing permanent discontent and opposition amongst the whole of the labouring classes. It was determined to rate the whole of the cottages, and make the occupiers (or ultimately the owners) contribute towards the payment of the poor's rates.

In Cookham –

The measure which excited the most tumult was the rating of the cottages, and the refusal to contribute to the payment of rents; finding many of this class most tumultuous, it was thought by the vestry prudent to take a few from each division of the parish as examples. One of the ringleaders (William Sexton), who had never paid rent or rates, and who had behaved very insolently in consequence of his son (a lad of sixteen who was out of work) being refused relief, was selected to be made an example of; and the demand for rates was enforced upon him. He has since constantly paid his rates and rent, and though his family has much increased since that time, he has never received any parochial relief. He has become an orderly and respectable person, and shows great attachment to Mr Whately, to whom formerly he behaved in a dogged and ungracious manner. I saw the account of this person in the savings' bank, and for his station the money was considerable. The lad above alluded to is now a respectable shopman in London. He came to see Mr Whately, and thank him for all past favours, the greatest of which was the refusing him relief. Had the old system of relief been continued, this boy and his brothers would probably have been paupers for life.

In Southwell –

The parish paid as much as £184 per annum for rents of cottages. After Captain Nicholls had succeeded in abolishing this custom, his next step was to assess all the cottages to the rates. When he had succeeded in carrying this measure, he directed the permanent overseer to give formal receipts to all the payers, though for sums no greater than 2½d. or 3d.

The poor looked upon these receipts in the light of testimonials of their independence, and proud of showing that they, as well as their richer neighbours, contributed to the parish burdens, they hung them up in the windows of their cottages. Captain Nicholls had ordered the overseer to treat them, when he was receiving their contributions, with respect, but he was surprised at this unexpected result, and at finding that they were loth to be in arrear, and generally brought their money without solicitation on the day it was due.

Mr Borser states, with relation to the improved condition of the labouring classes in that parish, that —

They have themselves told him they are better-off, and it is notoriously the fact. Though he collects money for the poor-rates, and all their cottages are now assessed, none of the labouring class now are ever uncivil to him. Has observed, since cottages were rated, that the tenants become very jealous of those who receive relief; they give him such information as they think will prevent his granting relief where it is not merited; will often come to his house and tell him when they think he has been imposed upon by any one pretending to be ill. Since cottages were rated, such as apply for relief without real necessity are looked upon very shily by others; they call it 'attempting to impose on one another'. They are very jealous of those who receive relief, thinking and saying it is given out of their earnings.

In Bingham it is stated —

Great good resulted from refusing to pay rents for cottages and from rating all cottages and strictly enforcing payment; thinks more good came from this than almost from anything else; it made all those who paid rates jealous of any one receiving relief. Only last week a woman, to whom he went for her rate, said, 'I say, I shan't pay any more rates if my money is thrown away. I hear that idle fellow Jack, ——, had 5s. from the parish some weeks ago, because he said his child was ill; I shan't pay my money to such like.' He has seen many instances of the jealousy of the poor in this respect; if they pay rates, they say, they don't like to be giving their earnings to their neighbours, who are only idle; and now they abuse those who want to get help from the parish.

It might be conceived, *a priori*, that the standard of comparison, i.e., the condition of the lowest class of independent labourers, is indefinite; but when examined, it is found sufficiently definite for the purpose: their hours of labour in any neighbourhood are sufficiently uniform; the average of piecework which able-bodied labourers will perform may be correctly ascertained, and so may the diet on which they actually sustain health.

In several instances opposition to the enforcement of labour, on the ground that it was too severe, was defeated by a direct comparison between the work exacted from the paupers and that cheerfully performed by the independent labourers.

At Cookham —

Mr Knapp, the assistant overseer, stated that when the able-bodied paupers were first set to work at trenching, they pretended that they could not do so much work as would enable them to get a living at the prices fixed. Knowing this to be false, I paid an independent labourer, an old man of seventy, to work, and as he did a great deal more than two of the stoutest young men amongst the paupers pretended they were incapable of doing, they declared 'We must cut this; this work won't suit us'; and they took their departure to search out regular employment.

Mr Barnett, the permanent overseer of the parish of St Mary, Nottingham –

began by offering piece-work to every applicant for relief, and employed an intelligent labourer to fix the price. Forthwith sixty or seventy paupers would appeal to the magistrates every week, complaining that they were not strong enough to perform the quantity of work which, at his rate of pay, would entitle them to receive a sum adequate to the maintenance of their families. Anticipating this manoeuvre, he had provided himself with men of less than the average physical strength, whom he produced before the mayor, and who deposed to their ability to perform a greater quantity of work than that allotted by Mr Barnett. By expedients of this nature he baffled the complaints of the paupers, their opposition grew gradually weaker and weaker, and now there are, speaking generally, no applications to the magistrates.

The circumstance of a rural parish being, to a considerable degree, an independent community separated by the barriers of the Law of Settlement from other parochial communities, and the general knowledge possessed by the witnesses of the principal circumstances of all or most of the individuals of its labouring population, give a very high value to the results of the experiment made in each of the rural parishes which we have mentioned. The uniform success of the principle, and the remarkable similarity of its incidents, in different parishes, in different parts of the country, and under different circumstances, appear to us to prove its correctness, and to leave no doubt that it would be productive of similar effects throughout the country.

Further evidence of the beneficial operation of the principle on which the improvements described in the preceding statements were founded is afforded in almost every pauperized district: first, by the comparative character of those resident labourers who, having a distant settlement, can only claim temporary relief, and that subject to an order of removal to their own parishes; and secondly, by the condition of that part of the labouring population which still remains independent of parochial aid. We have already stated that in every district the condition of this class is found to be strikingly distinguishable from that of the pauper, and superior to it, though the independent labourers are commonly maintained upon less money.

'I found', says Mr Chadwick,

the witnesses in all the parishes, town or country, agreed as to the superior value of non-parishioners as labourers. Mr J. W. Cockerell, the assistant overseer of Putney, stated that many of the paupers who had applied for relief from his parish had withdrawn their claims when they were told that they would be removed to their parishes in the country; and in answer to further questions as to what became of these persons who so refused, he stated (in common with all the other witnesses with similar opportunities of observation) that these persons remained, and afterwards attained a much better condition than they had ever before attained while they considered that parochial resources were available to them on the failure of their own. He cited the cases of nine persons who had applied for relief, but had refused it when they were told that they would be removed. Six of these families had not only been saved from pauperism, but they were now in a better situation than any in which he had ever before known them. In two instances particularly, the withdrawal of dependence on parochial relief had been the means of withdrawing the fathers from the public-houses and beer-shops, and making them steady and good workmen. 'Indeed', said he, 'it is a common remark amongst the employers of labourers in our parish that the non-parishioners are worth three or four shillings a week more than the parishioners. This is because they have not the poor's rate to fly to. The employers also remark, that the non-parishioners are more civil and obliging than the others.' In this parish the usual wages of the single labourer are about 12s. per week; and the deterioration of the labourer by the influence of the present system of administering the Poor Laws, may therefore, according to the witness's statement, be set down as from five-and-twenty to more than thirty per cent. Other witnesses declare that the deterioration is much more considerable.

This superiority, indeed, is so notorious as to be the argument most frequently employed against facilitating the acquisition of settlements. The Rev. Henry Pepys, a magistrate and clergyman of extensive experience, in a letter deprecating the facilitation of settlement, states —

that the objections to the operation of a poor's rate do not apply to the unsettled labourer, as the latter knows full well that should he neglect to provide against sickness, should he be unable to support his family upon the wages of his labour, or should he fail to get employment, his only resource would be an application to the overseer who, as a matter of course, would immediately take him before the nearest magistrate for the purpose of having him removed to his place of legal settlement, where he is perhaps a stranger, with all the inconvenience of having to quit the house in which he may have been born, to remove with him at a considerable expense, or sell at a probable loss, his household furniture, and separate from the companions with whom he has associated from infancy. That a poor man should be subject to such a distressing alternative may perhaps appear harsh; but the consequences are most beneficial, even to himself, for from it he derives that inducement (which we have been all seeking as the only remedy for the present evils of the Poor Laws) to depend upon his own industrious exertions and not upon parish relief, to belong to a savings' bank or benefit-society, that he may not become chargeable, and thereby removable in the event of sickness, to abstain from wasting his wages at a public-house, and thus, by frugality and industry, to render himself capable of maintaining his family, however large, upon his own resources; in short, with regard to him the Poor Laws are perfectly harmless, he still remains a sample of the industrious, sober, honest, and independent labourer, such as we are taught to believe constituted the peasantry of England before the statute of Elizabeth was passed.

Should we not pause then before, by facilitating the acquisition of settlements, we reduce all to the same level of idleness and intemperance? It is true that when the unsettled inhabitants of a parish are residing in the neighbourhood of their own parishes, they will sometimes apply for assistance to their own overseer, who is occasionally disposed to accord it without requiring them to be previously removed home by an order of removal. But the relief which under such circumstances is administered, will be administered with a much more sparing hand than in the case of settled inhabitants, and only because the overseer is himself satisfied that it is really required. The *unsettled* poor are well aware they have no legal claim upon their overseer; *the magis-*

trates have no right to interfere between them,* and hence the relief which is given, though probably much more scanty than in the case of settled inhabitants, is thankfully received as a *boon* instead of being claimed as a right.

If, while the general administration of the Poor Laws were allowed to remain on its present footing, such occasional or partial relief as that which is available to the settled labourers of a parish were rendered equally available to the unsettled labourers, we cannot doubt that such a proceeding would demoralize and depress this respectable and valuable class to the level of the settled and pauperized labourers. This is ample reason against assimilating the condition of the unsettled to that of the settled labourers, but none against placing the settled on the same footing as the unsettled. The present practice, as to unsettled labourers, is almost exactly that which we propose to make the rule for all classes, both settled and unsettled.

The non-parishioner has no right to partial relief; to occasional relief; to relief in aid of wages, or to any out-door relief whatever from the parish in which he resides; and yet the assurance which we propose to preserve to every one, that he shall not perish on the failure of his ability to procure subsistence, is preserved to him. If that ability actually fail him, he is assured that he can immediately obtain food until he can be passed home to his own parish, where he will be saved from perishing and be maintained at the public charge. By this course, however, he would be taken wholly out of employment, and reduced to the condition of a permanent pauper; and that condition being less eligible to him than the condition of an independent labourer, he struggles with all the occasional difficulties from which, if he were a parishioner and improvident, the usual administration of the Poor Laws would relieve him. Relief is accessible to him whenever a case of necessity occurs; it is indeed accessible to him whenever he chooses to avail himself of it; it is simply *ineligible* to him so long as he can subsist by his own industry. The ordinary workhouse of his own distant parish, with the inconveniences of removal superadded, produces on him effects of the same description as those which we find produced on parishioners by a well-regulated workhouse.

We attach much importance to the general superiority of the

conduct and condition of the non-parishioners, the unsettled labourers. Although the evidence afforded from the dispauperized parishes appears to us to be conclusive as to the effects which may be anticipated from a similar change of system throughout the country, it is still liable to the objection, however unreasonable, that these parishes are individual and scattered instances, too few to establish a general conclusion; but the evidence afforded by the character and condition of the unsettled labourers pervades the whole country. Every body of labourers resident and labouring within a parish of which they are not parishioners, and where the distance of their own parishes and the administration of the poor's rates does not render partial relief available, may be referred to in proof of the general effects which would follow an improved system of administering relief. These labourers make no complaints of their having no right to partial relief, and we have not met with an instance of their having suffered from the want of it. The fact of the non-settled labourers maintaining an independent condition, whilst they have a right by law to return at the public expense to their own parishes and claim parochial aid proves that they themselves consider their present condition more advantageous than that of paupers, and that so considering it they are anxious to retain it.

From the above evidence it appears that wherever the principle which we have thus stated has been carried into effect, either wholly or partially, its introduction has been beneficial to the class for whose benefit poor laws exist. We have seen that in every instance in which the able-bodied labourers have been rendered independent of partial relief or of relief otherwise than in a well-regulated workhouse:

1. Their industry has been restored and improved.
2. Frugal habits have been created or strengthened.
3. The permanent demand for their labour has increased.
4. And the increase has been such, that their wages, so far from being depressed by the increased amount of labour in the market, have in general advanced.
5. The number of improvident and wretched marriages has diminished.
6. Their discontent has been abated, and their moral and social condition in every way improved.

[PRINCIPLE OF LEGISLATION]

RESULTS so important would, even with a view to the interest of that class exclusively, afford sufficient ground for the general introduction of the principle of administration under which those results have been produced. Considering the extensive benefits to be anticipated from the adoption of measures founded on principles already tried and found beneficial, and warned at every part of the inquiry by the failure of previous legislation, we shall, in the suggestion of specific remedies, endeavour not to depart from the firm ground of actual experience.

We therefore submit, as the general principle of legislation on this subject, in the present condition of the country:

That those modes of administering relief which have been tried wholly or partially, and have produced beneficial effects in some districts, be introduced, with modifications according to local circumstances, and carried into complete execution in all.

The chief specific measures which we recommend for effecting these purposes, are —

FIRST, THAT EXCEPT AS TO MEDICAL ATTENDANCE, AND SUBJECT TO THE EXCEPTION RESPECTING APPRENTICESHIP HEREIN AFTER STATED, ALL RELIEF WHATEVER TO ABLE-BODIED PERSONS OR TO THEIR FAMILIES, OTHERWISE THAN IN WELL-REGULATED WORKHOUSES (i.e., PLACES WHERE THEY MAY BE SET TO WORK ACCORDING TO THE SPIRIT AND INTENTION OF THE 43 ELIZABETH) SHALL BE DECLARED UNLAWFUL, AND SHALL CEASE, IN MANNER AND AT PERIODS HEREAFTER SPECIFIED;* AND THAT ALL RELIEF AFFORDED IN RESPECT OF CHILDREN UNDER THE AGE OF SIXTEEN SHALL BE CONSIDERED AS AFFORDED TO THEIR PARENTS.

It is true that nothing is necessary to arrest the progress of pauperism except that all who receive relief from the parish should work for the parish exclusively, as hard and for less wages than

* See below, p. 419.

independent labourers work for individual employers, and we believe that in most districts useful work, which will not interfere with the ordinary demand for labour, may be obtained in greater quantity than is usually conceived. Cases, however, will occur where such work cannot be obtained in sufficient quantity to meet an immediate demand; and when obtained, the labour, by negligence, connivance, or otherwise, may be made merely formal, and thus the provisions of the legislature may be evaded more easily than in a workhouse. A well-regulated workhouse meets all cases and appears to be the only means by which the intention of the Statute of Elizabeth, that all the able-bodied shall be set to work, can be carried into execution.

The out-door relief of which we have recommended the abolition is in general partial relief, which, as we have intimated, is at variance with the spirit of the 43 Elizabeth, for the framers of that act could scarcely have intended that the overseers should 'take order for setting to work' those who have work and are engaged in work: nor could they by the words 'all persons using *no* ordinary and daily trade of life to get their living by', have intended to describe persons 'who *do* use an ordinary and daily trade of life'.

Wherever the language of the legislature is uncertain, the principle of administration, as well as of legal construction, is to select the course which will aid the remedy; and with regard to the able-bodied, the remedy set forth in the statute is to make the indolent industrious. In proposing further remedial measures we shall keep that object steadily in view.

And although we admit that able-bodied persons in the receipt of out-door allowances and partial relief may be, and in some are, placed in a condition less eligible than that of the independent labourer of the lowest class; yet to persons so situated, relief in a well-regulated workhouse would not be a hardship: and even if it be in some rare cases a hardship, it appears from the evidence that it is a hardship to which the good of society requires the applicant to submit. The express or implied ground of his application is, that he is in danger of perishing from want. Requesting to be rescued from that danger out of the property of others, he must accept assistance on the terms, whatever they may be, which the common welfare requires. The bane of all pauper legislation has been the legislating for extreme cases. Every exception, every violation of the general rule to meet a real case of unusual hardship, lets in a whole class of fraudulent cases by which that rule must in time be destroyed. Where cases of real hardship occur, the remedy must be applied by individual charity, a virtue for which no system of compulsory relief can be or ought to be a substitute.

[FURTHER EFFECTS OF PROPOSED ADMINISTRATION]

THE preceding evidence as to the actual operation of remedial measures relates principally to rural parishes. We shall now show, from portions of the evidence as to the administration of relief upon a correct principle in towns, that by an uniform application of the principle which we recommend, or, in other words, by a recurrence to the original intention of the Poor Laws, other evils produced by the present system of partial relief to the able-bodied will be remedied. The principal of the further evils which it would extirpate is the tendency of that system to constant and indefinite increase, independently of any legitimate causes, a tendency which we have shown to arise from the irresistible temptations to fraud on the part of the claimants. These temptations we have seen are afforded –

first, by the want of adequate means, or of diligence and ability, even where the means exist, to ascertain the truth of the statements on which claims to relief are founded:*

secondly, by the absence of the check of shame, owing to the want of a broad line of distinction between the class of independent labourers and the class of paupers, and the degradation of the former by confounding them with the latter:

thirdly, by the personal situation, connections, interests, and want of appropriate knowledge on the part of the rate distributors, which render the exercise of discretion in the administration of all relief, and especially of out-door relief, obnoxious to the influence of intimidation, of local partialities, and of local fears, and to corrupt profusion, for the sake of popularity or of pecuniary gain.

* See pp. 115–17.

1. The offer of relief on the principle suggested by us would be a self-acting test of the claim of the applicant.

It is shown throughout the evidence that it is demoralizing and ruinous to offer to the able-bodied of the best characters more than a simple subsistence. The person of bad character, if he be allowed anything, could not be allowed less. By the means which we propose, the line between those who do and those who do not need relief is drawn, and drawn perfectly. If the claimant does not comply with the terms on which relief is given to the destitute, he gets nothing; and if he does comply, the compliance proves the truth of the claim – namely, his destitution. If, then, regulations were established and enforced with the degree of strictness that has been attained in the dispauperized parishes, the workhouse doors might be thrown open to all who would enter them and conform to the regulations. Not only would no agency for contending against fraudulent rapacity and perjury, no stages of appeals (vexatious to the appellants and painful to the magistrates), be requisite to keep the able-bodied from the parish; but the intentions of the Statute of Elizabeth, in setting the idle to work, might be accomplished, and vagrants and mendicants actually forced on the parish; that is, forced into a condition of salutary restriction and labour. It would be found that they might be supported much cheaper under proper regulations than when living at large by mendicity or depredation.

Wherever inquiries have been made as to the previous condition of the able-bodied individuals who live in such numbers on the town parishes, it has been found that the pauperism of the greater number has originated in indolence, improvidence, or vice, and might have been averted by ordinary care and industry. The smaller number consisted of cases where the cause of pauperism could not be ascertained rather than of cases where it was apparent that destitution had arisen from blameless want. This evidence as to the causes of the pauperism of the great mass of the able-bodied paupers is corroborated by the best evidence with relation to their subsequent conduct, which has corresponded in a remarkable manner with the effects produced in the dispauperized parishes of the rural districts. Ill-informed persons, whose pre-possessions as to the characters of paupers are at variance with the statements of witnesses practically engaged in the distribution of relief, commonly assume that those witness form their general conclusions from exceptions and that their statements are made from some small proportion of cases of imposture; but wherever those statements have been put to a satisfactory test, it has appeared that they were greatly below the truth. The usual statements of the permanent overseers in towns are that more than one half or two thirds of the cases of able-bodied paupers are cases of indolence or imposture; but it rarely appears that more than five or six in a hundred claimants sustain the test of relief given upon a correct principle. We select the following instances in illustrations of these statements.

Mr Thomas Langley, examined.

I have been in office fourteen years, principally as out-door inspector of the parish of Marylebone.

When you were here before, you stated that the result of your having offered work in the stone-yard to 900 able-bodied paupers at piece-work, at which they might have earned from 10s. to 18s. a week, was, that only eighty-five out of the 900 remained to work. If, instead of paying the men in the stone-yard such wages as those from 10s. to 18s. a week, you had given them piece-work at about 1s. a day for a full day's work, and that 1s. had been given, not all in money, but chiefly in kind, that is to say, if you had given them at the end of each day's work a three pound loaf of brown bread, and cheese or other food, and 3d. to pay for the night's lodging, how many out of eighty-five, who remained to work at the full wages first mentioned, would have remained to work for the remuneration of the latter description? – I do not think that ten of them would have remained.

Would less than six have remained to work? – Never having seen such an experiment tried, I could not undertake to speak confidently; but there might, out of so large a number, be half a dozen who are so peculiarly situated as to accept work on such terms for a time.

Then you consider that it would in any case only be for a time, meaning, I presume, for a short time? – Yes, some of them might stay one day, others three or four, but none of them, I conceive, more than a week or so.

Would you consider the fact of a man accepting such work on such terms a sure test of his condition? – Yes, it would certainly be an infallible test of his being in a state of distress, and disposed to work, and unable to get work anywhere.

If I were to open a stone-yard in your parish, and offer to give to all comers such work on such terms, how many square yards of stone do you think I should get broken? – I think none, or if any, very few, although three pounds of bread is a good allowance of food, and far above a starving point.

What evasions do you think could be resorted to? – The only evasion I can see is in the cases where a man evaded the work by pretending to be ill, which is a trick now resorted to where men say they have a pain in their insides, and the doctor is not able to say positively that they have not; but these cases, judging from our present experience, would be very few.

Might not these cases be met by workhouse regulations, confining a man as a sick patient, and on a low diet? – Yes, that I think would fully meet the case I have supposed.

Do you see any cases in which such regulations (making the condition of the pauper on the whole less eligible than that of the independent labourer of the lowest class) do not constitute a self-acting test? – I certainly conceive it is a test which would go to the root of pauperism, if it were carried into full execution. I can see no mode of evasion but pretended sickness.

Do you see any difficulty in the way of the execution of those regulations? – None whatever.

Mr Leonard, overseer of St Giles, Middlesex, examined.

In the year 1831, we tried the application of labour at stone-breaking in 260 cases of able-bodied labourers at piece-work, at 2s. per ton, at which work they might have earned about 2s. per day with tolerable application. That was in the summer; but during the winter we gave them 2s. 6d. per ton. The labour performed from amongst the whole number only amounted to £9 18s. 2d. during six weeks. There were never more than five or six at work at the same time. The effect of the introduction of the stone-yard, and of the work in the house, and generally for the able-bodied, was to produce such peace and order as had not existed before. I am sure that where there is no work there will certainly be disorder. Where I have heard of disorder in workhouses and riots of paupers, I conclude, from the mere mention of such occurrences, that labour is not there properly applied, or the workhouses properly regulated.

I am certainly of opinion that if regulations could be enforced which would place the pauper in every case below the condition of the lowest class of independent labourers, that these regulations would supersede investigations of officers with relation to able-bodied paupers. This, in fact, is the principle of our employment for able-bodied paupers at the stone-yard, and has produced the effects anticipated, so far as it has been carried into operation.

Mr W. Hickson jun., of the firm of Hickson & Sons, wholesale shoe warehouse, Smithfield, examined.

We once engaged to supply the workhouse of St Giles's with shoes, on condition that we should give work to all the journeymen shoe-makers who were then receiving relief from the board. This was about four years back. We expected a great number to apply, and made preparations for upwards of a hundred; the number of applicants were however under twenty. Of these some endeavoured to spoil the work, that they might be dismissed and have an excuse for returning to the board; others ran away with the materials; and, finally, but one man remained, who was steady and industrious, and is working for us to this day.

Mr Teather of Lambeth, examined.

If you could get hard work for your able-bodied out-door poor, so as to make their condition on the whole less eligible than that of the independent labourer, what proportion of those who are now chargeable to the parish do you think would remain so? – On a rough guess, I do not think that more than one out of five would remain.

Have you any facts which you can adduce to justify that conclusion? – From the instances of the proportions who have left on the occasions of their having had work given them. Some time ago, for instance, we had a lot of granite broken: there were not above twenty per cent of the men who began who remained to work at all; there were not above two per cent who remained the whole of the time during which the work lasted. Many of them, however, were not idle men, but they found other jobs: they were doubtless more stimulated to seek work by the stone-breaking. I think it would save much money if the parish officers were to advertise to break stones for the roads for nothing, for all persons who chose to bring the granite and take it away again.

'Mr Richard Spooner, who resides near Worcester', says Mr Villiers,

mentioned to me the following instance, illustrative of the calculation made by paupers with respect to parish work. A bridge was to be built in his neighbourhood, and it was determined to employ all the able men who applied for relief. While the bridge was building, not a single pauper who was able to work applied to the overseer for relief. A short time afterwards, and when the work was completed, the overseer had frequent applications for relief, and having no work to give them, he was compelled, as usual, to relieve them in money.

John Hooper, assistant guardian, Poole, St James's, Dorset.

No allowance is ever given to any able-bodied man, nor are we ever applied to by such for relief, unless he is ill or cannot get work; we then give him piece-work as before stated, and it is seldom he remains in such work many days before he finds employment at his trade or calling. This number is very small, and generally consists of shoemakers, bricklayers, and such as are not so fully employed in winter; but previously to our purchasing twenty acres of land for the purpose of giving them employment, we had many such applications during the winter, and all the idle and lazy were a great pest to us almost continually; but this is now at an end, as they say they may as well work for other parties as for the parish.

Mr Butt, the secretary of the Surrey Asylum for Discharged Prisoners, states –

In the year 1824, I availed myself of a hint which I got from the Mendicity Society, and with the sanction of our committee, entered into an agreement with Messrs Thorington and Roberts, who at that time kept a stone wharf on the Regent's Canal, and who undertook to furnish employment to as many able-bodied men as we chose to send them, at breaking stones for the roads, finding them in tools and paying them at the rate of 8d. per ton for flints, and 1s. 8d. for granite. After some discussion and difficulty, I prevailed on the Committee of the Refuge for the Destitute at Hoxton, of which I was then a member, to adopt the same plan. Both institutions were, however, soon obliged to discontinue it, because they found that the orders for work were scarcely ever presented, though the price paid was notoriously sufficient to enable any man with common industry to support himself. The men to whom orders were given by the Surrey Asylum, were almost exclusively taken from the five worst classes in the house of correction at Brixton, which from its proximity to London, contains perhaps as bad a description of people as could possibly be found, and we soon ascertained that about three and three quarters per cent of the orders given were presented, i.e., about one man out of twenty-seven went to work. I soon afterwards learnt from an active member of the Mendicity Society, that of the working tickets issued to *beggars* by the subscribers to that institution, about one in twenty-three was used, or about four and a quarter per cent.

When witnesses have answered that they have tried the application of labour in the case of the able-bodied paupers, and that it has failed, it has appeared on further examination that the failure was merely a failure to yield pecuniary profit, or to meet their expectations of immediate results. Considerable sagacity and patience are requisite to conduct such proceedings without being misled by false appearances of failure. It is found that paupers are in general well aware that the enforcing labour is an experiment, and therefore resist. They view the contest as one in which it is worth while to hazard the labour of a week or a month, or a much longer period, for a year or a life of comparative ease, and the inexperience or the ignorance of the person superintending the experiment sometimes gives them the victory.

The most efficient application of the principle is usually by means of a workhouse. The following extracts from the evidence and communications from different parts of the kingdom show at once the uniformity of its effects, and the general nature of the evil to be contended against.

Mr Oldershaw, the vestry clerk of Islington, states:

It sometimes costs us more (the grinding corn by a mill) than the wheat ground; but then it keeps numbers away, and in that way we save. When in consequence of the stoppage of the mill it became known that we could not get work for the whole of our able-bodied, we had, in two or three days, one third more of this class of applicants, and unless we had been able to provide work of some sort, so as to keep the great body of the able-bodied employed, we should have been inundated with them.

Mr Henderson states, in his report from Liverpool, that –

The proceedings of the select vestry show that the workhouse is frequently used as a test of the real necessities of applicants for relief; and that while some, who pretend to be starving, refuse, others, really in want, solicit admission.

The introduction of labour thinned the house very much: it was sometimes difficult to procure a sufficient supply of junk, which was generally obtained from Plymouth; when the supply was known to be scanty, paupers flocked in; but the sight of a load of junk before the door would deter them for a length of time.

Mr Atkinson, comptroller of the accounts for the township of Salford, states that —

Finding work for those who apply for relief, in consequence of being short or out of work, has had a very good effect, especially when the work has been of a *different kind* from that which they have been accustomed to. In Salford, employment to break stones on the highways has saved the township several hundred pounds within the last two years; for very few indeed will remain at work more than a few days, while the bare mention of it is quite sufficient for others. They all manage to find employment for themselves, and cease for a time to be troublesome; although it is a singular fact that when the stock of stones on hand has been completely worked up before the arrival of others, they have, almost to a man, applied again for relief, and the overseers have been obliged to give them relief; but so soon as an arrival of stones is announced they find work for themselves again. This fact is in itself sufficient to show the nature and effects of pauperism. I sincerely believe, that if, instead of giving relief in money, all persons were taken into workhouses, and there made to work, and have no other benefit than a bare maintenance, that would almost *immediately reduce pauperism one third*, and in less than twenty years nearly annihilate it.

Mr Huish, the assistant overseer of St George's, Southwark, examined.

What do you think would be the effect of putting an end altogether to the system of out-door relief, and enacting that all persons should either be wholly on or wholly off the parish, and that those who are on should be relieved in a strict workhouse? — I am convinced that in the first year of any attempt to take all the poor into the workhouse, no more than one in ten of the out-door paupers will remain in the parish, and that this tenth person would, in a great proportion of the cases, do so to tease them.

I am convinced that in the second year not one out of twenty of the out-door poor would remain chargeable to the parish.

Do you assume that the workhouses are to be conducted much as at present? — Nearly the same; but all the workhouses should be managed alike, which can only be done by Government; for whilst the world lasts, parishes will not unite to do anything.

On what grounds do you form your opinion that the reduction of pauperism would be at the rate you mention? – As a practical man, I form my opinion on the proportion who have always, since I have been in office, refused to go into the workhouse when it has been offered them, and the instances where they have continued to get their living without parochial relief.

Mr Osler, in an account of the introduction of the improved workhouse system at Falmouth, states that in the first instance –

A select vestry was appointed and a good house built, but the improvement effected was not so considerable as it might have been because the house was inefficient. There was a total want of discipline; the dormitories were the common sitting rooms of their inmates, who cooked their own food, and the whole house was, in consequence, dirty and disorderly: finally, it was regulated upon principles agreeing with those explained in my former report, and all proper cases were ordered in. The effect was, not only to cut off a great number of out-paupers, but also actually to diminish the numbers in the house.

Last year before the use of the new workhouse –

Year ending 1820 ...	...	...	...	...	£2,321	13	0½
Select vestry and workhouse, but without discipline—							
1821 (Population 4,392) ...	...	...	...	2,112	6	2½
1822	...	...	...	...	...	1,888	15	5½
1823	...	...	...	...	...	1,903	14	6
1824	...	...	...	...	...	1,686	5	3½
1825	...	...	...	...	...	1,670	6	6½
1826	...	...	...	...	...	1,599	19	10
1827	...	...	...	...	...	1,511	1	9
1828	...	...	...	...	...	1,492	14	1
1829	...	...	...	...	...	1,938	3	3*

Introduction of moderate regularity into the house with increased strictness in ordering paupers—

1830	...	...	...	...	...	£1,378	1	8

Introduction of efficient domestic discipline; no relief given out of the house except in casual or peculiar cases—

1831 (Population 4,761) ...	...	...	...	£1,151	11	2
1832	...	...	...	...	...	1,029	12	7

* 'The casual list for 1829 is enormous, owing to a cargo of distressed German emigrants who remained for several months, their vessel being un-

Profit is not to be expected from workhouse labour. If it were practicable to convert workhouses into manufactories, which it is not, the measure would be most impolitic; for every shilling thus earned in the house would be at the expense of a labourer out of doors.

The true profit of parish labour is to form industrious habits in the young, and to deter the indolent; and the perfection of a parish establishment is for its inmates to be scarcely equal to its own work. Into such a house none will enter voluntarily; work, confinement, and discipline will deter the indolent and vicious; and nothing but extreme necessity will induce any to accept the comfort which must be obtained by the surrender of their free agency, and the sacrifice of their accustomed habits and gratifications. Thus the parish officer, being furnished with an unerring test of the necessity of applicants, is relieved from his painful and difficult responsibility; while all have the gratification of knowing that while the necessitous are abundantly relieved, the funds of charity are not wasted upon idleness and fraud.

Under the present system it is found that wherever relief is permitted to remain eligible to any except those who are absolutely destitute, the cumbrous and expensive barriers of investigations and appeals erected to protect the rates serve only as partial impediments, and every day offer a more feeble resistance to the strong interests set against them. To permit this system to continue, to retain the existing permanent officers, and yearly to subject a larger and larger proportion of those who are pressed into the public service as annual officers to a painful and inefficient struggle in which they must suffer much personal inconvenience and loss, a loss which is not the less a public loss because borne by only a few individuals, must excite great animosity against themselves, and ultimately be borne down in a conflict in which the ingenuity and pressing interests of a multitude of paupers, each having his peculiar case or his peculiar means of fraud, are pitted against the limited means of detection and the feeble interests in the prevention of fraud of one of a few public officers.

In the absence of fixed rules and tests that can be depended upon, the officers in large towns have often no alternative between indiscriminately granting or indiscriminately refusing relief. The

seaworthy. The extraordinary charge thus incurred included a rate of £122 7s., raised expressly for contributing to the hire of a vessel to carry them to their destination.'

means of distinguishing the really destitute from the crowd of indolent imposters being practically wanting, they are driven to admit or reject the able-bodied in classes. Now however true it may be that the real proportion of cases which are found to have the semblance of being well founded may not exceed three or four per cent of the whole amount of claims, yet since each individual thus rejected may possibly be one of that apparently deserving minority, such a rejection, accompanied by such a possibility, is at variance with the popular sentiment; and it is found that the great body of the distributors of relief do prefer, and may be expected to continue to prefer, the admission of any number of undeserving claims, to encountering a remote chance of the rejection of what may be considered a deserving case.

On the other hand, the belief which prevails that under the existing system some claims to relief *are* absolutely rejected operates extensively and mischievously. It appears that this belief, which alone renders plausible the plea of every mendicant (that he applied for parochial relief, and was refused), is the chief cause of the prevalence of mendicity and vagrancy, notwithstanding the existence of a system of compulsory relief; a system which, if well administered, must immediately reduce and enable a police ultimately to extirpate all mendicity. If merit is to be the condition on which relief is to be given, if such a duty as that of rejecting the claims of the undeserving is to be performed, we see no possibility of finding an adequate number of officers whose character and decisions would obtain sufficient popular confidence to remove the impression of the possible rejection of some deserving cases; we believe, indeed, that a closer investigation of the claims of the able-bodied paupers and a more extensive rejection of the claims of the undeserving would, for a considerable time, be accompanied by an increase of the popular opinion to which we have alluded, and consequently by an increase of the disposition to give to mendicants.

We see no remedy against this, in common with other existing evils, except the general application of the principle of relief which has been so extensively tried and found so efficient in the dispauperized parishes. When that principle has been introduced, the able-bodied claimant should be entitled to immediate relief on the terms prescribed, wherever he might happen to be; and should be received without objection or inquiry; the fact of his compliance with the prescribed discipline constituting his title to a sufficient, though simple diet. The question as to the locality or place of settlement, which should be charged with the expense of his maintenance, might be left for subsequent determination.

On this point, as on many others, the independent labourers may be our best teachers. We have seen that in the administration of the funds of their friendly societies they have long acted on the principle of rendering the condition of a person receiving their relief less eligible than that of an independent labourer. We have now to add that they also adopt and enforce most unrelentingly the principle that under no circumstances, and with no exceptions, shall any member of their societies receive relief while earning anything for himself. Mr Tidd Pratt was asked whether, in the rules for the management of friendly societies framed by the labouring classes themselves, he had ever found any for the allowance of partial relief; such as relief in aid of wages, or relief on account of the number of a family. He answers, 'No, I never met with an instance.'

Then do the labouring classes themselves, in the rules submitted to you, reject all partial relief or relief on any other ground than the utter inability to work? – Invariably.

By what penalties do they usually endeavour to secure themselves from fraud on the part of persons continuing on the sick list after they have become able to work? – In all cases by utter expulsion and enforcement of the repayment of the money from the period at which it was proved the party was able to work.

Does that utter expulsion take place whatever may have been the period at which the party had contributed towards the society? – Yes; and all his contributions are forfeited to the society; and so strict are they in the enforcement of these regulations, that I have known them expel a party for stirring the fire, or putting up the shutters of his window, these acts being considered by them evidence of the party being capable of going to work. A small shopkeeper has been expelled for going into his shop; and the only exception I have found in favour of such a rule is that of a party being allowed to sign a receipt, or to give orders to his servant. They are perfectly well aware, from experience, that to give relief in an apparently hard case would open the door to a whole class of cases which would ruin them. The other day the steward of a friendly society came to consult me as to the reinstatement of a member who had been expelled for having neglected to pay his quarter's subscription on the regular quarter night half an hour after the books were closed. The party had been a member thirty-two years, and during that time had received little or no relief. The case struck me as an extremely hard one, and I endeavoured to prevail on the steward to reinstate the member, but the steward stated to me so many facts, showing that if they yielded to this one case, that it would determine a whole class of cases and let in so much abuse that I was ultimately forced to agree in the necessity of the decision of the society. These rules may appear to be capricious and arbitrary, but my observation leads me to believe that they are necessary to protect the society. Although there is an extremely severe enforcement of them, societies are seriously injured and frequently ruined by the frauds committed under this mode of relief, notwithstanding the incessant vigilance exercised against them.

What description of vigilance is that? – It is generally provided by the rules that a domiciliary visit shall be paid by the stewards, or by a member, generally every day; these visits are to be paid at uncertain times, that they may increase the chances of detection. It is also usually provided that a sick member shall not leave his house before or after such an hour, and that on his leaving home at other times he shall leave word in writing where he has gone, by what line of road he has gone, and by what line he intends to return, in order that the stewards or members may track him. In some instances the members follow up these precautions by requiring a member, when he 'declares off' the box, to swear that he was unable to work during the whole time that he has been receiving relief of the society.

Are these precautions effectual? – No; notwithstanding the utmost vigilance, serious frauds are committed, especially by the members of those trades who can work at piece-work within doors; such, for example, as tailors, shoemakers, watchmakers and weavers. An operative of these trades keeps his door shut and works, and when the visitor comes, the work is put under the bed clothes or otherwise concealed, and he is found in bed apparently sick. I find that in those societies where the members' work is of a nature to render fraud liable to detection, such as painters, plumbers, glaziers, stonemasons, carpenters, and any other occupation that takes a man out of his own room, the money paid for sickness in the course of a year is less than in societies composed of equal numbers of the class of members before mentioned.

From the opportunities of fraud, I always judge of the certainty of fraud, and from those opportunities the certainty of the ruin of societies may be predicted.

This vigilance in the administration of out-door relief to the sick, a vigilance to which we have never found any parallel in the administration of the poor's rates, would, *a fortiori*, be requisite in the case of the administration of out-door relief to the able-bodied. But this is obviously impossible. No salaried officer could have the zeal or the knowledge of an inspector of a friendly society, who is always of the same class, and usually of the same trade as the claimant. And if it were possible, we believe that it would not be effectual. The labouring classes themselves find these daily visits and strict regulations inadequate substitutes for the means of supervision and prevention which well-regulated workhouses afford, and which those classes, if their circumstances permitted, would doubtless adopt. In fact, the experiment has long and often been tried, and always with the same ill-success. Visits are made to the claimants, their residences are inspected, and it appears that at these visits and inspections, false and fraudulent scenes are prepared with little more difficulty and much more effect than fraudulent stories, and that those who disregard all statements and trust only to what they call the evidence of their senses are often the most completely deceived. The testimony of the most experienced and intelligent of our witnesses shows the extensive opportunities for fraud which the most rigid inspection leaves; and in the case of paupers, much more than in the case of the sick members of friendly societies, from the extent of the opportunities may the extent of fraud be predicted. Mr Pratt is asked:

Have you as a barrister had much Poor-Law practice? – Yes, I have practised ten years at sessions, I have also edited Bott's *Poor Laws*, and other works connected with the subject.

Would you apply to the progress of out-door relief by parishes the same rules as are founded on the experience of the labouring classes in benefit societies? – Certainly; and considering a parish as a large friendly society (the members being mostly honorary, or persons who contribute without the intention of partaking of the benefits of the contribution, as the majority in most parishes are), I should look to them much more rigidly.

If the regulations of a parish, or of a friendly society consisting of a parish, were brought to you to authorize under the Statute of Elizabeth, would you certify them if you found in them rules for granting partial relief of any sort, or relief in aid of wages, or relief according to a bread-money scale, or relief in proportion to the number of a family, or out-door relief of any description? – As a lawyer I should undoubtedly consider all such allowances entirely at variance with the spirit and intention of the Statute of Elizabeth, and I should without hesitation reject them. My experience, also derived from the observation of less dangerous regulations in friendly societies, would enable me to pronounce them to be mischievous and ruinous to whatever community adopted them. I am sure that no members of any benefit society, incomplete as their knowledge is, would ever frame rules upon such ruinous principles. The only definite ground of relief, as it appears to me, is utter inability to work, and so it appears to the labouring classes themselves, for whose benefit and with whom I act, for their allowances are always made upon that ground.

In what way do the members generally regard parochial assistance? As discreditable? – In their rules it is generally provided that in the case of the death of a member, notice be given to the treasurer, who summonses two of the stewards; and, says the rule, 'They both shall attend such funeral, and see that the corpse is decently interred, *and free from parish grants*', or it is expressed as in the following rule: 'That the president and vice-president shall attend funerals of members and their wives, see they be decent, *and free from parochial assistance*; and if either of them neglect so to do, he shall be fined 5s.; but for such attendance each of them shall receive 2s. 6d. from the fund.'

We believe that the following evidence expresses the sentiments of a large proportion of the most respectable mechanics:

Launcelot Snowden examined.

Are you acquainted with the operative classes? – Yes, having been a journeyman printer twenty years, and one half of the time foreman, and having been in different situations in our own societies, as well as connected with various other societies of operatives, I believe I am well acquainted with them.

In what way do they regard the fact of any one of their body receiving parochial relief? – I know that none but the worst characters would ever think of applying for parish relief; and that the respectable workmen consider it disgraceful. The other day, a list of those who received out-door parish relief was brought to a printing-office to be printed. One of the men saw on the list the name and address of one of the journeymen in the same office. This man was challenged with the fact which he did not attempt to deny. He had been receiving as much as 6s. or 8s. a week out-door relief, during two years, for four children, although he had been in receipt of 36s. a week steady wages during the same time. The men stated the circumstances to the employer, and he was discharged.

Did they request that he might be discharged? – The proceeding was tantamount to that, and of course the master acceded.

Suppose the whole of the relief were regulated by an independent or, say, a Government authority on a fixed rule, that of not rendering the condition of the pauper within the workhouse so good as that of the lowest class of workmen living by his labour out of the house? – That of course. No reasonable man would, I should conceive, expect to have his condition in the workhouse bettered. I think a Government authority would be much the best, as the parish officers are now, in ninety-nine cases out of a hundred, interested parties.

2. Little need be said on the next effect of the abolition of partial relief (even independently of workhouse regulations) in drawing a broad line of distinction between the paupers and the independent labourers. Experience has shown that it will induce many of those whose wants arise from their idleness to earn the means of subsistence; repress the fraudulent claims of those who have now adequate means of independent support, and obtain for others assistance from their friends, who are willing to see their relations pensioners, but would exert themselves to prevent their being inmates of a workhouse.

3. It will also remove much of the evil arising from the situation of the distributors of relief.

It has been shown that destitution, not merit, is the only safe ground of relief. In order to enable the distributors to ascertain the indigence of the applicant, it has been proposed to subdivide parishes and appoint to the subdivisions officers who it is supposed might ascertain the circumstances of those under their care. But when instances are now of frequent occurrence where a pauper is found to have saved large sums of money, without the fact having been known or suspected by the members of the same family, living under the same roof, how should a neighbour, much less a parish officer, be expected to have a better knowledge of the real means of the individual? We are not aware that our communications display one instance of outdoor pauperism having been permanently repressed by the mere exercise of individual knowledge acting on a limited area. What our evidence does show is that where the administration of relief is brought nearer to the door of the pauper, little advantage arises from increased knowledge on the part of the distributors, and great evil from their increased liability to every sort of pernicious influence. It brings tradesmen within the influence of their customers, small farmers within that of their relations and connections, and not unfrequently of those who have been their fellow workmen, and exposes the wealthier classes to solicitations from their own dependants for extra allowances, which might be meritoriously and usefully given as private charity but are abuses when forced from the public. Under such circumstances, to continue out-door relief is to continue a relief which will generally be given ignorantly or corruptly, frequently procured by fraud, and in a large and rapidly increasing proportion of cases extorted by intimidation – an intimidation which is not more powerful as a source of profusion than as an obstacle to improvement. We shall recur to this subject when we submit the grounds for withdrawing all local discretionary power and appointing a new agency to superintend the administration of relief.

Many apparent difficulties in the proposed plan will be considered, and we hope removed, in a subsequent part of this Report. One objection, however, we will answer immediately; and that is that it implies that the whole, or a large proportion, of the present paupers must become inmates of the workhouse. One of the most encouraging of the results of our inquiry is the degree in which the existing pauperism arises from fraud, indolence, or improvidence. If it had been principally the result of unavoidable distress, we must have inferred the existence of an organic disease, which, without rendering the remedy less necessary, would have fearfully augmented its difficulty. But when we consider how strong are the motives to claim public assistance, and how ready are the means of obtaining it, independently of real necessity, we are surprised not at the number of paupers but at the number of those who have escaped the contagion. A person who attributes pauperism to the inability to procure employment, will doubt the efficiency of the means by which we propose to remove it, tried as they have been, and successful as they have always proved. If such a person had been present when the 900 able-bodied paupers applied to the Marylebone officers on the ground that they could find no work, he would have treated lightly the proposal of getting rid of them by the offer of wages and the stone-yard. He would have supposed that work must have been provided for the 900, not for the eighty-five who actually accepted it. If a workhouse had been offered, he would have anticipated the reception of the 900, not the eighty-five, or rather, according to the opinion of the officer, the ten who would probably have entered it. He would have come to the same conclusion respecting the twenty shoe-makers to whom relief was offered by Mr Hickson. We have seen that the test showed that among the twenty there was one deserving person: if the test had not been applied, and to meet the chance of there being one such person, the whole twenty had received out-door relief, even that person would have received relief instead of wages, and nineteen persons really capable of earning their support would have been converted into permanent paupers, besides those whom the example would have attracted. Before the experiment had been tried, the sixty-three heads of pauper families at Cookham might have been confidently pronounced to be a surplus population, and emigration have been urged as the only remedy. 'The low rate of wages', it might have been said, 'proves the redundancy, and the certain effect of throwing upon the depreci-ated labour-market nearly one third more of competitors (rendered desperate by their privations) will be to increase the prevalent misery; the proposal to take them into the workhouse, which will require expensive preparations for the whole of them, is impolitic, and indeed impracticable.' Such, in fact, were the anticipations of persons deemed competent judges as to the number of the pauper-ized labourers who would remain permanently chargeable. It is stated in the report from Cookham that 'The work provided was trenching; an acre of hard gravelly ground was hired for the pur-pose. Some of the vestry, at the outset, considered that this quantity of land would be utterly inadequate. Many of the farmers thought the parish officers would have to trench the whole parish; but it turned out that not more than a quarter of an acre was wanted for the purpose.' In several others of the dispauperized parishes, the erection of workhouses and other remedial measures were strongly and sincerely opposed on similar grounds. In answer to all objections founded on the supposition that the present number of able-bodied paupers will remain permanently chargeable, we refer to the evidence which shows the general causes of pauperism, and to the effects produced by administration on a correct principle, as guaranteeing the effects to be anticipated from the general application of measures which have been tried by so many experiments. But we cannot expect that such evidence will satisfy the minds of those who sincerely disbelieve the possibility of a class of labourers subsisting without rates in aid of wages; and we have found numbers who have sincerely disbelieved that possibility, notwithstanding they have had daily presented to their observation the fact that labourers of the same class, and otherwise no better circumstanced, do live well without such allowances; still less can we expect that such evidence will abate the clamours of those who have a direct interest in the abuses which they defend under the mask of benevolence.

Such persons will, no doubt, avail themselves of the mischievous ambiguity of the word *poor*, and treat all diminution of the expenditure for the relief of the poor as so much taken from the labouring classes, as if those classes were naturally pensioners on the charity of their superiors, and relief, not wages, were the proper fund for their support: as if the independent labourers themselves were not, directly or indirectly, losers by all expenditure on paupers; as if those who would be raised from pauperism to independence would not be the greatest gainers by the change; as if, to use the expression of one of the witnesses whom we have quoted, the meat of industry were worse than the bread of idleness.

We have dwelt at so much length on the necessity of abolishing out-door relief to the able-bodied, because we are convinced that it is the master evil of the present system. The heads of settlement may be reduced and simplified; the expense of litigation may be diminished; the procedure before the magistrates may be improved; uniformity in parochial accounts may be introduced; less vexatious and irregular modes of rating may be established; systematic peculation and jobbing on the parts of the parish officers may be prevented: the fraudulent impositions of undue burthens by one class upon another class – the tampering with the labour-market by the employers of labour – the abuse of the public trust for private or factious purposes, may be corrected; all the other collateral and incidental evils may be remedied; but if the vital evil of the system, relief to the able-bodied, on terms more eligible than regular industry, be allowed to continue, we are convinced that pauperism, with its train of evils, must steadily advance; as we find it advancing in parishes where all or most of its collateral and incidental evils are, by incessant vigilance and exertion, avoided or mitigated.

*

It has been strongly, and we think conclusively, urged that all local discretionary power as to relief should be withdrawn. Mr Mott, when he was examined on the subject of workhouse management, was asked whether, under a well-regulated system, he thought that the local officers might be entrusted with the power of modifying the dietaries. He answers –

I am decidedly of opinion that no such authority can be beneficially exercised, even by the local manager and superintendent of any place; whatever deviation there is in the way of extra indulgence has a tendency to extend and perpetuate itself which cannot be resisted. If you give to particular people an extra allowance on special grounds, all the rest will exclaim, 'Why should not we have it as well as they?' and too often they get it. That which was only intended to be the comfort of the few, and as an exception, at last, one by one being added to the list, becomes the general rule; and, when once established, there are few annual officers who will interfere to abridge the accustomed allowance.

Thus uniformity of excess is produced; and then again it is often deemed necessary to make distinctions in the way of increase, which increase is again diffused, and the whole is again equalized to the profuse standard. Uniformity in the administration of relief we deem essential as a means, first, of reducing the perpetual shifting from parish to parish, and fraudulent removals to parishes where profuse management prevails from parishes where the management is less profuse; secondly, of preventing the discontents which arise among the paupers maintained under the less profuse management from comparing it with the more profuse management of adjacent districts; and, thirdly, of bringing the management, which consists in details, more closely within the public control. The importance of the last object will appear more clearly in our subsequent statement. The importance of uniformity in reducing removals appears throughout our evidence. We have found that the confirmed paupers usually have a close knowledge of the detailed management of various parishes (although the managers rarely have), and act upon that knowledge in their choice of workhouses. Many of the out-door paupers, when they have the means, avoid those parishes in which there are workhouses. The Rev. Rowland Williams, Vicar of Myfod, Montgomery, states in his communication –

It is notorious that when paupers come to swear their settlements, they show a strong inclination to be removed to parishes where there are no workhouses. Those magistrates who are experienced in such removals exercise great caution in believing testimony given under such influence.

[A CENTRAL BOARD OF CONTROL]

THE next subject for consideration is the agency by which partial relief to the able-bodied may be abolished, and a continued administration of relief, on the principle suggested by us, maintained.

The simplicity of that principle and the effects which it has produced, and apparently with ease, in the dispauperized parishes naturally suggest to those who have observed only these striking instances that the change may be effected by a single enactment. That there would be much able and correct administration of any law which the legislature might pass we entertain no doubt, since we find much ability, and often eminent ability, displayed in the administration of the existing system; neither do we doubt that the number of cases of voluntary improvement would greatly increase; for we have been informed of some instances where improvements have actually been commenced in consequence of the light thrown upon the subject by the published extracts from the reports of our Assistant Commissioners; but the evidence collected under this Commission proves that whilst the good example of one parish is rarely followed in the surrounding parishes, bad examples are contagious and possess the elements of indefinite extension. The instances presented to us throughout the present inquiry of the defeat of former legislation by unforeseen obstacles, and often by an administration directly at variance with the plainly expressed will of the Legislature, have forced us to distrust the operation of the clearest enactments, and even to apprehend unforeseen mischiefs from them, unless an especial agency be appointed and empowered to superintend and control their execution.

While we find on the one hand that there is scarcely one statute connected with the administration of public relief which has produced the effect designed by the Legislature, and that the majority of them have created new evils and aggravated those which they were intended to prevent, we find on the other hand that the obstacles to the due execution by the existing functionaries of any new legislative measure are greater than they have ever been. The interests of individuals in maladministration are stronger, the interests in checking abuses are proportionately weaker; and the dangers to person and property from any attempts to effect the intention of the Statute of Elizabeth are greater than any penalties by which the law might be attempted to be enforced. That the existing law admits of a beneficial administration of the provisions of that statute is proved by the instances of the dispauperized parishes; but those instances were produced by the circumstance of there being found within each of those parishes, an individual of remarkable firmness and ability, often joined with a strong interest in good administration, great influence to overcome opposition, and leisure to establish good management. In the majority of instances the change originated with the clergyman or some of the largest holders of land within the parish. In the absence of these fortunate accidents the example has not been followed. In Cookham and White Waltham the benefits of the improved administration have been manifested since the year 1822, but manifested without imitation.

In Faringdon, Berks., which we have already cited as an instance of improvement, the governor of the workhouse was asked:

Are the surrounding parishes aware of the effects produced in your parish by the change of system? – They are quite aware of them.

If legislative measures were taken for the adoption of such a system as that adverted to by you, do you think that obstacles would be found to prevent their execution? – If the adoption of the measures were not enforced by some strong means, I do not believe they would be extensively carried into effect voluntarily.

Are those parishes heavily or lightly burthened? – Most heavily burthened. Property is a great deal deteriorated in value in consequence of the progress of pauperism. One gentleman the other day mentioned to me that lately, in consequence of the heavy burthen of the poor's rates, by which for the last two or three years he had lost upwards of a hundred a year upon the farm his family had held for upwards of two centuries, he had thrown up that farm and gone to another parish which was not yet so heavily burthened with poor's rates. I know that in the surrounding parishes capital is fearfully diminishing and property deteriorating.

Are you aware of any steps being taken in those parishes to follow the example of your parish? – I am not aware of any steps being taken to follow the example. I have indeed heard some persons say they should be very glad to see the same system followed.

What are the obstacles which stand in the way of their following it? Partly fear, and partly the want of persons of influence and energy to come forward to take the first steps.

The Commissioner who examined Cookham visited Bray, and made inquiries of persons connected with that and other adjacent parishes why they did not adopt the means of reducing their heavy rates, which (as they were well aware) had been found so efficient and salutary in Cookham. The answers were usually to this effect: 'The farmers are so disunited and unwilling to stir.' 'The members of the vestry are so jealous of each other that they can do nothing.' 'We have no one to take the lead.' 'We have no one who will take upon himself the responsibility.' 'It never can be done unless we have among us a man of the talent and influence of Mr Whately.'

Mr Whately himself was asked:

Do you think your example would be followed if extensively known? – I very much doubt it. I believe it is pretty extensively known, but it has been followed only in one or two solitary cases so far as I am aware of.

Are you aware that any pains have been taken by the neighbouring parishes to ascertain the nature of your system? – Yes; many have made themselves fully acquainted with it by personal application to me; but either through indolence or want of firmness, or some other cause have not availed themselves of the information they have received; nor have I any reason to hope that a great national benefit can be effected by the personal exertions of individuals, who must necessarily expose themselves to considerable obloquy, if not to great loss of property, and who in many cases have no immediate personal interest.

If you were to withdraw your exertions, do you think that the present system would be carried on in your parish? – Many of the principal rate-payers with whom I act are of opinion that it would not.

In the communication of Messrs Cameron and Wrottesley will be found an account of the ignorance and apathy prevalent amongst the rate-distributors of the adjacent parishes, with relation even to the important pecuniary results of the change of system at Cookham. Mr Whately having been prevented by a severe illness from attending the vestry, the effects of his absence soon exhibited themselves in the management of the poor; and some of the members of the select vestry were convinced that the safety of the reformed system depended upon his restoration to health. It appears from Major Wilde's report that when the master of the workhouse at Southwell, who had long been accustomed to manage that establishment under the admirable superintendence of Mr Becher, went to another parish, he soon relapsed into the common habits. In Hatfield the management fell back during the short illness of the permanent overseer, who is a person excellently qualified; and it appears from various other instances that the voluntary adoption and continuance of an improved system is dependent on obtaining within each parish an individual of great firmness, ability, and disinterestedness to originate it and carry it on; or in other words, that the good general administration of the existing system is dependent on a perpetual succession of upwards of fifteen thousand men of firmness and ability agreeing upon a system and conducting it voluntarily.

We must again state that while there is no province of administration for which more peculiar knowledge is requisite than the relief to the indigent, there is no province from which such knowledge is more effectually excluded. The earlier part of our Report shows the consequences of acting upon immediate impressions, or upon conclusions derived from a limited field of observation. At present, the experience which guides the administration of relief is limited to the narrow bounds of a parish, and to a year of compulsory service. The common administration is founded on blind impulse or on impressions derived from a few individual cases; when the only safe action must be regulated by extensive inductions or general rules derived from large classes of cases, which the annual officer has no means of observing. Capacity for such duties comes by intuition even to persons of good general intelligence as little as an intuitive capacity to navigate a ship or manage a steam engine. The influence of the information and skill which any officer may acquire, may be destroyed by other officers with whom his authority is divided, and even though he may prevail, it usually departs with him when he surrenders his office. The improvements which he may have introduced are not appreciated by his successor. In petty and obscure districts, good measures rarely excite imitation, and bad measures seldom yield warning. 'I have seen', says Mr Mott,

sets of officers succeed sets; I have seen a great many plans and systems suggested and tried; I have seen them tried by officers of the highest respectability and intelligence, and the little good derived from the practical operation of their plans utterly defeated by their successors, who, though equally honest, come into office with different opinions and views. Here and there an extraordinary man will come into office and succeed very satisfactorily. But when he goes, there is generally an immediate relapse into the old system. His example works no permanent change in his own parish, still less is it attended to in the adjacent parishes. In short, I am quite convinced from all my experience that no uniform system can be carried into execution, however ably it may be devised; nor can any hopes of permanent improvement be held out, unless some central and powerful control is established.

Such being the qualifications essential to the performance of parochial offices, our evidence abounds with indications that in devising any new legislative measures it would be necessary to guard not only against adverse interests, but against the actual incapacity of the persons usually filling parochial offices. The following are instances from our communications.

The Rev. Robert Ellison, the rector of Slaugham, in Sussex:

The accounts of eight or ten surrounding parishes should be audited by a person with a proper salary, resident in an adjoining town. It is difficult to get a proper person in villages to audit accounts. My vestry clerk is a pauper, and not a good character; the two last overseers could neither read nor write. Need I say more? The rates rose last year 9s. in the pound, which amounted to near £700 additional. The poor cost upwards of £1,600; the population not 800.

Major General Marriott, an acting magistrate of the Pershore division, containing sixty-six parishes, of Worcester, states that some of the overseers (small farmers) –

can scarcely write their names, and few can keep accounts (witness the Returns made to Parliament), and are so ignorant or inattentive to

A Central Board of Control 403

the magistrates' orders, wishing to slip through their half year with as little trouble as possible, that many appeals against removals and other expenses are very unnecessarily incurred which would have been saved to the parish by a regular assistant, and at a trifling expense. In the above sixty-six parishes there may be twelve or fifteen where gentlemen or clergymen reside, and take part in parish affairs; in most of the rest, I fear, I might draw too exact a picture by saying their affairs are managed by some few principal farmers and landholders, generally at open variance, and formed into two inveterate parties; the poor parishioners are obliged to take one side or the other, and are favoured or oppressed as their party prevails. *Such are the persons for whom it is necessary to legislate (as well as for inhabitants of large towns) in making or altering laws for the poor.*

Although clear and often able replies to our queries have been received from the officers of the town parishes, some of the answers, even from the metropolis, were evidently written by illiterate and ignorant men. One of the population returns from Middlesex, to which we had occasion to refer, was attested by the mark of the returning officer. The revision of the lists of votes under the Reform Act, however, brought to view in some respects much more completely than the present inquiry the qualifications of the general body of overseers; and it appears from the information of the revising barristers, that the inability of a large proportion of them was not confined to the comprehension of legal distinctions, but extended to the execution of the most simple directions.

'The class of persons', says Mr Moylan,

whom I have seen in the office of overseer are generally men who, far from being able to fulfil the duties imposed upon them, seem unable to comprehend those duties. The general ignorance and stupidity of the overseers in country parishes with whom I came acquainted as Revising Barrister in Cheshire and Nottinghamshire, surpassed anything which I could have previously conceived. In some of the agricultural parishes we found a × substituted for the overseer's signature to the list of voters. Many lists were made out and signed by the village schoolmaster, or some other person who accompanied the overseer in attendance upon our court, and was alone competent to answer on his behalf any inquiries we deemed it requisite to make. In some cases where the overseer had not had recourse to the aid of others, his blunders were ludicrous. Instead of making the list a fair transcript of the claims, he would perhaps undertake to insert what he thought a more accurate description of the qualification, which would prove, in point of fact, no qualification at all.

'In 1832', says Mr Maclean, 'I revised the list of voters for the western division of the county of Sussex, and in the present year I have revised the lists of the northern division of the county of Essex.'

In both counties I met with many overseers apparently perfectly unable to comprehend, from reading the Reform Act, what they were required to do. Many were unable to write at all, and others could with difficulty affix their names to the lists. Some appeared unable to copy accurately the schedule of the Act according to the form there given. Those lists which had any pretension to correction had been invariably written out by the parish schoolmaster, or under the advice and direction of some resident gentleman. Few were capable of furnishing any information, or of understanding that any distinction existed between a freehold and leasehold qualification. Through ignorance or obstinacy, many had neglected several of the duties distinctly pointed out in the Act; such as to publish the names which were upon the register of the preceding year, or to sign the lists previous to affixing them on the church door. I met with few lists which did not require considerable alteration. Attempts at an alphabetical arrangement seemed to have completely failed. Several had omitted to make out lists at all. In one instance I was attended by a female overseer, and it is due to her to state that the list furnished by her, and in her own handwriting, was one of the most correct I met with.

Mr Flood, revising barrister for the northern division of the county of Leicester, states –

I found very great difficulty in revising the list of voters owing to the illiterate character of the overseers of many of the parishes. In one instance where there were two overseers, one had not acted and did not sign the list, though he was able to write; and a mark × was substituted for the signature of the other. There were, I think, three or four lists unsigned, none of the overseers being able to write, and about the same number only signed by one overseer. In about sixteen or eighteen lists the overseers had resorted to the assistance of the parish schoolmaster or some other person to assist them. In not more than ten parishes did the overseers appear in the least to comprehend the duties they were required to perform. I found, however, the overseers of the parishes of Loughborough, Castle Donington, Melton Mowbray and Ashby-de-la-Zouch exceedingly intelligent men, while in the eastern side of the county, where the population is exclusively agricultural, I met with a degree of ignorance I was utterly unprepared to find in a civilized country.

Mr Villiers, when acting as a revising barrister in North Devon, found that not less than one fourth of the overseers were unable to read, and he mentions one overseer who had not that qualification and yet was intrusted with the distribution of rates to the amount of £7,000 per annum.

Such being the *capacity* of a large proportion of the distributors, we shall find the state of their *motives* to either the commencement or the support of improvement equally unpromising. Persons engaged in trade have represented the management of parochial affairs to be analogous to the management of a bankrupt's estate by creditors where although each creditor has an interest in the good management of the estate, yet, as the particular creditors who were appointed assignees had not an interest sufficient to incite them to exertions which necessarily interfered with their other and stronger interests, no estates were ever so extensively mismanaged or so frequently abandoned to plunder, until a special and responsible agency was appointed for their protection. The common fallacy in which the management by overseers, that is, by two or three persons, is treated as a management by the people of the 'people's own affairs', and an 'attention to their own interests', meaning the affairs and interests of some hundreds or thousands of other persons may be exposed by a slight examination of the evidence. It will be found that the private interests of the distributors of the rates are commonly at variance with their public duties, and that the few pounds, often the few shillings, which any parish officer could save to *himself* by the rigid performance of his duty, cannot turn the scale against the severe labour, the certain ill-will, and now, in a large proportion of cases, the danger to person and property, all of which act on the side of profusion. And it must be recollected that the consequences of a large proportion of the existing mismanagement do not fall on the parishes in which they have originated, but upon those against whom, under the present system of parochial warfare, they are aimed, and that much of that mismanagement is consequently mismanagement by the officers and by the vestries, not of their own affairs, but of the affairs of other parishes, or of the public at large. Even if the whole power were left to the vestry, and the vestry were composed of the proprietors as well as of the occupiers, it could not be said, except in very small parishes, that the governing body were the managers of their own affairs. Numerous bodies are incapable of managing details. They are always left to a minority, and usually to a small minority; and the smaller that minority, the greater, of course, is the preponderance of private and interested motives.

It must be added, as indeed might have been expected, that as parochial duties become more arduous, as they require more leisure and ability, those who have that leisure and ability appear less and less inclined to undertake them. This is shown in the great falling off in the number of representative vestries, in consequence of the difficulty of obtaining the attendance of those who were the best qualified; although such vestries are amongst the best existing instruments for systematic management, with the least annoyance to those who perform the duties. It has been stated to us that in one district where the income of the proprietors was reduced nearly one half, chiefly by the progressive increase of the rates, several of them declared that they would abandon the remainder rather than encounter the annoyance of having to contend against the system. The property of the whole parish of Cholesbury was abandoned to pauperism, apparently without a struggle.

We need only revert to the evidence, quoted in the earlier part of our Report, to mark the extent to which interests *adverse* to a correct administration prevail amongst those who are entrusted with the duties of distributing the fund for relief.

We must anticipate that the existing interests, passions, and local habits of the parish officers will, unless some further control be established, continue to sway and to vary the administration of the funds for the relief of the indigent; and that whatever extent of discretion is left to the local officers will be used in conformity to those existing interests and habits. Wherever the allowance system is now retained, we may be sure that statutory provisions for its abolition will be met by every possible evasion. To permit out-door relief as an exception would be to permit it as a rule. The construction which has been put on the 59 Geo. III [1818], shows that every case would be considered 'a case of emergency'; and under provisions directing that the able-bodied shall be relieved only in the workhouse, but allowing relief in money to be continued to the sick, we must be prepared to find allowances continued to many of the able-bodied, as belonging to the excepted class. We have had instances where, after the use of fermented liquors in workhouses had been forbidden, they were found in use in extraordinary quantities as medicines.

In addition to these strong elements for the perversion of any legislative measures, we cannot omit to notice again the comparatively new and still more powerful element of intimidation now openly avowed in the most pauperized districts.

The labouring men in a large proportion of the districts where the allowance system prevails must have seen and felt what indeed the labourers who have been examined explicitly declare, that the discretion and irresponsible power allowed to the distributors of relief are often used prejudicially to them. We believe, however, that the acts of injustice properly imputed to those who have so exercised that power, bear no proportion to the injustice imagined and erroneously attributed to them by the receivers, under the notion generated by the indefiniteness of the existing system of relief, that the poor's rates are an inexhaustible fund, from which all who call themselves poor are prevented drawing to the extent of their desires only by the cupidity or partiality of parish officers.

However groundless this suspicion may be, its existence appears to us a sufficient reason for endeavouring to remove its pretext. Every man ought, in fact, to distrust his own judgement and his own actions in the affairs of others in proportion as his interests and affections are concerned. Our law, in its jealousy of the influence of similar interests, has rendered the taint of pecuniary interest a ground for incompetency in the case of a witness, and for exclusion from the execution of trusts, and in both cases to a degree which is very inconvenient. The powers vested in the overseers by the Statutes of Elizabeth can only be accounted for on the supposition that the distribution of the poor's rates was little more than an occasional distribution of alms from the poor's box, too small in its amount and influence to be regarded. Not a century had elapsed, however, before the evils of the 'unlimited power of the overseers' and their 'giving relief upon frivolous pretences, but chiefly for their own private ends, to what persons and number they thought fit', had been stated and attempted to be remedied. The remedy however was, as we have seen, unsuccessful, indeed worse than unsuccessful. It gave, or was construed as giving, powers to the justices, of which we have described the effects, and it does not, in practice, appear to check the powers of the overseers, powers which enable them to reduce the value of the labour of which they themselves are the purchasers, and even to throw on others a part of its price to increase the productiveness of their own property, and depreciate that of their neighbours, and generally to gratify their own feelings and promote their own interests at the expense of every other portion of the community.

Whatever may have been the various causes of the agricultural riots in various districts, whether the object was to force an increase of wages or a reduction of tithes or rent, the one effect has been to prove that the discretion exercised in the distribution of the poor's rates can be effected by intimidation, and the rate-receivers every week show themselves more completely aware that intimidation may be made as efficient a means of producing maladministration as the corrupt interests of the distributors. Various communications made to us in 1833 correctly anticipated the continuance of incendiarism during the present winter. Intimidation is not unfrequently exercised in the town parishes, and the police called in for the protection of the distributors. To such an extent has it been carried in a large parish in the metropolis that the officers thought it necessary for their safety to go armed to the vestry.

Under these circumstances, any discretionary power left to the local officers must be a source of suspicion, and so far as their persons or properties are obnoxious to injury, a bounty on intimidation. The ignorant rarely estimate, or even take into account, the motives which lead men to pursue any line of conduct except the narrow tract pointed out by their own immediate interest, and are prone to exaggerate any power that may be used against them, and to fear and hate those who exercise it. It is matter of common observation that acts of incendiarism have been most frequently committed against persons who had done 'nothing to excite animosity', or who were 'distinguished for their kindness', or were 'the last persons who would have been expected to become the victims of such revenge'. We see no ground for expecting that any purity in act or intention in the distribution of rates will render the distributors less obnoxious to hatred, which is always the stronger as they are the more closely connected with the rate-receivers. A refusal by a person who is nearly an equal excites more animosity than one by a person who is comparatively a stranger and has greater authority. Can a farmer at a vestry be expected to refuse relief and endanger his own property and person to save funds to which he is only one of many contributors, when in proportion to his belief that the applicant is undeserving must be his conviction of the capability of that applicant to resort to any criminal means of obtaining compliance with his demands, or of gratifying his revenge? But the immediate distributors of relief are not the only persons obnoxious to such motives. Mr Villiers states that a magistrate declared to him that in his neighbourhood, if a gentleman living upon his own property were strictly to perform his duty in a large proportion of the cases where paupers appealed from their overseers, he would be in danger of having his property destroyed. Such dangers, it is to be observed, are generally incurred by refusals to increase allowances, which are *now* wholly illegal; and, therefore, to expect the voluntary execution of new and strict regulations by persons placed under such circumstances appears unreasonable. Mr Day, the magistrate at Maresfield, to whose communication we have before referred, in the following passage forcibly expresses opinions which we have reason to believe are entertained by a numerous class.

I must here guard against an impression that may be conveyed by these remarks, which might lead to a fatal disappointment. The workhouse system is at present legal, and funds for emigration may, in many instances, be raised by voluntary contributions. But were the plan advocated by me attempted to be put in execution at the mere instigation of an individual, or by a vote of vestry, it would probably induce an irritation that would lead to disastrous consequences. When in the parish of Mayfield it was rumoured that I intended interfering to reduce the rates, it was immediately suspected by the paupers that I was opposed to their interest. On the door of the first vestry I attended I found affixed a notice that they intended washing their hands in my blood. In 1826, a threat of that kind was readily disregarded; at present it would be consummated in a riot or fire. But if the alteration be the act of the Legislature, it assumes a different aspect. It comes with the sanction of the law, and however it may be murmured at, the odium is removed from the obnoxious vestryman, or the individual magistrate, The complaining pauper looks round to the adjacent parishes and the neighbouring benches. He sees his lot the lot of all; and is told that however he may meet with sympathy, there is no power of redress. He may hope to intimidate a vestry, but he cannot dare to oppose a government.

We believe, however, that general regulations made under the immediate control of the executive would meet with comparatively ready obedience; not from despair of the success of resistance, but from confidence in the disinterestedness of the source from which the regulations emanated. We are happy in having found no distrust of the Government amongst the labouring classes in the pauperized districts: we rather apprehend that they entertain extravagant expectations of what can be accomplished by legislative interference. In the instructive letters from emigrants of the labouring classes to their friends in England, we see few traces of discontent with the political institutions, or the general government of their former country; few expressions of satisfaction that they now live under other institutions; but we do find, in those letters, felicitations that they are no longer under local control or parochial management: 'Here' say the labourers, in speaking of their new abodes, 'there are no overseers to tread us under foot.' Wherever in the course of this inquiry it has been deemed requisite to communicate directly with the labouring classes, the Commission appears to have been regarded with entire confidence. Our written communications from labouring men on the subject of the labour-rate are abundant; our Assistant Commissioners found their inquiries answered with alacrity by all the labourers who were examined. Under the conception that the Commissioners were invested with extraordinary powers, the labourers have appealed to us for interference against local malversations. One of the Sussex labourers was asked in the course of his examination:

What alterations of the Poor Laws are talked about by the labourers? – They have hopes that Government will take it in hand, as they would then be contented with what was allotted to them; they would be sure that they would have what was right, and would not be driven about by the overseers.

Are you sure that the labourers would be pleased to see the overseers deprived of their power? – Yes, that they would, for they often fail, and take the parishes in; and besides, all parish business now goes by favour. Many people do now say that they talk about reform in the Government, but there wants reform in the parish.

Suppose that the workmen were deprived of the allowance in aid of wages, but deprived in such numbers that the farmers would be compelled to pay wages to the same amount, how do you think such a measure would be received by the workmen? – That would give a great deal more content, and I am sure that they would do the farmer more work. The parish money is now chucked to us like as to a dog.

The jealousy felt by the labourers towards the local authorities, from a suspicion of their being under the influence of adverse interests, combined with distrust of their possession of knowledge qualifying them to interfere with advantage, was strongly displayed in framing the present Act for the Regulation of Friendly Societies.

Dr James Mitchell, examined.

We are informed that you have paid great attention to the formation of friendly societies, and the legislative proceedings with relation to them – I have lectured and published works on the subject of benefit societies, and took an active part in assisting the delegates of the working men of the benefit societies in London in framing the present Act of Parliament under which benefit societies are regulated, and, as an actuary, I am very often consulted on the subject.

Was the appointment of a central authority or control, under the authority of the Government, to revise the regulations of the benefit societies, and enforce conformity to the will of the Legislature, popular with the representatives of the working classes? – Yes; in order to prevent the capricious control of the various local authorities, each of whom had his own notions, which probably differed from the notions of everybody else, and were formed from very limited experience and observation, and often from no observation whatever, the working men thought it would be very beneficial to get one person appointed to revise the rules of all the societies throughout the country, in order that their administration might be rendered uniform, and that the detailed regulations might be the result of more extended information. The chief object of the labouring men was to prevent capricious local interference, which might often be the interference of employers. The clause for the purpose was framed by the delegates themselves.

In the various dispauperized parishes, the enforcement of one inflexible rule of administering relief prevented the exercise of any discretionary power by the employers of labour. The contentment which followed is, to a considerable extent, attributable to this circumstance.

The circumstances which tend gradually to drive discreet and trustworthy persons from voluntarily undertaking the management of the poor's rates leave it in fact either to compulsory service, performed by officers whose authority is transient, who have no appropriate knowledge, and whose only interest is to get through their service with the least personal inconvenience to themselves, or to voluntary service by persons who have either a strong private interest, or who are actuated by ardent feelings. If those feelings are well directed they produce indeed the effects which have followed at Southwell, Bingham, Cookham, and Farthinghoe, but in ill-disciplined minds they may be more injurious than the basest self-interest. On these grounds many of the most respectable parochial officers who have been examined under this Commission have urged the necessity of withdrawing from themselves and from their associates and successors all discretionary power in the distribution of relief. They implore, even as a mere protection, that they may be released from that discretion, and declare that while it lasts they *dare* not pursue the course which they deem the most beneficial even to the paupers by whom the intimidation is exercised.

The following extracts exhibit the tenor of the independent communications to the Board, as well as of the reports of our Assistant Commissioners as to the state of opinion on this subject in the most pauperized districts.

Mr Okeden's report, Appendix A p. 4 – The magistrates of that county (Oxfordshire) are so fully aware of this [the evils produced by the scale and head-money system] that they are ready to concur in and support any measures proposed by Government for averting the increasing curse.

Mr Majendie, Appendix A p. 188 – The vestries held every fortnight for determining relief are very ill-attended, the parishioners seeming to despair of any improvements; and anxious hopes are expressed of the interference of Government.

ibid., Appendix A p. 198, Disturbed Districts – The allowance system is represented to be so established, that without some legislative enactment, neither overseers, vestries, nor magistrates can make any effectual change.

ibid., Appendix A p. 216 – It was observed to me at Maidstone that the management of the poor is beyond the power of parish officers, and requires the superintendence of Government.

Mr Power, Appendix A p. 240, Cambridge – I have reason to think that opinion points rather to a total change of the system than to partial and palliative amendments.

ibid., p. 249, Bottisham – They have no workhouse there at present; an assistant commissioner ten years hence would probably find them with double rates, and no workhouse still; so little chance is there of the mere propagation of opinion on the subject of that system inducing its general adoption, without some active interference by the legislature to that effect.

The conclusion of most examinations of witnesses in the deeply pauperized districts is usually of the following tenor:

The parish officers of the parish of Bethnal Green, London, examined.

Mr Hooker –

My trade is declining; so is the trade of my neighbours. From year to year my returns are less; so are theirs; and respectable people are leaving the place, which makes it still worse.

The condition of your parish being such as you describe, sunk deep in debt, if not absolutely bankrupt; houses deserted in consequence of the pressure of the rates; the pressure increasing; rents declining, and ruin impending; what remedies have presented themselves to the minds of those who govern the parish; what new courses are they prepared to take? – I do not know; I have not heard of anything; we cannot do anything; we must depend on Providence; I do not see what is to save us from ruin, if Government does not do something for us.

Mr Brushfield of Spitalfields –

The outcry for the establishment of some strict regulations is very generally increasing throughout our parish. They ask, 'what remedy is there for the increasing evil?' I have said I see no way but by some superior and central control being established. Since I was here before the subject has been the topic of conversation at our Board of Governors, and it is agreed on all hands that some powerful central control ought to be established.

Mr Thomas Single of Mile End Old Town, says –

I hear it very frequently said in the parish that it would be a very excellent thing if the Government would take the parish affairs in their own hands, for the inhabitants see no chance of the present rates being reduced under the present system. Some regulating power should be established.

I consider it a very necessary interference for the protection of the good order of society, against the worst misgovernment. I think it necessary for the protection of property which is now giving way, and must continue to give way, under the pressure of pauperism. Rents are now much reduced in consequence of the heaviness of the rates. We have 800 empty houses in our parish, and persons are constantly leaving it to go to other parishes where the rates are lower. As the owner of houses, I can speak to these effects from my own knowledge.

The Rev. Thomas Pitman, vicar of Eastbourne, Sussex –

I have no hope void of the interference of Government. If Government take up the administration, we may be relieved, and the present laws, upon revision, may effect this; but as long as the system which is at present adopted here and in the neighbourhood is permitted to continue (and we have no means void of the interference of Government of having it discontinued), we have no prospect but the destruction of our property, the corruption of our people, and the distress of all.

A recommendation that the Legislature should divest the local authorities of all discretionary power in the administration of relief appears to us to follow as a necessary consequence from the mass of evidence to which we have adverted.

[POWERS AND DUTIES OF THE CENTRAL BOARD]

WITNESSES when speaking of the necessity of withdrawing all discretionary power from the distributors, in their own parishes usually express a hope that the relief may be fixed, and to the 'smallest detail unalterably prescribed by the legislature'. The evidence, however, proves that little more reliance can be placed on the voluntary execution by the present agency of any regulations, than on their correct execution of any general principle of management prescribed to them.

It appears, too, that the actual condition of the pauperized districts does not admit of legislation in detail. The differences in the modes of administering the law in different districts have produced habits and conditions of the population equally different. The best-informed witnesses have represented that the measures applicable to adjacent districts are totally inapplicable to their own; and it appears to us that measures which might be safely and beneficially introduced into the majority of parishes in a district might, if immediately introduced, be productive of suffering and disorder to the remainder. Even if the simultaneous and complete execution of so great a change of system throughout the country were practicable, we consider it desirable to avoid it.

It must be remembered that the pauperized labourers were not the authors of the abusive system and, ought not to be made responsible for its consequences. We cannot, therefore, recommend that they should be otherwise than gradually subjected to regulations which, though undoubtedly beneficial to themselves, may, by any sudden application, inflict unnecessary severity. The abuses have grown up in detail, and it appears from our evidence that the most safe course will be to remove them in detail.

We deem uniformity essential; but, in the first instance, it is only an approximation to uniformity that can be expected, and it appears that it must be obtained by gradations in detail, according to local circumstances. And although uniformity in the amount of relief may be requisite, it may not be requisite that the relief should be invariably the same in kind. In Cumberland, and some others of the northern counties, milk is generally used where beer is used in the southern counties. The requisite equality in diet would probably be obtainable without forcing any class of the inmates of the workhouses in the northern counties to take beer, or those of the southern counties to take milk.

The most practical witnesses concur with Mr Mott in representing the voluntary adoption of detailed regulations hopeless, and legislation on details ineligible, if not impracticable. He is asked, 'Do you think it practicable to bring parishes to the voluntary adoption of any uniform regulation when their importance is proved to them?' – He answers,

I certainly do not think it practicable. I think it utterly impossible to bring the 14,000 or 15,000 parishes in England and Wales to one mind upon any one subject, however clear the evidence may be; much less so to act with uniformity in any one point. The Commissioners must be well aware that great frauds are committed by paupers in the metropolis receiving relief from different boards on different board days. I have known instances of paupers receiving pensions from three or four different parishes. It was proposed some years ago, and it has been proposed from time to time, to remedy this evil, which all the parishes are aware is very great by one simple but effectual expedient, which it would be very easy to adopt – namely, by all the parishes paying on the same day; but they never could be got to do this. Individual conveniences prevented the remedy being applied, and the system of fraud still prevails, and will continue to prevail, so long as the present management prevails. Now, if the parishes in the metropolis cannot be got to act in concert for the suppression of an evil which affects only one part of the system, I think it will be seen that I am justified in my opinion, that any reform or co-operation in the country is quite hopeless without the establishment of a strong central management; nothing else will check the system.

Might not such general regulations as those to which you have alluded be prescribed by Act of Parliament? – No, certainly not. The regulations of any system must be very numerous; and though they may be uniform, it would be necessary to vary them from time to time; and unless Parliament was to do nothing but occupy itself with discussions on detail of workhouse management, it would be impossible to effect any great alteration in that way. Many regulations, however ably devised, must be experimental. Unforeseen and apparently unimportant details might baffle the best plans, if there were not the means of making immediate alteration. Suppose a general regulation were prescribed by Act of Parliament, and it was found to want alteration; you must wait a whole year or more for an Act of Parliament to amend it, or the law must be broken. A central authority might make the alteration, or supply unforeseen omissions in a day or two. Besides, a central board or authority might get information immediately on the matters of detail. If they had, for instance, to settle some uniform diet, they could at once avail themselves of the assistance of men of science, physicians, or chemists; but you would find that Parliament, if it could really attend to the matter, and would do anything efficient, must have almost as many committees as there are different details. If there was a central board established, and it were easily accessible, as it ought to be, persons in local districts would consult them or make suggestions, who would never think of applying to Parliament. Who would think of applying to Parliament to determine whether four or five ounces of butter should be used as a ration in particular cases, and whether the butter should be Irish or Dutch? or, if Irish, whether Cork or Limerick; or to determine whether the old women's underpetticoats should be flannel or baize, and how wide or how long? Yet on details of this sort, beneath the dignity of grave legislators, good or bad management would depend.

By many it is considered that the only means by which the system can be effectually amended is the management of the whole Poor Law administration as a branch of the general government. The advocates of a national rate, and those who are willing and desirous that the Government should take upon itself the whole distribution of the funds for the relief of the poor, do not appear to have considered the expense and difficulties in the way of obtaining such an agency throughout the country.

We have received no definite plan for the purpose, and have prepared none. We trust that immediate measures for the correction of the evils in question may be carried into effect by a comparatively small and cheap agency, which may assist the parochial or district officers, wherever their management is in conformity to the intention of the Legislature; and control them wherever their management is at variance with it. Subject also to this control, we propose that the management, the collection of the rates, and the entire supervision of the expenditure, under increased securities against profusion and malversation, shall continue in the officers appointed immediately by the rate-payers. This course, we believe, will be the most easily practicable, and will best accord with the recommendations of the majority of the witnesses and with the prevalent expectation of the country.

The course of proceeding which we recommend for adoption is in principle that which the legislature adopted for the management of the savings' banks, the friendly societies, and the annuity societies throughout the country. Having prescribed the outline and general principles on which those institutions should be conducted, a special agency (which, in this instance, was constituted by one barrister only) was appointed to see that their rules and detailed regulations conformed to the intention of the law. This agency, we believe, has accomplished the object effectually. From magistrates and clergymen who act as trustees and managers of savings' banks we have learned that it is found to work satisfactorily to them and to the members at large, because they are aware that the decision by which any regulation is established or disallowed is made on extended information derived from all similar institutions throughout the kingdom, instead of being made only on such as the neighbourhood might chance to afford. We believe that the control has also been found beneficial by the members of friendly societies, and has put a stop to many which were founded, either ignorantly or dishonestly, on principles fraught with ruin to the contributors. Since the adoption of this measure, there has been only one appeal against the barrister's decision, and that appeal was disallowed.

WE RECOMMEND, THEREFORE, THE APPOINTMENT OF A CENTRAL BOARD TO CONTROL THE ADMINISTRATION OF THE POOR LAWS, WITH SUCH ASSISTANT COMMISSIONERS AS MAY BE FOUND REQUISITE; AND THAT THE COMMISSIONERS BE EMPOWERED AND DIRECTED TO FRAME AND ENFORCE REGULATIONS FOR THE GOVERNMENT OF WORKHOUSES, AND AS TO THE NATURE AND AMOUNT OF THE RELIEF TO BE GIVEN AND THE LABOUR TO BE EXACTED IN THEM, AND

THAT SUCH REGULATIONS SHALL, AS FAR AS MAY BE PRAC-
TICABLE, BE UNIFORM THROUGHOUT THE COUNTRY.

We have already recommended the abolition of partial relief to
the able-bodied, and particularly of money payments. It appears
to us that this prohibition should come into universal operation at
the end of two years, and as respects new applicants, at an earlier
period, and that the Board should have power, after due inquiry
and arrangements, to shorten these periods in any district: one of
their first proceedings should probably be the gradual substitution
of relief in kind for relief in money.

With such powers the Central Board might discontinue abusive
practices and introduce improvements gradually, detail after detail,
in district after district, and proceed with the aid of accumulating
experience.

Another advantage of this course, as compared with that of a
simultaneous change, is that trouble and expense may be spared
to all those parishes where abusive modes of administration do
not exist.

The Commissioners would assist those who were willing to
exert themselves in bringing about the change, and would exonerate
from responsibility those who found it too heavy, or who could
not sustain it beneficially. Since the Commissioners would have
no local interests or affections, they would enforce the law without
ill-temper on their parts, and without exciting animosity. Unless
those measures which have hitherto caused a decrease of pauperism,
and diminished its peculiar burthen, the only measures which it
would be the duty of the Commissioners to enforce, should produce bad effects instead of good, the benefits of the change in the
first districts in which it will be effected must be such as to remove
from the minds of the ill-informed or the timid all the undefined
apprehensions which beset the subject, and suppress the interested
opposition with which every such change will be assailed.

As one barrier to increase of expense in the detailed management, the Commissioners should be empowered to fix a maximum
of the consumption per head within the workhouses, leaving to
the local officers the liberty of reducing it below the maximum
if they can safely do so.

The following are exemplifications of the regulations which might be transferred from district to district, when found applicable by the Commissioners. An officer of Whitechapel parish, in London, was asked:

What sort of work have they in the workhouse? – They have various sorts of work in the workhouse. Out of the workhouse we employ them as general scavengers for cleansing the parish, contracting for carting only, and making the paupers cleanse all the lanes, alleys, and streets and fill the carts, giving them a small allowance.

What has been the effect of this regulation? – It had been in operation some years before I came into office, and has been found very beneficial. The parish is much better cleansed, and is more healthy than if left to contractors only. The contractors generally shuffle off cleansing the alleys as they cannot get the cart up them, but we make our men take the wheelbarrows up the avenues. The paupers are by this system made spies to prevent any nuisances that may occasion them trouble. If they see any one throwing down filth, they fetch the superintendent and the party is made to take it up again. For this purpose we find that the paupers are better than the police. The efficiency of this system depends mainly on the superintendent, who is paid to attend the labour of the paupers. The parish was fortunate in making choice of a proper officer.

In Mr Codd's report, there is a similar instance. In the parish of St Paul, Covent Garden, the able-bodied paupers were employed to cleanse the streets:

'Our parishioners', the witness states, 'say that the streets were never kept so clean as they have been since the new system prevailed. The fact is that it is the interest of the contractors to employ as few labourers in the work as possible and to leave the streets until they are so dirty that large portions may be removed at once.'

In the answer from Penrith, it is stated by the assistant overseer –

We have at present about ten acres of land, two of which are planted with potatoes every year by the paupers, with the spade; the remainder is sown with corn and hay-grass. We also collect manure from the streets, which we farm of the Duke of Devonshire for that purpose, and for the sake of cleanliness and employment for the poor. The streets are kept clean by those in the workhouse; and at times, when able-bodied out-door paupers apply for relief, we offer them work in the streets, which they invariably refuse. By this means, and that of spade husbandry, we get rid of both our male and female applicants.

Mr Tweedy states that at Huddersfield –

Two years ago a number of men (fifteen) applied for relief as out of work, and were ordered to come next morning and have employment in cleansing the streets. Out of the fifteen but one came the next morning, who said the others had got jobs elsewhere.

The same results may always be expected where the applicant cannot plead actual inability; and the labour of cleansing the streets can be offered in every town. The reports of the various local Boards of Health on the state of the densely-peopled neighbourhoods show how grievously this source of employment has been neglected. Even where it has been introduced, it has seldom been enforced with regularity and upon principle: even the success of the experiment does not ensure its repetition, still less its imitation.

Another instance is the mode in which the out-door paupers are paid in some of the large parishes in the metropolis. The vestry clerk of the parish of St Luke, Middlesex, states that –

For several years past a new system of paying the pensioners has been adopted in our parish. Formerly they came in crowds, the regular pensioners being then about 800, and were paid promiscuously on the presentation of their cards. It was found that some persons obtained payment twice over by getting other persons to present their cards after they had been once paid. The whole coming together, a large proportion of them was kept waiting a considerable time, and in addition to the time lost by the paupers, there was much mischief done by an extension of the opportunities of communication, and the formation of vicious acquaintances. The mothers of bastard children might form acquaintances with others still more depraved. The children of more creditable people became familiar with the confirmed paupers.

The improvement consisted in the pensioners being paid in sets of one hundred each; each hundred is paid, and each payment entered within a quarter of an hour. Any person within the same hundred may be paid within the same quarter of an hour; the quarter of an hour, it may be observed, is printed on each ticket. If the party does not attend at the proper time their pension is suspended during the ensuing week. An hour and a half of the pauper's time is thus saved; and on an average, the crowd is reduced from 800 to 50, and the commission of fraud by repeated payments on the same ticket is rendered impossible.

The regulation might probably be made much more efficient, but such as it is, it appears to have been little imitated. The overseer of the adjacent parish of St Matthew, Bethnal Green, states in his evidence –

There were 400 people with new faces for me to pay the first night I sat. I had no one to assist me or inform me, and I gave money away on the mere statements made to me; I am confident I paid some of the people twice over that night.

These crowds are kept often the whole day, and usually during several hours congregated together in the most corrupting state of idleness around the workhouse door. The conduct of these crowds is thus described by the governor of St Pancras workhouse:

Even this course has not entirely got rid of the evil; for while they are congregated round the workhouse doors, their language and conduct are so degrading and obscene as to be a subject of heavy complaint with the neighbours and passengers; no decent female can approach them without being insulted; and I grieve to say that the young women especially seem to have entirely lost all sense of propriety, or rather of common decency; it is no unusual sight to see them upon these occasions in situations of indecency that are most revolting.

These very shameful practices have not subsisted for more than five or six years; but they have increased in force and frequency within that time, and we have tried every means of prevention within our reach, without success. We have called in the aid of the police, have taken the parties before the magistrates, &c., but all to no purpose.

Other witnesses, whose own parishes are the boundaries of their knowledge as well as of their experience on the subject, assert that such evils are incurable. One parish evinces perfect ignorance of regulations which have long been in force as efficient remedies in adjacent parishes. The instance mentioned at St Pancras relates to a form of relief which we hope to see abolished; but during the period of its unavoidable continuance provision should be made for the introduction of regulations by which its evils may be abated. Some valuable practical improvements of the existing system are found in the voluminous codes and by-laws under which incorporations are managed.

If the sum of the good regulations which are found in single and separate, and therefore partial operation, scattered amidst a multitude of parishes, were carried into complete execution in every parish or district to which they were found applicable, the improvement would probably be greater than can be hoped for from untried enactments. We recommend, therefore, that the *same* powers of making rules and regulations that are now exercised by upwards of 15,000 unskilled and (practically) irresponsible authorities, liable to be biassed by sinister interests, should be confined to the Central Board of Control, on which responsibility is strongly concentrated, and which will have the most extensive information. Even if the Board were to frame bad regulations (and worse regulations than those now in practice they could scarcely devise), it would be a less mischievous arrangement than the present, inasmuch as the chances of opposition to a pernicious measure would be increased in proportion to the extension of the jurisdiction, and success in such opposition would be success throughout the jurisdiction. Those who are now maintainers of their own errors would be vigilant and unsparing censors of the errors of a distant authority. Under the existing system, when opposition is made to the continuance of a bad practice, and the opposition is successful, the success is limited to one parish, or to one fifteen-thousandth part of the whole field in which the practice may prevail. In the next parish, and in other parishes, the form of the abuse is generally varied, and requires a varied as well as a renewed opposition. These variations elude legislative enactments, and divide and weaken the force with which the opinion of the intelligent part of the community would act against them. But if a bad practice is rendered uniform, it becomes obnoxious in proportion to its extent, to the full force of public opinion; the aggregate of its effects, immediate or collateral, which may appear insignificant and unworthy of attention, in the single and obscure parish or in any group of parishes, may be correctly estimated, and brought completely within the cognizance of the Legislature. For this purpose, therefore, in addition to the others which we have already laid down, we consider that uniformity of management would in many cases be essential to improvement and to the permanency of any improved system. To the accomplishment of these objects, other measures, to which we shall shortly advert, appear to us to be requisite. By means, however, of the agency which we have proposed, by alterations of detail after detail, with which the Legislature could not occupy itself, bad practices may be weeded out of every district, good practices may be planted in every district. The precedent which we have adduced with relation to the control of savings' banks and friendly societies illustrates this course of operations. Mr Tidd Pratt states –

I invariably forward to all the institutions suggestions of the expediency of adopting rules which have been found to work beneficially; and I also warn them of mischievous results experienced from particular rules in other places. For example, with regard to the former, I found in one of the savings' banks (the Exeter) a rule which allowed the trustees to apply to the member's benefit any portion of the deposits in case of insanity or imbecility; and not one of the other savings banks possessed such a rule. The consequence was that when a member became insane, they would have had no other mode to enable them to apply the member's money to his use than an application to the Lord Chancellor. Sometimes the sums to be applied were only £10: this rule I communicated by circular to the members of every savings' bank, with a recommendation that it should be adopted: many of them have already adopted it; and I believe that in a short time it will be generally adopted. Where I find a good rule, I send it to all; and when I find a bad rule, I stop it in all, and the chances of finding good rules are just in proportion to the extent of the jurisdiction.

The central agency instituted by the Legislature for the control of the administration of the Poor Laws, would form a depository of comprehensive information to guide the local officers in cases which, from their comparatively limited experience and knowledge, might appear to them to be, or which really were, anomalous. Applications in cases of this nature have already been made to the Commissioners. Their information would be received with the conviction of its being the best existing upon the subject. The last witness cited was asked, with reference to this point,

Are you often consulted in cases of difficulty experienced by magistrates and others who are managers of the several societies within your supervision? – Yes; and by chairmen of quarter sessions, by members of both Houses, under the supposition, as I conceive, that I am paid by salary, and that, being a servant of the Crown, they are entitled to apply to me in cases where they themselves feel difficulty. I invariably give the assistance asked, although it takes up a great deal of a professional man's time.

The chief remedy for the principal evil of the system, the increase of the number of the able-bodied paupers, having been shown to be their reception in a well-managed workhouse, we shall next consider by what means by which such workhouses can be provided and the requisite management enforced.

The first difficulty arises from the small population of a large proportion of the parishes. Of the 15,535 parishes (including under that name townships maintaining their own poor) of England and Wales, there are 737 in which the population does not exceed fifty persons; 1907 in which it does not exceed a hundred; and 6,681 in which it does not exceed 300. Few such parishes could support a workhouse, though they may have a poor-house, a miserable abode occupied rent-free by three or four dissolute families, mutually corrupting each other. Even the parishes which are somewhat more populous, those containing from 300 to 800 inhabitants, and which amount to 5,353, in the few cases in which they possess an efficient management, obtain it at a disproportionate expense.

In such parishes, when overburthened with poor, we usually find the building called a workhouse, occupied by sixty or eighty paupers, made up of a dozen or more neglected children (under the care, perhaps, of a pauper), about twenty or thirty able-bodied adult paupers of both sexes, and probably an equal number of aged and impotent persons, proper objects of relief. Amidst these the mothers of bastard children and prostitutes live without shame, and associate freely with the youth, who have also the examples and conversation of the frequent inmates of the county gaol, the poacher, the vagrant, the decayed beggar, and other characters of the worst description. To these may often be added a solitary blind person, one or two idiots, and not unfrequently are heard, from among the rest, the incessant ravings of some neglected lunatic. In such receptacles the sick poor are often immured.

In the former part of the Report we have given instances of the condition of the larger workhouses in the metropolis. The statements with respect to those in the provincial towns and in the rural districts are equally unfavourable: we annex a very few instances.

Captain Pringle states that in

Portsea workhouse, in the women's yard all characters mix together, excepting that the very old have small rooms, in each room three or four; in these, and in the large day-rooms, in which were nurses with bastards, they had fires in August, and were cooking, making tea, &c. The general character of the house, both as to the persons of the paupers, their day-rooms and bed-rooms, is slovenly and dirty. The space so limited also, that in rooms containing from twenty to thirty beds, they were so close as merely to allow a person to pass between them.

In that at *Rumsey*, in which the inmates amount to forty-eight, they are farmed at the price of 3s. weekly, children included. There is no scale of diet, that being left to the farmer or contractor, who also employs the paupers where and how he pleases. The house was dirty, the old men particularly so; the younger men and boys were out at work. On inquiring for the boys' dormitory, I found they slept each with one of the men; the mistress said this was done to keep them quiet. The overseer, who accompanied me, and whose duty it was to inspect the house, stated that he was not aware of the placing men and boys to sleep together; that he never had any complaints either as to diet or beds, and he believed all were comfortable. And as a further proof of the little attention paid by these constituted authorities to the duties confided to them, one of the girls, it appeared, had a child by the brother of the contractor. The overseer did not consider this as a circumstance of any importance. Nothing was said to the contractor, and his brother was still allowed to be about the house.

With regard to classification it may be observed that in the small poor-houses, with the exception of Millbrook, I never found it more than nominal; and even in the larger poor-houses, classification and other regulations appeared never to be carried into effect in an efficient manner, for which the master was probably often less to blame than those under whose control he held his situation. The children are the sufferers from this neglect, as may be inferred from so large a portion turning out badly.

In the small agricultural parish of *Tandridge*, with a population of 478, a double tenement has been hired as a poor-house: in one of the rooms, in one bed, sleep the master with two boys, aged fifteen and twelve; in the other bed, a girl of fifteen with a boy of eleven; in another very small room, a man and wife, and two children, lie in one bed, and two children on the floor. The parish cage, the interior of which is about eight feet square, is used as the habitation of four persons – a man, his wife, and two children; a grated opening in the wall admits light and air.

In *Dover* workhouse the number of inmates is 250; the average expense of diet 2s. 7¾d; seven lunatics are confined here, two of whom are very dangerous, and are chained to their beds; one of them was lately at large in the yard, and had very nearly put one of the paupers to death, who was saved by the master coming in time to rescue him. In many workhouses in this county there are idiots and insane persons who are a great annoyance to the inmates in general; probably this nuisance will not exist much longer, as the asylum near Maidstone is nearly completed.

Mr Osler, in his communication, gives the following instances of the condition of the workhouses in the vicinity of Falmouth:

Mabe House, a ruinous hovel, utterly unfit for the residence of a human being, two men, four women, three children; of whom four receive 8s. 9d. weekly, and a man, his wife, and three children, have only shelter. A married couple occupy the same room with two women.

Mylor – Eight men, seventeen women, seven children, who are placed in the different rooms, supporting themselves either by an allowance of money from the parish, or by their own labour. A barber, who carries on business in the house, has his pole hung out at the door. No governor, or domestic authority of any description.

In such places, when questions of the following tenor are put – Why is no labour found for the able-bodied? Why are not the children placed under proper tuition? Why is not proper care taken of the lunatic? – the usual answers are, 'The parish is too poor to pay for a keeper'; 'We cannot keep a schoolmaster for so few children'; 'To provide a superintendent to keep half a dozen or a dozen men at work would be too heavy a charge'. Even the superintendence of the whole of these various classes, and the management of the house, is often found a pecuniary burthen disproportionately heavy; and the parish officers attempt to diminish it by confiding the whole to one who is in reality, and sometimes avowedly, a pauper.

Constantine House – Ten men, nineteen women, two children. The governor has been dismissed for the sake of economy, and an infirm old pauper regulates the diet and keeps the accounts. All rooms, except the kitchen, close, dirty, and offensive. Bedsteads, clumsy wooden ones. Men's dormitory, their sitting-room, very low, with windows too small for ventilation; excessively dirty, and an abominable musty smell. The fish dinners are cooked here. House appeared not to have been whitewashed from time immemorial. Two men slept in the women's rooms, but the new overseer expressed an intention to correct these evils.

The Rev. Peyton Blackiston, the curate of Lymington, Hants, states –

It appears to me that parochial workhouses are in most places very inefficient, owing to their want of a proper and extensive subdivision, so that the bad may be completely separated from the good. All the parish officers with whom I have conversed upon the subject have at once acknowledged the evil; but they say that the parishes could not afford the expense of such subdivisions.

The result of my inquiries and observations respecting the moral and religious education of the children in the parochial workhouses is that it is greatly neglected. Even in the workhouse of Lymington there was no such instruction previous to the year 1831, with the exception of about an hour a day, in which the girl who cooked taught the children to read. This has also contributed to make them turn out badly. At this moment the generality of parochial workhouses in Hampshire do not supply any effective religious and moral instruction; the children cannot do even the coarsest needlework in a creditable manner, nor are they practised in that kind of work which, as domestic servants, they would be required to perform. I dare say the parish officers will endeavour to gloss over the matter, and from shame would make it appear that the moral and religious instruction of the parish children was well attended to; but as an eye-witness of many parochial workhouses, and having conversed with many of my brother clergy on the subject, I can state that such is not the case. In the workhouse of Lymington parish, which is one certainly of the most improved provincial towns I know, a school was established in 1831, when an able woman was appointed to give instruction in reading and religious duties, and to teach and superintend needlework. The advantages were most striking. It is almost past belief that about two months ago the vestry discontinued the schoolmistress, although her salary was only £10 per annum and her dinner.

Even in the larger workhouses internal subdivisions do not afford the means of classification, where the inmates dine in the same rooms, or meet or see each other in the ordinary business of the place. In the largest houses, containing from eight hundred to a thousand inmates, where there is comparatively good order, and in many respects superior management, it is almost impossible to prevent the formation and extension of vicious connections. Inmates who see each other, though prevented from communicating in the house, often become associates when they meet out of it. It is found almost impracticable to subject all the various classes within the same house to an appropriate treatment. One part of a class of adults often so closely resembles a part of another class as to make any distinction in treatment appear arbitrary and capricious to those who are placed in the inferior class, and to create discontents, which the existing authority is too feeble to suppress, and so much complexity as to render the object attainable only by great additional expense and remarkable skill. Much, however, has been accomplished in some of the existing houses, but much more it appears to us, may be effected, and at a less expense by the measures which we proceed to suggest.

At least four classes are necessary: 1. The aged and really impotent; 2. The children; 3. The able-bodied females; 4. The able-bodied males; of whom we trust that the two latter will be the least numerous classes. It appears to us that both the requisite classification and the requisite superintendence may be better obtained in separate buildings than under a single roof. If effected in the latter mode, large buildings must be erected, since few of the existing buildings are of the requisite size or arrangement, and as very different qualities, both moral and intellectual, are required for the management of such dissimilar classes, each class must have its separate superintendent. Nothing would be saved, therefore, in superintendence, and much expense must be incurred in buildings. If, however, a separate building is assigned to each class, the existing workhouse might in most cases be made use of. For this purpose the parishes possessing these houses must, for certain purposes, be incorporated. By these means four parishes, each of which has at present no means of classification, might at once obtain the means of the most effectual classification; and though so small a number of parishes as four might be sufficient for an incorporation, it is obvious that a much larger number might unite and obtain the advantages of wholesale management and good superintendence, not only without any increase, but with a great diminution of expense.

The salary of the masters of separate workhouses in towns does not usually exceed fifty or sixty guineas per annum; the aggregate expenses of management of four such workhouses may be stated to be two hundred or two hundred and forty guineas, and yet no special provision is usually made for the superintendence of the labour of the able-bodied, nor for the education of the children. Under a system of combined management a less salary would probably suffice for the person who superintended the poorhouse or receptacle for the old, whilst a larger salary might be given to a person of appropriate qualifications to act as taskmaster or superintendent of the workhouse, properly so called, for the reception of the able-bodied, and also to a person properly qualified to act as a schoolmaster. Each class might thus receive an appropriate treatment; the old might enjoy their indulgences without torment from the boisterous; the children be educated, and the able-bodied subjected to such courses of labour and discipline as will repel the indolent and vicious. The principle of separate and appropriate management has been carried into imperfect execution, in the cases of lunatics, by means of lunatic asylums; and we have no doubt that, with relation to these objects, the blind and similar cases, it might be carried into more complete execution under extended incorporations acting with the aid of the Central Board.

Apprehensions are frequently expressed of the evil consequences from congregating 'large bodies of sturdy paupers together in workhouses'. Such consequences have not ensued in the instances of the dispauperized parishes, and we believe that the most effectual means of preventing them is the classification which we propose. It is natural, indeed, for those who judge from the conduct of the able-bodied paupers in small classes under the existing system to anticipate that in larger classes their conduct will be proportionably worse, and that the difficulty of controlling them will be increased, and could be overcome only in edifices constructed for the purpose. We should admit this opinion to have weight, if the able-bodied paupers were brought together in larger classes, without being placed under better management; the probable mischief of an *ill*-regulated and *idle* class being proportionate to the chances of there being found within the class persons able to give it a mischievous direction, and all other things remaining the same these chances are of course increased by the increase of the class; but by good management those chances are almost annihilated. The evidence which we have received appears to establish that continued tumult on the part of able-bodied paupers is conclusive proof of inexperience or incapacity on the parts of those charged with their management. The testimony upon the subject of Mr Mott, a witness of the most extensive practical experience of any witness examined under this Commission, is corroborated by that of others.

'The refractory poor', he states,

occasion great mischief and confusion in all workhouses; but the mischief arises more from the bad example of the *few*, than from the *many*, for all my experience has shown that the number of refractory paupers is not great, as compared with the gross number of paupers in any parish or district, perhaps not much above five per cent, certainly not ten per cent; and the conduct even of persons of this class must be attributed to the inducements offered by the present defective system rather than to any innate disposition to act unlawfully. They know that their customary allowances and the rules of management are *discretionary* in the breasts of the parish officers; they have daily proof that the most refractory frequently obtain their ends, and get their condition 'bettered', partly through the fear or dislike of the officers to come in contact with such characters, and partly from a desire of the stipendiary manager to save himself trouble, well knowing that a complaint to the magistrates is only a waste of time, because the punishment awarded is in fact no punishment whatever. These refractory characters are generally the most expert work-people (of those who apply for relief) under proper guidance. If I had a given quantity of work to get done in a certain time, by paupers, I should say to the parish officers, 'Let me have your most refractory characters'; as I find that, with mildness and persuasion, but with a determined conduct, constant superintendence, and suitable encouragement, they may be brought to do much more work than other paupers. They are not to be calculated upon as permanent paupers under a good system, and I do believe that to a man they would run to steady industry, if compelled by superior authority to conform to regulations rendering such industry preferable.

The success of the management of various institutions in the metropolis which give no partial relief, such as the Philanthropic Society, where the children of criminals are educated and brought up to useful trades; the Refuge for the Destitute, in which young persons who have been discharged from prison are supplied with the means of instruction and reformation; and the Guardian Society, in which females who have become outcasts from society are provided with a temporary asylum and suitable employment until their conduct affords assurances of their amendment, are instances of what might be done by the good management of separate classes of the existing paupers.

These societies take for their subjects persons trained up in vice, and are stated, in a large proportion of cases, to reclaim them. The children who enter an ordinary workhouse, quit it, if they ever quit it, corrupted where they were well disposed, and hardened where they were vicious.

The circumstances which appear to conduce to the success of the excellent institutions to which we have referred (and to which we might add the Asylums for the Indigent Blind, the Schools for the Deaf and Dumb, the Marine Society's Schools), appear to be; first, that by classification of the objects of relief, the appropriate course of treatment is better ascertained, and its application and the general management rendered less difficult; secondly, that the co-operation of persons of leisure and information is obtained. The institutions for females are generally superintended by ladies' committees.

The following extracts from some evidence given by Mrs Park, wife of Mr Adam Park, surgeon, Gravesend, the brother of the celebrated traveller, will serve to show that under good arrangements much voluntary service might be made available in a great proportion of the workhouses throughout the country.

About two years ago the state of our workhouse attracted my attention, from the condition in which I learned that it was during my inquiries respecting Mr Park's patients, he being then the surgeon of the parish. There were then fifty females in the workhouse. Of these, twenty-seven were young, stout, active women, who were never employed in doing anything whatever. There were five of these young and able women who were accustomed to go to bed in the forenoon, solely to pass off the time. There was no separation of the sexes during the day, and the most frightful demoralization was the consequence. Four old females did the whole of the work of cooking and cleaning the house.

The younger females, the children, were brought up much in the same way; they were educated by an exceedingly ignorant, ill-conducted man, a pauper, who acted as the parish schoolmaster. These females were brought up in the same school with the boys, and very great disorders prevailed.

The old females were also very ill regulated. I found that they made it a practice to send the children to the public-house for spirits. How they obtained the money was a mystery which I have never been able to penetrate. On the whole, the workhouse appeared to me, from all I saw and all I could learn, a frightful and increasing source of demoralization to the labouring classes, and of burthens to them in common with the higher classes.

Seeing this I got several ladies to form a committee, and we tendered our services to the church wardens and the parish officers to educate the children, and to make the young and able-bodied paupers of our own sex work a certain number of hours a day, and conform to industrious and religious habits.

The first object was to bring all the inmates to more industrious habits. Instead of four old persons always doing all the work in the house, our intention was, that the requisite number of persons should perform the cooking and other work in turn, so that these young women might learn household work, and form useful domestic habits, instead of bad habits and immorality.

The exertions of these ladies were greatly impeded by the parish officers; much good was nevertheless accomplished. The witness states that –

The elder paupers were taught knitting stockings, and the younger females needlework. Before we went to the workhouse they were badly clothed, and some of them were almost in a state of rags and nakedness. We wished to have the whole clothed in one way, with gowns of blue linsey-woolsey, check aprons, dark handkerchiefs, and close white caps. After violent opposition from the mistress of the house and the females themselves, this was acceded to. Hitherto they had purchased the most gaudy prints for the females, and ready-made slop shirts for the men in the house, whilst the young women were lying in bed idle. One of the paupers, a girl of eighteen years of age who refused to work, was dressed in a dashing print-dress of red and green, with *gigot* sleeves, a silk band, a large golden or gilt buckle, long gilt earrings, and a lace-cap, turned up in front with bright ribbons, in the fashion of the day, and a high comb under the cap and abundance of curls. A general order was given that the hair of the females should be braided, and put under their caps, and no curls or curl-papers seen. We got the whole of the young females clothed in the manner we designed in two months during the first year. This was done by their own labour, under the instructions we gave them. The benefit of this dress was, that whenever they went out of the workhouse they were known and liable to observation, and could not act as they had been accustomed to act when they could not be distinguished. In the next place the parish saved money. They were thus clothed comfortably for 10s. each; the clothing consisting of one chemise, one apron, one cap, gown, and petticoat, stockings, handkerchief, and all for 10s.

After that we procured them needlework, in which we had no difficulty, though we were opposed, in the first instance, under the notion that we should injure the National School, where work is taken in. It was supposed also that it would injure industrious poor people in the neighbourhood. But, according to the statement of the National School Society, the amount of the labour done was not diminished. Neither could we ascertain that any industrious people out of the house had been injured by it; we never had any complaint, nor ever heard of one from any industrious people. I believe the fact to be that a great part of the work we procured was work created, or which would not have been done had it not been taken in at the workhouse. But it would have been much better that the work which might be done in wealthy families should be done in the workhouse, that these paupers should be occupied usefully, and instructed. The ladies paid great attention to the work, and employed one of the most intelligent and active of the inmates of the house as the general superintendent. The work was remarked for its neatness; no slovenly or indifferent work was permitted to go out; and the committee were so particular, that the instruction they received was necessarily much better than that which they would have obtained in the houses of their own parents. One effect of this partial discipline in the house was that in almost two months about one half of the workers left. Some of them called themselves widows; others said that they did not come in to work; they merely came in until they could accommodate themselves, until they could get themselves another situation; but they would not remain to work, indeed, that they would not; they would take a room and keep themselves when they were out of place, sooner than put on a dress, and be made to work! One refractory person said, 'The poor were not going to be oppressed by work.'

If you had been seconded in your exertions, and been allowed to carry into effect the alterations which you thought desirable, what further effects do you believe, judging from your experience, would have been practicable? – In the first place, we should have had the hours of work at least doubled. I am well convinced that the workhouse might, as regards females, be made a school of industry, and a place of wholesome restraint, instead of a school of vice. Whilst no one would come to it under the influence of the inducements afforded by indolence, those who must necessarily come there, orphans, and the great numbers of young people who have been born on the parish, might be so instructed as to be made superior servants and good nurses, and superior wives of working men. In the first place, the workhouse affords the means of giving to females instruction in household work and in domestic economy, which at present is their great want, and which so frequently occasions the ruin and misery of labouring men when they take wives from this class. That which is done by the Guardian Society in London might be done in every workhouse throught the kingdom. If matrons, with proper qualifications, were appointed, they might conduct the system, and might obtain the assistance of the ladies of the vicinity. I was told at the outset that ladies could not be got to form a committee, but I found no difficulty whatever in getting a committee of the age and qualifications to command respect. The household work, scouring, cleaning, washing, plain cooking, needlework, knitting, mending and making up carpets, and economical industry might under such a system be taught in a much higher degree than they could be learned in a cottage, or even in the house of a person of the middle classes. They might also receive superior instruction in another respect; they might be well qualified to act as nurses when sickness occurred in the families of their employers or in their own families. There are always poor people sick in the workhouse, and they might be usefully taught to wait upon the sick people. There are very few females capable of acting as nurses; in fact, it requires good instruction of a nature which might be given by the physician who attends the workhouse. The ladies' committee might maintain a very high order of domestic instruction in these places; and the children of misfortune, who are now a prey to every vice, might be good servants, and in every respect good members of society. This is, in fact, accomplished by the ladies of the Guardian Society in London.

Did you attempt to make any classification in the house? – In such a house classification was nearly impossible. We did on some occasions separate the very old from the young, which was deemed by the old a very great blessing. Some attempt was made to separate the very bad females from the others who were less depraved, but we never could effect it. In short, it appears to me that the only classification which could be made, would be by placing them in separate houses, which might be effected, I am sure, without any addition to the present number of houses. When I look at the parishes around here and their houses, I see no difficulty whatever in making a good classification of the inmates, provided they were under one general management. The persons who are placed as superintendents should have no local interests, and therefore should not be locally appointed. So surely as they are, so surely will there be disorder. The rules will not be so rigidly applied as they ought to be from the numbers in the house who are connected with them or known to them. The mischief which we find to result from this exercise of partiality goes beyond the violation of some rules and the weakening of all others, in the ferment and discontent and disorder excited in the minds of the other paupers by the injustice done by the exercise of this partiality. If the class were large, as it would be for a time, from such a district, it might be worth while to employ as the superintendent of the house for the females a person of education and respectability. Such persons as the widows of non-commissioned officers would be extremely glad to accept such situations; and they might also be made acceptable to such persons as the widows of poor clergymen, and it would be cheap to the public in the end to obtain the services of such persons. They would be incapable of the low cunning and petty jobbing which exist at present.

The different effects of different modes of education and treatment upon the same descriptions of persons are strikingly exemplified in some portions of the evidence collected under this Commission, in which it is shown that whilst nearly the whole of the children of one parish where their education and training is neglected, become thieves or otherwise pests of society, nearly the whole of the children of another parish where better care of them is taken, are rendered industrious and valuable members of the community. In the latter case much of the beneficial results may be ascribed to the attention of persons of education who visited and superintended the schools. One great advantage of the classification obtainable by means of a combination of work-houses would be that the aid of voluntary associations or local committees, of the class of persons who have conducted useful public institutions, might be more extensively obtained, to super-intend the education of the workhouse children, as well as of the other classes of paupers adverted to by the lady whose testimony we have cited.

Although our evidence does not countenance the apprehension that under a good system of management a large proportion of the existing able-bodied paupers would continue permanently dependant on the poor-rates, it appears that in the first instance the chief arrangements must be made with reference to this class of paupers. But we do not apprehend that in many instances new workhouses would be requisite for their reception. It is another of the advantages held out by the aggregation of paupers from a district for the purpose of classification, that the separate classes of the proper objects of relief might be accommodated temporarily in ordinary dwelling-houses, and it is a fortunate district in which there are no empty tenements available for their reception. The tenements belonging to the parish might be rendered available for the separate accommodation of one class of paupers, and the poor-house itself for that of the able-bodied; and on the whole it appears from the evidence that although a considerable proportion of the parishes are without workhouses, there are a few districts in which, by combined management, and under good regulations, the existing workhouse-room would not suffice.

By assigning one class of paupers to each of the houses com-prehended in an incorporation, a greater number of persons might be received within each house. In small districts there are consider-able fluctuations of the numbers of persons in each class; in the workhouse of a single parish the rooms appropriated for the reception of the sick must often be empty; in a house for the reception of the sick from a number of parishes, the absence of patients from one parish would be met by an influx from another, and a more steady average number maintained, and so with the other classes of inmates. The rooms left empty by these fluctuations or reserved for emergencies under the existing management cannot, without great inconvenience, be immediately appropriated to the use of the redundant class. If any rooms on the female side of the house be left unoccupied, they cannot be readily appropriated to the use of an extra number of male paupers. The witness last cited states –

In Lambeth, under the present arrangement, 800 is as great a number as we can reasonably calculate upon accommodating; whereas if the whole workhouse was appropriated to the reception of only one class of persons, from 900 to 1,000 might be fairly accommodated. If you add to this the room that would be obtained by the discharge of those of the present inmates who *would not* submit to the restraint of strict workhouse regulations, I think ample accommodation might be made for all those who *would* avail themselves of the workhouse dietary and accommodation, when their money allowance was discontinued.

Although such is the general tenor of the evidence, we cannot state that there may not be some districts where new workhouses would be found requisite, but we have no doubt that where this does occur, the erection of appropriate edifices, though apparently expensive, would ultimately be found economical. Under a system of district management the workhouses might be supplied under one contract at wholesale prices. Mr Mott states that if 500 persons cost £10 per head, or £5,000; 1,000 persons would cost only £9 per head, or £9,000. He also states, that there would be no more difficulty in managing five or six combined workhouses than five or six separate wards or rooms in one house. Considerable economy would also be practicable in combined workhouses, by varying the nature of the supplies. In the smaller workhouses the children receive nearly the same diet as the adults; if they were separated they might receive a diet both cheaper and more wholesome.

TO EFFECT THESE PURPOSES WE RECOMMEND THAT THE CENTRAL BOARD BE EMPOWERED TO CAUSE ANY NUMBER OF PARISHES WHICH THEY MAY THINK CONVENIENT TO BE INCORPORATED FOR THE PURPOSE OF WORKHOUSE MAN-

AGEMENT, AND FOR PROVIDING NEW WORKHOUSES WHERE
NECESSARY, TO DECLARE THEIR WORKHOUSES TO BE THE
COMMON WORKHOUSES OF THE INCORPORATED DISTRICT,
AND TO ASSIGN TO THOSE WORKHOUSES SEPARATE CLASSES
OF POOR, THOUGH COMPOSED OF THE POOR OF DISTINCT
PARISHES, EACH DISTINCT PARISH PAYING TO THE SUPPORT
OF THE PERMANENT WORKHOUSE ESTABLISHMENT, IN
PROPORTION TO THE AVERAGE AMOUNT OF THE EXPENSE
INCURRED FOR THE RELIEF OF ITS POOR, FOR THE THREE
PREVIOUS YEARS, AND PAYING SEPARATELY FOR THE FOOD
AND CLOTHING OF ITS OWN PAUPERS.

The power of incorporation for workhouse purposes appears to
us to be absolutely necessary. It also appears to us that parishes
may be beneficially incorporated for some other purposes. As
this opinion depends in some measure on a further opinion that
extended management is in certain points and within certain
limits economical, and as this opinion is at variance with a prevalent impression in favour of the general economy of small districts, we shall support it at some length. In the minds of many,
management on a large scale, and large establishments, are associated with large expenses and general profusion: where every
thing is magnified, abuses, which though greater in proportion
would have been imperceptible on a smaller scale, become visible
and striking; but we find that in the small parishes the expense
per head of the persons entitled to relief is generally the greatest,
and that, although the actual burthen per pound on the rental is
often small, that is effected not by diminishing but by shifting
and often aggravating the real burthen, by destroying cottages,
preventing settlements, and driving the labourers into the adjoining
district. The following answer by Mr Mott both states the comparative economy of the larger parishes and accounts for it. He
was asked, 'What would be the effect of dividing Lambeth into
as many independent parishes as there are in the city of London?'
He replies –

The chief effects which appear to me to be likely to ensue are,
that we should have ninety-six imperfect establishments instead of
one; ninety-six sources of peculation instead of one; ninety-six sets of
officers to be imposed upon by paupers instead of one set; ninety-six

sources of litigation and of expense for removals and disputed settlements instead of one; and ninety-six modes of rating instead of one.

It appears that the ninety-six city parishes (many of which are extremely wealthy, and lightly burthened with poor), with a population of 55,000, expended for the relief of the poor in the year 1831 £64,000. Lambeth, with 32,000 more people, and many densely-peopled districts containing very poor people, expended on the relief of the poor only £37,000 during the same year. In the wealthy parishes of the city of London, the money annually paid as poor's rates amounted to £1 3s. 3¼d. per head; whilst in Lambeth the amount annually paid is 8s. 6d. and a fraction per head. The adults of Lambeth parish are now supported in the workhouse at 3s. 11d. a week per head; whilst in the city of London, the greater proportion of all classes of poor, including children, are farmed out at an expense of from 4s. 6d. to 7s. each, and the expense of those maintained in the small city workhouses varies from 5s. to 8s. per head per week for all classes.

The following is a recapitulation of an examination of the comparative expense of the poor's rates per head, in the largest, the least, and the intermediate sized parishes; comprehending all the parishes from which we have received returns, belonging to the first seven counties, taken in alphabetical order, referred to in our supplement.

	Population	Rate per Head
		£ s. d.
BEDFORDSHIRE:		
16 Parishes	12,224	1 0 0¾
5 Largest	6,163	0 16 5
6 Intermediate	4,012	1 6 10¾
5 Least	2,049	0 17 8½
BERKS.:		
30 Parishes	40,971	0 14 7½
10 Largest	29,489	0 12 10¼
10 Intermediate	8,401	0 17 7½
10 Least	3,081	0 19 3½
BUCKS.:		
35 Parishes	34,456	0 14 5¼
12 Largest	22,655	0 11 8¼
11 Intermediate	8,386	0 18 7½
12 Least	3,415	1 4 1½

CAMBRIDGE:

					£	s.	d.
41 Parishes	...	...	...	...	59,016	0 13	1¼
12 Largest ...	...	...	...	37,114	0 11	9½
12 Intermediate	...	...	...	11,830	0 14	8½
12 Least	...	...	...	...	5,410	0 14	10¼

CHESTER:

					£	s.	d.
17 Parishes	...	...	...	...			
6 Largest ...	...	...	...	6,481	0 7	0¾
5 Intermediate	...	...	...	1,568	0 6	8¾
6 Least	...	...	...	...	871	0 9	9¼

CORNWALL:

					£	s.	d.
30 Parishes	...	...	...	...	60,121	0 6	1¼
10 Largest ...	...	...	...	43,328	0 4	9½
10 Intermediate	...	...	...	11,520	0 9	7
10 Least	...	...	...	...	5,273	0 9	5

CUMBERLAND:

					£	s.	d.
46 Parishes	...	...	...	...	45,607	0 5	8
12 Largest ...	...	...	...	32,979	0 5	4¾
12 Intermediate	...	...	...	6,419	0 6	3
12 Least	...	...	...	...	2,223	0 7	11¾

Of these seven counties,   s.   d.
The 67 largest parishes give   ...   9   0¾ per head on the population
The 66 intermediate parishes ...   14   4   ditto.
The 67 least parishes   14   11¾   ditto.

Of all England,

The 100 absolutely largest parishes, containing a population of 3,196,064, give 6s. 7d. per head.

The 100 intermediate parishes, containing a population of 19,841, give 15s. per head.

The 100 least parishes, from which Poor Rates Returns are made, with a population of 1,708, give £1 11s. 11½d. per head.

The 100 intermediate parishes are of the size of which there is the greatest number, and where the population is not too large, to allow the parish officers to obtain a personal knowledge of the individuals relieved.

We have no recent returns of proportions of paupers in the
parishes referred to in the preceding statement; but on referring
to the Parliamentary Returns of the number of paupers in each
parish in the years 1803 and 1813 it appears that the number of
persons relieved in the large and small parishes bears some proportion to their relative amount of rates. In the three hundred
parishes of which the comparative amount of the poor's rates on
the population has been stated, the

	1803	1813
Average number of persons relieved was, in the 100 largest parishes	1 in 16, or 6¼ per cent	1 in 13, or 7¾ per cent
100 intermediate ditto	1 in 10, or 10 per cent	1 in 8, or 12½ per cent
100 smallest ditto ...	1 in 6, or 16⅔ per cent	1 in 4, or 25 per cent

	In 100 largest parishes	In 100 intermediate	In 100 smallest
The increase of pauperism on population from 1803 to 1813 was ...	1½ per cent	2½ per cent	8⅓ per cent

The economy of extended management in the rural districts is
also proved by the evidence derived from the incorporated hundreds. These hundreds are on the whole distinguished by the
economy and general superiority of their administration, as compared with the unincorporated hundreds. From a comparison
of the expense of the eight unincorporated hundreds of Suffolk
with the expense of the nine incorporated hundreds of the same
county, making the calculation on the basis of the real property
assessment of 1815, it appears that the expense of maintaining
the poor, during the year from 1824 to 1831, was 53 per cent in
favour of the incorporated hundreds.

Captain Pringle, who appears to have examined carefully the administration of the poor's rate in the Isle of Wight, the whole of which is incorporated, shows that notwithstanding much general ill management, the result, after a trial of sixty years, is greatly in favour of incorporation. On a comparison of the amount of property assessed in the year 1815 with the amount of rates raised in the year 1829, it appears that the rate per pound for the whole county was 3s. 6d.; for the county exclusive of the island 3s. 8d.; for the island exclusive of the rest of the county, 1s. 10d. In this incorporation, however, litigation about settlements and the expense of removals are almost entirely avoided.

Much of the saving is attributable to the efficiency of the officers of the incorporations, and to the more methodical transaction of their business. Mr Meadows White, a solicitor of great experience in the management of incoporated hundreds, states that each of the parishes incorporated in Blything hundred for less than £10 per annum obtains for the management of the in-door poor the services of a

		£	s.	d.
chaplain ... ... at a salary of		50	0	0
governor and a matron	„	100	0	0
schoolmistress	„	20	0	0
superintendent of the labour (a weaver)	„	20	0	0
clerk	„	140	0	0
visiting guardian	„	40	0	0
house surgeon	„	52	0	0
TOTAL for 46 parishes		£422	0	0

If it were possible that the several functions performed by each of these officers could be performed by any one person at least five times the amount of money paid by each of the parishes incorporated would be requisite to obtain the services of such a person. But it is obviously impossible that one officer could execute these functions: the performance of the duties of the schoolmaster or matron of the workhouse imply a neglect of the duties of the school, in which it appears that there are rarely less than 100 or 120 children; neither could the business of the superin-

The Poor Law Report of 1834

tendent of the pauper labour, nor the business of the clerk (an attorney, whose salary includes the remuneration for all his attendances, journeys and law business in the county) be performed unless at the expense of other duties.

In the establishments of the larger parishes, whilst there is great gain in efficiency by the division of labour, there is also frequently gain by the concentration of labour where it may be concentrated without interfering with the performance of other equally important duties. One of the assistant overseers of Lambeth parish, in reciting his duties, states –

Besides inquiring into the cases of applicants for relief, I inquire into the cases of the non-payment of poor's rate, and whether the neglect or refusal proceeds from inability to pay, or from any other causes, and I report the same to the overseers. It is also my duty to inform the vestry clerk of all houses newly erected in the parish, and of all houses, noted in the rate-book as empty, which have become inhabited; I report them in order that they may be assessed to the rate; I enter this in a book kept for the purpose, and called the draught-book. This serves as a check on the collectors and on overseers, who, from favouritism or other causes, might be disposed to overlook the houses of friends. The overseers or parish officers may be persons in business who are desirous of favouring friends. By imposing these duties on the assistant overseers, who have to traverse districts for purposes relating to the paupers, they are performed at a very little additional expense, as it is all done under one head. I find frequently that when I am inquiring of a person about a house, he can also give me information with relation to a pauper.

To these advantages may be added the greater facility of obtaining securities against embezzlement.

One of the most prominent suggestions of those who have written on Poor Law amendment is compelling the adoption of a uniform and well-arranged system of accounts, a provision which they often appear to consider a sufficient check on peculation. There can be no doubt that arrangements to insure completeness, clearness, uniformity and publicity of parochial accounts are as requisite in this as in any other department of public administration.

WE RECOMMEND, THEREFORE, THAT THE CENTRAL BOARD BE EMPOWERED AND REQUIRED TO TAKE MEASURES FOR THE GENERAL ADOPTION OF A COMPLETE, CLEAR, AND,

AS FAR AS MAY BE PRACTICABLE, UNIFORM SYSTEM OF ACCOUNTS.

But it appears to us that new arrangements as to the mode of transacting the business in question and the establishment of self-acting checks (which are partly independent of accounts) are equally requisite. It is one advantage of management on a large scale that it admits of these arrangements and securities without any increase of expense. Thus in the incorporated hundreds there are six distinct functionaries for the collection and the expenditure of the rates. 1. The assessments are fixed by the board of guardians. They are collected by, 2, the overseers of the several parishes incorporated, who are compelled under a penalty to pay within a certain time to, 3, the treasurer, the money collected. The latter gives security. 4. The clerk of the incorporation receives the commodities supplied, and enters an account of them into the stock-book. 5. The governor of the workhouse attends to the distribution of the goods supplied and, is answerable for it. 6. It is the duty of the visiting guardian to see that the goods received are in conformity to the contracts, and, in fact, to act as a check on the two last-mentioned officers. In the parishes of the unincorporated districts one person, the overseer, is usually assessor, collector, treasurer and distributor, and the checks derived from the performance of the business by separate individuals are lost.

Similar advantages to those of the incorporations are possessed by the larger parishes.

In Lambeth, containing 87,000 persons, a population equal to that of 1,300 of the smaller parishes, under 1,300 sets of officers, the money is assessed by ...   } 1. The churchwardens and overseers.

It is collected by ...   .   2. A paid collector.

By whom it is paid into the hands of   3. A banker or treasurer.

On the other hand, for the distribution of relief there are ...   ...   } 4. The annual overseers.

Who in the majority of instances are assisted by the inquiries of ...   ...   } Assistant overseers or paid officers.

And when relief is ordered it is given by ticket on ...   .   } 5. The clerk at the workhouse.

Here then the parish being large, the business of collecting and distributing the fund is managed by five different hands, exclusive of the workhouse-keeper and other assistant officers. The following is the account which the vestry clerk gives of one simple expedient by which a check is obtained against peculation in the distribution of the casual relief.

Mr Watmore, vestry clerk of Lambeth, examined.

Each overseer relieves the casual poor in cases within his district which are cases of necessity; and this relief is by a little printed ticket on the clerk of the workhouse. The overseer relieving signs his name and the amount on the ticket, and this serves as a voucher for every one, the smallest item.

Before the establishment of the checks, I have known casual poor obtain relief from the whole eight overseers. Frauds have been committed with the tickets; one woman was prosecuted for increasing the amount of the ticket, but frauds in this way cannot be very extensive. I see every day the benefits of this check as regards officers as well as the applicants, and I can see no reason why it should not be adopted in other parishes. In our parish the overseers neither receive nor pay any money; the collectors are bound to pay in every week to the bankers the money collected; we have eight collectors, with securities of £1,000 each.

Some large parishes, however, neglect these precautions, and commit to one person the whole distribution of the rates. In one case the overseer draws from the treasurer a sum of money which he distributes at his discretion; in another, the money is paid into the hands of several overseers who severally distribute it as they think proper, and account for it at the end of the year; the only check being their honour. It appears, however, that this check is not always sufficient, and that cases occur in which the officers mix fictitious names in the crowd of items, and overcharge the sums paid to real characters; thus, where 1s. 3d. has been given, 1s. 9d. is charged; where 1s. 6d. has been given, 2s. or 2s. 6d. is often charged. The following portions of the examination of the parish officers of Bethnal Green show the danger of omitting proper checks.

The parish officers of Bethnal Green, examined.

Mr Bunn – The overseers do not pay by ticket, but pay money out of their own pockets, which they charge to the parish, and account for the money at the end of the quarter; my last weekly account of the casual relief for one division was £27 odd; this was paid away in shillings and sixpences. It is paid in advance for the quarter, and we receive no interest for the outlay.

Has this been the usual course of proceeding for years past? – I believe it is; there has been no alteration.

Is this expenditure discretional with the annual overseer? – Yes, the casual relief is.

Does he frequently sit alone, or is he assisted by other parish officers? – On Thursdays and Saturdays we sit alone, unless some governor by chance drops in in the course of the day, but generally we sit alone.

And are you not regularly assisted by any permanent officer? – No, we are not assisted by any one.

Do you not find that you are frequently imposed upon? – In spite of all an annual officer can do, we are frequently imposed upon. There were 400 new faces for me to pay the first night I sat. I had no one to assist me or to inform me, and I gave money away on the mere statements made to me. I am confident that I paid some of the people twice over that night.

Have you had overseers serving more than one year? – Mr Davis – Yes. Since I have been in office two have served three years, and one two years.

Have you had others who have been desirous of serving? – Mr Davis – Those who last served were known to have been desirous of serving again.

What reason did they allege for being desirous of serving again? – Mr Davis – I do not know.

Mr Bunn – For my own part I would have gladly paid to have been excused. I have offered £60 to be excused from serving after I was in office; I also offered to put down £50 as a subscription to extricate the parish from its difficulties, but not a soul followed my example. I was offered by my predecessors, when I entered into office to have my duties performed for me, but this offer I declined as I must have been responsible for all monies.

Can you judge or state what you suppose to have been the object of the parties in again serving so burdensome an office? – I know their object, Sir, but that I must, if you please, decline stating.

Have there been any cases of malversation in your parish? – Never, that I am aware of.

Nor any suspicions or rumours of malversation prevalent in the parish? – There have been such rumours.

Have there been no grounds for such rumours? – I do not know of any of my knowledge, and cannot speak to them.

Are you ready to swear that you know of no grounds? – All that I can say is, that the expenditure this year is less than it was last year; I cannot say how that was.

But in a parish like yours, where there are a number of small tradesmen whose credit is not very good, and where large sums pass through the hands of parish officers with considerable opportunities for malversation on the part of any one who has the inclination, is not the parish exposed to very considerable danger unless a prudent choice be made? – Certainly. I have heard such persons boast that if they were in office they would take care of themselves.

Mr Masterman, another parish officer of Bethnal Green, examined.

What other opportunities has the system afforded for considerable malversation? – The payment of the casual poor, and the out-door relief, affords very great opportunities for fraud on the parts of the overseers, as well as the paupers, but I cannot say that I know of any instances. I suggested the payment by tickets, but the suggestion was not adopted.

What is the popular opinion on this subject? – That to be an overseer and take care of the poor is a very good thing.

On what grounds has that opinion been founded? – They have seen a person's condition greatly improved after having served the office of overseer; they have seen this take place without seeing any increase in his business, and without having heard or known of any money having been left to him; having, in short, no ostensible reason except that he has been in office.

Is the remark common? – Yes, it is.

In the smaller parishes the state of things is still worse. There one officer collects and distributes, and unless he have some personal adversary who inspects the accounts and objects to them, this officer accounts really to no one, for the audit by the magistrates is confessedly a form.

Many parishes have been agitated by contests to obtain publicity of accounts; these accounts have accordingly been published and peace has ensued; but the statements published leave the satisfied rate-payers almost as much in the dark as ever.

The items are usually published in the following form:

					£	s.	d.
Beer and ale ...	...	...	...	...	440	0	6
Bread and flour	...	...	...	...	1,779	7	6
Butcher's meat	...	...	...	...	1,694	11	11
Butter, cheese, and bacon	...	...	...	691	13	6
Candles and soap	...	...	...	...	120	15	6
Coals ...	...	...	...	...	...	238	13	0
Grocery	...	...	...	...	...	324	19	0
Clothing for paupers	...	...	...	175	9	0

The parishioner knows not from such items what was the character of the purchases; whether 3s. or 7s. per pair was paid for shoes, if any were included in the general item *Clothing*. If the account were made out in detail, the other shoemakers or the other bakers of the parish might judge of the reasonableness of the charges; but even these details would still leave room for fraud in the misstatement of the *quantity* of goods supplied, and as to the actual consumption of the whole quantity supplied.

We consider, therefore, that any uniform and good system of accounts would not of itself suffice, unless the operations or the mode of doing business were clearly arranged. One system of accounts might be prescribed to the two parishes, Lambeth and Bethnal Green: it might be required in both that every item of casual relief given should be entered in the accounts; but whilst in Lambeth the security against fraud, derived from the checks arising from the method of doing business, would perhaps be found nearly complete, in Bethnal Green the accounts would afford little or no security whatever; the names of the parties alleged to have been relieved may be fictitious; the amount of the payments may be misstated; and yet the accounts may, *prima facie*, afford to the auditor no means of detection. Clearness does not ensure truth. Captain Pringle, who has had much experience in the examination of the accounts of commissaries, states that he generally found that the greatest peculators had the clearest accounts. Clear accounts, then, must be based on good arrangements of the modes of transacting business. Uniformity as to some points in the modes of keeping accounts would be of great service for the purpose of comparing the detailed expenditure of one district with another, and would form a necessary means of any general system of management, but the same forms in every point cannot suit every parish. The forms requisite in Marylebone, containing 122,206 inhabitants, would be unsuited to the 1,657 parishes, containing, collectively, only 122,170 inhabitants, and managed by 1,657 different sets of officers.

The sources of peculation will be to a great extent extirpated by the abolition of money-payments; by the supply of goods on public contract, under proper securities, and by the adoption of the checks rendered practicable by more extended management. In a large proportion of the smaller parishes, it would be requisite to obtain in each the services of a good book-keeper. In the larger establishments this is accomplished without difficulty and at a comparatively trivial expense; one set of books serves instead of forty or fifty sets; and the officers of the establishment are usually competent to the task of keeping them.

A further advantage of extended districts arises from the comparative facility of providing for the paupers' useful employment. Opportunities for such employment are wanting in many parishes; in others, exist in forms too large to be undertaken; and in still more numerous instances exist uselessly, in consequence of the jealousies which always act most powerfully in small neighbourhoods. It appears that one of the first preliminary measures must be the preparing for the able-bodied more of this employment than we believe that they will accept.

Employment of some kind can, indeed, be always provided, but it appears to us it ought to be useful employment. Parish officers, whilst they have had sufficient labour of this description before their doors, in their unwillingness or their inability to take upon themselves the trouble of superintendence, or to make any immediate pecuniary sacrifice for the purpose of enforcing the performance of that labour, have resorted to the expedient of sending paupers on fictitious errands, with baskets full of stones, or blank paper directed as letters, and other devices of the same nature, obviously intended to torment them. Such contrivances are pernicious in the revengeful feelings which they generate in the minds of the paupers themselves, and they are also pernicious in exciting sympathy in behalf of the indolent and vicious, and in the obstacles which they create to the use of legitimate labour and salutary discipline. We believe that they ought to be carefully prevented. The association of the utility of labour to both parties, the employer as well as the employed, is one which we consider it most important to preserve and strengthen; and we deem everything mischievous which unnecessarily gives to it a repulsive aspect. At the same time we believe that in extended districts the requisite sources of employment will be easily found. The supply of the articles consumed in workhouses and prisons would afford a large outlet for the manufactures carried on in the house; and, with respect to out-door employment, it is probable that there are few districts to which such evidence as that contained in the following extracts would not be applicable. Mr William Winkworth, overseer of the parish of St Mary's, Reading, whilst advocating the necessity of the incorporation of the parishes in that town, states –

The town, for example, wants draining. We have brickmakers and carpenters, and other labourers on the parish receiving relief; and the whole town might be well drained by the labour of these paupers at the expense of materials only; bricks, wood, mortar, and sand. This, however, is a work which the parishes cannot or will not undertake separately; it is prevented by petty jealousies and dissensions, and the want of able officers to direct the work of the paupers. The owners of premises well situated and well drained, say, 'Drainage is a benefit to the owners of the property, and we do not see why we should be called upon to contribute money for their benefit.' The owners of the houses where the drainage is most wanted, say, 'We can get no rents to pay for the work, and the nuisances which are caused by the want of it must therefore continue.' No account is taken of the necessity of finding work of any sort for the able-bodied paupers; nothing can be done with the separate parishes governed by open vestries, no cordial co-operation can be got, and the benefit of considerable labour is lost. As the surveyor of the road from this town to Basingstoke, and also of the road from hence to Shillingford, I can state, from my observation of the several parishes (nineteen in number) through which these roads pass, that very considerable labour might be found, under good direction, in improving their private roads. This is an instance of the sort of work which might frequently be found for paupers. In some of the parishes the roads are kept in very good order, but this is mere accident; whilst in the immediately adjoining parishes more money will be expended, and the roads will nevertheless be in so bad a state that the parish is indictable for them. The farmers steadily adhere to their old practices and never willingly conform to any improvements; they employ waggons where carts would serve much better; they throw down on the roads materials totally inapplicable, and think they can mend them with big loose stones, which stones would really be useful if they were broken up.

The Rev. James Randall, rector of Binfield, Berks., states —

In this parish I think the poor might be beneficially employed in making roads; the parish having been lately inclosed, many cottages and many fields are only approachable by drift ways, which are mere green lanes, almost impassable in winter, the soil being a stiff clay. The inhabitants of these houses are consequently cut off from the village, and remain in a very uncivilized state. It would be a public benefit to turn these lanes into good roads; but the vestry will never agree to such a measure, unless under legislative compulsion, because it would require an immediate outlay from which temporary occupiers would derive no advantage, and also because the chief benefit, after all, would be to the cottagers, not to the large rate-payers.

Mr Villiers states that an opinion was expressed to him —

by many different persons, that from the present state of the communication in many parts of the county of Worcester, that if the roads were placed under any general system of superintendence and properly attended to, assuming that the same number of paupers as at present should remain dependent upon their parishes, that employment for the five next years at least might be found for them, and with the greatest advantage to the county, a fact which is worth considering if an immediate change in the system of maintaining the poor is contemplated.

WE FURTHER RECOMMEND, THEREFORE, THAT THE CENTRAL BOARD BE EMPOWERED TO INCORPORATE PARISHES FOR THE PURPOSE OF APPOINTING AND PAYING PERMANENT OFFICERS, AND FOR THE EXECUTION OF WORKS OF PUBLIC LABOUR.

We must not, however, conceal our fear that the appointment of efficient permanent officers will be difficult.

Those only who have a full knowledge of the peculiar nature of the duties to be performed would be qualified to judge of the fitness of the agents to perform them; a knowledge which, as it does not influence the daily practice, can scarcely be presumed to exist in the districts where abusive systems prevail. In the dispauperized parishes the appointment of fitting officers was found to be attended with great difficulty, and was rarely accomplished without opposition. The person appointed as the permanent overseer and master of the workhouse at Hatfield had been a drill-serjeant and paymaster-serjeant in the Coldstream Guards. One of the witnesses states –

that the parish was entirely indebted for the change to the talents and personal energy applied to the work by the Marquis of Salisbury, and to the peculiar personal qualifications of the person appointed by him to serve the office of permanent overseer. This appointment would never have been made had the matter been left in the hands of the rate-payers at large. Many of them openly said that a stranger ought not to be brought into the parish; that they ought to appoint a person from amongst themselves, some poor person, who wanted a comfortable home; when the duties of the office required a person of peculiar firmness and habits of command, and were such as ninety-nine out of a hundred in the parish would have been unable to execute.

The success of this appointment occasioned similar appointments to be made in some adjacent parishes where the larger proprietors attempted to amend the administration. The Hon. and Rev. Robert Eden states that in Hertingfordbury,

A permanent overseer was appointed who was also to collect the rates in the adjoining parishes of Bayford and Little Berkhampstead, and to keep the accounts and superintend the men employed at parish work. He had been a pay-serjeant in the Guards; his appointment was opposed chiefly on the ground of his being a stranger.

The Rev. Ralph Clutton, curate of Welwyn, states –

A permanent overseer has been appointed who is also the governor of the poor-house; he was serjeant in the Coldstream Guards, a married man, and not a parishioner. It is to the efficiency of himself and his wife that the success of the undertaking thus far must in a great measure be attributed. His chief qualifications are firmness, order, clearness and accuracy in his accounts, unconquerable resolution and integrity; and on the part of his wife, extraordinary cleanliness, and a sincere desire to better the condition of those (especially the young) under her care.

The wife herself stated that the selection of her husband had excited great displeasure, because it was considered that none but a parishioner ought to have been appointed. In Waltham, where some improvements were carried into effect,

A permanent overseer has been appointed who is also governor of the workhouse, but is not a parishioner: having been in the army, his qualifications for the discipline and management of the workhouse, by the aid of that order, regularity, and system in which he had been there initiated, together with a perfect ability as to the arrangement and keeping of the accounts, are his merits. Dissatisfaction was manifested to this appointment: the principal objections were his being a stranger, and not a parishioner.

The statement of Mr Richard Gregory, of Spitalfields, is characteristic of the circumstances under which the permanent officers are frequently appointed in the town parishes:

Might not paid and responsible officers be elected by the parishioners? – He answers, No; I think you would never get such offices well filled, unless it was by accident. The people have no conception of what sort of men are requisite to perform properly the duties of a parish officer. If such a situation were vacant, what sort of a man would apply for it? Why, some decayed tradesman; some man who had got a very large family, and had been 'unfortunate in business', which, in ninety-nine cases out of a hundred, means a man who has not had prudence or capacity to manage his own affairs; and this circumstance is usually successful in any canvass for a parish situation to manage the affairs of the public. Men who have before been in office for the parish would obtain a preference. And what sort of men are those who would be likely to be at liberty to accept a vacant situation? The situations of overseer and churchwarden are by some considered situations of dignity, and dignity always attracts fools. I have known numbers of small tradesmen who were attracted by 'the dignity of the office', and succeeded in getting made overseers and churchwardens. Their elevation was their downfall. They have not given their minds to their own business as before. The consequence of this was that they have lost their business and have been ruined. Now and then a good man of business will be desirous of taking office when he thinks he is slighted, or has had an affront put upon him by being overlooked; but in general, any man in decent business must know, if he has the brains of a goose, that it will be much better for him, in a pecuniary point of view, to pay the fine than serve. I could name from fifteen to twenty people in our parish who have been entirely ruined by being made churchwardens. These would be the people who would succeed best in parochial or district elections; for the people would say of any one of them, 'Poor man, he has ruined himself by serving a parish office, and the only recompense we can give him is to put him in a paid office.' This always has been the general course of parish elections, and I have no doubt would always continue to be so. There is infinitely more favouritism in parish appointments than in government appointments. In appointments by the government there is frequently some notion of fitness; but in the case of parish appointments, fitness is out of the question. When I was the treasurer of the watch department of the parish, I took great interest in the management of the police of the district, and determined to make it efficient. You would conceive that the inhabitants would have been so guided by their own apparent interests, as to get active men appointed, but I had solicitations from some of the first and most respectable houses in the parish to take their old and decayed servants and put them on the watch. I had also applications from the parish officers to put men up on the watch who were in the workhouse. As I was determined to make the police efficient, I resolutely resisted all these applications.

It is also clear that such officers should be selected as would not be biassed by local interests or partialities. The most fitting persons must often, as in the instances we have cited, be sought for in distant districts and, *caeteris paribus*, would be preferable to persons within the same districts.

These premises appear to lead to a conclusion that the Central Board ought to be empowered to appoint the permanent and salaried officers in all parishes, or at least in those which they should incorporate. But we do not venture such a recommendation. In the first place, because we doubt the power of a single Board to select a sufficient number of well-qualified persons; secondly, because such a duty would occupy too much of their time and attention; and, thirdly, because the patronage, though really a painful incumbrance to them, would be a source of public jealousy. But believing that, after all, more will depend, as more always has depended, on the administration of the law than on the words of its enactments, and that the good or bad administration will mainly rest on the selection of the inferior administrators, we think that no security for good appointments should be neglected, and no means of preventing the effects of bad appointments omitted. We think that the first object might be aided if the Commissioners were directed to prescribe some general qualifications, in the absence of which no person should be eligible as a salaried officer, and we think that the number of competent persons who must in time come under their observation would enable them frequently to assist parishes and incorporations by recommending proper candidates; we also think that they might to a great degree both aid and support the well-disposed and prevent the continuance in office of improper persons if they were invested with the power of removing them. Some of the ablest of the permanent officers who have been examined under the authority of this Commission have urged that they ought to be immediately responsible to the authority whose regulations they are to enforce; that it ought to be obvious that they really have no discretion, that the rule of duty is inflexible, and that if they violate or neglect it, suspension or dismissal must be the consequence. If the permanent officers continue responsible only to the annual officers or to the vestry, a screen will be interposed between the Central Board and the actual administrators of relief which will encourage and protect every form of malversation.

WE RECOMMEND, THEREFORE, THAT THE CENTRAL BOARD BE DIRECTED TO STATE THE GENERAL QUALIFICATIONS WHICH SHALL BE NECESSARY TO CANDIDATES FOR PAID OFFICES CONNECTED WITH THE RELIEF OF THE POOR, TO RECOMMEND TO PARISHES AND INCORPORATIONS PROPER PERSONS TO ACT AS PAID OFFICERS, AND TO REMOVE ANY PAID OFFICERS WHOM THEY SHALL THINK UNFIT FOR THEIR SITUATIONS.

The alteration of some portions of the existing law with respect to contracts for the supply of food and other necessaries to the workhouses will be requisite to protect the public from continued jobbing, fraud and mismanagement. The extensive prevalence of these evils is indicated not only by the direct testimony contained in our Appendix, but by the recurrence in the answers to our circulated query as to the propriety of giving relief in kind, of apprehensions of peculation. Such an alteration is necessary also in order to facilitate a change, which in many districts will be more strenuously opposed by the few who will lose, than supported by the many who will gain by more rigid management. Private interest, often apparently inconsiderable, has always created the strongest and the most successful opposition to improvement. The Hon. and Rev. Robert Eden states —

In the year 1827 I endeavoured to unite, under Sturges Bourne's Act, the parishes of Hertingfordbury, Essendon, Little Berkhampstead and Bayford. Could I have succeeded, we should have built a central workhouse and have had under superintendence a population of 2,000 persons, and been able to pay a really efficient officer. My plan failed, partly from the lukewarmness of the landowners, from the unwillingness of the occupiers (being tenants at will) to contribute to the formation of a new building, and from the opposition of the tradesmen of the various parishes, who were employed occasionally in the old repairs of the old workhouses, but had no chance of getting the tender for building the new.

In Cookham and other parishes, as soon as the general benefits of improved management had become apparent, a renewed opposition was organized by publicans and beer-shop keepers, who found that they were losers by the frugality created among their customers. In many instances, the profusion which prevails in the workhouse management has been directly traced to the tradesmen who took the most active part in the parochial business.

Mr Richmond, one of the guardians of the poor in St Luke's parish, Middlesex, states —

When I came into office it was a recognized principle that the purchase of commodities for parochial consumption should be confined to the tradesmen of the parish. The effects of the patronage incident to the purchase of goods to the amount of upwards of £20,000 per annum from shopkeepers within the parish, patronage exercised by a board who are themselves shopkeepers or connected with shopkeepers, may well be conceived. For several years I have contended, but unsuccessfully, for the universal application of the principle that contracts should be taken from those who made the lowest tenders, wherever they resided, provided they gave the requisite securities for the due performance of the contract. On investigating the purchases of goods within the parish, I found that some of the charges were upwards of forty per cent above the market prices. Whatever opposition may be made against an extensive or efficient reform or generalization of the management of the funds for the relief of the poor will be based on the retention of the parochial patronage and power, although such a motive will never be ostensibly avowed. I have no doubt they will even assume that extended management will be more profuse than their own.

What may be expected is also indicated in the following extract from the evidence collected by Mr Codd:

Before we had a select vestry, it was not unusual for our overseers to be quite willing to take the office, and even to continue in it for more than one year; and it was well understood that this was because they had the means of spending money on behalf of the parish with their neighbours, or with whom they pleased. Since the establishment of the select vestry, however, we purchase everything by open contracts, and the consequence has been that our rates are 25 per cent at least below what they were prior to the formation of the select vestry. Our tradesmen now cry out against being exclusively called upon to serve as overseers, and they have said that they will insist upon having the gentry included with themselves.

WE RECOMMEND THAT THE CENTRAL BOARD BE EMPOWERED TO DIRECT THE PAROCHIAL CONSUMPTION TO BE SUPPLIED BY TENDER AND CONTRACT, AND TO PROVIDE THAT THE COMPETITION BE PERFECTLY FREE.

This will prevent much indirect fraud. Direct embezzlement must also be guarded against more effectually than while left to voluntary prosecution. It is vain to expect men to proceed, on public grounds, against their own neighbours, friends, or connections. It is to local influence, not to the absence of peculation, that we ascribe the rarity of prosecutions against parochial defaulters; and the prosecutions which do take place are often attributed, truly or falsely, to private motives and public sympathy becomes enlisted in favour of the criminal.

WE RECOMMEND THAT THE CENTRAL BOARD BE EMPOWERED AND REQUIRED TO ACT IN SUCH CASES AS PUBLIC PROSECUTORS.

The pecuniary loss by bad management, or the pecuniary gain from good management, are of course insignificant when weighed against the moral evils of the existing system. It will be necessary, however, to guard sedulously against pecuniary mismanagement, as it is usually a primary cause of the extension of pauperism, and we trust that it will be found that the measures which we have proposed, though recommended by us chiefly as beneficial to the labouring classes, will also be found the means of pecuniary saving.

Not one instance has been met with where a permanent increase of expenditure has followed any moderately well-directed efforts to repress abusive modes of administration. Where select vestries have been established and a strict management has been introduced, even under the existing law, the expenses have been reduced by an amount seldom less than one third. In the dispauperized parishes, the real reduction has seldom been less than half the expense. In Durham and Cumberland, paupers are kept well and contented at a weekly expense of 1s. 6d. per head for food. In most of the southern counties the expense varies from 3s. 6d. to 4s. 6d., 5s., and 6s. per head. The average is probably not less than 4s. per head; the expense may in all probability be reduced to 2s. per head, the common expenditure of a labourer's family, and the legitimate objects of relief be much better provided for. The whole evidence proves that if a Central Board be appointed, consisting of fit persons and armed with powers to carry into general effect the measures which have been so successful wherever they have been tried, the expenditure for the relief of the poor will in a very short period be reduced by more than one third.

*

From the metropolis, from the provincial towns, and indeed from nearly every district, complaints have been received that large classes of persons who obtain during particular seasons such wages as would enable them to maintain themselves and their families until the return of the season of work and provide by insurance against sickness and other casualties, spend the whole of their earnings as fast as they receive them, and when out of work throw themselves and their families on the parish, and remain chargeable until the period of high wages returns. The alternations of dissipation and of privation to which such persons have become habituated render it probable that even under an improved system of administration, many of them would endure the most rigid workhouse discipline during the winter, to gain freedom from self-restraint during the spring, summer, and autumn.

The following extracts from the evidence describe the nature of the evil, and suggest the remedy.

Mr John Coste, relieving overseer of St. Leonard, Shoreditch:

We have frequently amongst our paupers mechanics who obtain very high wages during particular periods, and when work fails, immediately come upon the parish. These men are, generally speaking, the greatest drunkards. I formerly carried on the business of a willow-square maker, and have paid as much as £4 or £5 a week to particular men for months together. I do not believe that one of these men ever saved a pound; several of them are now in the workhouse, and receiving relief, who might have provided for themselves by means of savings' banks until they got some other description of profitable labour. The sawyers are another set of men of the same description. It would be of great advantage to parishes if relief were given to all these classes in the way of loan, and power were conferred to attach a portion of their wages for repayment.

Mr Teather, an assistant overseer of Lambeth, when examined as to the condition of some of the paupers, stated –

We have had many bootmakers and shoemakers who might have saved enough money when in work to keep them from the parish when they are out of work. Amongst the barbers there are several who have been master barbers, who might have saved enough money to keep them from the parish; one man I know could not have got less than £3 or £4 a week; he boasted that he made 30s. on a Sunday. Amongst the tailors are many who might save money. Some of them on the parish are very good workmen who could earn about 6s. a day, and when they chose to work over-work, about 7s. One of them now on the parish, a man named M'Innis, is said by persons in the trade to be one of the best workmen in London. He is now just out of the tread-mill for neglecting his family. The greater part of sawyers could save enough to keep them from the parish during the intervals of work. The greater part of them, that is, all the able men, before the saw-mills came up could have put by at least £1. Before the saw-mills were established a pair of sawyers have, during the whole year, earned £5 a week; they have acknowledged to me, in blaming their own improvidence, that there have been times when they have earned as much as

£10 a week; they have acknowledged also that when they have been earning money they have never taken their families more than £1 a week regularly; they have paid rent and bought coals besides; but they have themselves lived at the public-house with the rest of their money. Barge-builders are men who could save money; they have 6s. a day standing wages. The coal-porters earn a great deal; they have been known to get as much as 9s. or 10s a day, but they are very rarely known to save anything.

Mr Robert Oldershaw, vestry clerk of Islington:

Amongst the able-bodied labourers are many brick-makers, men who during seven or eight months in the year work hard and obtain very high wages. They sometimes earn £6, £8, or £10 a week per gang. Some of these gangs are children. The adults will, I have been informed, earn from £2 to £3, £4, or £5 a week. The head of the gang, I am informed, often earns as much as £5 per week. They drink much beer, and perhaps their labour requires it; but they might out of the wages wholly or in part make provision for the winter if they were so inclined; but they spend all; they make no provision whatever for the winter, and when the weather sets in they throw themselves upon the parish as a customary thing. We have tried to make savings' banks available against this course of improvidence, but without effect. Formerly, however, their wives have made small deposits in the savings' banks to provide for their confinement, or the payment of their rent in the winter, unknown to their husbands. If their husbands knew they had the money, they would beat them to force it from them, and would then spend it improvidently. I was a member of the savings' bank, and have seen the poor women bring their little pittances there. They have besought me to keep it secret from their husbands.

Mr Money, builder and master brick-maker, Shaw-cum-Donnington, Berkshire, was asked with respect to the men in his own employment, of the class adverted to by the last witness –

What do you think would be the effect of an enactment enabling the parish to order the employers of men of this class to receive a portion of their wages to repay the parochial expenditure of the winter? – This would be of great advantage, and I believe would be entirely practicable.

You would perhaps say that if the deduction were too great, he would abscond? – There is certainly that danger.

What deduction do you think might be made from a brick-maker's wages without material danger of his absconding? — I think in the instance of any labourer in my employment a deduction might be made, from Lady-day to Michaelmas, of about 5s. a week.

I should recommend that no relief whatever be *given* to able-bodied single men or women, but let the officers have authority to advance small sums of money by way of loan, upon receiving some acknowledgement or security for the repayment of the same. With regard to applicants for relief who may have families, or where there is sickness, the local board should have discretionary power either to relieve them under the same conditions, or otherwise, according to the circumstances of the case and when the parties get into work, the overseer should have the same power of recovering the sum advanced from their employers, either by instalments or otherwise, as they now have of claiming seamen's wages in the merchants' service, or the pension for past services in the navy or army, for money advanced either to the parties themselves or to their families. There is a provision already made to authorize overseers to advance small sums of money in this way; but there is no power to enable the overseers to enforce a repayment of the money so advanced from the employers.

Mr Hollands, sometime vestry clerk of Bermondsey, examined.

When in office I found that the provisions of the 59 Geo. III, c. 12, enabling parish officers to stop the wages of merchant seamen and to receive those of men in the king's service, were provisions of the greatest utility. They were satisfactory to the well-disposed poor, and the parishes were greatly benefited. I have had deserted wives express the highest gratitude for wages saved from vagabond and unprincipled husbands. I have no doubt that these provisions might be profitably extended to all classes of workmen. Parish officers would not make the deduction from wages too heavy.

In the returns of the occupations of the depositors of the savings' banks, we have found a number of mechanics of each of the large classes, whose unworthy members we see in the condition of paupers. These habits detract extensively from the support of savings' banks and friendly societies, so meritoriously sustained by a large proportion of the working classes. Eleemosynary aid, even in cases of sickness, to those who, from their condition, will probably have wherewithal to repay it, is a bounty on improvidence. Statements to the following effect have been made to us from various quarters:

'We are of opinion', say the trustees of the Marylebone Savings' Banks,

that if the facilities given to the able-bodied of obtaining parochial relief or public charity (and we are induced to lay much stress upon the latter) were removed, the number of members of such institutions as ours would be increased.

We are unable to state in what proportion the increase would take place; but we think that wherever any considerable number of a class of labourers and others are found to be depositors in banks for savings, almost all such persons might follow their example, and probably would do so, were they not encouraged in their thoughtless and improvident habits by the expectation of obtaining relief from some established public charity in almost every circumstance of difficulty or distress to which they can be exposed.

The Rev. William Otter, vicar of Kinlet, Salop. states –

When I first came to this living, the landlord and myself persuaded the farmers to join in the establishment of an institution which was intended to combine the advantages of a sick club and a savings' bank. In the former capacity, after doing some good, it has gradually declined, because it was found difficult to make the members contribute steadily and regularly; and there seemed, besides, to be a notion prevalent that in case of sickness the parish doctor might always be had recourse to for nothing.

On this subject, as well as the general question of the Poor Laws, we have had ample evidence tendered by some of the most respectable of the workpeople themselves. Launcelot Snowdon, the witness whose evidence we have before cited, was asked –

Do you find any effect produced by men obtaining parochial relief readily when they are out of work or have anything the matter with them? – I have always seen that men who have had parish relief have been very careless of work and of their money ever afterwards. It has also acted very mischievously on the benefit societies, as these men would never contribute to them. We had a large and very good society of our own which failed some time ago, and I have known the societies of other trades fail: and it has been a common complaint amongst us that but for the parish, they would have stood firm. I am myself confident that but for the parish, they would have stood firm.

Do you think that rendering a workman's wages attachable, when in work, as repayment for any relief which he may have had from the parish, would be serviceable as a remedy for the evil you have mentioned? – Yes, I think it would be highly useful in every point of view. I have no great hopes of the old ones who have had parish relief, but I have no doubt that it would make many of the young ones subscribe, and keep themselves from the parish.

Do you think the body of operatives with whom you are acquainted would agree with you in this view? – Of course those who have been paupers would not agree; but all the respectable workmen would decidedly agree. I think that in instances of real misfortune, which I have known occur, it would be thought better of if the relief was given as a loan and not as a charity. But the workmen would generally object to any compulsory payment to guard against future liabilities.

Do you think the process of collecting this sort of repayment would be difficult? – I think not.

A large proportion of those who become in any way chargeable to the parish are incapable of self-control or of altering their habits and making any reservation of money when once it is in their possession, although they acknowledge their obligations and are satisfied to perform them.

It appears that from the Chelsea pensioners there are about 3,500 quarterly assignments, or 14,000 annual assignments, of pensions to parish officers, and 1,480 pensions annually claimed by virtue of magistrates' orders, in cases in which pensioners have allowed their wives or families to become chargeable to the parish; and that from the Greenwich out-pensioners 1,200 pensions, amounting to £12,530, were attached and recovered last year. The parish officers examined upon this subject agree that but for the provisions of the act, the whole amount of these pensions would be lost to the parish, and would be injuriously wasted by the pensioners, from their incapacity to take care of large sums of money.

Any collection from the labourer himself must be weekly, and the labour of collecting these small instalments would often prevent its being undertaken; but if wages were attached in the hands of the master, the payments might be at longer intervals or in liquidation at once of the whole demand.

Tradesmen declare that they should feel it no grievance to be compelled to make reservations of wages to satisfy such demands, and that whatever money was recovered, would be recovered from the ginshop. The more important object of the measure is the reimposing motives to frugality on those who possess the means of being frugal; on this account we consider that it would be deserving of adoption, though the greater number of labourers defeated the claims upon them by absconding. By a tolerably vigilant administration of the proposed law, however, much money might be recovered from them. A large proportion of the labour of the classes in question is of a nature not to be found everywhere. A tailor may run away, but a brickmaker can only get work in the brick-fields, where he may be found. During the period when the labourer is in the receipt of full wages, if he spend them he will have in prospect the necessity of absconding in search of work at the commencement of another season; and if subjection during the interval to strict workhouse regulation be comprehended in the view, there can be little doubt that he will often be impelled to have recourse to the savings' banks to avoid the inconvenience.

It appears, then, that if power were given to parish officers of attaching wages, or of ordering the reservation of such instalments as they deemed expedient for the liquidation of debts due to the parish, a proportion of those debts would be recovered.

We are further of opinion that such a measure might be made still more useful if the principle on which the 29th, 30th, 31st, and 32nd clauses of the 59 Geo. III, cap. 12 [1818], are founded were acted on more extensively. The 29th clause enables the officer to whom it appears that the applicant for relief might, but for his extravagance, neglect, or wilful misconduct, have been able to maintain himself or to support his family, to advance money to him weekly or otherwise by way of loan. It appears from our evidence that in some places this clause has been acted upon beneficially, but that in general little use is made of it, partly because a person who has not been guilty of extravagance, neglect, or wilful misconduct, is excluded from its operation, and partly because the existence of the clause is not notorious. It appears to us advisable that under regulations to be framed by the Central Board parishes should be empowered to treat any relief afforded to the able-bodied or to their families, and any expenditure in the workhouse, or otherwise incurred on their account, as a loan, and recoverable, not only in the mode pointed out by the clause to which we have referred, but also by attachment of their wages, in a way resembling that in which the 30th, 31st, and 32nd clauses of the same act direct the attachment of pensions and seamen's wages.

WE THEREFORE RECOMMEND, THAT UNDER REGULATIONS TO BE FRAMED BY THE CENTRAL BOARD, PARISHES BE EMPOWERED TO TREAT ANY RELIEF AFFORDED TO THE ABLE-BODIED, OR TO THEIR FAMILIES, AND ANY EXPENDITURE IN THE WORKHOUSES, OR OTHERWISE INCURRED ON THEIR ACCOUNT, AS A LOAN, AND RECOVERABLE NOT ONLY BY THE MEANS GIVEN BY THE 29TH SECTION OF THE 59 GEO. III, C. 12, BUT ALSO BY ATTACHMENT OF THEIR SUBSEQUENT WAGES, IN A MODE RESEMBLING THAT POINTED OUT IN THE 30TH, 31ST, AND 32ND SECTIONS OF THAT ACT.

In our recommendation of the prohibition of partial relief to the families of the able-bodied, we proposed that relief by apprenticing should, to a certain extent, be excepted from that prohibition. In the instructions given by us to our Assistant Commissioners, we directed them to ascertain 'the practice in the different parishes as to the apprenticing of poor children, inquiring to what class of persons they are apprenticed, and whether such persons take them voluntarily or by compulsion, and if the latter, according to what principle they are distributed; whether any and what care is taken to see that they are well treated and taught; and whether there are any grounds for supposing that a power to bind for less than seven years would be expedient'.

But we regret to say that we have received less information on this subject than on any other. The most important is that collected by Captain Chapman and Mr Villiers, but even that is contradictory; and if it were consistent, too meagre to afford grounds for legislation. It is a mode of relief expressly pointed out by the 43 Elizabeth [1601], and so much interwoven with the habits of the people in many districts that we should hesitate, even if its evils were much more clearly ascertained, and even if we believed that those evils will not be much diminished by the alteration which we shall propose respecting settlement, to recommend its abolition until it has been made the subject of further inquiry, and until the effects of the measures now likely to be introduced have been ascertained by experience.

At the same time we think it probable, perhaps we might say certain, that further inquiry will show that the laws respecting the relief to be afforded by means of apprenticeship are capable of improvement, particularly those portions of them which render the reception of a parish apprentice compulsory.

WE RECOMMEND, THEREFORE, THAT THE CENTRAL BOARD BE EMPOWERED TO MAKE SUCH REGULATIONS AS THEY SHALL THINK FIT RESPECTING THE RELIEF TO BE AFFORDED BY APPRENTICING CHILDREN, AND THAT AT A FUTURE PERIOD, WHEN THE EFFECT OF THE PROPOSED ALTERATIONS SHALL HAVE BEEN SEEN, THE CENTRAL BOARD BE REQUIRED TO MAKE A SPECIAL INQUIRY INTO THE OPERATION OF THE LAWS RESPECTING THE APPREN- TICING CHILDREN AT THE EXPENSE OF PARISHES, AND INTO THE OPERATION OF THE REGULATIONS IN THAT RESPECT WHICH THE BOARD SHALL HAVE ENFORCED.

On the subject of vagrancy, a large mass of evidence is contained in the Appendix, particularly in the reports of Mr Bishop, Mr Codd, Captain Chapman, and Mr Henderson. It appears from this evidence that vagrancy has actually been converted into a trade, and not an unprofitable one; and it also appears that the severe and increasing burden arises from the vagrants by trade, not from those on account of destitution. We state in proof of this, and the state-ment is more valuable as it points out the remedy as well as the cause of the evil, that in those few districts in which the relief has been such as only the really destitute will accept, the resort of vagrants has ceased, or been so much diminished as to become only a trifling inconvenience. But it appears vain to expect the remedy from detailed statutory provisions. The tendency of legislation respecting the poor to aggravate the evils which it was intended to cure, a tendency which we have so often remarked, is strikingly exemplified in that portion of it which respects vagrancy. The early statutes attempted to repress it by severity. 'This part of our history', says Dr Burn, 'looks like the history of the savages in America. Almost all severities have been exercised against vagrants except scalping; and as one severity fell short, it seemed naturally to follow that a greater was necessary.' But such was their effect that every successive preamble admits the inefficiency of the former law down to the 1 and 2 Geo. IV, c. 64 [1821], which recites 'that the provisions theretofore made, and then in force, relative to the apprehending and passing of vagrants, were productive of great expense, and that great frauds and abuses were committed in the execution thereof'; and to the 5 Geo. IV [1824], c. 83, which declares that it is expedient to make further provision for the suppression of vagrancy. Nor has the last-mentioned act been more successful than those which preceded it. As one among many instances in which its provisions have been perverted, we will mention the effect of the 15th clause, which allows the visiting justices of prisons to grant a certificate or other instrument enabling any person discharged from prison to receive relief on his route to his place of settlement. The intention of the clause was to enable prisoners, after having undergone their punishment or trial, to go *from* prison to their own homes without temptation to further crime. The effect has been 'for the benefit of the pass' to convey *into* prisons paupers, and families of paupers, as if the legislature intended that they and their children should have all the terrors of a prison obliterated from their minds, and receive instruction in the worst schools of vice; as if provision ought to be made to increase the stock of juvenile delinquents, already more numerous in England than in any other European country. By what foresight could the benevolent author of this clause have guarded against such an administration of the enactment as that of which one of the witnesses, a gaoler, thus describes?

It is a melancholy thing that poor people are sent into prison as vagrants that they may be passed home. There is now a mother, a widow with five children, under my care; the boys are from five to fifteen years of age. The mother was committed, not for any crime, but having been found sitting in the open air. Now what, I beg to ask, can be the effect of sending these children with their mother to a gaol? What can they not learn? In general, vagrants are told that they are sent to prison, not for their punishment, but for their benefit. Prisons should not, in any case, as I humbly conceive, be held out as places where people are to be *benefited*. They are now looked upon as a places of *relief*, and the large class of vagrants are told that they are sent to prison avowedly for their advantage.

'When the law', says another witness,

was made restricting pauper passes to Scotch and Irish, very few for a time came to Westmoreland or Cumberland; but the vagrants soon found that they might easily resume their trade by swearing they belonged to those countries; and the expense became as large as ever. When this again was checked by making the contract for a fixed sum annually to convey all paupers with passes by cart through the country, the number of vagrants calling themselves discharged prisoners (and therefore not subject to these regulations) began to increase, and has continued to do so progressively.

Feeling convinced that vagrancy will cease to be a burthen if the relief given to vagrants is such as only the really destitute will accept; feeling convinced that this cannot be effected unless the system is general; and also convinced that no exactments to be executed by parochial officers will in all parishes be rigidly adhered to, unless under the influence of strict superintendence and control –

WE RECOMMEND THAT THE CENTRAL BOARD BE EM-POWERED AND DIRECTED TO FRAME AND ENFORCE REGULA-TIONS AS TO THE RELIEF TO BE AFFORDED TO VAGRANTS AND DISCHARGED PRISONERS.

*

We have now given a brief outline of the functions for the due performance of which we deem a new agency, or Central Board of Control, to be requisite; and we have inserted none which the evidence would warrant us in believing attainable by any existing agency. The length of this Report precludes the statement in further detail of the powers and duties of the proposed board. The extent of those powers and duties must be measured by the extent and inveteracy of the existing evils, and by the failure, or worse than failure, of the measures by which their removal has been attempted. If for that purpose the powers which we have recommended are necessary, to withhold those powers is to decree the continuance of the evil. The powers with which we recommend that they should be invested are in fact the powers now exercised by 15,000 sets of annual officers. By far the majority of those officers are ignorant of their duties, influenced by their affections, interests and fears, and restrained by scarcely any real responsibility. The Commissioners would act upon the widest information, under the direct control of the Legislature and the supervision of the public, and under no liability to pecuniary or private bias, partiality or intimidation. They would have the immediate advantage of having well-defined objects assigned to them, powerful means at their disposal, and clear rules for their guidance; and they would soon have the aid of varied and extensive experience; and it appears to us that the best means of preventing their negligent or improper use of the discretion with which it appears to be necessary to invest them will be, not to restrict that discretion, but to render their interest coincident with their duty and to let them be removable at Your Majesty's pleasure.

We entertain, however, no hope that the complicated evils with which we have to contend will all be eradicated by the measures which we now propose. The mischiefs which have arisen during a legislation of more than 300 years must require the legislation of more than one Session for their correction. In order to secure the progressive improvement from which alone we hope for an ultimate cure; and in order to bring the proceedings of the Commissioners more constantly and completely within the superintendence of the executive and the legislature, we propose that the Commissioners should be charged with the duty, similar to that which we now endeavour to perform, of periodically reporting their proceedings and suggesting any further legislation which may appear to them to be desirable.

WE RECOMMEND, THEREFORE, THAT THE BOARD BE REQUIRED TO SUBMIT A REPORT ANNUALLY, TO ONE OF YOUR MAJESTY'S PRINCIPAL SECRETARIES OF STATE, CONTAINING – 1. AN ACCOUNT OF THEIR PROCEEDINGS; 2. ANY FURTHER AMENDMENTS WHICH THEY MAY THINK IT ADVISABLE TO SUGGEST; 3. THE EVIDENCE ON WHICH THE SUGGESTIONS ARE FOUNDED; 4. BILLS CARRYING THOSE AMENDMENTS (IF ANY) INTO EFFECT, WHICH BILLS

THE BOARD SHALL BE EMPOWERED TO PREPARE WITH PROFESSIONAL ASSISTANCE.

We consider that three Commissioners might transact the business of the Central Board. The number of the Commissioners should be small, as they should habitually act with promptitude, as responsibility for efficiency should not be weakened by discredit being divided amongst a larger number, and as the Board, whenever the labour pressed too severely, might avail themselves of the aid of their assistants. The Central Board would probably require eight or ten Assistant Commissioners, to examine the administration of relief in different districts, and aid the preparations for local changes. As the Central Board would be responsible for the performance of the duties imposed upon them by the legislature –

WE RECOMMEND THAT THE CENTRAL BOARD BE EMPOWERED TO APPOINT AND REMOVE THEIR ASSISTANTS AND ALL THEIR SUBORDINATE OFFICERS.

[FURTHER LEGISLATIVE AMENDMENT]

―――――――

[SETTLEMENT AND BASTARDY]

WE now proceed to two of the most difficult and most important of the questions submitted to us: the laws respecting Settlement and Bastardy.

We have seen that the liability to a change of settlement by hiring and service, apprenticeship, purchasing or renting a tenement, and estate, are productive of great inconvenience and fraud; and it does not appear that those frauds and inconveniences are compensated by any advantage whatsoever. We have seen that these heads of settlement were introduced as qualifications of an arbitrary power of removal, and then indeed they were necessary. If they had not been created the parish officers would have been empowered to confine almost every man to the place of his birth. Now that power is at an end. No man can be removed until he himself, by applying for relief, gives jurisdiction to the magistrates. The slightest evil arising from enactments, the motive for which has ceased, would be a sufficient ground for their repeal. It has been shown, however, that the evils are very great. We recommend, therefore, the immediate but prospective abolition of all these heads of settlement. For this recommendation we have the sanction of the great majority of those whose opinions we have taken. It is true that those opinions advocate most strongly the repeal of settlement by hiring and service, apprenticeship and renting a tenement, and with respect to the last, rather recommend raising the rent necessary to give a settlement from £10 a year to £20, or some larger sum, than the abrogation of the law. It appears that the witnesses are led thus to restrict their recommendations chiefly from the circumstance that these are the most common modes of settlement, and therefore those of which the evil is most apparent, and that all the grounds which exist for making a change of settlement by renting a tenement more difficult, are also grounds for making it impossible. And we believe that if these modes of settlement are destroyed, and settlement by purchase and estate are allowed to continue, we shall be holding out temptation to perjury and fraud, not only without an adequate motive on our part, if any motive could be adequate, but with no motive whatever.

WE RECOMMEND, THEREFORE, THAT SETTLEMENT BY HIRING AND SERVICE, APPRENTICESHIP, PURCHASING OR RENTING A TENEMENT, ESTATE, PAYING RATES, OR SERVING AN OFFICE, BE ABOLISHED.

There will remain parentage, birth, and marriage; with respect to parentage, however, there is this difficulty. If while the modes by which a male can lose his settlement are abolished, settlement by parentage is continued unaltered and every male child is to acquire his father's settlement, to have no means of changing it, and to transmit it, equally unchangeable, to his children and his children's children, settlement will in time be reduced to a question of pedigree, and the expense of ascertaining it become intolerable. On the other hand, if settlement by parentage is totally abolished the parents and their infant children will often be settled in different parishes.

It appears to us that the best mode of meeting these difficulties is to continue settlement by parentage during that period of a child's life during which it is dependent on its parents, and to put an end to it at the age at which that dependence has so nearly ceased as to render their separation comparatively unimportant. This age may be said, in general, to commence at fifteen or sixteen years. At fifteen or sixteen a child can generally earn his own maintenance, and if his parents cannot maintain him, it cannot be advisable that he should continue a member of their family.

WE RECOMMEND, THEREFORE, THAT (SUBJECT TO THE OBVIOUS EXCEPTIONS OF PERSONS BORN IN PRISONS, HOSPITALS, AND WORKHOUSES) THE SETTLEMENT OF EVERY LEGITIMATE CHILD BORN AFTER THE PASSING OF THE INTENDED ACT, FOLLOW THAT OF THE PARENTS OR SURVIVING PARENT OF SUCH CHILD, UNTIL SUCH CHILD

SHALL ATTAIN THE AGE OF SIXTEEN YEARS, OR THE DEATH
OF ITS SURVIVING PARENT; AND THAT AT THE AGE OF
SIXTEEN, OR ON THE DEATH OF ITS SURVIVING PARENT,
SUCH CHILD SHALL BE CONSIDERED SETTLED IN THE PLACE
IN WHICH IT WAS BORN.

It will be seen that we do not recommend the introduction of
settlement by residence. We are aware of the advantages of that
mode of settlement; it is the most natural and the most obvious,
and its adoption would often prevent inconvenience to particular
parishes, from the return in age or infirmity of those who have
left them in youth and vigour, and inconvenience to the paupers
themselves, from being removed from friends and residences to
which they have become attached, to places in which they have
become strangers.

But these advantages, great as they are, appear to us to be over-
balanced by objections still more powerful. It appears from the
evidence that the existing modes by which a settlement can be
changed are productive of perjury and fraud, and that they tend
to injure the employers of labour by restricting them in the choice
of their servants – the owners of property, by distributing the
labouring families according to rules not depending on the demand
for their services, or the fund for their support – and above all,
the labourers themselves by depriving them of the power of selling
all that they have, their labour, to the best advantage. We fear
that settlement by residence would aggravate all these evils. At
present, a labourer may be steadily employed for years in a place
in which he is not settled, by means of successive hirings, each
hiring being for less than a year. But if settlement by residence
were adopted, this would be impossible. We should have the constant occurrence of one of the worst consequences of the existing
law, the separation of master and man notwithstanding their
mutual utility, and their mutual attachment, to the injury of both,
but to the greater injury of the most numerous and the most helpless class – the labourers. Again, the demolition of cottages, and
the forcing the agricultural population into the towns and the
parishes in which property is much divided, though we fear that
they must to a certain degree arise under any law of settlement
whatever, would be much promoted by a law which would fix

on a parish every labourer who should have been allowed to reside there for any given period, unless the period were so long as to render the law almost inoperative. Another objection to settlement by residence, which has been dwelt on by many of our most intelligent witnesses, arises from its effect on the unsettled labourers. At present they are confessedly superior, both in morals and in industry, to those who are settled in the parishes in which they reside. Make that residence give a settlement, and they will fall back into the general mass. With respect to the hardship on those who may be removed, we must repeat, first, that a person who applies to be maintained out of the produce of the industry or frugality of others must accept that relief on the terms which the public good requires; and secondly, that in the small proportion of cases in which his claim is not founded on his own indolence, or improvidence, or misconduct, the duty of rescuing him from the hardship of a removal falls peculiarly within the province of private and uncompulsory charity; a virtue so deeply implanted by providence in human nature that even the existing system has rather misdirected than destroyed, or even materially diminished it.

We further recommend that instead of the present mode of first removing a pauper and then inquiring whether the removal was lawful, the inquiry should precede the removal. We find this measure in a bill brought into the House of Commons in 1819, and printed in the Parliamentary Papers of that year, Number 211. That bill empowers the justice who shall order a removal to suspend its execution, and to forward (which might be effected through the Post Office) a copy of the examination of the pauper, and of the order of removal, to the overseers of the parish in which the pauper has been adjudged to be settled. It then enables the parties who think themselves aggrieved by the order to appeal to the quarter-sessions within twenty-eight days, and the sessions to decide on the question as if the removal had actually taken place. In the absence of appeal the order is to be conclusive. The expediency of this measure is so obvious that it is difficult to account for its rejection in 1819, unless we are to believe a tradition that it was defeated by a combination of persons interested in creating litigation and expense.

It will be observed that in our exposition of the evils arising from the Law of Settlement, we have not dwelt on the expense of litigation and removals; we have passed it over slightly, not because we doubt its magnitude, but because we believe that in this as in every other branch of the evils connected with the administration of the Poor Laws, the pecuniary loss, great as it may be, is utterly unimportant when compared with the moral mischief. The collection, burthensome as it is, is far less ruinous than the expenditure. If twice the number of millions were annually thrown into the sea, we might still be a moral, industrious, and flourishing nation. But if the whole of our poor-rates could be raised without inconvenience; if they were paid to us, for instance, as a tribute by foreigners, and were still applied as they are now applied, no excellence in our laws and institutions in other respects could save us from ultimate ruin. And we must add that we think it would be rash to expect from, the alterations which we have recommended in the Law of Settlement, much diminution of expense.

Some diminution, however, we anticipate from them, particularly with respect to litigation. The simplicity of the rule which we propose will exclude all questions of law, and in all cases reduce the question to a matter of fact; and when a general registration of births shall have been established, a measure which cannot be long delayed, the proof of the fact of birth will be much easier. We anticipate, however, a much further diminution, both of litigation and removals, from the operation of our general measures. In proportion as there is an approximation to uniformity of management, the motives on the part of paupers to shift from a parish where there may be rigid management or 'a bad parish' to a parish where there is profuse management or 'a good parish' will decrease. In proportion as there is an approximation to our main object, that of rendering the condition of the able-bodied pauper less eligible on the whole than that of the independent labourer, it is proved by all experience, that the able-bodied will cease to avail themselves of any settlement whatever, whether immediate or distant.

Mr Thomas Langley, out-door inspector of the parish of Marylebone, a witness whose evidence has already been cited, was asked what effect regulations upon the principle last mentioned would have upon removals, and upon the general operation of the law of settlement. He answers –

I think the Law of Settlement would then be of very little consequence. Where a pauper has a doubtful settlement, it is now our practice to offer him labour or to take him into the workhouse, as an experiment. We even take families in, and we now, under all our disadvantages, get rid of three out of four of such cases. If we were under such regulations as would make a pauper's condition, whether in or out of the workhouse, not so good as the condition of a hardworking labourer of the lowest class, the experiment being much cheaper, we should naturally resort to it more frequently. In fact, if such regulations were established, I think we should very seldom incur the expense and trouble, or the risks, of a removal in any case.

Would the Law of Settlement remain then of any consequence in any case? – I do not know that it would; I cannot see that it would.

And in order to afford further facilities to the proof of a birth settlement –

WE RECOMMEND THAT WHENEVER THERE SHALL BE ANY QUESTION REGARDING THE SETTLEMENT BY BIRTH OF A PERSON, WHETHER LEGITIMATE OR ILLEGITIMATE, AND WHETHER BORN BEFORE OR AFTER THE PASSING OF THE INTENDED ACT, THE PLACE WHERE SUCH PERSON SHALL HAVE BEEN FIRST KNOWN BY THE EVIDENCE OF SUCH PERSON, BY THE REGISTER OF HIS OR HER BIRTH OR BAPTISM OR OTHERWISE TO HAVE EXISTED, SHALL BE PRESUMED TO HAVE BEEN THE PLACE OF HIS OR HER BIRTH, UNTIL THE CONTRARY SHALL BE PROVED.

With respect to the BASTARDY laws, the evidence shows that as a general rule they increase the expense which they were intended to compensate, and offer temptations to the crime which they were intended to punish, and that their working is frequently accompanied by perjury and extortion, disgrace to the innocent, and reward to the shameless and unprincipled, and all the domestic misery and vice which are the necessary consequence of premature and ill-assorted marriage. We advise, therefore, their entire abolition.

What we propose in their room is intended to restore things, as far as it is possible, to the state in which they would have been if no such laws had ever existed; to trust to those checks, and to those checks only, which Providence has imposed on licentiousness, under the conviction that all attempts of the Legislature to increase their force or to substitute for them artificial sanctions have tended only to weaken or pervert them.

First, with respect to the child – In the natural state of things a child, until emancipated, depends on its parents. Their legal domicile, or, as it is technically called, place of settlement, is also the settlement of their offspring. And such is the existing law with respect to legitimate children. Only one of the parents of an illegitimate child can be ascertained.

WE RECOMMEND THAT THE GENERAL RULE SHALL BE FOLLOWED, AS FAR AS IT IS POSSIBLE, AND THAT EVERY ILLEGITIMATE CHILD BORN AFTER THE PASSING OF THE ACT, SHALL, UNTIL IT ATTAIN THE AGE OF SIXTEEN, FOLLOW ITS MOTHER'S SETTLEMENT.

The immediate effect will be to prevent a great amount of waste, suffering, and demoralization. At present an unmarried pregnant female, though asking for no relief, is hunted from parish to parish, her feelings deadened by exposure, and her means of supporting herself and her child destroyed, and all this evil is incurred merely to save expense to the parish in which she is resident, at the much greater expense of the parish to which she is removed. We feel confident that if the woman were allowed to remain unmolested until she asked relief, she would, in many cases, by her own exertions and the assistance of her friends succeed in maintaining herself and her infant; but as the law now stands she has not power and inducement to do this. If she is settled in the parish in which her pregnancy took place, she has no inducement. The parish offers her a pension generally equalling, often exceeding her incumbrance, to be obtained without any additional disgrace. If she is unsettled she has no power. However willing or anxious she may be to toil for her own and her child's subsistence rather than to be dragged in shame to the scene of her youth, she is not allowed the choice. The officers know that if the child is born in their parish, they are responsible for its support throughout life, and for the support of its posterity. The consequences which her removal will produce to the child, to the mother, and to her parish, are no concern of theirs. They remove her as a matter of course.

Secondly, with respect to the mother –

AS A FURTHER STEP TOWARDS THE NATURAL STATE OF THINGS, WE RECOMMEND THAT THE MOTHER OF AN ILLE-GITIMATE CHILD BORN AFTER THE PASSING OF THE ACT, BE REQUIRED TO SUPPORT IT, AND THAT ANY RELIEF OC-CASIONED BY THE WANTS OF THE CHILD BE CONSIDERED RELIEF AFFORDED TO THE PARENT.

This is now the law with respect to a widow; and an unmarried mother has voluntarily put herself into the situation of a widow: she has voluntarily become a mother, without procuring to herself and her child the assistance of a husband and a father. There can be no reason for giving to vice privileges which we deny to misfortune.

This course, or a course as nearly resembling it as the existing law will allow, has been tried, and with uniform success. 'In Swallowfield, Berks.,' says Mr Russell,

a few years ago we adopted the practice of paying to the mother as much only of the allowance from the father as was absolutely necessary for the immediate support of the child. The effect upon the mother was precisely what we expected and desired it to be; and if we could have persevered in the practice, I have no doubt it would have been productive of very salutary consequences; but a question having arisen as to its legality, we were compelled reluctantly to abandon it. At present a bastard child, instead of being an incumbrance, is a source of profit to the mother.

In Cookham, Berks., the same plan was adopted and persevered in by Mr Whately. The result has been that in a population of 3,337 persons, but one bastard has been christened during each of the last five years. In 1822 there were twenty-six bastards; now ten years after, notwithstanding the increase of population, there are but five.

It appears from Mr Cowell's report that at Bingham, in Nottinghamshire, as soon as the parish adopted measures which prevented the mothers from recurring to the parish, bastardy, which had been previously prevalent, almost ceased. For the first three years there was not one illegitimate birth in the parish, except in the case of a woman who was an idiot, and for the last twelve there appears to have been only one woman who has had a second. The same principle has been acted on, and for a longer period, with equal success in the United States. An instructive article on the Poor Laws in the twenty-seventh number of the *American Quarterly Review*, the part of which relating to America we have inserted in Appendix F, states that –

In Boston, Baltimore, and Salem, the principle has long been acted upon that the public will not undertake to bring up illegitimate children without expense to the mother. The consequence is that in 1826, but ten cases came under the notice of the public officers at Boston, and but two at Salem; while in Baltimore the public was put to no expense whatever in regard to them. In the same year, in Philadelphia, the number of bastards under the care of the guardians of the poor was two hundred and seventy two.

Further evidence in favour of this plan is afforded by the conduct of those whom it would principally affect, the labouring classes themselves. Mr Tidd Pratt, to whose evidence we have so often referred, was asked, 'What is the course adopted by the labouring classes in their friendly societies, with regard to illegitimate children? He answered,

In female societies, which are numerous and increasing, they utterly deprive the parties of relief, and expel them. In male societies they allow no benefit on the birth of a child, unless such child is born in wedlock. In those societies which allow an annuity or other payment to a widow on the death of a member, such benefit is forfeited by her having lived apart from her husband during his lifetime, or having had an illegitimate child after his death. Their rules are usually of the tenor of the following:

'We do also agree to and with each other, that if any widow pensioner of this society, who shall be proved to be with child, or be delivered of a child, either alive or still-born, at any time after she has been a widow eleven months, that then and from thenceforth every such widow shall forfeit all her right and title to the pension of ten pounds per annum, and to be for ever debarred from every part thereof.'

'No benefit will be allowed for the birth or death of a child that is not born in wedlock.'

Then in all cases they utterly disallow relief to a woman who has a bastard child? – Yes, both male and female societies.

In those classes of society which are above the labouring classes the burthen of supporting an illegitimate child in the first instance falls of course on the mother. The labouring classes throw it upon her when they frame regulations for themselves. It appears, therefore, that the plan of exempting her has been rejected wherever there has been the power of rejecting it, and has been adopted only where one class has legislated for another.

One great advantage which will follow from giving an unmarried mother no advantage over a widow with a legitimate child will be that her parents will be forced, if it is necessary, to contribute to her support and to that of her infant. In a natural state of things they must do so, whether the child be legitimate or not; and when we consider that, in the vast majority of cases, the neglect, or ill example, and in many cases the actual furtherance of those parents has occasioned their daughter's misconduct, it appears not only just, but most useful, that they should be answerable for it.

WE RECOMMEND THAT THE SAME LIABILITY BE EXTENDED TO HER HUSBAND.

The general law of the country throws on the husband all his wife's liabilities; he is bound to pay her debts, he is answerable for her engagements, even though he may not have been aware of them, though they may have been carefully concealed from him; and there seems no reason why this peculiar liability, a liability which must almost always be notorious to him, should be expected. We certainly consider it no objection that this will make it more difficult for a woman who has misconducted herself to obtain a husband: and we must add that if this plan be not adopted, it will be difficult to follow out the system of giving no relief to the child independently of the mother, and of giving that relief in the workhouse.

ON THE OTHER HAND, WE RECOMMEND THE REPEAL OF THAT PART OF THE 35 GEO. III, c. 101, s. 6, WHICH MAKES AN UNMARRIED PREGNANT WOMAN REMOVABLE, AND THE 50 GEO. III, c. 51, s. 2, WHICH AUTHORIZES THE COMMITTAL OF THE MOTHER OF A CHARGEABLE BASTARD TO THE HOUSE OF CORRECTION.

The first of these enactments will cease to be applicable as soon as the child follows the mother's settlement. The second appears by the evidence to produce on the whole much more harm than good, and we object to them both as unnecessary interferences. If our previous recommendations are adopted, a bastard will be what Providence appears to have ordained that it should be, a a burthen on its mother, and, where she cannot maintain it, on her parents. The shame of the offence will not be destroyed by its being the means of income and marriage, and we trust that as soon as it has become both burthensome and disgraceful it will become as rare as it is among those classes in this country who are above parish relief, or as it is among all classes in Ireland. If we are right in believing the penalties inflicted by nature to be sufficient, it is needless to urge further objections to any legal punishment. We may add, however, that the effect of any such punishment would probably be mischievous, not only by imposing unnecessary suffering on the offender, but by making her an object of sympathy.

Thirdly, as to the Father – In affirming the inefficiency of human legislation to enforce the restraints placed on licentiousness by Providence, we have implied our belief that all punishment of the supposed father is useless. We believe that it is worse than useless. Without considering the numerous cases in which that punishment falls upon the innocent, without dwelling upon the perjury by which that injustice is accomplished, we will confine ourselves to the effect produced on the woman's mind by her power of calling for that punishment. That power is the security to which the woman looks at present; she expects that the parish will *right her*. If she is ill disposed, this adds to the force of her temptation; if she is well disposed, this removes the prop which should support her self-control. Marriage will always be preferred by the woman if she can attain it, and she ought not to be placed in circumstances in which marriage shall be most easily attainable by previous concession.

'One day', says a witness examined by Mr Chadwick,

I went into the house of one of the people who work at the chalk quarries at Northfleet to buy fossils, and a young woman came in for a few minutes whose appearance clearly showed approach to maternity.

When she went out, I said to the woman of the house, 'Poor girl, she has been unfortunate.' She replied, 'Indeed she has, poor girl, and a virtuous good girl she is too. The fellow has betrayed her, and gone to sea.' I said, 'She should not have trusted him till she had been at church.' To this observation the woman replied, and let me observe *her own children were all about her*, 'What could she do, poor girl? If she did not do as other girls do, she would never get a husband. Girls are often deceived, and how can they help it?'

WE RECOMMEND, THEREFORE, THAT THE SECOND SECTION OF THE 18 ELIZ., CAP. 3, AND ALL OTHER ACTS WHICH PUNISH OR CHARGE THE PUTATIVE FATHER OF A BASTARD, SHALL, AS TO ALL BASTARDS BORN AFTER THE PASSING OF THE INTENDED ACT, BE REPEALED.

Cases will no doubt occur of much hardship and cruelty, and it will often be regretted that these are not punishable, at least by fine upon the offender. But the object of law is not to punish, but to prevent: and if the existing law does not prevent, as is too clear, it must not be maintained against its proper design with a view to punishment; still less must it be maintained if it acts as an incentive. It must be remembered too that we do not propose to deprive either the woman or her parents of their direct means of redress: she may still bring her action for breach of promise of marriage, and her parents may still bring theirs for the loss of their daughter's service.

One objection, however, may be made to our plan, which deserves an answer in deference, not to its force, but to the religious and moral feelings in which it originates. It may be said that throwing on the woman the expense of maintaining the child will promote infanticide. It appears from Mr Walcott's report that infanticide, and in one of its worst forms, is promoted by the existing law; but we do not, in fact, believe that we have to choose between the two dangers: we do not believe that infanticide arises from any calculation as to expense. We believe that in no civilized country, and scarcely in any barbarous country, has such a thing ever been heard of as a mother's killing her child in order to save the expense of feeding it.

We have still to consider a subject which, though not expressly

mentioned in our Commission, appears to us within its spirit, and
that is –

EMIGRATION

BEFORE we examine the expedience of resorting to measures for
facilitating emigration, as principal or auxiliary remedies for the
evils which we have described, it is necessary to consider the
questions whether there exists in any part of England a population
which materially exceeds the actual demand for labour, and
whether such an excess is likely to exist after the measures which
we have already recommended shall have been put in force.

After a system of administration, one of the most unquestionable
effects of which is the encouragement and increase of improvident
marriages among the labouring class, has prevailed in full vigour
for nearly forty years, it is a remarkable proof of the advance of
the wealth of this part of the kingdom that a question should arise
as to the existence of a surplus population; and a mere inspection
of the comparative account of the numbers of the people, especially
in the agricultural districts, at the times of the three last enumera-
tions would seem to remove any doubt which may have arisen
on such a question. Not only has an increase of population, which
would have been heretofore deemed extraordinary in a long-settled
country, taken place in the manufacturing counties, but the increase
has been nearly as rapid in those purely agricultural districts from
which we have received general complaints of a decrease of the
capital of the farmer. In the county of Bedford, for instance, the
increase of population has been, in the ten years ending 1821, 19 per
cent; in the ten years ending 1831, 14 per cent; in Buckinghamshire,
14 and 19 per cent; in Northamptonshire, 15 per cent and 10 per
cent; in Essex, after similar rates for the same periods; and in
Cambridgeshire, 20 per cent and 18 per cent.* In the communication, so often referred to, Mr Day has given the following statement.

Our division of petty sessions comprehends the following eleven
parishes, the population of which is almost exclusively agricultural, and
the censuses of which I subjoin:

* Some allowance must be made in this case for the rapid increase of the
town of Cambridge.

PLACE	1801	1811	1821	1831
Buxted	1,063	1,292	1,509	1,642
Chiddingly ...	673	793	870	902
East Hothly ...	395	468	510	505
Framfield	969	1,074	1,437	1,468
Horsted	207	235	286	300
Isfield	334	464	569	581
Maresfield ...	960	1,117	1,439	1,650
Mayfield	1,849	2,079	2,698	2,738
Rotherfield ...	1,963	2,122	2,782	3,085
Uckfield	811	916	1,099	1,261
Waldron	752	840	965	997
TOTAL ...	9,976	11,346	14,164	15,129

Increase in 30 years	50 per cent
Ditto in last 20 years	33 —
Ditto in last 10 years	6·8 —

Note. The increase in the *whole county* (exclusive of the towns of Brighton, Chichester, Hastings and Lewes) in the last twenty years is from 161,577 to 204,707, or 26 + per cent. This population I apprehend to be purely agricultural. It gives an average increase of about 158 souls in each parish, the average present population being 752.

The accuracy of the census of 1801 has been generally disputed; assuming then the census of 1811 for the purpose of my argument, we find that there are now 133 labourers to do the same work that was then done by a hundred. I say the same work, but I should be justified in saying less; for as the profits of agriculture have declined, and the capital of the farmer deteriorated, so has the state of tillage and the general cultivation of the land. As I consider this point of the argument to be of vital importance to a just view of the subject, I beg to explain that I mean that the same physical force which effectuated a certain state of cultivation in 1811 (without reference to what was left undone) would effect the same in 1831; and if that is now done by the application of a greater number of labourers, it must be by assigning less work to the share of each.

In the answers to the questions addressed by us to individuals in agricultural districts of the middle, southern and eastern counties, we find frequent cases stated of a great excess of labourers above the means of employment in the respective parishes. And we find the statement confirmed by the fact of multitudes of able-bodied young men wasting their time on the roads and in gravel-pits at the expense of the rate-payers, who deem it cheaper to pay them for the idleness than for their labour. The excess in some districts of labourers beyond the actual demand must be taken to be established beyond dispute.

But in the case of labour, as of commodities, the extent of the demand, as compared with the supply, will depend in some degree on the quality of the article offered. The present state of the administration of the Poor Laws does not allow us to ascertain, in the great majority of parishes we have referred to, what the demand for labour would be if work were sought for with energy, and performed with diligence. It is to be observed too that although not employed, all the population in the parishes which complain of its excess is at any rate clothed and fed, and that the income which maintains an able-bodied pauper in idleness would, if not so expended, be applied directly or indirectly to the employment of labour. It does not necessarily follow, indeed, that the demand for labour which would arise from the saving of the farmer through the diminution of rates would be felt within the same parish or district within which the poor-rates are now expended, and we have therefore looked with some anxiety to the effect on the demand for labour in those parishes where a reform in the administration of the Poor Laws has been effected. We have already had to state, among the most gratifying results of this reform, that the dispauperized labourers have found employment to a greater extent than the most sanguine friend of the change could have anticipated in the parishes where they were previously relieved as paupers.

One of the parishes which we have mentioned among those in which an improved administration of the law has been introduced (Uley), was the seat of an apparently large surplus population, and of a declining manufacture. No circumstances could be conceived apparently less favourable to the absorption of surplus labour. Yet of 1,000 persons who, before the introduction of the reform, were on the parish books (out of a population of 2,641), and who are now chiefly maintained by their own exertions, few have left the parish; and this statement is supported by a list showing the actual occupations and present means of support of all who received parish pay before the workhouse was opened. No evidence can be more satisfactory or complete.

These results lead us to a conviction that even in the parishes where the greatest surplus above the actual demand exists it would be rapidly reduced and ultimately disappear if relief were no longer granted, except in return for actual labour, and subject to the restraints of a workhouse.

But no expedient by which the reduction of the surplus labour can be accelerated and the suffering of the labourer during the progress of the change diminished, should be disregarded; and we are of opinion that emigration, which has been one of the most innocent palliatives of the evils of the present system, could be advantageously made available to facilitate the application of the remedies which we have already suggested.

Numerous instances are stated in our evidence of emigration at the expense of parishes, and the results have generally been satisfactory; we believe they have been uniformly so wherever the experiment has been made on a considerable scale. In the case of Benenden, in Kent, where the effects of emigration, unconnected with other remedies, have been carefully detailed by Mr Law Hodges, the result has been that the annual parochial expenditure, exclusive of the emigration expenses, has been reduced in four years by one third; that within the same time the debt incurred on account of emigration has been nearly liquidated; that the whole expense of the poor, including the sums applied to this liquidation, has been considerably reduced from the very year the emigration commenced, while the moral condition of the labourers has been decidedly improved. But emigration has hitherto been resorted to under many discouragements and difficulties. The same causes which make those who are dependent on the poor-rates listless in seeking employment at home render them unwilling to undergo the temporary privations and inconvenience which must attend their settlement in another country. Those persons are generally most forward to emigrate who are least corrupted by the abuses of the system of relief. Those are most willing to remain a burthen to their parishes who are most thoroughly profligate and useless.

Mr Stuart, speaking of the counties of Norfolk and Suffolk, where emigration to a greater or less extent has taken place in many of the parishes, observes –

It is, however, vain to hope that emigration can be carried to an extent equal to effect any diminution on the expenditure on the poor, so long as the parish funds are open to all comers. It is a matter of complaint by the farmers that emigration only carries off the industrious and well-behaved, and leaves them encumbered with the idle and profligate; and it cannot be otherwise while everyone is sure of a liberal maintenance whether they are idle or industrious. Mr Turner has taken the trouble to extract from the overseer's books the parish allowances paid to those who removed from Kettleburgh, from which it will be seen that men with seven children were in receipt of 14s. a week, and others in proportion. It is surprising that any inducement could be discovered sufficiently strong to influence any person to forego the certainty of so liberal a pension, to encounter the violent change of feelings and habits which must accompany emigration under any circumstances. It is universally known that those who are in receipt of parish relief leagued together for the purpose of keeping it up and augmenting it for their own benefit, or extending it to others; and as they are less scrupulous in the means they resort to, they are better able to carry through their designs of encroachment than the rate-payers are their endeavours to resist them. The progressive increase of the expenditure on the poor would seem to prove this. In such a state of things, it cannot be expected that the expenditure on paupers can be diminished by lessening the numbers of the population, unless it be carried to a greater extent than seems to be possible, so long as compulsory relief exists; the chances being that whatever diminution of expense might take place from that cause would be no saving to the rate-payers, as fresh candidates for relief would immediately start up. Where the parochial fund is considered as a property on which all have a claim, there is little difficulty in contriving pretences to make the claim good; and as long as the fund exists for the purposes to which it is now directed, it is not by the diminution of the numbers of the population which could be effected by emigration that it can be brought within reasonable bounds.

'If chargeable paupers would go,' says Mr Maclean, speaking of Dorking, 'the parish would be willing to raise a large sum; but this class of persons naturally prefer an idle but certain dependence on the parish at home, to an uncertain independence abroad, to be procured by industry and good conduct.'

The following extract from Mr Majendie's report shows the pecuniary saving which has been effected by emigration. It is valuable also as showing that emigration alone is an inadequate, and must be a transient remedy. We have seen in the cases of Cookham, Swallowfield, and other parishes, that the evils of the Poor Laws disappear under the influence of the system we have recommended, notwithstanding an apparent surplus of population. We see in the evidence we are about to quote that although the supernumerary labourers be removed by emigration, yet, in the absence of other changes, the abuses of the allowance system may continue to abound, and that the charge for the poor may be 27s. per head on a population where no pretence of a surplus continues to exist.

EWHURST
POPULATION

In 1801	In 1811	In 1821	In 1831
847	1,032	1,225	1,200

Rates in the £	Value	Total Expenditure, 1832
11s.	$\frac{2}{3}$	£1,630

Wages, 2s. 3d. Allowance, 1s. 6d. for third child.

In the year ending March 1822, the total expenditure was £3,371. The reduction of rates in the parish of Ewhurst has been effected partly by adopting money payment, but principally by emigration. Since the year 1818, a hundred persons have emigrated, so that there are now no supernumerary labourers. In a parish which has incurred the expense of emigration to such an extent as to leave no more labourers than are requisite for the cultivation of the soil, in which 400 acres of hops afford employment to women and children, winter and summer, and where the rate of weekly wages is 13s. 6d., the allowance for children must be considered as compulsory, and to that must it be ascribed that rates are still 27s. per head on the population, and 11s. in the pound on a two-thirds value.

The rector, from benevolent motives, has offered small allotments to the labourers at a low rent: he has been able to let three acres only, and his offer of nine acres more has been rejected.

Even in Benenden, where emigration has been so well managed, the expenditure on the poor is still above 20s. per head on the whole population. The abolition of partial relief will remove the main discouragement to emigration, while it will ascertain the extent to which emigration may be useful; it will increase the disposition to emigrate on the part of those whose emigration is to be desired. We believe, therefore, that in proportion as our other remedies are applied, there will be an increased disposition on the part of parishes to supply the means to paupers desirous of emigrating, if they be enabled by law so to do.

WE RECOMMEND, THEREFORE, THAT THE VESTRY OF EACH PARISH BE EMPOWERED TO ORDER THE PAYMENT OUT OF THE RATES RAISED FOR THE RELIEF OF THE POOR, OF THE EXPENSES OF THE EMIGRATION OF ANY PERSONS HAVING SETTLEMENTS WITHIN SUCH PARISH, WHO MAY BE WILLING TO EMIGRATE; PROVIDED, THAT THE EXPENSE OF EACH EMIGRATION BE RAISED AND PAID, WITHIN A PERIOD TO BE MENTIONED IN THE ACT.

We think it also would be expedient to adopt the measures for facilitating and regulating emigration contained in the Bill introduced into the House of Commons in 1831 and to be found (as amended by a committee) in the Parliamentary Papers of that session (No. 358).

It has occasionally happened that emigrants have returned to burthen the parishes at the expense of which they have been removed; and to remedy this evil, it has been proposed that every person who should, with his own consent, be removed to the Colonies at the expense of his parish, should lose his settlement. But we do not think it expedient that this proposal should be adopted. We do not believe the instances of the return of emigrants are now frequent enough to affect the profit to a parish of an emigration judiciously conducted, and we believe that the instances would be still more rare if it were known that the emigrant on his return would not be entitled to relief otherwise than in a well-managed workhouse. But the chief objection is that to deprive the emigrant of his settlement – while it might operate to prevent the pauper emigrating by the threat of an imaginary forfeiture – would only enable returned emigrants to be relieved as casual poor in any places, not excluding their own parishes, where they might be pleased to fix themselves.

We should propose rather that the expenses which any parish shall have defrayed or contracted to pay for the removal of any voluntary emigrant shall, upon the return to England of the emigrant, become a debt due to the overseers for the time being, and shall be recovered by an attachment of any wages to which the debtor may become entitled, as we have before recommended in the case of other expenses incurred on account of a pauper or his family.

We forbear to enter upon a consideration of the modes in which emigration may be most beneficially conducted because it has already formed the subject of minute inquiries by Parliamentary Committees, and because, if the Emigration Bill which we have referred to be passed into a law, the commission to be appointed under its provisions must soon be able to avail itself of information much more ample and detailed than we have had access to. But there is one suggestion of which we feel the value, from all the evidence we have received as to the state of feeling of the pauper emigrants. Under the influence of the system which at once confines the labourer to a narrow neighbourhood and relieves him from the care of providing for his subsistence, he has acquired, or retained, with the moral helplessness, some of the other peculiarities of a child. He is often disgusted to a degree which other classes scarcely conceive possible by slight differences in diet; and is annoyed by any thing which appears to him strange and new. We believe the novelty of food and manners in the Colonies and the longing for old associates and old associations have concurred, with a retrospect of the ease and security of pauperism, to bring back to their parishes some of the least energetic emigrants, who, to justify themselves, spread discouraging accounts of the Colonies from which they have returned. In Mr Stuart's report will be found a letter from an emigrant at Montreal who, being able to save money enough from his wages to pay his passage back, declared his intention to return to the parish in which he had been a trouble-

some pauper; apparently moved to that determination as much
by the want of well-tasted beer in Canada and a longing for old
associations as by the fact that he was obliged punctually to pay
rent for his lodgings instead of being provided with a cottage at
the parish expense. We suggest that to diminish distaste to the
Colonies on imaginary grounds, the emigrants from particular
parishes and neighbourhoods in England should be directed, as
far as possible, to the same townships or districts in which the
new comers would thus find old acquaintances and manners with
which they would be familiar. We believe that this precaution
would commonly lessen their aversion to a new country, and that,
if any returned, their misrepresentations would be more effectually
checked by the accounts continually received from their colonial
neighbours.

*

There are some other matters connected with the objects of our
inquiry on which we do not propose the immediate adoption of
any specific measures, because we should be unwilling to embarass
the progress of the remedies we deem of paramount importance
by any change not necessarily connected with them. The following
subjects appear to us, however, to deserve the consideration of the
Legislature.

[RATING]

THE first is the present method of rating the property chargeable
with the relief of the poor. The mode of rating is now, like many
other parts of the administration of the Poor Laws, in the highest
degree uncertain and capricious. 'It will be seen', says one of our
Assistant Commissioners, 'by a reference to the Return recently
made to Parliament, that in the first *ten* parishes named, viz.
Abingdon, Andover, Arundel, Ashburton, Aylesbury, Banbury,
Barnstable, and the parishes of St Michael, St Peter and St Paul
and Walcot, in the city of Bath, *nine* different rates of assessment
are now in operation, and these vary in the proportion of *one fifth*
of the rent or actual value, as assessed at Ashburton, to the full or

actual value as assessed at Bath; while at Bridgnorth, a little further on in the Return, it appears that in the seven parishes of the *same* town five different modes of assessment are adopted.'

Nor is the fractional part of the value on which the rate is professedly made always fixed or ascertainable within each parish.

The Commissioner whom we have quoted says, 'Appeals are frequently made to me (as a magistrate) upon this subject, and although it has been my duty as well as my desire to ascertain the fractional part of the real value (for we do not rate on the rack-rent) upon which the assessment *professes* to be made, in Kensington, where I reside, I have been unable to do so, because I could not find any man in the parish who could state it with accuracy; and my conviction is that when once the simple rule of real value is departed from a door is opened to much partiality and much abuse.'

In the town of Southampton, according to Captain Pringle, the assessment for the poor-rates is on a valuation made sixty years since. New buildings are assessed by the guardians, and at a much higher rate; many of the old being rated at about one third of the rack-rent, whilst the new are nearly two thirds.

That the mode of rating should be uniform; that it should be according to the actual value, and not any alleged, much less any uncertain or variable fractional part, is too obvious to be doubted; and we may observe that besides affording a temptation and a cover to partiality and abuse, the present system, or want of system of rating, enables parishes at their discretion to render nugatory the salutary provisions of the 58 Geo. III, c. 69 [1817], as to the manner of voting in vestries.

It would be unjust, however, to assume the actual value of rateable property to be identical with the rack-rent. The value according to which property should be rated appears to us to be the rent which a tenant, taking upon himself the burthen of repairs, could afford to pay under a twenty-one years' lease.

We have incidentally observed, in a former part of our Report, on the evils which arise from the exemption from rates enjoyed by the cottages or apartments inhabited by the poor, and of the payment of their rents by the parish. The enactment of the 59 Geo. III, c. 12, s. 19 [1818], was directed against these evils; but it has been found defective, inasmuch as it *empowers*, and does not enjoin, parishes to rate the owners instead of the occupiers, and because dwellings let at a rent of less than £6 a year, or for three months, or any longer term, are exempted from the operation of this power. The remedies we have already recommended will lessen the interest of the owners of the dwellings of the poor in the maladministration of the parochial fund; but we think that for effecting an improvement in the composition and conduct of vestries, and for securing the more full and punctual payment of the rates, it is desirable that the owner of every dwelling or apartment let to the occupier at any rent not exceeding £15 for any less term than seven years should be rated instead of the occupiers.

[MILITIA-MEN'S FAMILIES]

THE Act of the 43 Geo. III, c. 47 [1803] (for consolidating the laws for the relief of the families of militia-men), to which we have already referred, appears to us to be within the range of the inquiries which we have been directed to make, and it deserves to be reconsidered by the Legislature. It enacts in substance, that if a militia-man be called into actual service, leaving a family unable to support themselves, an allowance, after a rate not exceeding the price of one day's labour, nor less than 1s. per head, for the wife and each of the children under ten years of age shall be paid upon the order of one justice to such family by the overseers of the parish where they dwell.

The justices in quarter-sessions may settle the rate of allowance for such county, and the allowance so settled is binding on the individual justices. The payment made by the overseers of the place where the family dwell to be reimbursed by other parishes and places in a manner immaterial to our purpose.

These payments are open to many of the objections to the 'allowance system'. They are made not in reward of the services of the father, or in proportion to those services, but in proportion to the assumed necessity of the family, and this necessity is assumed to be in proportion to their numbers; for although, perhaps, the words of the act would authorize a justice to refuse to make an order where the mother was manifestly able to maintain all her children, yet it is clear that if he give anything, the magistrate must give the full allowance for all the members of the family; and we believe the act is commonly construed (as without violence it may be) as not even leaving the justice satisfied of the fact of marriage, and the number and age of family, any discretion to withhold the allowance. We have already stated that this act, or rather the acts which it consolidates and amends, largely contributed in many parts of the kingdom to familiarize both magistrates and parish officers with the allowance system, and it diminished the shame of applications for parochial assistance, because it exhibited as receivers of relief by the hands of the over-seers numerous families to whom no moral blame could be justly attributed. We feel great difficulty, however, in proposing the abolition of the provisions in question, depending as it does on the method established by law of recruiting for the militia by lot. It is not within the province of our Commission to pronounce an opinion on this mode of recruiting; but whatever may be its advantages, we may be permitted to state our belief that it has tended – it must tend when it is no longer dormant – to discourage the course of steady industry, and to increase the excuses for improvidence. It adds a factitious chance of ruin to those inevitable accidents of health and fortune which make the reward of steady industry in some degree precarious, and must render the strict administration of the Poor Laws more difficult by multiplying the cases of blame-less destitution.

[CHARITIES AND EDUCATION]

CLOSELY connected with the relief provided by the Poor Laws is the relief provided by charitable foundations. As to the administration and effect of those charities which are distributed among the classes who are also receivers of the poor-rate, much evidence is scattered throughout our Appendix, and it has forced on us the conviction that, as now administered, such charities are often wasted and often mischievous. In many instances being distributed on the same principle as the rates of the worst managed parishes, they are only less pernicious than the abuse in the application of the poor-rates, because they are visibly limited in amount. In some cases they have a quality of evil peculiar to themselves. The majority of them are distributed among the poor inhabitants of particular parishes or towns. The places intended to be favoured by large charities attract, therefore, an undue proportion of the poorer classes, who, in the hope of trifling benefits to be obtained without labour, often linger on in spots most unfavourable to the exercise of their industry. Poverty is thus not only collected, but created, in the very neighbourhood whence the benevolent founders have manifestly expected to make it disappear.

These charities, in the districts where they abound, may interfere with the efficacy of the measures we have recommended, and on this ground, though aware that we should not be justified in offering any specific recommendation with respect to them, we beg to suggest that they call for the attention of the Legislature.

We have now recommended to Your Majesty the measures by which we hope that the enormous evils resulting from the present maladministration of the Poor Laws may be gradually remedied. It will be observed that the measures which we have suggested are intended to produce rather negative than positive effects; rather to remove the debasing influences to which a large portion of the labouring population is now subject, than to afford new means of prosperity and virtue. We are perfectly aware that for the general diffusion of right principles and habits we are to look, not so much to any economic arrangements and regulations as to the influence of a moral and religious education; and important evidence in the subject will be found throughout our appendix. But one great advantage of any measure which shall remove or diminish the evils of the present system is that it will in the same degree remove the obstacles which now impede the progress of instruction, and intercept its results; and will afford a freer scope to the operation of every instrument which may be employed, for elevating the intellectual and moral condition of the poorer classes. We believe that if the funds now destined to the purposes of education, many of which are applied in a manner unsuited to the present wants of society, were wisely and economically employed, they would be sufficient to give all the assistance which can be prudently afforded by the state. As the subject is not within our Commission, we will not dwell on it further, and we have ventured on these few remarks only for the purpose of recording our conviction, that as soon as a good administration of the Poor Laws shall have rendered further improvement possible, the most important duty of the Legislature is to take measures to promote the religious and moral education of the labouring classes.

All which we humbly certify to Your Majesty,

C. J. LONDON	(L. S.)
J. B. CHESTER	(L. S.)
W. STURGES BOURNE	(L. S.)
NASSAU W. SENIOR	(L. S.)
HENRY BISHOP	(L. S.)
HENRY GAWLER	(L. S.)
W. COULSON	(L. S.)
JAMES TRAILL	(L. S.)
EDWIN CHADWICK	(L. S.)

Whitehall Yard,
20 February 1834

INDEX

TO

REPORT OF POOR LAW COMMISSIONERS

MORE ABOUT PENGUINS
AND PELICANS

Penguinews, which appears every month, contains details of all the new books issued by Penguins as they are published. From time to time it is supplemented by *Penguins in Print*, which is a complete list of all titles available. (There are some five thousand of these.)

A specimen copy of *Penguinews* will be sent to you free on request. For a year's issues (including the complete lists) please send 36p if you live in the United Kingdom, or 60p if you live elsewhere. Just write to Dept EP, Penguin Books Ltd, Harmondsworth, Middlesex, enclosing a cheque or postal order, and your name will be added to the mailing list.

In the U.S.A.: For a complete list of books available from Penguin in the United States write to Dept CS, Penguin Books Inc., 7110 Ambassador Road, Baltimore, Maryland 21207.

In Canada: For a complete list of books available from Penguin in Canada write to Penguin Books Canada Ltd, 41 Steelcase Road West, Markham, Ontario L3R 1B4.

THE PELICAN CLASSICS

'A boon to students young and perennial ... The admirable introductions by reputable scholars are required reading' – *The Times Literary Supplement*

Some volumes in this series